The Whips

In *The Whips*, C. Lawrence Evans offers a comprehensive, system-atic, and historical exploration of party coalition building and legisla-tive strategy in the US House and Senate, ranging from the relatively bipartisan, committee-dominated chambers of the 1950s to the highly polarized congresses of the 2000s. In addition to examining roll call votes, personal interviews with lawmakers and staff, and other standard techniques of congressional scholarship, Evans utilizes the personal papers of dozens of former members of the House and Senate lead-ership, especially former whips. These records allow Evans to create and draw on a database of nearly 1,500 private leadership polls about evolving member preferences on hundreds of significant bills across five decades of recent congressional history.

The result is a rich and sweeping contribution to scholarly and public understanding of congressional party leaders at work. Since the whips regularly provide leaders and members with valuable political intelligence and fulfill a host of other critical duties, examining them is essential to understanding how coalitions are forged and deals are made on the most important legislation considered on Capitol Hill. But their impact—and the impact of other leaders in the lawmaking process—is far more nuanced and interesting than is implied by other treatments of partisan coalition building in Congress.

C. Lawrence Evans is the Newton Family Professor of Government at the College of William & Mary.

LEGISLATIVE POLITICS & POLICY MAKING

Series Editors
Janet M. Box-Steffensmeier, Vernal Riffe Professor of Political Science,
The Ohio State University

David Canon, Professor of Political Science, University of Wisconsin, Madison

RECENT TITLES IN THE SERIES:

For a complete list of titles in this series, please see www.press.umich.edu.

THE WHIPS

Building Party Coalitions in Congress

C. Lawrence Evans

University of Michigan Press
Ann Arbor

Copyright © 2018 by C. Lawrence Evans
All rights reserved

Published in the United States of America by the
University of Michigan Press
Manufactured in the United States of America
Printed on acid-free paper

First published August 2018

A CIP catalog record for this book is available from the British Library.

Library of Congress Cataloging-in-Publication data has been applied for.

ISBN 978-0-472-13082-5 (hardcover)
ISBN 978-0-472-03730-8 (paper)
ISBN 978-0-472-12387-2 (e-book)

To W. Lee Rawls

Contents

List of Figures

List of Tables

Preface

To my knowledge, the pages that follow are one of the few scholarly research projects about the congressional legislative process to be denounced on the floor of the US Senate. In October 2009, then Senator Tom Coburn, who I admire a great deal, regaled his colleagues and the C-SPAN audience with a litany of political science projects funded by the National Science Foundation (NSF) that he viewed as, well, less than optimal recipients of taxpayer support. Included on the list was my research about the role of party whips in our national legislature, which had received much-appreciated funding from the NSF. "Who cares?" Coburn asked on the Senate floor that day about my investigation of the whip systems of Congress. "Nobody should care about that," he continued.[1] With all respect to a principled public servant, this book can be viewed as an attempt to explain why the Senator's characterization was off base.

My focus is the party whips in Congress—who they are, what they do, and why they matter so much. The primary subjects include leadership, persuasion, bargaining, party politics, and the construction of legislation from the 1950s into the 2000s. The whips, you will see, have been vital components of Washington national politics for over a century now. Yet, as scholars and as citizens we know very little about their work, which largely takes place outside the public eye on the most significant policy disputes on the national political agenda. Drawing on nearly 30,000 pages of archived materials from the papers of former leaders and members of Congress, the analysis of roll call votes and other observable indicators of congressional politics, and close observations of party leaders at work, the chapters that follow are intended to fill this unfortunate gap—and to do so in a manner that is compelling to scholars and interested non-specialists alike. The overriding goal is to make the internal operations of Congress more transparent.

Along the way, I also hope that this book can convince scholars of American politics to rethink how they have come to conceptualize law-making in Congress, particularly the roles played by parties and leaders. Far more attention, I argue, needs to be devoted to the processes through which individual members form preferences and positions on legislative issues, and perhaps less to anecdotes about arm-twisting and the manipulation of procedure. The two major political parties certainly matter in the congressional legislative process, but broad claims for "party government" tend to obscure as much as they reveal and probably should be discarded. My guess is that most readers will be surprised by significant portions of this volume.

Preparing it has not been an easy task. For one, the project required that I comb through more than 10,000 documents and other leadership records maintained in dozens of libraries and archives located around the country; the coding and analysis of massive data sets based in part on information included in the aforementioned archives; and more than a decade of research and writing as I attempted to make sense of all this evidence. Along the way, many debts were incurred.

As mentioned, the NSF provided important seed money at the beginning of my endeavor (NSF Award SES-0417759). By expanding knowledge about government, NSF sponsored research empowers citizens. I hope this book will be viewed as a noteworthy part of that broader effort. Important financial support also was provided by the Newton Family Endowment and The Roy R. Charles Center of the College of William & Mary, The Carl Albert Congressional Research and Studies Center of the University of Oklahoma, The Thomas S. Foley Institute for Public Policy and Public Service at Washington State University, and The Dirksen Congressional Center. The Dirksen Center, in particular, has funded hundreds of research projects about the Congress, and over the past few years I have been honored to serve on their advisory board.

During my many trips to examine the papers of former congressional leaders, I relied extensively on the assistance of a legion of professional archivists. Their names and the main libraries and research centers that I visited are included in the appendix, as well as notes throughout the text. At the heart of this book are unique new data sets that capture the evolving positions of members prior to major floor votes, as revealed to the relevant party whips at the time and as reported in contemporaneous whip records. Over 50 William & Mary students helped me compile, enter, and analyze these data. Their names also are listed in the appendix, but the contributions of seven are especially noteworthy: Pierce Blue, Erin Bradbury, Ryan Davidson, Logan Feree, Nicole Gaffin, Claire Grandy, and Laura Minnichelli.

Over the years, dozens of former members and staff have spoken with me candidly about whip operations in the House and Senate, including two former Speakers, several additional congressional leaders, and many leadership aides. I particularly appreciate the candor of former Rep. Robin Hayes of North Carolina, whose pivotal decision to vote for Fast Track in 2001 provides the illustrative narrative in Chapter 2. My first direct exposure to the whips at work was as a professional staffer to the venerable Rep. Lee H. Hamilton of Indiana. Mr. Hamilton allowed me to experience and observe aspects of congressional operations that are hidden to most scholars of the institution, and I cannot thank him enough.

My primary intellectual home is the international community of legislative scholars, and over the years many valued colleagues have read and commented on conference papers and presentations where I reported preliminary findings about the work of the whips. Among others, these scholars include Scott Adler, Richard Bensel, Bill Bianco, Sarah Binder, Jon Bond, Barry Burden, Jamie Carson, Michael Crespin, Chris Den Hartog, David Dessler, Christine DeGregorio, Larry Dodd, Dick Fenno, Chuck Finnochiarro, John Gilmour, John Griffin, Rick Hall, Marc Hetherington, John Hibbing, John Hilley, Chris Howard, Brian Humes, Jeff Jenkins, Eric Jensen, Sean Kelly, Greg Koger, Keith Krehbiel, Frances Lee, Dan Lipinski, Burdett Loomis, Tony Madonna, Bryan Marshall, Matthew McCubbins, Kris Miler, Nate Monroe, Mark Oleszek, Walter Oleszek, Bruce Oppenheimer, John Owen, Jeremy Pope, Ron Rapoport, Janna Rezaee, Jason Roberts, David Rohde, Cathy Rudder, Eric Schickler, Wendy Schiller, Patrick Sellers, Steve Smith, Randy Strahan, Sean Theriault, Rob Van Houweling, Ryan Williamson, Don Wolfensberger, and especially Joe Cooper and Barbara Sinclair. Portions of this book also were presented to political science audiences at Duke University, Indiana University, Northwestern University, Princeton University, the University of Georgia, the University of Miami, Vanderbilt University, the annual History of Congress Conference, and of course my own institution, the College of William & Mary. My appreciation to all of the discussants and seminar/conference participants who provided feedback along the way.

I am especially indebted to eight people who read and commented on the penultimate version of this book: Larry Bartels, Larry Dodd, Dick Fenno, Walter Oleszek, Wendy Schiller, Steve Smith, Rick Valelly, and an anonymous referee.

Supplemental data sets for the project were provided by David Canon and Charles Stewart, David Rohde and his colleagues in the Political Institutions and Public Choice Program, E. Scott Adler and John Wilkerson of the Congressional Bills Project, Gary Jacobson, Larry Dodd, Joshua Clinton, and of course the inestimable Keith Poole and his colleagues at the Voteview project. For the University of Michigan Press, I benefited from the assistance of a succession of capable editorial staff that included Melody Herr, Meredith Norwich, Scott Hamm, Danielle Cody, and Elizabeth Demers, as well as series editors David Canon and Jan Box-Steffensmeier.

The rest of my debts are more personal. My wife, Susan, and our children, Jack and Rebecca, have been a source of encouragement and toleration for my obsession with party politics in Congress for a long time. Susan's sharp editorial eye, in particular, has substantially improved the quality of my writing. Jack's spouse, Megan, is a welcome addition to our family. Together, they keep me sane, more or less.

Since my graduate school days at the University of Rochester, Richard F. Fenno, Jr., has been the model for how a scholar should work and behave. I will never approach the high standard he set throughout his illustrious career, but this book is much better because that standard exists. Indeed, the behavioral theory of the congressional whip process introduced in Chapter 2 is largely an extension of Dick Fenno's landmark studies. For that and much more, thank you.

Most important, this book would not have been written without the encouragement and assistance provided by the late W. Lee Rawls. With Lee Rawls, I do not know where to begin. A longtime aide to Senator Pete Domenici during the 1970s and 1980s, Assistant Attorney General of the United States during the administration of George H. W. Bush, Chief of Staff to former Senate Majority Leader Bill Frist in the 1990s and early 2000s, and then Chief of Staff and Counsel to FBI Director Robert Mueller in the years after the September 11 attacks, Lee's was a savvy voice of good judgment, integrity, and welcome humor in the halls of government across four decades. For nearly 20 of those years, he communicated with me regularly about congressional politics, read and commented on everything I wrote, and traveled to Williamsburg a dozen or more times a year to teach his popular seminar to a generation of William & Mary undergraduates. Susan and I came to cherish dinners with Lee and his wife, Linda, during those visits. More generally, Lee's guidance shaped every page of this book. It is only appropriate, then, that the final product be dedicated to his memory.

Introduction

Within the hallways of the US Congress, the leaders of the two political parties play a central role in most of the legislative and other work that helps shape the content of public policy and America's place in the world. The Speaker of the House of Representatives, for example, has enormous influence over which bills are considered by that body. And on both sides of the partisan aisle, House leaders have significant say over which of their fellow partisans are assigned to sought-after committees, where important early decisions about legislation often are made, and where most rank-and-file lawmakers are best positioned to influence policy and curry favor with the groups and constituencies so important to their reelection. Republican and Democratic leaders are also highly visible public spokespersons for their parties, as they seek to translate their respective legislative priorities into viable communications strategies for the next election campaign. On the Senate side of the US Capitol Building, the majority leader lacks most of the formal powers that have been extended to party leaders in the House. Yet Senate leaders, like their House counterparts, still exert considerable sway over the chamber agenda and the content of legislation, and are also highly visible players on the national political scene. I could go on. But the many and varied roles played by party leaders in Congress ultimately rest on one critical challenge—the ability to secure the votes of individual lawmakers on the floor on matters important to the party agenda. It is just that challenge—the cracking of the party whip on the most significant policy disputes of the day—that is the focus of this book.

Whipping Fast Track

On a Thursday afternoon in early December, 2001, scores of Democratic members stood on the floor of the House, clapping their hands in applause as it appeared that legislation providing President George W. Bush with enhanced authority to negotiate international trade agreements was about to lose on a nearly party-line vote. As the 15-minute period that is standard for conducting recorded votes in the House came to a close, hundreds of members from both parties milled around on the floor, talking with their colleagues and looking up at the wall panels behind the Speaker's desk where the roll call choices of individual legislators are displayed. The official tally indicated that the majority Republicans, who mostly backed the measure, had fallen just short of the votes necessary to prevail, 210–214. Such an outcome was not unexpected, but still would constitute a significant political defeat for Bush and a major blow to the Republican agenda in Congress.

The measure, known as "Fast Track," or alternatively, "enhanced trading authority," was a top legislative priority for the new president and provided that any international trade agreements negotiated by the administration would receive swift legislative action on Capitol Hill with no amendments. Decisions about whether to grant or withhold fast track negotiating privileges had been controversial on Capitol Hill for decades because international trade agreements can affect the material well-being of powerful constituencies throughout the country and many members of Congress are reluctant to delegate extensive authority over their contents to the executive branch, especially one controlled by the other party. Fast Track was first adopted as part of a 1974 trade bill, and bipartisan majorities renewed the authority in 1979 and again in 1988. In the 1990s, however, the politics of Fast Track became more partisan, typically dividing GOP free-traders from congressional Democrats concerned about foreign imports and the lax labor and environmental standards set by many US trading partners. Long-term extensions of Fast Track were defeated in the House in 1991, 1994, and 1998.

For these reasons, the Bush administration and Republican leaders in Congress knew that they faced an up-hill fight in passing fast track authority in 2001 and they fully recognized that the toughest test would be in the House, where the smaller constituencies of lawmakers were more likely to be dominated by producers and workers concerned about foreign competition. Moreover, the Republican majority in the House that year was a razor-thin three votes.

Dozens of House members would play important parts during the fight over Fast Track. Included were Bill Thomas, R-Calif., and Philip Crane, R-Ill., chairs, respectively, of the Committee on Ways and Means and its trade subcommittee, and authors of the main GOP proposals; Speaker Dennis Hastert, R-Ill., who worked with the Bush administration to convince wavering Republicans to support passage; Minority Leader Richard Gephardt, D-Mo., who operated mostly behind the scenes to coordinate the opposition; Sander Levin, D-Mich., Crane's minority counterpart on the trade subcommittee and the author of the main Democratic alternative; and Calvin Dooley, D-Calif., leader of the centrist "New Democrats Caucus" that was potentially pivotal to the outcome. However, especially as the critical floor votes neared, the key players within the chamber were Tom DeLay of Texas, the Republican whip, and David Bonior of Michigan, who served as whip for the minority Democrats.

In both chambers of Congress, the two major political parties each have a "whip," and the four whips in turn are each assisted by an organization of other members who serve as their assistants or deputies. The whip and the relevant assistants comprise the whip operation for their party within that chamber. And together, the four whip operations constitute the whip systems of Congress.

The whips fulfill a range of important tasks, such as helping formulate party strategy, informing other members about the legislative agenda, canvassing the viewpoints of rank-and-file lawmakers about party legislative priorities, and convincing wavering or opposing members to stay loyal on important roll call votes. Within the House, the majority whip is the third highest member of the leadership after the Speaker and majority leader. For the House minority party, the minority whip is the second highest leadership position after minority leader. On the Senate side of the Capitol, the whips likewise are critical members of the leadership for their respective parties, second only to the majority and minority leaders. The whip function, we will see, is at the very heart of the legislative process in Congress.

Early Skirmishes

Although President Bush and the US Trade Representative, Robert Zoellick, both pushed for quick passage of Fast Track, Hastert and DeLay were wary because of their small majority and the dozens of GOP members representing districts that had lost jobs due to foreign competition.

On March 13, 2001, they surveyed a sample of 78 House Republicans, asking them whether they would vote for legislation granting the president enhanced powers over trade.[1] The leadership did not poll committed free-traders such as Philip Crane, R-Ill., or David Dreier, R-Calif., nor did they approach likely opponents such as Bob Ney, R-Ohio. Instead, the whips contacted the GOP lawmakers likely to be in play, as well as newly elected members without voting records on trade.

"Whip polls," also called "whip counts" and "whip checks," are critical tools for effective party leadership in Congress. Prior to major floor votes important to the party program, the top leadership often will ask the whip organization to canvass the positions of the members from their party on the question. Party leaders use whip counts to signal to rank-and-file members that an issue or vote is important to the party, to gauge the level of support that exists for the party position, and to identify which members are in need of further lobbying or "whipping" if they are to stay loyal to the party program. The results of these counts are very closely held, seldom shared with members outside the extended party leadership, and almost never released to the media or the public. Usually, the positions of members are categorized as "yes," "leaning yes," "undecided," "leaning no," or "no" on the polled question. On the March survey, only 47 members responded as yes or leaning yes when asked whether they were inclined to support a Fast Track measure, 29 were undecided or opposed, and two could not be reached.[2] Even this preliminary tally showed Republican House leaders that the quick adoption of Fast Track was not going to happen.

Throughout the spring of 2001, other aspects of the Bush legislative program dominated the congressional agenda, especially a trillion-dollar tax cut, patients' rights legislation, and the "No Child Left Behind" education reforms. But on June 13, House Republican leaders coalesced around a streamlined Fast Track proposal, introduced by Trade Subcommittee Chair Philip Crane, which would have required an up-or-down vote on trade agreements within 90 days of their submittal and no amendments.

There was no mention in the Crane bill of the labor and environmental standards so important to Democrats. The main purpose of the bill, GOP leaders acknowledged, was to give DeLay concrete language upon which to whip and to gauge how much compromise would be necessary to prevail on the floor.

The whip count on the Crane bill took place during June 19–20 and the results were yet another signal that Fast Track was in deep trouble. Just 131 Republicans indicated they would vote for the legislation in its current form, with another 31 members leaning yes. Twenty-seven were undecided, 17 were leaning no, and 15 were opposed. With Democratic support unlikely to exceed 15 or 20 members, the Crane bill was at least 40 votes short of a House majority. So in July, Thomas began meetings with Democratic centrists, attempting to craft compromise language capable of passage on the floor. The main sticking points continued to be the priority to be placed on labor and environmental protections in future trade negotiations and whether or not these protections would be enforced by mandatory sanctions if violated. Most Republicans did not want sanctions in the bill. Most Democrats would not vote for Fast Track without them.

On the other side of the partisan aisle, Democratic leaders also prepared for the looming floor fight over trade. In mid-April, under the leadership of David Bonior, Democratic opponents of Fast Track formed an informal task force called the "Fast Track Working Group" to begin whipping against the emergent Republican position. There were divisions over trade within the Democratic Caucus. In addition, a number of groups and constituencies that Democratic leaders viewed as potential sources of financial and other assistance for their party in campaigns, including the high-tech industry, were actively lobbying for Fast Track. The Fast Track Working Group held regular meetings every other week or so when the House was in session, from late April 2001 until the critical roll call in December. Group members began polling their colleagues the week of May 3, asking them if they would oppose Fast Track unless labor and environmental standards were included and backed up with sanctions. The initial results were mixed: 73 Democrats were opposed to Fast Track without sanctions, another 60 were leaning that way, 41 were undecided, and 24 were with the other side.[3] Among the potential defectors was Calvin Dooley, an ideological moderate and House co-chair of the New Democrats Caucus, a group of party centrists that had been pivotal to the adoption of several trade measures during the 1990s.

Escalation

In the contemporary Congress, the party whip operations typically work hand in hand with interest groups and outside advocacy coalitions, who themselves lobby wavering members and engage in extensive grassroots campaigns aimed at influencing the votes of lawmakers by mobilizing and shaping the views of their constituents. In late July, as members prepared to return home for the monthlong August recess, the outside groups associated with both sides of the issue ran television and radio commercials in the districts of members that were viewed as "in play."

On July 26, for example, the AFL-CIO began airing television ads in 19 congressional districts. The ads explicitly referenced the Crane bill, claiming that it would give Bush "the power to slam through trade deals like NAFTA ... stripping Congress of the right to add rules that would safeguard the environment and workers' rights."[4] Trade unions, environmental organizations, and other groups opposed to Fast Track also conducted hundreds of meetings with the members on their target lists, both in Washington and at home in their districts. These contacts were coordinated with the efforts of the Democrats' Fast Track Working Group on Capitol Hill.

For Tom DeLay, the seamless integration of corporate lobbyists and grassroots pressure with the House GOP whip organization was central to his coalition-building success throughout his tenure in the leadership. Here, the outside lobbying effort was orchestrated by a broad-based coalition of roughly 500 corporations and industry groups, called "US Trade," that by mid-summer 2001 was running pro-trade television ads in swing districts, lobbying members directly in favor of adoption, and organizing grass roots campaigns across the country in support of the GOP-backed measure.[5]

Thomas' efforts to win the support of centrist Democrats continued during the August congressional recess and stepped up when members returned to Washington after Labor Day. On September 11, the terrorist attacks altered calculations about the adoption of Fast Track, along with much of the political and cultural landscape in the United States. In a September 24 speech, Trade Representative Zoellick linked the passage of Fast Track to the war on terrorism and claimed that parochial interests in their districts primarily motivated opponents of the initiative.[6] Charles Rangel and other Hill Democrats quickly swung back. "As a combat veteran and as a person whose city has been attacked and suffered devastating losses as a result," Rangel stated, "I am offended by the strategy of the current US Trade Representative to use the tragedy in New York and at the Pentagon to fuel political momentum behind a partisan 'Fast Track' proposal."[7]

On October 3, Ways and Means Chair Thomas and three Democratic moderates, Dooley, William Jefferson, La., and John Tanner, Tenn., jointly released a compromise Fast Track bill that provided for timely consideration and an up-or-down vote on trade agreements, and which mentioned labor and environmental standards but did not include mandatory sanctions. Democratic leaders immediately opposed the legislation and the Fast Track Working Group, now including dozens of active members, polled the party rank and file, asking them if they would oppose the Thomas bill. The results indicated only 12 Democrats were with Thomas or leaning that way, while another 25 were undecided. Almost all the rest were opposed. Based on the whip count, Democratic leaders were increasingly optimistic about their chances on the floor. Working with the outside coalition of advocacy groups, the Bonior task force stepped up its whipping against the compromise.

The same day the Thomas bill was introduced, Republican leaders polled their colleagues about the measure. Only 146 Republicans, they found, were yes or leaning yes, 18 were undecided, 42 were no or leaning no, and 9 were nonresponsive. Three Republicans were undecided or opposed, but assured the whips they would vote with the leadership "if needed" to pass the measure. On the whole, the results constituted more bad news for the Republican leadership on Fast Track. Compared with the July whip poll about the Crane version, GOP support had actually dropped by 16 members, in part because free-market conservatives were opposed to even the weak protections for labor and the environment included in the Thomas compromise, and also because of mounting anxiety about imports among Republicans from agricultural and textile districts. Even with the 12 Democrats that had indicated support for the compromise bill, the Republican leadership still needed to pick up the votes of another 50 to 60 members to win on the floor. Repeatedly, they were forced to put off floor action in pursuit of more votes for the legislation.

Endgames

During the last week of November, Republican leaders announced that the House vote on Fast Track would occur on Thursday, December 6. They were still short on votes, but believed there was enough support that last-ditch lobbying might put them over the top. In the days leading up to the roll call, Bush met with several dozen wavering members at the White House. Republican House leaders also emphasized to their rank-and-file colleagues the importance of staying loyal to the party program and a GOP president, especially on international economic issues in a time of war. The pitch was sufficient to convince Duncan Hunter, R-Calif., a long-time opponent of trade agreements who had been leaning no on the Crane bill and undecided on the Thomas compromise, to vote for Fast Track. Before casting his vote, Hunter explained: "In early September, I was gearing up as usual to oppose this Fast Track. And then our country was attacked ... I do not like free trade. But I like less the idea of weakening this President in this time of great national emergency."[8]

The leadership also made substantive adjustments to the content of their bill and utilized other legislative vehicles in the search for votes. Members from Florida were pushing for modifications that would exclude citrus from future trade agreements. GOP leaders rejected that demand, but did add language instructing US trade negotiators to consult with Congress before accepting proposals that might damage domestic producers, including citrus. The day before the vote, Thomas offered to add language making future reductions in US agricultural tariffs contingent upon similar cuts by America's trading partners, and Hastert and DeLay released a letter pledging that $20 billion would be allocated to helping the unemployed in a stimulus bill expected to move through Congress in the next few months. The next day, hours before the vote, Republican leaders scheduled and the House passed a bill extending by six months benefits for workers who lost their jobs due to imports. All of these proposals were intended to shore up support for Fast Track. GOP leaders also knew that during House consideration they would benefit from a closed rule, which was traditional on trade measures and would effectively preclude the Democrats from offering any floor amendments to the Thomas bill.[9]

As the roll call began at about 4:00 in the afternoon on December 6, Rep. James DeMint, a Republican from a textile district in South Carolina, arrived on the floor and voted against the Thomas bill. DeMint, however, had also brought with him a draft letter that, if signed, would constitute a commitment by the GOP leadership that the next trade agreement passed by the House would include language requiring African and Latin American clothing manufacturers to use cloth produced in the United States, which would significantly benefit textile producers in his constituency. DeMint was willing to switch his vote in exchange for the commitment. Sensing that they now needed the votes of DeMint and other textile-state Republicans, Hastert and DeLay signed the letter and DeMint changed his vote. Later, DeMint and several other Republicans cited the letter as pivotal to their decisions to vote yes.[10]

On the Democratic side of the aisle, Gephardt, Bonior, and other members of the Fast Track Working Group, assisted by their allies in the interest group community, kept the pressure on wavering Democrats, urging them to vote no. A key strategic decision was whether to focus exclusively on defeating the Republican measure, or to also whip in favor of a Democratic alternative, which had been introduced by Levin and Rangel in early October. Bonior, however, believed the party would be better positioned by whipping against the Republican measure, and not simultaneously whipping for Levin-Rangel.[11] As one of his top aides later explained, "In the majority it is really important to count votes, and in the minority it was really important to throw monkey wrenches."[12] As the floor vote neared, Democrats focused almost exclusively on bringing down the Republican proposal.

One of the undecideds on the Democrats' whip count was Marion Berry, a moderate from Arkansas who had voted the previous year for trade normalization with China. Gephardt promised Berry that he would help him secure a coveted seat on the House Appropriations Committee if the Arkansan voted against Fast Track. Berry voted no and was appointed to the panel at the end of the following year.[13] Thirteen Democrats who had responded on whip counts as favorable to the Thomas bill also promised not to cast their votes until the very end of the roll call.[14] Unable to count on the support of these Democrats, DeLay would not be able to release as many cross-pressured Republicans to vote their constituency interests over the party line, potentially undermining their reelection prospects.

As the interval for conducting roll calls came to a close, it looked like the yearlong fight over Fast Track had ended in a stunning defeat for Bush and the Republican leadership and a significant policy and political victory for Bonior and other Fast Track opponents. At this point, Republican leaders extended the vote, holding it open for another 20 minutes, as they attempted to reverse the apparent outcome. The GOP numbers edged upward. With the tally now tied at 214–214, Republican leaders approached Rep. Robin Hayes of North Carolina, who had run a hosiery mill before his 1998 election to Congress and represented one of the most textile-dependent districts in the country. Hayes intended to vote against the Thomas compromise, but GOP leaders convinced him to vote yes and the roll call was quickly gaveled to a close, 215–214. From the gallery above the House floor, onlookers could see DeLay and Hayes sitting together, the whip with his arm around the North Carolinian, promising that the party would "move heaven and earth" to provide economic assistance to his constituents.[15]

The December 6 vote did not ensure the enactment of Fast Track. Ahead lay Senate action in spring 2002, further modifications to the legislation, difficult bicameral negotiations between the House and Senate over a final package, and two more tight votes on the House floor during summer 2002. Still, initial House passage in December 2001 was the critical step toward the eventual adoption of Fast Track, and Republican leaders rightly portrayed it as a major victory for the White House and their party.

Why Whips Matter

The debate over Fast Track was one of the classic political fights that often occur on Capitol Hill on major legislation, including the critical role played by the whips and other party leaders. Indeed, the story illustrates why a book called "The Whips" is worth reading.

First, the policy stakes were enormous. The whips and other leaders tend to be active on the legislation and issues that matter the most to the two political parties and the American people. Evidence reported in this book will show that whips for the House majority party conducted over 1,000 whip polls during the five decades that followed World War II, touching on most of the significant measures considered on Capitol Hill over the period. During the 1950s and 1960s, among many other issues, the list of "whipped" questions included federal aid to education, civil rights, the creation of Medicare, and US involvement in Vietnam. During the 1970s and 1980s, the whips were highly active during the congressional investigation of the Watergate scandal, the epic 1977–78 debate about national energy policy, the enactment of the Reagan economic plan in 1981, and the 1980s debates over military assistance to the Nicaraguan "Contras." For the 1990s, the list of whipped matters includes the landmark Clinton budget of 1993, the bills that comprised the House GOP's "Contract with America" in 1995–96, and the adoption of sweeping welfare reforms in the late 1990s. During the opening years of the George W. Bush administration, the party whips were active on dozens of major bills, including the massive tax cuts of 2001, campaign finance reform, the authorization of US military intervention in Iraq, and of course the fight over Fast Track.

Second, the legislative process was fluid and the outcome uncertain. Even though members mostly divided along party lines on Fast Track, significant numbers of Democrats and Republicans were also cross-pressured by the interests of their constituents, the demands of advocacy groups, and the imperatives of party and ideology. Dozens of members changed sides or remained uncommitted until the day of the vote. The positions taken by rank-and-file lawmakers, the contents of the main legislative alternatives, and the prospects for passage all changed markedly over the year. The fluidity that characterized House action on Fast Track is actually a pervasive and under-appreciated feature of the congressional legislative process. Only rarely does the majority leadership in either chamber have a winning coalition firmly in place until relatively late in that process, if at all. We cannot understand coalition building in Congress without considering the work of the whips.

Third, the tactics used to whip Fast Track illustrate the breadth of strategies available to party leaders in Congress. Democratic and Republican leaders used whip intelligence to gauge their prospects and identify potential opponents among the rank and file. Powerful interest groups were arrayed on both sides of the issue, and the integration of Washington lobbying with grassroots mobilization that characterizes coalition building in the modern Congress was on full display. Party leaders attempted to frame the Fast Track debate to advantage their side of the fight, with Republicans emphasizing linkages between trade and the war against terrorism, and Democrats focused more on the implications for worker rights and environmental protection. On the majority side of the partisan aisle, the leadership made substantive changes in the legislation and struck special deals to secure the votes of wavering lawmakers. Disputes over procedure and legislative substance were inseparable, as the majority leadership used its scheduling powers to keep the bill off the floor until they were within reach of victory. On the Democratic side, party leaders relied especially on pressure from outside groups important to the campaigns of their members and on the special favors that are available even to leaders of the minority to minimize defections and otherwise highlight their policy differences with the majority party.

Fourth, Fast Track shows how the broader role played by party leaders depends on the whips. Some scholars claim that party influence in the House mostly occurs at the agenda setting stage, rather than during votes on the floor, and that the work of the whips may not be essential to party power. The agenda setting choices of the House majority leadership, however, only have force if voting majorities on the floor can be mustered to back them up. The closed amendment procedure on Fast Track was made possible by a near party-line vote on the "rule" for considering the bill, and the special rules that contemporary House leaders use to structure the floor agenda are often themselves the subject of whip counts. Also, leadership decisions about whether and when to schedule legislation for floor action often are based on political intelligence gathered by the whips. Still other scholars emphasize the influence party leaders may exert in committee, where the crucial early work on legislation occurs, rather than the struggle for votes on the floor. But House and Senate committees often draft their bills with an eye toward what is passable in the full chamber, which in turn is a function of the prospects for effective floor whipping. On Fast Track, both parties extensively canvassed and lobbied individual members many months before formal committee action even took place. The work of the whips, in other words, is an essential linchpin for party influence exerted throughout the congressional legislative process.

Fifth, and most important, Fast Track illustrates the tenuous and highly tactical nature of party leadership in Congress under even the best of circumstances. Especially for the majority, intensive whipping is as much a sign of party weakness as it is an indicator of party strength. As a result of party building reforms adopted during the 1970s and 1990s (enhanced control over the floor agenda, valued committee assignments, and the like), House Republican leaders in 2001 had significant advantages relative to the majority leaderships of prior decades. Moreover, the majority rank and file of 2001 was relatively unified on most policy matters and generally provided Hastert and DeLay with a firm base of support for building coalitions. A president of their party also had made the adoption of Fast Track an administration priority and was actively lobbying for passage. The measure and the period, in other words, were very conducive to effective leadership by the House Republican majority.

Yet, as we have seen, majority coalition building for Fast Track was an up-hill fight from the beginning, modifications to the bill and related legislation proved essential to the outcome, and in the end the GOP leadership still barely prevailed. Moreover, the party whipping that occurred took place within a broader context of intensive presidential and interest group lobbying. The movement of votes toward and away from the GOP position resulted in part from the efforts of the Bush administration and the advocacy community, rather than the work of congressional leaders alone. The whips, to be sure, can be critical players in the legislative game. But House action on Fast Track—and the evidence presented in this book more generally—demonstrates that the references to various forms of "party government" that have become so common among scholars of American politics in recent years both exaggerate and mischaracterize the real impact of leaders in Congress.

What's Ahead

This book provides a comprehensive, systematic, and historical treatment of the whip systems of Congress during a transformative era for the national legislature. Although I touch on the origins and operations of the whip process during the late nineteenth and early twentieth centuries, the primary focus spans from the 1950s to the 2000s, extending from the relatively bipartisan, committee-oriented congresses of the 1950s and

1960s to the intensely partisan era of the 1990s and 2000s. The broad sweep of the project allows us to investigate whip operations and leadership coalition building across a range of partisan configurations and stages in the institutional development of Congress. Indeed, we cannot understand the impact of parties and leaders in the current Congress, as polarized as it is along partisan lines, without also evaluating what the whips did during prior decades when lawmaking on Capitol Hill was less like a battle between two warring partisan camps.

Although there has been an explosion of scholarly and popular interest in the congressional parties in recent years, no books and relatively few articles have been published about the congressional whips, primarily because what they do is mostly invisible to scholars, the media, and the general public.[16] The whip meetings that take place each week in the House and Senate, for example, are open only to members and a select group of leadership staff. The whip polls crucial to partisan vote gathering are conducted privately and the results are seldom shared with members or staff outside the leadership circle, much less with scholars, the media, or the public. Beginning in 2001, Republican leaders stopped releasing even the names of the members who were part of the House GOP whip system because they did not want Democrats to use their whip status against them in campaigns. Not much is known about what the whips do, in other words, because so much of their work occurs outside the public eye.

The research reported in this book relies in part on the standard techniques of congressional scholarship—the analysis of roll call votes, evidence from media accounts and congressional documents, personal interviews with members and staff, and so on. But the most informative evidence derives from the personal papers of dozens of former members of the House and Senate leadership, especially former whips. These records include the political intelligence, memos, and other strategic materials about party coalition building that are so closely held when the relevant legislation is under active consideration. Over almost a decade of work in archives and libraries across the country, including the photocopying of nearly 30,000 pages of records and the creation of whip count databases comprising almost 1,500 whip polls and a half million member positions, it was possible to piece together nearly comprehensive evidence about what occurred within the whip systems of the House from the 1950s to the 2000s. The evidence available for the Senate is less expansive, but still instructive. By integrating this archival evidence with publicly available sources, the roll call record, and interviews with key participants, it is possible to provide a uniquely rich and systematic portrayal of partisan coalition building across nearly five decades of transformation on Capitol Hill. In a sense, my aim is to provide an "over the shoulder" perspective on partisan coalition building, akin to the up-close observational studies of Fenno and other scholars, but relying on the tally sheets, internal memoranda, scribbled notes, and other materials that the whips themselves used as they went about their work.[17]

The pages that follow are structured by 10 chapters, with the first two-thirds or so of the book focusing mostly on the House. We begin with the background necessary for understanding who the whips are, what they do, and why they do it. Chapter 1 describes how the whip systems of the House developed over time from individual leadership positions to large, complex organizations. Chapter 2 presents a conceptual framework capable of guiding our investigation of the whips at work. As you will see, a proper understanding of party coalition building in Congress requires that we step back from scholarly theories grounded in the predetermined ideological viewpoints of lawmakers and focus instead on the behavioral processes through which rank-and-file members make up their minds on major issues.

The next two chapters are a largely quantitative overview of partisan whipping in the House across the entire time span from the 1950s to the 2000s. In Chapter 3, we test whether expectations produced by the afore-mentioned conceptual framework are actually consistent with the distribution of whip activity across bills and over time. Chapter 4 evaluates whether analogous hypotheses about the ability of House party leaders to gather votes and prevail on the floor also mesh with aggregate evidence about member preferences, position changes, and leadership wins and losses.

Following this broad-brush treatment, we divide the 1955–2002 time span into four distinct periods, which enables a closer and more detailed look at whip tactics at different stages in recent House history. In Chapter 5, the emphasis is on 1955–72, which covers the last decade or so of the "Textbook Congress." Here, the Democratic House majorities were often deeply divided along sectional lines, especially on matters of civil rights and race, committees had significant autonomy vis-à-vis the majority leadership, and by most accounts party leaders were relatively weak. Chapter 6 concerns 1973–82. As a result of the 1960s enfranchisement of black Americans and the shift among southern conservatives toward the GOP, the long-standing sectional cleavage within the majority Democratic Caucus grew substantially less important. The large Democratic majorities of the era were deeply divided on the major issues of the day, however, constraining the leadership, and during 1981–82, the party confronted an effective

Republican president with an ambitious legislative program. The focus of Chapter 7 is 1983–94 and the transition toward heightened partisanship and more active House leaders. Following the Democratic Party's strong performance in the 1982 midterm elections, the House majority leadership stepped up its opposition to the Reagan policy program and party unity within the Democratic Caucus began to rise. Chapter 8 is an exploration of the Republican House majorities of 1995–2002. Although there was considerable internal agreement within the GOP conferences of the era, their majorities were much smaller than previous Democratic margins, which created different but still daunting challenges for the Republican whips. As you will see, the different strategic configurations associated with the four periods had consequences for whip behavior and success.

Next, our attention shifts from the US House to the Senate. Chapter 9 describes the institutional development and internal operations of party whip operations in the Senate, and then provides a systematic analysis of member decision making and party success on the items targeted for whipping by the Republican Senate majorities of 1997–2002. In the epilogue chapter, I review trends in party coalition building since 2002 within both chambers, and sum up what we have learned about the whips and the nature of party influence in Congress.

My hope is that the mix of detailed illustrations and examples, systematic quantitative evidence, and tentative generalization that makes up this book can convey the profound importance of legislative strategy and the day-to-day activities of members of Congress and other political elites. The work they do is far too important and interesting to be relegated to academics or journalists. The whips, it will be clear, provide an illuminating perspective on the most significant legislative debates that have occurred on Capitol Hill over many decades, and we simply cannot understand American government without shining a bright light on the whip systems of Congress.

ONE

Origins and Operations

Who are the whips? How have the whip role and the nature of the whip networks they run changed over time? To address these questions, this chapter reviews the historical evolution of whip operations in the House, paying particular attention to the initial creation of the office, the kinds of individuals who have served as Democratic and Republican whip, the processes used for choosing them, the emergence of the whip organizations, and the general trajectory of whip activity over time. For now, the focus is exclusively on the House. The history and contemporary operations of the Senate whip systems are topics for Chapter 9.

Antecedents

Depending on the context, the people who work in the US Congress or observe its inner operations use the term "whip" to refer to formal positions of party leadership, the organizations that have developed over time around these positions, and the various tasks and activities that have come to be associated with the whips and the whip organizations they lead. As both a noun and a verb, the renowned British statesman and political philosopher, Edmund Burke, first applied the term to coalition building in legislatures on May 8, 1769, during a heated debate in the House of Commons over the seating of a member from Middlesex. Advocates of the move had sent representatives to Paris and the north of England to bring back absent members for the vote and Burke sarcastically referred to the search parties as "the whippers-in," after the assistant responsible for keeping the hound dogs organized during fox hunts. The terminology and the role quickly caught on.[1] By the early 1800s, members of Parliament were being designated as "whippers-in" and eventually "whips" for the government, responsible for determining the schedule for debate and the timing of votes.

The US Congress has firm roots in the British parliamentary tradition and periodic references to "cracking the party whip" and "the party whip and spur" could be heard on the floor of the House early in the Reconstruction Era that followed the American Civil War.[2] To be sure, the tasks of canvassing member viewpoints, building coalitions, and ensuring that members were present on the floor for major votes were important features of congressional politics from the very beginning. Rep. De Alva Alexander, a Republican House member from New York during 1897–1910, and author of a richly detailed history of the chamber, reported that in the early Congress the chair of the committee with jurisdiction over a measure often played the role of whip, informally. For instance, Alexander described Rep. John W. Taylor, R-N.Y., first as Chair of the Committee of Elections (1815–18) and then as Speaker (1819–20 and 1825–26), as "a vigorous whip." Rep. Taylor, Alexander wrote, "knew the sentiment of members, carried a list of absent ones, and kept adherents informed of an approaching vote."[3] John Bell of Tennessee, a longtime Chair of the Committees on Indian Affairs and Judiciary, as well as Speaker during 1833–34, also had a reputation for highly effective whipping.

The constitutional structures and electoral systems of the United States, however, are much less conducive to strong parties than is the case in Britain, and the internal organization of the two congressional parties was relatively thin until the very end of the nineteenth century. Before the 1830s, the organizational role of political parties in US elections was still developing, and during the 1840s and 1850s the deep intersectional divide that existed between northern and southern states likewise limited the incentives for rank-and-file members to establish a centralized party infrastructure on Capitol Hill. Following the Civil War, however, party cleavages became more pronounced in the electorate and also within the halls of Congress. Moreover, the size of the House grew markedly, from just 234 members in 1855 to almost 360 members in 1895, complicating the task of coalition building. The legislative workload also increased substantially during the second half of the nineteenth century, creating further incentives for members to provide their leaders with enhanced powers over the agenda.

For these reasons, in 1890 the House adopted "the Reed Rules," which enabled the Speaker, as head of the majority party within the chamber, to curtail obstructionist tactics by the minority. And during the early 1890s, the leadership-dominated Committee on Rules was given enhanced procedural authority over the floor agenda, which further empowered the Speaker and the majority party. Tom DeLay and Dennis Hastert notwithstanding, by most accounts the two decades from 1890 to 1910, often called the era of "Czar Rule," constitutes the high-water mark for party leadership influence in the US House.

The position of party whip took form during this period, first as an informal role and then as an official position within the two party caucuses. (The organization of all House or Senate Democrats is called the Democratic Caucus for that chamber, while the organization of all Republican members is referred to as the Republican Conference.) As the major issues of the day increasingly divided members of Congress along party lines in the 1870s and 1880s, the whipping and other coalition-building activities that occurred also took on an increasingly partisan cast, with individual members being tapped to informally play the role of whip for their parties. For example, Alexander characterized Rep. James Wilson, R-Iowa, as "whip for his party" during the late 1870s.[4] And the legendary Thomas Brackett Reed, R-Maine, who spearheaded the party-building reforms of 1890 that still bear his name, was an effective whip for the majority Republicans during the early 1880s, while serving as Chair of the Judiciary Committee. In 1897, Reed, now serving as Speaker, formally established the position of Republican whip and asked James A. Tawney, R-Minn., an influential member of the Committee on Ways and Means, to serve as the first official whip for his party. In establishing the position, Reed was institutionalizing a role and function that had been developing informally for several decades. The central importance of the role, however, is signified by the Republicans' decision to establish the whip position two years prior to that of majority leader, and by the Democrats' decision in 1899 to follow suit and also establish the positions of whip and minority leader on their side of the partisan aisle.

Unfortunately, historical treatments and congressional biographies shed little light on the details behind the timing of the Republicans' decision to establish the position of party whip, and there are no contemporaneous media accounts. The reasons for the decision, however, are fairly obvious. The positions of Republican and Democratic whip were both established during a period in congressional history when the parties were deeply polarized on major issues and rank-and-file members were taking significant steps to strengthen their leaders in the House. In 1897, Reed and the Republicans had a solid partisan majority within the chamber, but the number of GOP members had fallen sharply relative to the previous Congress, from 254 to 206 members. Moreover, in 1896 Reed's main rival within the Republican Party, William McKinley, was elected president and the shift to unified GOP control of the legislative and executive branches fueled expectations that the 55th Congress, 1897–99, would be the most productive in years.[5] Indeed, the best scholarship about legislative productivity indicates that the substantive importance of the measures enacted during 1897–99 exceeded those passed during the previous three Congresses.[6] The key causal factors behind the creation of the position of Republican whip in 1897, then, appear to be the intense partisan polarization of the 1890s and the resulting centralization of power within the House, in conjunction with the heightened legislative demands that confronted the majority Republicans after winning the White House in 1896. In establishing the positions of Democratic whip and minority leader in 1899, the Democrats apparently were attempting to cope with analogous challenges on their side of the aisle.

Party Whips as Individuals

Summary information about the individuals that have served as House Democratic or Republican whip is provided in Table 1.1.[7] Since only 19 individuals have been whip for the Republicans and 23 have filled the position for the Democrats, it is important not to overgeneralize. Still, the most striking characteristic of the individuals that have served as party whip in the House is the extent to which their regional backgrounds have changed over time, reflecting broader developments in the geographic strengths of the two political parties.

Within Congress, the Democrats were disproportionately a southern party from the early 1900s until at least the 1930s, when the percentage of non-southerners in the House Democratic Caucus began to climb steadily. In contrast, the Republicans did not begin to regularly win House races below the Mason-Dixon line until the 1960s, but then took on an increasingly southern cast, with the percentage of southerners in the House Republican Conference reaching about 40 percent by the early 2000s. Interestingly, 10 of the first 13 Democratic whips (from Oscar W. Underwood, D-Ala., through Hale Boggs, D-La.) were from southern or border states, and of the 10 members who have served as Democratic

TABLE 1.1. Party whips of the US House

Republicans	State	Years	Prior Service	Post-Whip Status	Party Ideological Quintile
James A. Tawney	Minn.	1897–1905	4	Chm., Approps Cmte	3
James E. Watson	Ind.	1905–09	8	Defeated for governor	3
John W. Dwight	N.Y.	1909–13	6	Retired	4
Charles H. Burke	S.Dak.	1913–15	12	Defeated for Senate	4
Charles M. Hamilton	N.Y.	1915–19	2	Retired	5
Harold Knutson	Minn.	1919–23	2	Chm., Pensions Cmte	5
Albert H. Vestal	Ind.	1923–31	6	Not in leadership	4
Carl G. Bachmann	W.Va.	1931–33	6	Defeated for House	2
Harry L. Englebright	Calif.	1933–43	6	Died	3
Leslie C. Arends	Ill.	1943–75	9	Retired	4
Robert H. Michel	Ill.	1975–81	18	Min. Leader	5
Trent Lott	Miss.	1981–89	8	Elected to Senate	4
Dick Cheney	Wyo.	1989	10	Sec. of Defense	5
Newt Gingrich	Ga.	1989–95	10	Speaker	4
Tom DeLay	Tex.	1995–2003	10	Maj. Leader	5
Roy Blunt	Mo.	2003–09	6	Defeated for Min. Leader	4
Eric Cantor	Va.	2009–10	8	Maj. Leader	4
Kevin McCarthy	Calif.	2011–14	4	Maj. Leader	3
Steve Scalise	La.	2014–	7		4

Democrats	State	Years	Prior Service	Post-Whip Status	Party Ideological Quintile
Oscar W. Underwood	Ala.	1899–1901	5	Future Maj. Leader	3
James T. Loyd	Mo.	1901–08	4	Chm., Campaign Cmte	4
Thomas M. Bell	Ga.	1913–15	8	Not in leadership	5
William A. Oldfield	Ark.	1921–28	12	Died	5
John McDuffie	Ala.	1929–33	10	Defeated for Speaker	3
Arthur H. Greenwood	Ind.	1933–35	10	Not in leadership	3
Patrick J. Boland	Penn.	1935–42	4	Died	4
Robert Ramspect	Ga.	1942–45	12	Resigned	4
John J. Sparkman	Ala.	1945–46	9	Elected to Senate	3
John W. McCormack	Mass.	1947–49	18	Maj. Leader	4
J. Percy Priest	Tenn.	1949–53	8	Future Chm., Comm Cmte	3
John W. McCormack	Mass.	1953–55	24	Maj. Leader	4
Carl Albert	Ark.	1955–62	8	Maj. Leader	4
Thomas Hale Boggs	La.	1962–71	17	Maj. Leader	3
Thomas P. O'Neill	Mass.	1971–73	18	Maj. Leader	4

TABLE 1.1. *(Continued)*

Democrats	State	Years	Prior Service	Post-Whip Status	Party Ideological Quintile
John J. McFall	Calif.	1973–77	16	Defeated for Maj. Leader	3
John W. Brademas	Ind.	1977–81	18	Defeated for House	5
Thomas S. Foley	Wash.	1981–87	16	Maj. Leader	3
Tony Coelho	Calif.	1987–89	8	Resigned	4
William H. Gray III	Penn.	1989–91	10	Resigned	4
David E. Bonior	Mich.	1991–2001	15	Resigned, ran for governor	5
Nancy Pelosi	Calif.	2001–03	15	Min. Leader	5
Steny Hoyer	Md.	2003–07	22	Maj. Leader	2
Jim Clyburn	S.C.	2007–10	14	Asst. Democratic Leader	4
Steny Hoyer	Md.	2011–	26		3

whip since Boggs, only Jim Clyburn of South Carolina has hailed from the south. On the GOP side of the aisle, the opposite regional trajectory is evident. Reflecting the paucity of southern Republicans at the time, none of the first 10 GOP whips (through Leslie Arends, R-Ill.) was from that region, although one early whip did represent the border state of West Virginia (Carl G. Bachmann, 1931–33). Since the 1975 retirement of Arends, though, six of the nine individuals serving as House Republican whip have been from southern or border states.

The importance of the whip position on the congressional career ladder has also changed over time. Table 1.1 provides information about the number of years of House service that a whip completed prior to selection, and about the career status of the whips after leaving the position. On the Democratic side, the level of prior experience in the House appears to have increased over time, as does the likelihood that a whip will use the position as a springboard to higher positions within the leadership. From John McCormack's, D-Mass., first selection as whip in 1947 to the present, 10 of the 15 Democratic whips served 15 years or more in the House before filling the position, whereas none of the 9 individuals who were whips prior to McCormack had more than a dozen years of previous House service. Moreover, beginning with McCormack, a noticeable leadership trajectory also emerged on the Democratic side of the aisle, with whips often moving up to majority leader and then eventually to Speaker. McCormack, Albert, O'Neill, Foley, and Pelosi all traveled this path, and Boggs and

Hoyer rose from whip to majority leader. Prior to McCormack, none of the Democratic whips progressed to Speaker, and the only one that rose to majority or minority leader (Oscar Underwood, D-Ala.) was selected for that position a full decade after failing to be reappointed as whip.

On the Republican side of the aisle, the pattern is fairly similar, although dampened somewhat by Leslie Arends' three-decade stretch as whip, 1943–75, and the party's long period in the minority, 1955–1994. The nine individuals that served as GOP whip prior to Arends had on average less than six years previous experience in the chamber, while after Arends the average level of past service increased to nine years. Since the 1970s, a career trajectory from whip to floor leader or Speaker also has become discernible among Republicans. From Leslie Arends in the 1970s backward in time, not a single House Republican whip successfully rose in the leadership (although Arends tried and failed). Since then, Robert Michel, Newt Gingrich, Tom DeLay, Eric Cantor, and Kevin McCarthy have become floor leader or Speaker. As with the Democrats, there were noteworthy exceptions. Trent Lott and Dick Cheney left the chamber to pursue other ambitions, and Roy Blunt was defeated in his race for minority leader in 2008. Yet, on both sides of the aisle, it appears the stakes that the parties place on the position of whip have increased over time, with more senior members being tapped for the position and more whips rising within the relevant leadership as their House careers progressed.

It also is instructive to consider the ideological views of the individuals selected as whip since 1897. Do the parties tend to tap ideological extremists or party moderates for the position? Within the scholarly literature, there are two main hypotheses about the selection of party leaders in Congress. One claim, called the "middleperson hypothesis," is that the parties tend to pick for leadership positions members near the center of the distribution of viewpoints within the relevant caucus or conference, because these individuals would be most likely to advance an agenda acceptable to the party membership as a whole.

The alternative claim is that leaders disproportionately come from the ideological extremes of a party. Ideological extremists, according to this view, may make the best negotiators with leaders of the opposite party, the other chamber, and the executive branch. Moreover, leaders may be drawn from the area of the ideological spectrum within their party where there are especially large clusters of members. In other words, along with the median or mean of the distribution of preferences within a party, we also need to consider the extent to which that distribution is skewed to the left or right. If there are disproportionately large numbers of ideological extremists in a party caucus or conference, these members may work together to place their fellow ideologues in the leadership. Since the policy preferences of Democratic lawmakers are skewed sharply to the left, while those of Republicans are skewed to the right, leaders may indeed be drawn from the ideological extremes.

The best research demonstrates that party leaders in both the House and the Senate, including the whips, are disproportionately likely to be near the median viewpoint within their respective caucus or conference than would occur by chance. Clearly, the process of leadership selection is not random. But Democrats also tend to pick as leaders members who are slightly left of the median position within their party, while Republicans tend to pick leaders who are just to the conservative side of the ideological median for their rank and file.[8] The available evidence, in other words, supports both the "middleperson" and the "party extremist" hypotheses.

This finding is reflected in the final column of Table 1.1, which denotes the within-party ideological quintile of the whips based on the roll calls they cast during the Congress immediately prior to their selection to the position.[9] A quintile value of "5" for a Republican whip, for example, means that the individual was among the 20 percent most conservative GOP members of the House the two years prior to becoming whip, while a "5" for a Democrat indicates that the legislator was among the 20 percent most liberal members of the Democratic Caucus during the preceding Congress. If most of the whips had fallen in the fifth quintile, this would have been strong support for the extremist hypothesis. Along those lines, quintile rankings of "3" indicate that the member was in the middle 20 percent of the relevant caucus or conference the Congress before becoming whip, which would be supportive of the middleperson hypothesis. As you can see, Table 1.1 indicates that 12 of the 19 GOP whips had ideological views that were located near the center of the Republican Conference, or somewhat to the right of that median, while 17 out of the 23 Democratic whips had voting records that placed them near the ideological median or just to the left of that median within the Democratic Caucus.

To some extent, then, the basic strategic logic of the middleperson and extremist claims appear to illuminate the selection of party whips in the House on both sides of the aisle, extending back to the late 1890s. Not surprisingly, members want as their whips colleagues who are broadly representative of viewpoints within the relevant caucus or conference. But within each party, the cluster of extremists located toward the far end of the ideological continuum may skew the selection of whips somewhat to the left for Democrats and to the right for Republicans. In addition, rank-and-file members may believe that whips and other party leaders with viewpoints somewhat to the ideological extreme will make better negotiators for them vis-à-vis the other party, the other chamber, and the White House.

Theme

The Selection Process

One area where the House parties have differed is in the method for selecting their whips. As mentioned, Speaker Reed appointed James A. Tawney, the first GOP whip, and Republican leaders (either as Speaker or minority leader, depending on whether the party was in the majority or minority) continued to choose the party whip until 1919. From 1919 to 1965, the choice of Republican whip was made by a committee of party leaders, contingent upon acceptance by the full GOP Conference. And since 1965, the selection method has been a formal vote of the Republican rank and file. On the Democratic side of the aisle, in contrast, the whip was appointed by the floor leader (in consultation with the Speaker when the party had majority status) until a party rule change in 1984. Since then, the selection of Democratic whip also has been by election within the Democratic Caucus. In both parties, leadership elections are conducted by secret ballot. The whips must be designated at the beginning of each new Congress, but most of these decisions have been unanimous, especially when the whip was continuing on from the previous year. Still, certain whip elections have been heavily contested. The results of contested whip elections, 1964–2018 for the Republicans and 1986–2018 for the Democrats, are reported in Table 1.2.

Although party leaders in the House, including the whips, tend to have ideological views near the center of the relevant party caucus or conference, but tilted somewhat to the extreme, the outcomes of contested leadership races are not generally determined by ideology. In other words, if two or three members are running for whip, we cannot predict the outcome by looking at their policy views. Instead, the impact of ideology mostly occurs through the initial decision about whether or not to run for a leadership post. Members out-of-step with the policy views of most of their partisan colleagues generally do not throw their hats in the leadership ring.[10]

Among the Republican whips, for example, Leslie Arends was considerably more conservative than his challenger for the whip post in 1965, Peter Frelinghuysen, N.J., but their main differences were stylistic and generational. Frelinghuysen's challenge was part of a broader revolt of younger Republican members that year that resulted in Gerald Ford, R-Mich., defeating and replacing Charles Halleck, R-Ind., as minority leader. A decade later, Robert Michel, Ill., handily won the whip position based on the close ties he had developed with other Republican members as chair of the party campaign committee. The 1980 contest between Trent Lott, Miss., and Bud Shuster, Penn., to replace Michel when he moved up to minority leader likewise turned on personal style and relationships, rather than ideology.[11]

Perhaps the most consequential whip contest on the Republican side of the aisle occurred in 1989 when Dick Cheney, the newly elected GOP whip, resigned to become Secretary of Defense and Newt Gingrich, Ga., and Edward Madigan, Ill., competed to succeed him. The main differences

TABLE 1.2. Contested whip elections in the House, 1964–2018

Congress	Republican Candidates	Votes
89th (1965–66, organizational vote)	Leslie C. Arends (Ill.)	70
	Peter H.B. Frelinghuysen (N.J.)	59
94th (1975–76, organizational vote)	Robert H. Michel (Ill.)	75
	Jerry Pettis (Calif.)	38
	John Erlenborn (Ill.)	22
97th (1981–82, organizational vote)	Trent Lott (Ill.)	96
	Bud Shuster (Penn.)	90
101st (Replacement election on March 22, 1989)	Newt Gingrich (Ga.)	87
	Edward Madigan (Ill.)	85
104th (1995–96, organizational vote)	Tom DeLay (Tex.)	119
	Robert Walker (Penn.)	80
	Bill McCollum (Fla.)	28
113th (Replacement election on June 19, 2014)	Steve Scalise (La.)	NA
	Peter Roskam (Ill.)	NA
	Marlin Stutzman (Ind.)	NA

Congress	Democratic Candidates	Votes
100th (1987–88, organizational vote)	Tony Coelho (Calif.)	167
	Charles Rangel (N.Y.)	78
	W. C. "Bill" Hefner (N.C.)	15
101st (Replacement election on June 14, 1989)	William Gray (Penn.)	134
	David Bonior (Mich.)	97
	Beryl Anthony (Ark.)	30
102nd (Replacement election on July 11, 1991)	David Bonior (Mich.)	160
	Steny H. Hoyer (Md.)	109
104th (1995–96, organizational vote)	David Bonior (Mich.)	145
	Charles Stenholm (Tex.)	58
107th (Replacement election on October 10, 2001)	Nancy Pelosi (Calif.)	118
	Steny H. Hoyer (Md.)	95

Source: Amer (2006), supplemented by relevant issues of *CQ Weekly Report*.

between Gingrich and Madigan concerned their strategic postures toward the majority Democrats. Gingrich was an informal leader of a group of mostly junior House Republicans who advocated a more confrontational approach to dealing with the majority party. As whip, he pledged to clarify the policy differences between the two parties and undermine public confidence in the Democratic leadership, thereby facilitating a GOP takeover of the House. Madigan, in contrast, had served as chief deputy whip under Lott and (briefly) Cheney and also as ranking Republican on the House Agriculture Committee, and his aim as whip would have been to build bridges more effectively to moderate and conservative elements within the Democratic Caucus. Unlike the insurgent Gingrich, Madigan was viewed as the candidate of the Republican establishment and a personal favorite of Minority Leader Michel.

As Table 1.2 indicates, Gingrich narrowly prevailed, 87-85. An analysis of the head counts that Gingrich and his allies conducted before the Conference vote in March 1989 indicates support for Gingrich among rank-and-file Republicans was strongest among ideological conservatives, junior members, and Republicans preferring a more activist stance toward the Democratic leadership.[12] Gingrich's one-vote victory in the 1989 whip contest was historic. It signaled a turn toward more confrontational and aggressive tactics for House Republicans and set the stage for his elevation to the speakership.

With the election of a Republican House majority in 1994, Gingrich became Speaker and Dick Armey, R-Tex., was the unopposed pick for majority leader. In the House that year, the most heated leadership contest was between Tom DeLay, Robert Walker, R-Penn., and Bill McCollum, R-Fla., to be the Republican whip, and thus the individual with line responsibility for gathering the votes necessary to pass the Contract with America and the rest of the new majority's legislative program. Walker, who was chief deputy whip under Gingrich, and DeLay, then the Secretary of the Republican Conference, were the leading candidates. By most accounts, Walker was the more adept parliamentarian and also Gingrich's closest friend in the House. But DeLay, through assiduous fundraising, had accumulated wide support among the Republican rank and file, especially newly-elected freshmen. In the early 1990s, his political action committee, "Americans for a Republican Majority," contributed over $200,000 to GOP House candidates, his personal campaign committee donated another $100,000, and a party campaign panel he headed was responsible for $1.3 million in financial support for Republican candidates.[13] Contrary to the optimistic projections of Walker and McCollum, DeLay accurately predicted that he would win the whip contest by a comfortable margin.

The most recent contested election for House Republican whip occurred in June 2014, following the stunning defeat of then Majority Leader Eric Cantor, R-Va., in a primary election and his replacement as leader by Kevin McCarthy, R-Calif., who previously had been whip. Initially, McCarthy's top deputy, Peter Roskam, R-Ill., was viewed as the likely successor. But the conservative unrest within the GOP Conference that eventually would bring down the speakership of John Boehner in fall 2015 was already apparent, and Roskam was challenged by two members of that faction, Steve Scalise, R-La., and Marlin Stutzman, R-Ind. As chair of the influential Republican Study Committee, Scalise was perceived as the more pragmatic of the two and he quickly emerged as the top contender to Roskam. By most accounts, Scalise simply outworked the mild-mannered chief deputy. Among other tactics, he built an effective organization of 40 close allies to help lobby for his selection, rewarding them the night before the vote with baseball bats engraved in red with "Bring the Wood."[14] Although the Conference did not release vote tallies, Scalise won on the first ballot and readily cleared the 117 votes necessary to prevail.

On the Democratic side of the aisle, during the eight decades when the floor leader was responsible for appointing the whip, the selection often reflected attempts to broaden the geographic and factional representation within the leadership. Not surprisingly, personal alliances and relationships also mattered a great deal. In 1937, for example, the decision of the Pennsylvania delegation to support Sam Rayburn, D-Tex., for majority leader was contingent upon Rayburn's pledge to retain their in-state colleague, Patrick J. Boland, as whip.[15] In 1955, when Democrats regained majority control of the House and Rayburn and John McCormack, D-Mass., became Speaker and majority leader, respectively, the choice of whip was between two close Rayburn allies, Carl Albert, Okla., and Hale Boggs, La. Albert got the nod, in part because Rayburn believed it politically unwise to have two Roman Catholics in the Democratic leadership (McCormack and Boggs) and also because Albert would be more supportive of the oil depletion allowance, which was critical to Rayburn's Texas delegation.[16] In 1971, when Albert became Speaker and Boggs moved up to majority leader, Boggs' personal preference for whip was his close friend Dan Rostenkowski, Ill., then Chair of the Democratic Caucus. Albert, however, disliked and distrusted Rostenkowski and vetoed the choice. The position instead went to Thomas P. "Tip" O'Neill, Mass., a respected member of the Rules Committee who had provided Boggs with critical support during his race for majority leader.[17]

During the 1970s, Democrats adopted a number of institutional reforms aimed at opening up the legislative process and curtailing the power of committee chairs relative to the leadership and rank-and-file members. As part of the reform effort, pressure mounted to make the whip position subject to election by the full Democratic Caucus. Advocates of the change argued, correctly, that the whip often progressed up the leadership ladder and thus should be elected and not appointed. Other members, however, maintained that the Democratic floor leader should be allowed to pick as whip an individual who would work well with other members of the leadership. Throughout the decade there were regular calls from rank-and-file Democrats to change the selection method for their whip to election by the caucus, and following the 1984 elections, the change was finally adopted.

The first elected whip for the Democrats was Tony Coelho, Calif., who previously had served for six years as Chair of the Democratic Congressional Campaign Committee, raising tens of millions of dollars for the campaigns of his Democratic colleagues. Coelho easily won the whip race in 1986 over two challengers. Indeed, his campaign for the position was so exhaustive and systematic that he even asked his campaign manager, Vic Fazio, D-Calif., how he would vote. "You can't be serious," Fazio reportedly replied, "I'm your campaign manager."[18]

In 1989, Speaker Jim Wright resigned when an ethics investigation instigated by Newt Gingrich found he had violated House rules. That same year, Coelho also found himself a potential subject of ethics charges and chose to resign as whip. The spirited contest to replace him quickly turned into a two-way fight between William Gray, D-Penn., the chair of the Democratic Caucus, and David Bonior, then the chief deputy whip. Gray defeated Bonior, 134-97, largely because he had successfully built a majority coalition among his Democratic colleagues just the year before to become Caucus Chair, while Bonior, as chief deputy whip, had been appointed to his position and had not previously campaigned caucus-wide for a leadership post. After Gray himself resigned in 1991, Bonior easily defeated Steny Hoyer, Md., a party moderate, for the whip position, and then three years later withstood a challenge from conservative Democrat Charles Stenholm, Tex., following the party's defeat in the 1994 midterm elections.

The final contested race for Democratic whip occurred in 2001, when Bonior stepped down from the position to run for governor of Michigan.[19] Throughout the year, Nancy Pelosi and Steny Hoyer had been positioning themselves to be the next whip as it became apparent that Bonior would soon resign. Indeed, the race between Pelosi and Hoyer really began in

1999, in anticipation of a possible Democratic takeover of the House in 2000, which would have opened up the whip position (with Richard Gephardt advancing to Speaker and Bonior to majority leader). Both candidates developed extensive networks among their colleagues that kept track of the views of unpledged members in the race for whip. Tim Roemer, D-Ind, who was undecided between Pelosi and Hoyer until the week before the caucus vote, remarked, "For the last year, every time I've walked on the floor, it feels like a whip saw going in both directions. If two Pelosi people got me on the floor, a Hoyer person would walk with me back to my office. Then 12 calls would be waiting for me from former members calling on behalf of one or the other."[20] The morning of the vote, Pelosi reserved several private planes in case any of her supporters needed last-minute transportation to Washington.[21] In the end, she won the position, 118-95, setting the stage for her elevation to floor leader and then Speaker in 2007.

By the beginning of the twenty-first century, then, the incumbent leadership or a cohort of senior members no longer dominated the selection of party whip, as had been the case during the formative years of the two whip operations. Instead, a vacancy in the whip post now generated elaborate and highly organized lobbying campaigns that themselves showcased the fundraising, organizational, and canvassing prowess of the candidates for the position—yet another indicator of the vital importance of the whips in the modern Congress.

The Whips as Organizations

The whips, of course, are organizations as well as individuals. Histories of the chamber and contemporaneous media accounts indicate that in 1900 the Democratic Caucus established the position of "assistant whip," which for a brief period was filled by Sydney Epps, D-Va., and the House Republican whip received staff assistance as early as 1905.[22] Neither party, however, developed much of a whip organization until the early 1930s.

On the Republican side of the aisle, Carl Bachmann, W.Va., who served as whip during 1931–33, established the basic system the party was to use for the next half century. In 1931, the GOP retained majority control of the House, but the size of their margin had dropped to just two seats. Confronted with a national economic emergency and a small majority, the Republicans needed a more extensive whip operation to exert even a semblance of control. As a result, Bachmann divided the country into two regions, each headed by an assistant whip, and then within each state that had elected Republicans to the House, he selected a member to serve as the contact person for the whip operation vis-à-vis that delegation.[23] Decisions about when to conduct whip counts and other mobilization activities during the period typically were made by a party committee, with the floor leader and whip playing a significant role in the strategizing. The Republican whip would notify the regional assistants that canvassing had been called for, the regional whips would contact the whip representatives within each state delegation, and they in turn would touch base with rank-and-file members and report back the results.

Although Bachmann's whip structure remained in place for decades, the extent to which it was actually staffed and used varied considerably over time, especially during the many years when the Republicans were in the minority. In an April 1942 letter to Minority Leader Joe Martin, R-Mass., for example, Charles A. Plumley, a Republican member from Vermont, observed that, "There is a lot of criticism of the fact that we have no Whip Organization. Nobody dares say anything to you about it, but they talk a lot to me. [GOP Whip Harry L. Englebright] hasn't notified a single person in the 77th Congress [1941–42] that they were members of the whip organization."[24] But Plumley also emphasized the potential importance of an effective whip operation, even for the House minority party during the 1940s. "If we are to get anywhere in the next few months preliminary to the campaign," he wrote, "we have got to have an organization, whether or not it is called upon to act.... The Republican membership should have notice as to whose orders they should heed, if orders are issued."[25]

The next year, Leslie Arends began his long tenure as House Republican whip. Arends formalized and expanded the system over time to include three regional whips (for the eastern, midwest, and western/southern divisions), and 13 assistant whips who were responsible for canvassing Republican members in particular states or clusters of states.[26] From its inception in the early 1930s to the current House, the GOP whip has always appointed all participants in the Republican whip organization.

For House Democrats, the whip had been given several assistants by the late 1920s, but as was the case for the Republicans, the establishment of a full-fledged whip organization on that side of the aisle also did not occur until the 1930s. Under Arthur Greenwood, Democratic whip from 1931 to 1933, the party created a system comprised of 15 assistant whips, each responsible for a zone of members from a particular state or geographic area. In contrast to the Republican setup, on the Democratic side of the aisle the assistant or "zone" whips were not appointed by the leadership,

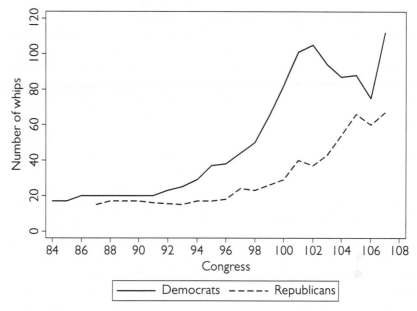

Figure 1.1. House whip organizations (1955–2002)

but instead were selected by the rank-and-file members from their zones, or picked by the most senior member of the relevant delegation. To some extent, the Democrats probably were simply following the Republicans' lead in setting up a whip organization for their party. But there also were more instrumental reasons. Although the Democratic majorities of the 1930s were very large, they also were deeply divided along sectional and ideological lines, complicating the leadership's ability to pass the Roosevelt administration's large and ambitious legislative agenda. The Democrats, in other words, also needed to create a whip organization to build winning majorities under daunting circumstances. Interestingly, the Greenwood system also was largely unchanged until the early 1970s. Indeed, the only alterations to it were the establishment of the position of deputy whip in 1955 (as a consolation prize for Hale Boggs after he was passed over for whip) and the addition of three more zones in 1957, which increased the number of assistant Democratic whips to 18.

Then, from the 1970s to the 1990s, the whip organizations for both parties were remarkably transformed, with the majority Democrats moving first. Figure 1.1 shows the total number of members included in each whip organization from 1955 until 2002 (the last year for which authoritative information is available).[27] As the figure indicates, the number of Democratic whips was fairly stable until the 93rd Congress (1971–72), when the leadership split the deputy whip role into two offices and appointed John McFall and John Brademas to the positions. Two years later, when McFall became whip, Brademas was made chief deputy and two other members were tapped as deputy whips. In 1975, the leadership appointed three "at-large" whips to ensure the full representation of African Americans, women, and freshman lawmakers in the party whip operation. In 1976, the number of "at large" slots grew to 10.

During the 1980s, the number of appointive whips for the Democrats continued to increase, and in 1991–92, the position of chief deputy whip was divided into four separate positions to better integrate women, African Americans and other groups within the caucus in the upper echelons of the whip organization.[28] At the beginning of the 104th Congress, 1995–96, the zone structure for conducting whip counts was revamped to include 12 regional areas, each headed by two assistant or regional whips. This core group of regional assistants, it should be emphasized, was still selected by the rank-and-file Democrats from the relevant areas, but the remaining whips were appointed by the leadership, often in consultation with important groups and factions within the Democratic Caucus. The appointive whips selected by House Democratic leaders in the 1990s were more likely to be party loyalists than had been the case during the 1980s, when overall levels of partisan polarization had been lower.[29] By 2001–02, the number of Democratic whips reached 112, or just over half of the full caucus. As a result of the burgeoning size of the Democratic whip operation, by the mid-1980s the leadership regularly created and relied on issue-specific task forces, rather than the full whip organization, when major legislation important to the party was slated for floor action.

As shown in Figure 1.1, the size and organizational structure of the House Republican whip system did not change much during the 1970s. In 1981, however, with Ronald Reagan in the White House and a GOP majority in the Senate, the newly elected whip, Trent Lott, took steps to strengthen the House Republican organization. Over the next eight years, the number of members in the GOP whip system grew steadily from 18 members (including the whip) to almost 30. In 1981, Lott appointed two chief deputies, Tom Loeffler, Tex., and Sid Morrison, Wash. The selection of Loeffler was particularly important because of the Texan's extensive contacts with southern Democrats, such as Charles Stenholm, D-Tex., who would be pivotal to several important GOP victories on the floor that year. Lott also created a fourth regional division and expanded the number of regional and assistant whips. In 1985, he established whip positions for the freshman and sophomore classes. When Newt Gingrich became whip in 1989, he also added several assistant deputy whip slots and appointed five new "strategy whips" to help him set the stage for a GOP takeover of the House.

After being elected the House Republican whip in 1994, Tom DeLay further increased the size of the party whip operation. But more important, DeLay also streamlined its organizational structure and tightened up the lines of responsibility to promote effective coalition building on the floor. As the majority party, the Republicans' strategic posture had shifted from unraveling Democratic coalitions to building their own majorities and otherwise managing the flow of legislation in the chamber. In the 104th Congress, DeLay's vote-gathering operation included future Speaker Dennis Hastert as chief deputy, 13 deputy whips, and 39 assistants, all handpicked by the majority whip. Although DeLay would increase the number of deputies and assistant whips over the next few years, he maintained the basic hierarchical structure he first put in place in 1995. In 2001–02, the Republican whip organization, at 68 members, was not as large as its Democratic counterpart, but still encompassed almost one-third of the full GOP membership.

Whip Activity

Not surprisingly, the scope of whip activity also changed markedly over time. Shortly after the positions were created at the end of the nineteenth century, party whips in the House were involved in a range of coalition building activities, but ensuring the presence of members on the floor for contested votes was especially important. At the time, the technology available for transportation and communications was more primitive than in the modern Congress. Party leaders often had to reach members by wire and travel from the district to Washington could take many days. Moreover, without electronic voting in the House, the typical roll call could last 40 to 45 minutes, with undecided members wavering back and forth on the floor and the outcome hanging in the balance. As a result, a central task for the early whips was simply making sure that their likeminded colleagues were present in the chamber for major votes.

Champ Clark, D-Mo., a House member from 1893 to 1920 and Speaker during much of the presidency of Woodrow Wilson, characterized the ideal whip of the early 1900s in his autobiography:

> The whips are the right hands of the two leaders. To be efficient they must know the membership by sight; be on as friendly a footing with them as possible; know where they reside, both in Washington and at home; know their habits, their recreations, their loafing-places; the condition of their health, and that of their families; the number of their telephones; when they are out of the city; when they will return; how they would probably vote on a pending measure; what churches they attend; what theaters they frequent – in short, all about them.[30]

"The whip's principal duty," Clark continued, "is to have his fellow political members in the House when needed. On critical occasions, when great questions are to be decided, especially when a close vote is expected, much energy is expended by the whips in order to muster the full party strength."[31]

Securing the presence of members on the floor would continue to be a significant challenge for the whips for many decades, especially until regular access to jet air travel in the 1960s, which significantly eased member travel to and from Washington. In the early 1950s, for instance, GOP Whip Leslie Arends needed the vote of an absent Republican who was back home in the district. The member apparently was ducking Arends' repeated telephone calls to his residence, so the whip arranged for the local radio station in that district to announce periodically that any listeners running across their congressman should mention that he was needed back in Washington.[32]

In addition to getting members to the floor, the first whips also coordinated the process through which absent members arrange "pairs" with lawmakers on the opposite side of a vote. With such pairs, neither partner casts a roll call and their stands are printed in the *Congressional Record*. Due to the relative difficulty of traveling to and from Washington during the period, the ability to arrange "live pairs" (one member is present and the other is not) could be pivotal to the outcome. The Republicans were able to win a highly charged tariff fight on the House floor in February 1900, for example, because of their advantages in the arrangement of paired votes and the critical role played by the GOP whip, James A. Tawney.[33]

There also are many examples of successful lobbying and other persuasive efforts by the early whips on major legislation. On the tariff vote in 1900, Tawney's initial canvassing indicated the Republicans might lose. As a result, according to the *Washington Post*, "he set to work with great energy ... and all the machinery of the House was utilized to assist him."[34] According to one history of the period, John W. Dwight, R-N.Y., GOP whip during 1909–13, "might be seen daily, with whip's book in hand, taking note of the whereabouts of every member.... It became his business, also, to learn the disposition of members toward party measures and to report signs of disaffection.... Thus the labor of the whip mobilized the majority party, kept it within call, minimized defeat, and informed leaders of the strength of the Opposition."[35]

By most accounts, the role of the whips in counting votes and lobbying wavering members stepped up significantly during the 1930s, as the whip organizations became more developed. Patrick J. Boland served as a valued lieutenant to the Roosevelt administration and three Democratic Speakers during his tenure as majority whip, 1935–42. In a review of the first session of the 74th Congress in 1935, for example, the *Washington Post* reported that, "the House developed a new whip organization led by Pat Boland of Pennsylvania which showed such uncanny accuracy in forecasting how a vote would go that the vote itself was superfluous."[36] In 1936, Boland and his organization conducted a whip count on a farm mortgage-refinancing bill backed by the infamous radio priest and political demagogue, Father Charles E. Coughlin. The count demonstrated that the bill, which was adamantly opposed by Roosevelt and the House Democratic leadership, lacked the votes to win, enabling them to bring the measure to the floor where it was easily defeated.[37] In the lead-up to an historic roll call in 1939 repealing the US arms embargo, Boland was described as "constantly polling House sentiment," and correctly predicted that the leadership would carry the day.[38]

Boland's effectiveness as whip, however, was constrained by the sectional and ideological differences within the Democratic Caucus. On a landmark revision of the Neutrality Act in 1941 (the famous "Lend-Lease" program), he was unable to predict the outcome on the key roll call because 30 to 40 members remained undecided until the very end of the floor debate, and eventually supported the leadership and the White House only after impassioned floor speeches by Speaker Sam Rayburn and Majority Leader John McCormack.[39] After Boland's death in 1943, the role of the Democratic whip in the 1940s and 1950s was less systematic and generally more limited than during Boland's tenure, reflecting Rayburn's inclination to lobby individual members personally and informally.[40]

From the 1950s to the 2000s, because of the availability of archival records, the level of whip activity in the House can be gauged with more precision, using the number of whip counts conducted by Democratic and Republican leaders as an indicator. This information is provided in Table 1.3, along with several indicators of the broader legislative context. Two columns denote the total number of "whipped questions" that the relevant leadership put to its rank-and-file members during a two-year Congress, 1955–2002. In other words, if the leadership requests that the zone or regional whips ask their members three separate questions dealing with a single bill (perhaps about the rule, an expected floor amendment, and the vote on final passage), then the request would count as three polled questions. The missing entries in the table are for Congresses for which whip count data for the party are unavailable. Prior to 1975, for example, the Republicans regularly purged their whip files at the end of each Congress and we lack systematic archival traces for them for those years. And as noted in the table, for four of the cells whip count records do not

TABLE 1.3. Number of whipped questions in the House, 1955–2002

Congress	Years	Dem Ques	GOP Ques	Party Polarization	Party Sizes (D-R)	Roll Call Votes	White House
84	1955–56	20		.48	232–203	149	R
85	1957–58	8		.47	234–201	193	R
86	1959–60	5		.50	283–153	180	R
87	1961–62	15		.48	262–175	240	D
88	1963–64	18		.50	258–176	232	D
89	1965–66	27		.50	295–140	394	D
90	1967–68	30		.49	246–187	478	D
91	1969–70	21		.52	243–192	443	R
92	1971–72	26		.52	255–180	649	R
93	1973–74	68		.53	239–192	1,078	R
94	1975–76	20[1]	53	.52	291–144	1,273	R
95	1977–78	105	46	.51	292–143	1,540	D
96	1979–80	45	22	.53	276–157	1,276	D
97	1981–82	28		.56	243–192	812	R
98	1983–84	52		.59	268–166	906	R
99	1985–86	48		.62	252–182	890	R
100	1987–88			.63	258–177	939	R
101	1989–90	54[2]	98	.65	259–174	879	R
102	1991–92	49[3]	84	.67	267–167	901	R
103	1993–94	98	27[2]	.73	258–176	1,094	D
104	1995–96		168	.81	204–230	1,321	D
105	1997–98		144	.85	207–227	1,116	D
106	1999–2000		85	.87	211–223	1,209	D
107	2001–02		47	.90	211–221	990	R

[1] Through February 5, 1976
[2] First session
[3] After September 23, 1991

encompass the full Congress. Still, the available evidence indicates several instructive trends about House whip activity from the 1950s to the 2000s.

First, the level of activity has risen substantially over time. For the Democrats, the average number of whip counts per Congress for 1955–72 was about 19. During the 1970s transition, the average rose to just over 61 (excluding the 94th Congress for which only partial data are available). And during the turn to partisanship in 1983–94 (again, only including Congresses with full data), the average increased somewhat to 66. On the Republican side of the aisle, for the three Congresses in the 1970s for which evidence is available, the average number of counts per Congress was about 40. If we consider the Congresses since 1989 for which full data are available, in contrast, the average number of GOP whip counts was 104.

Second, although the number of years for which polling data are available for both parties is small, it does appear that whip activity is higher on the majority side of the aisle. This clearly is the case for the 1970s. Moreover, the high level of polling among House Republicans during 1995–2002 probably exceeded the amount of whip counts conducted by the minority Democrats, at least based on the comments of knowledgeable participants.[41] The reasons are straightforward. The majority party is more likely to be held responsible for managing the floor agenda by the media and the public, and thus has greater incentives to poll on a large number of questions, especially relating to appropriations bills and other must-pass legislation. The minority party, in contrast, is primarily concerned with highlighting the differences that exist between the two party programs and, when feasible, picking apart the majority coalition. Not surprisingly, then, they tend to whip a smaller and narrower set of issues.

Third, although the number of whip polls has increased over time, there were sharp spikes for the Democrats in the late 1970s and for the Republicans in the late 1990s. As mentioned, the four columns to the right in Table 1.3 include indicators of the broader legislative context that are a first step toward illuminating the changes that have occurred in whip activity over time. First, note that the level of partisan polarization in the roll call record has increased markedly from the 1950s to the 2000s. This trend comes as no surprise to even casual observers of American politics. In recent years, the Congress has become far more polarized along party lines. Here, polarization is measured by the distance between the mean DW-NOMINATE scores within the Democratic Caucus and Republican Conference.[42] These scores are a standard measure of the ideological liberalism or conservatism of individual members of Congress, as revealed by the roll calls they cast on the floor, and range in value from –1 (extremely liberal) to +1 (extremely conservative), with values near zero reflecting ideological moderation. Notice that the distance between the two party means was relatively low and stable from the mid-1950s until the late 1970s, and then began to climb steadily in the 1980s and reached very high levels in the 1990s. The upward trajectory in whip counts during the 1980s and 1990s accompanied increased partisan polarization in the chamber and a growing need for the majority party to build winning coalitions almost entirely from among its own members. But what about the 1970s spike for the Democrats, which occurred prior to the most significant increases in partisan polarization?

The next column in Table 1.3 provides information about party sizes in the House over the time period.[43] Notice that the GOP majorities during 1995–2002 were relatively small by recent historical standards. Indeed, early in 2001 there were only 221 Republicans in the chamber, a bare majority. The small size of the GOP margin during these years, combined with the high levels of partisan polarization, meant that the party needed to hold onto the votes of almost all of its members to win on the floor. One likely consequence was a highly active whip operation, which is reflected in the hundreds of counts that Tom DeLay conducted during the period. During the late 1970s spike in Democratic whip activity, however, the size of the majority caucus was very large, reaching almost 300 members. Again, why was the Democratic whip operation so active during these years?

The last two columns in Table 1.3 can help answer the question. One denotes, for each Congress, the number of roll call votes that took place on the floor of the House, and the other indicates the party of the president. As the table shows, the number of roll calls grew steadily during the 1950s and 1960s, and then surged in 1973–74 and remained high for the rest of the decade, before dropping somewhat in the 1980s and then increasing again in the 1990s. Prior to 1970, recorded votes on amendments were very rare in the "Committee of the Whole," which is the parliamentary device through which the House considers amendments in the full chamber. Before the 1970s, the fate of amendments was decided by voice vote, division (members stood to indicate their positions), or teller (members filed down the center aisle in "yes" and "no" lines). The Legislative Reorganization Act of 1970, however, provided for roll call votes in the Committee of the Whole, and thus on floor amendments, and in 1973 the House implemented electronic voting (which sharply decreased the time necessary to conduct roll calls). As a result, the number of floor amendments shot up during the 1970s. Much of the new amending activity was instigated by Republican members attempting to force the majority Democrats to cast public votes on politically divisive issues that could hurt them at home.[44]

Confronted with an avalanche of amendments and votes and a caucus that was large, but divided, the Democratic leadership significantly stepped up its whip activity. Moreover, the election of Jimmy Carter as president in 1976 meant that Democratic leaders were responsible for shepherding the administration's legislative agenda through Congress, reinforcing the need for accurate intelligence about the evolving positions of members and for effective lobbying on the floor. For these reasons, the incidence of majority whip activity increased markedly in the late 1970s. By the early 1980s, Democratic members had convinced Speaker O'Neill to clamp down on the floor amendment process via the use of more restrictive rules.[45] And because of the election of Ronald Reagan as president in 1980, the Democrats were no longer responsible for advancing the legislative program of the incumbent president through the House. Instead, they could focus more on playing defense. For a time, the number of Democratic whip counts fell, before rising again with the burgeoning partisan polarization in Congress.

From the inception of the formal whip system in the late 1890s to the contemporary era, the incidence of whip activity is related to both the degree of partisan polarization in the chamber and the magnitude of the legislative challenge confronting the relevant leadership. Depending on the period, the presidential context also made a difference, with the majority leadership often stepping up its whipping to advance the legislative agenda of a fellow partisan in the White House.

Overall, then, the emergence of the whips as a critical feature of the lawmaking process derived from important developments in the broader party system, and we cannot understand their role separate from the incentives that rank-and-file lawmakers confront as members of one or the other political party. They are referred to as *party* whips for a reason. Still, the preliminary look at the whips as individuals and organizations provided in this chapter also indicates the linkages that exist between party variables like the degree of polarization, on the one hand, and the organizational complexity and activity levels of the two whip systems, on the other, are neither simple nor direct. In the late 1930s, for example, Democratic leaders relied on a highly active whip operation to build majorities within a Democratic Caucus that was large but also deeply divided along sectional and ideological lines. During the late 1970s, House Democrats similarly expanded their whip system and the amount of polling and lobbying they conducted in response to a significant rise in floor amendments and the internal disagreements that existed within the Democratic Caucus. And the highly active GOP whip operations of the late 1990s partially resulted from party polarization, to be sure, but also from the narrow Republican majorities of that period. The important changes that have occurred in the whip systems of the House over the course of congressional history are as much a response to significant challenges confronting the leadership, as they are a reflection of heightened party unity or an indicator of leadership strength. This observation is important, and it needs to be front and center in the next chapter as we attempt to conceptualize about the role of the whips and of congressional leaders more generally.

TWO

Behavioral Foundations of the Whip Process

As mentioned at the beginning of the previous chapter, the title of "party whip" derives from a centuries-old metaphor that relates vote gathering within a legislature to the herding of hound dogs during foxhunts in the English countryside. Perhaps not surprisingly, journalistic coverage of the whips often is similarly couched in metaphor. Early in his tenure in the position, the media chose to nickname Tom DeLay, House GOP whip from 1995 to 2002, as "the Hammer" for his purported forcefulness at getting wavering Republicans to vote the party line. By one count, prior to DeLay's 2006 resignation from the House, there were 50 separate references to him as "the Hammer" in the *Washington Post* and over 30 in the *New York Times*.[1] Around Capitol Hill, one profile claimed, DeLay was infamous for being "the Meanest Man in Congress."[2] Richard Cohen, a respected columnist, even quoted a GOP insider in describing DeLay's whip operation as "a cross between the concierge at the Plaza and the mafia ... they can get you anything you want, but it will cost you."[3]

Such analogies to hand tools and the mob imply a certain narrative about the whips and legislating that might go something like this. First, prior to legislative action on the floor, members of Congress weigh the policy choices before them and develop preferences between the competing alternatives, perhaps rooted in their constituents' interests or their own views. Second, fearing an embarrassing loss for the party position on the floor because of the distribution of member preferences, the leadership

41

engages its whip networks and hammers away. Third, through a combination of aggressive browbeating, well-placed payoffs, and good old-fashioned threats, targeted lawmakers switch their positions and vote with the party. *Voilà!* The leadership wins, centrist opinion is undermined, and the majority party dominates the legislative game.

Interestingly, contemporary scholarship about party coalition building in Congress has come to reflect this narrative in important ways.[4] Prior to the 1980s, the dominant paradigm for studying legislatures, often referred to as "behavioralism," emphasized member goals and the representational relationships that exist between individual lawmakers and important constituencies back home and across the country. The policy preferences of legislators were treated as strategic manifestations of these relationships, and the process of preference formation was front and center in the analysis.

Since then, the field of legislative studies has shifted remarkably toward spatial models of lawmaking in which member preferences usually are treated as exogenously determined, or as if they derive from factors external to the lawmaking process. The intuition behind spatial theory is intuitively plausible and familiar to most observers of American politics.[5] Basically, members are assumed to have "preferences" that can be represented as ideal points along one or more underlying dimensions of evaluation, such as the liberal-conservative continuum. Legislative alternatives likewise can be represented as points in ideological space. Members base their votes on which alternative is located most spatially proximate to their "preferences." Unless some legislators are assumed to have procedural powers or other resources unavailable to their colleagues, the outcome according to this formulation should be the most preferred position of the median voter, or the legislator having an equal number of colleagues with ideal points located to her ideological left and right. Any proposals to move legislation in a conservative direction would be opposed by the median and the members to her left, and any attempts to move legislation to the left would be opposed by the median and her colleagues on the ideological right. Called the median voter theorem, this prediction is one of the best known conceptual claims in political science, and it resonates with popular intuition about the importance of swing voters and the political middle ground (Black 1958).

Among other scholars, Krehbiel (1998) and Brady and Volden (2006) have extended this rudimentary spatial setup to include additional legislators with preferences that might be pivotal in the legislative process. For instance, in the real world of congressional politics, a majority-favored bill may not pass in the Senate if there is a filibuster and

60 Senators—the number needed to invoke cloture and end the talkathon according to Senate rules—do not have ideal points located closer to the bill than to existing law, or the outcome that otherwise will occur if the bill dies. In addition, legislation favored by floor medians in both chambers may not become law if the president issues a veto and two-thirds supermajorities in the House and Senate fail to override the act. As a result, supermajorities may be required in one or both chambers to enact a piece of legislation and outcomes may need to diverge from the preferences of the floor median to pick up the additional votes. Like the median voter model, such extensions also include no meaningful roles for parties or for leaders. *Theme*

Within the field of congressional studies, there are two leading conceptual frames for thinking about legislative parties—the party cartel model and the conditional party government argument. Although neither theory was originally articulated as a spatial model, over time both have come to be presented in largely spatial terms. And both theories generate predictions of non-centrist, party-influenced outcomes precisely because they posit special powers for leaders of the majority party. Not hammers or mob enforcement, exactly, but powers sufficient to overcome the centripetal pull of the median voter or some other actor made pivotal by the rules of the game. *Cartel Model - Legislative parties*

The cartel model derives from two highly influential books by Gary Cox and Mathew McCubbins (1993, 2005) in which they argue that the majority party in the House has functioned as a form of procedural cartel since at least the late 1800s. Members of a party caucus, Cox and McCubbins assert, share a common electoral fate. If a party's public reputation among voters, or what they call the party "name brand," is positive, then members of that party can more easily get elected and maintain or secure majority status for their caucus. As a result, members of the partisan majority have given their leaders complete authority over which bills are considered by the chamber and which bills are kept off the agenda. If scheduling a bill for floor action would result in the passage of legislation that most members of the majority oppose, then the majority leadership should block consideration. According to the cartel model, party leaders are not presumed to have the leverage necessary to alter legislative content once a bill has been placed on the agenda. The median voter theorem should hold for the bills that move. But there will be many issue areas where something could pass and consideration is precluded because of leadership agenda control. Under such conditions, outcomes (or non-outcomes, if you prefer) diverge from centrist attitudes toward policy views within the majority party.

Conditional
Party Government.

The second major theory of party influence is the conditional party government argument of John Aldrich and David Rohde (Rohde 1991, Aldrich 1995). Their argument goes something like this. When the two parties are each comprised of members representing similar districts, and when there are stark differences between the kinds of constituencies that elect Democrats versus Republicans, the consequence will be a distribution of policy preferences within the chamber that is polarized along partisan lines. In spatial terms, the preferences of Republican members will cluster toward the ideological right, the views of Democrats will cluster toward the left, and there will be few ideological moderates from either party with ideal points located in the middle. When these conditions are met—ideological homogenization within each party and ideological polarization between them—Aldrich and Rohde maintain that the majority party will provide its leadership with important prerogatives and resources to push the party agenda through Congress. The potential costs to centralization are low under such conditions (majority party members are largely in agreement on the major issues of the day), while the potential benefits are high (members of the majority want an empowered leadership to overwhelm the dramatically different proposals backed by the opposition). The special powers granted to the majority leadership will include agenda control *a la* the cartel model, but also a range of additional prerogatives, such as control over valued committee assignments and other forms of institutional patronage, resources to aid the reelection campaigns of individual members, the ability to punish members who defect from the party position, and so on. As a result, when the distribution of ideological preferences is polarized along party lines, the majority leadership will have the leverage necessary to pull outcomes away from centrist preferences in the chamber toward the majority party program—not just for items that are blocked, but also for measures that advance.

As mentioned, the initial articulations of the cartel and conditional party government theories were not overtly spatial, or for that matter rooted in explicit assumptions about exogenously determined preferences. Fundamentally, the cartel logic posits that members of a congressional party will consider their common electoral interests in making up their minds about positions to take and votes to cast, and such calculations can take place as part of the whip process on the floor. With conditional party government, activist party leadership is predicted when the distribution of ideological preferences within the chamber is polarized along party lines, but that does not necessarily imply that member preferences about particular issues or votes are fully formed prior to the whip process. Scholars of the caliber of Cox and McCubbins or Aldrich and Rohde fully recognize that in the real world of congressional politics member viewpoints are not generally determined exogenously, and are more typically shaped by factors internal to the lawmaking process, including party considerations.

Yet, as spatial reasoning came to dominate legislative scholarship during the 1990s and 2000s, both theories were recast in largely spatial terms, with the main differences between them concerning the magnitude of the powers posited for the majority leadership and whether or not a polarized distribution of preferences is necessary for parties to affect outcomes (e.g., Cox and McCubbins 2005; Aldrich and Rohde 1998a). Now, when scholars attempt to generalize about the congressional parties, sharp distinctions are usually drawn between the independent effects of preferences and parties, which in turn implies that party influence is not primarily exerted via the process of preference formation. And legislative deviations from centrist viewpoints in the chamber—an overtly spatial construct—have become the *sine qua non* for party influence. In other words, if the spatial location of an outcome diverges from the ideological middle ground toward the majority position, then parties are said to matter in the legislative process. And if systematic evidence for such deviations cannot be found, then the inference is that party effects are absent.

Perhaps most telling, when contemporary scholars test the implications of cartel theory or conditional party government with quantitative data, preferences measures are almost always included as rival explanatory variables to party, which essentially mandates an underlying spatial logic. Indeed, the very measures that are used as indicators of member preferences illustrate the downside of taking preferences as given. These ideological scores are generally scaled from the roll call record, and thus are themselves shaped by partisan considerations, presidential lobbying, and all of the other factors lawmakers consider in deciding how to vote (Jackson and Kingdon 1992). It comes as no surprise, then, that scholars have had considerable difficulty identifying instances where party effects occur after controlling for preference effects. Conceptually, the distinction often makes little sense, and empirically, the preference measures scholars use are incapable of disentangling the independent effects of the two factors on lawmaking.

These limitations are especially problematic for us. Whipping concerns the development of member positions and preferences as part of the legislative process, with partisan and other factors shaping the process of viewpoint formation. Procedures and other structural arrangements certainly matter, but to understand the work of the whips, we need a conceptual framework capable of generating predictions about the internal mechanisms through which members make up their minds in the first place. Cartel theory and conditional party government provide insights, but we need to dig deeper. Fortunately, the aforementioned behavioral tradition in congressional studies provides ample guidance about how to proceed. And the main ingredients of a behaviorally grounded theory of the whip process can be identified by revisiting the pivotal decision of Robin Hayes to vote for Fast Track in the House in December 2001, as introduced in the opening narrative of this book.

Summary

Robin Hayes, the 8th District, and Fast Track

To be illuminating, an analysis of the decision-making process of a member of Congress, including the role played by party leaders and other elite-level pressures, should be grounded outside of the chamber, and within the district or state the lawmaker was elected to represent. The impact of congressional leaders is not solely or even primarily a Washington story. Instead, to understand how partisan coalitions are built on Capitol Hill, we first need to consider what individual members see when looking at their constituencies.

In his book, *Home Style*, Richard Fenno argued that these perceptions can be usefully conceptualized as a bull's-eye of concentric circles. The outermost circle is the *geographic constituency*, which is the member's district as defined by law or judicial decision, along with the people that reside within those physical boundaries. Within the geographic constituency, Fenno found, a member distinguishes between voters based on the likelihood that they will support him or her at the polls. Members tend to perceive a *reelection constituency*, in other words, comprised of their likely supporters on Election Day. Nested within the reelection constituency, lawmakers also perceive a third circle, the *primary constituency*, which is comprised of their strong supporters, or alternatively, the votes they would need to secure in order to prevail in a contested primary election. Finally, the innermost perceptual circle is for what Fenno labeled the *personal constituency*, or the people that are closest to the lawmaker and perhaps were instrumental in some way to her pre-congressional career and initial election to Congress.

Fenno's study of members at home was mostly conducted during the 1970s, when candidates for Congress were far less dependent on the national parties, political action committees, and other Washington-based

Theme reliance on greater party ⟩

organizations for campaign donations and infrastructure, polling, message, and other political intelligence necessary to win elections. By 2001, though, candidates for the House and Senate were heavily reliant on such outside sources for campaign assistance. As a result, contemporary members actually conduct two related campaigns to stay in office; one at home with the voters, and the other mostly in Washington and aimed at national party organizations, interest groups, and policy coalitions headquartered outside the geographic constituency (Herrnson 2012). The need to satisfy national party organizations and advocacy coalitions can shape the decisions members make within the Congress and the positions that they take on issues, which in turn can influence how they interact with the multiple constituencies they face at home. Along with the four nested constituencies that Fenno described, then, we add a fifth, the *outside constituency*, comprised of the national groups and organizations to which a member must be responsive in order to accumulate the resources necessary to win reelection.

In 2001, Robin Hayes was in his second term as a Republican member of the US House, representing the 8th District of North Carolina. His geographic constituency was located in the south-central portions of the state, adjacent to the border with South Carolina and extending from the Charlotte suburbs in the west almost to Fayetteville in the east. When Hayes cast the deciding vote on Fast Track, his district was geographically large, politically and economically diverse, and comprised of all or parts of 10 counties. Figure 2.1 portrays the district, including the percentage of the vote Hayes won at the county level in 2000.[6]

Asked to describe the 8th District in general terms, Hayes immediately emphasized its diversity and the significant geographic differences in partisan attachments that are apparent in the map. "The two key Republican areas are in the western part, Union and Cabarrus County," Hayes observed. "The eastern parts of the district are more Democrat. In the middle are counties that lean Democrat where I needed to do well to win."[7]

The solidly GOP counties that Hayes mentioned—Union, Cabarrus and Stanly—are proximate to Charlotte, and thus shaped by that city's late twentieth century emergence as a major national center of banking and finance. Union County, in particular, was growing rapidly in population and by 2001 had become a bedroom suburb of Charlotte. Union also includes a fairly large percentage of religious conservatives. Together, the three western counties included about 40 percent of the voters in the 8th District, and thus provided a fairly solid base for Hayes and other Republican candidates for office.

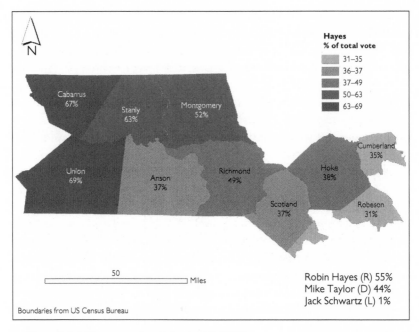

Figure 2.1. NC congressional district 08 (2000)

Within the western portions of the district, the Interstate 85 corridor runs northward from Charlotte through Cabarrus County, and in 2001 was still heavily dependent on the textile industry. The city of Kannapolis, for example, located in northern Cabarrus County, was named after Charles Cannon, the founder of Cannon Mills and grandfather of Rep. Robin Hayes. Earlier in his career, Hayes himself had run Mount Pleasant Hosiery Mills in eastern Cabarrus County. According to one account, the towns and small cities adjacent to Interstate 85 then constituted "the thickest concentration of America's textile industry—so thick you can almost see the lint."[8] Pillowtex Corporation, for instance, the successor firm to Cannon Mills, provided employment in the early 2000s to over 4,000 people in Cabarrus and nearby Rowan Counties alone.

As our attention shifts away from the Charlotte area and in the direction of Fayetteville in the east, the central counties within the district are mostly rural, dotted with small towns, and featuring economies that are heavily depended on agriculture, mining, small manufacturing, and the processing of poultry. Here, median incomes are lower than in the western counties, and the voters tend to be socially conservative and open to supporting moderate Democrats.

The eastern edge of the district bordered on the city of Fayetteville, located in the Sandhills region of North Carolina. In 2001, the overall population of the 8th District was about 26 percent African American, but black residents were mostly concentrated in the eastern portions and they voted overwhelmingly Democratic. Cumberland County, where Fayetteville is located, is also home to Fort Bragg and other smaller military installations. As a result, there was a strong military and veterans' presence in the eastern portions of the district that partially countervailed the area's pro-Democratic tilt.

Not surprisingly, the remarkable political and economic diversity of the 8th District produced a long succession of contested House elections. During 1975–98, Bill Hefner, a moderate Democrat who had survived many close races over the years, represented the district in the House. Late in 1997, Robin Hayes, a former state legislator and the 1996 GOP nominee for governor, announced that he would run against the 8th District incumbent; Hefner announced his retirement; and in November 1998 Hayes barely won the seat over a political newcomer named Mike Taylor, 51–48 percent, even though he outspent his Democratic rival roughly three-to-one. In 2000, Hayes once again prevailed over Taylor, but by a more comfortable margin of 55–44 percent. In 2001, as Hayes made up his mind about how to position himself on Fast Track, Democrats controlled the redistricting process within North Carolina and the expectation was that that they might drop from the district reliably Republican areas near Charlotte and replace them with pro-Democratic areas adjacent to Fayetteville. By any measure, then, the 8th District was highly competitive for the two political parties.

When issues arise on the floor agenda in the House or Senate, lawmakers confront an array of interested constituencies and audiences. To the extent that the major policy alternatives under consideration are concrete and widely known, these audiences may have preference orders over them. The representational task for the member is to weigh and balance these viewpoints. If the relevant constituency or group is part of the member's reelection constituency, then clearly that ordering will receive significant weight in the member's considerations. Since members rely on strong support from within their primary constituencies, if the issue activates the party base those preferences will be especially important. In addition, from guns and abortion to health care and defense, a member's primary constituency within the district and the outside constituency of national party organizations and affiliated groups will generally share similar perspectives on issues important to the party program, which reinforces the importance of these shared preferences in the member's decision calculus.

In his treatment of member home styles, Fenno emphasized that the policy preferences of even the most attentive and active constituencies may not be fully formed because of uncertainty about the main policy alternatives and the potential effects these alternatives might produce. As a result, by carefully framing explanations of their Washington activities, members can shape the environment of competing demands and views that they confront in an issue area and also reduce potential opposition from constituencies that may have preferred that the member take a different position or cast a different vote.

On many issues, there is little disagreement within the multiple constituencies confronting a member of Congress and the decision-making process for that lawmaker is fairly straightforward. During his first term in the House, Robin Hayes had a consistently conservative voting record, which resonated with GOP voters in the western counties and military families concentrated in the eastern portions of the district. His social conservatism also played well with residents of the rural central counties. In the 106th Congress for example, Hayes cast votes in favor of estate tax reduction and other tax cuts, defunding of the so-called abortion pill, and legislation to promote public displays of the Ten Commandments. For the most part, these and other initiatives central to the GOP agenda did not produce significant conflict within the audiences central to his primary and reelection constituencies.

Hayes also took steps to bolster his support within areas that leaned Democratic and among independent voters. His committee assignments, for example, included Agriculture, Armed Services, and Transportation and Infrastructure; all of which enabled him to promote important economic interests within the 8th District. By all accounts, he allocated significant effort to securing federal funds and projects for the district and state, including a $100 million payout for North Carolina tobacco farmers. On Armed Services, he took steps to ensure that the base closure process would not detrimentally affect Fort Bragg and other 8th District installations.[9]

Trade issues, in contrast, created vexing political and policy dilemmas for Hayes. The emergence of Charlotte as a major commercial center meant that significant portions of his primary and reelection constituencies favored enhanced international trade. There was also the potential for free-trade sentiment within the rural central portions of the district, where lower trade barriers might promote exports of locally produced soybeans, cotton, hogs, and poultry. And especially after 9/11, the military families and veterans in the eastern counties were responsive to arguments that blocking Fast Track might undermine the president's bargaining leverage within the international economy. The significant textile interests along the Interstate 85 corridor, however, were deeply concerned about the impact of reduced trade barriers on their industry and livelihoods. While there was pro-Fast Track sentiment in Union County and the rural center of the district, in other words, within the textile producing areas opposition to the measure was widespread and intense. And the textile towns and cities of Cabarrus County were potentially important parts of Hayes's reelection constituency. For Hayes, decisions about trade policy were multidimensional and based on far more than ideological liberalism or conservatism.

As Fenno emphasized, the positions members take and the votes they cast are integral to the representational relationships they develop with constituents, but such "Washington" activities are mediated at home by the act of explanation. In other words, explanations of positions and votes can matter as much or more than the positions and votes themselves, and members often make roll call choices in part based on their explainability.[10] For Robin Hayes, the intensity of the opposition to Fast Track from the textile interests in his district, in combination with his personal and family background in the industry, made "no" the most readily explainable vote to cast. The textiles dimension of his choice seemed the most straightforward to convey to voters and organized interests back home. Indeed, on the morning of the roll call on initial House passage, his chief of staff urged him to vote against the legislation for precisely this reason—a "no" vote would be far easier to explain.[11]

The Bush administration and the GOP leadership in Congress, however, had made adoption of enhanced trade promotion authority a major priority during 2001–02. In March 2001, when House Republican leaders polled a subset of new or wavering members about whether they could support fast track authority for Bush, Hayes was recorded as leaning yes, indicating that he could possibly support enhanced trade authority in the abstract. As the main alternatives took form and lobbying on both sides of the question heated up, textile interests within the 8th District coalesced strongly against the leading proposals. Hayes shifted his position to likely opposition. He was listed as "leaning no" on the June 2001 whip count about the initial Crane version of the legislation and the October 2001 whip count about the Thomas compromise. Shortly before the December vote on the Thomas language, Hayes stated publicly that he could not support Fast Track unless something significant was done to protect the textile industry, and he arrived on the floor fully expecting to vote no.

Hayes recalled in detail the sequence of events that led him to switch sides and cast the pivotal, last minute vote in favor of passage. He emphasized the combination of substantive concessions and direct appeals to party loyalty that secured his support.[12]

> Trade promotion authority was my first high profile, really pressured vote. My staff viewed it politically. Their advice was to go in there, vote no. On the day of the vote, I got a call from the Speaker's office. He said come on over, and I met with him. He said, "I never do this, but I really need your vote. Can I have your vote?" I told him I couldn't do that.
>
> I had given him a list of things I needed before I could vote for [trade promotion authority], and staff didn't think he could do it. He said, "You're right, I shouldn't have asked. But here's what I want to ask you to do." He asked me to hold off my vote and wait until the end....
>
> On the floor, it all fell into place. The things on the list were taken care of over the day. DeMint took care of some of that.

The DeMint concession was the letter that the South Carolinian convinced the leadership to sign on the floor promising that the next trade measure passed by the House would include language requiring that African and Latin American clothing manufacturers use US cloth. Hayes continued:

> It came down to the last thing on the list, a weaving and dying agreement with European countries. The Speaker was in the well of the House, I was sitting about thirty feet back, and he motioned to me. It was the last point. Hastert told me he would do it. Right there in the well on the floor.
>
> [Ways and Means Chair] Bill Thomas saw what was happening. He was furious about it, and said if that was going to be done he would bring the bill down himself. But he didn't. It was all right there in the well of the House. The press gallery was full, people hanging over the rails. Back in my office, my staff was totally in shock because of the political consequences.

Bush and other administration officials were part of the broader lobbying process, to be sure, but as the roll call drew to its dramatic close, Hastert and DeLay were the critical players.

The president wasn't really involved for me until after the vote. Before the vote it was the Speaker and Tom DeLay. But [Bush] called that night, told me he knew how hard a vote it was for me. He said, "I'll work with you, get this done [help for the 8th District]. Come over tomorrow and we'll talk."

The leadership's end game bargaining with Hayes exhibited the hallmarks of effective partisan coalition building in Congress. Republican leaders had accurate information about the precise leanings of members from multiple whip counts. As the roll call ended, Hastert targeted a member who was potentially "gettable" on the matter. The Speaker knew that Hayes' district was divided on trade issues and that his position against the measure primarily derived from opposition within the textile community that was intense, but concentrated.

On the floor, Hastert and DeLay emphasized to Hayes the importance of the vote to their fellow partisan in the White House and to the party program on Capitol Hill. Hayes, they knew, needed legislative concessions and economic assistance for his district in order to craft a credible explanation for a vote in favor of passage. He needed to be able to claim that the district economy benefited more from his cooperation with the leadership and the administration than would have been the case if he had voted no and the measure had been defeated. "When I first went to Congress," Hayes would later tell constituents,

My outlook was to vote no and stop these trade agreements. Well, obviously that wasn't working. Do you take something that's not working and hope for better results? I don't think so. Or do you slow down free trade and in the meantime, bring additional opportunities to the district?"[13]

Moreover, on two key roll calls related to Fast Track that occurred in the House the following year, GOP leaders did not need Hayes's vote to prevail and he voted "no" in both instances, and explained that language he opposed had been added to the measure after initial House passage in 2001. His anti-Fast Track votes in the second session helped blunt Democratic claims that he was undermining the district economy with pro-trade votes. Interestingly, Hayes's long personal and family association with the North Carolina textile industry appeared to cut both ways in crafting an explanation. On the one hand, his relationship with the industry meant that many constituents would be surprised by a vote in favor of the legislation.

On the other hand, Hayes's background in textiles also enhanced his ability to credibly claim that the myriad of deals he helped cut in exchange for his vote actually produced net benefits for the district economy.

Effective leaders also consider the relationship of a member to the partisan power structure when deciding who and how to pressure. Prior to his 1998 election to Congress, Hayes served two terms in the North Carolina House, and in 1995–96 was the majority whip in the state legislature. In 1996, as part of his unsuccessful campaign for governor, he built close working relationships within the GOP organization statewide. After losing his congressional seat in 2008, Hayes became Chair of the Republican Party in North Carolina. Throughout his political career, then, Robin Hayes was a consistent party loyalist. Indeed, during his first term in the US House, Tom DeLay chose to make him a member of the Republican whip organization. As Hayes recalled, "When I entered the House, I went to Tom and told him, 'I want to be on your team.' Being a whip was a natural and something I wanted to be part of. It's what I'm good at."[14] Cooperating with the leadership on a party priority like Fast Track, in other words, was conducive to the promotion of his power goals and fully consistent with his career-long strategic posture.

Finally, Hastert and DeLay knew that they could count on Hayes's outside constituency to help keep him in line on Fast Track. After the vote, as DeLay thanked Hayes in the House chamber, the whip promised that the national party and its allies in the interest group community would swing into action behind the North Carolinian's reelection, and that is precisely what occurred.[15] During the 2002 election cycle, Hayes was able to raise about $2.3 million, or nearly four times as much as his Democratic opponent. His largest contributors included Republican Party committees, political action committees associated with the GOP congressional leadership, and other House colleagues. President Bush and Vice President Cheney conducted fundraisers on his behalf. Indeed, over the course of the campaign, Bush made four trips to North Carolina to assist Hayes and GOP Senate candidate Elizabeth Dole. The National Republican Campaign Committee (NRCC) spent nearly $250,000 on ad buys in the 8th District alone. Although the AFL-CIO ran ads critical of Hayes's 2001 vote on Fast Track, the Business Roundtable countered with ads heralding his efforts to create jobs. The president of the AFL-CIO praised the votes that Hayes was able to cast against Fast Track in 2002, and these remarks were emphasized in pro-Hayes ads produced by the NRCC. Hayes also received extensive grassroots support from the National Federation of Independent

Business and the US Chamber of Commerce; two organizations that had spearheaded the advocacy campaign in favor of Fast Track. Although his Democratic opponent highlighted his pivotal 2001 vote throughout the campaign, in November 2002 Hayes was reelected by a solid margin of 54–45 percent.

Behavioral Preliminaries   *Theme*

The Hayes story provides a narrative outline of the behavioral theory of the whip process. To clarify and generalize that outline, we need to define precisely what constitutes a "preference" in the legislative process. For the purposes of analysis, a preference can be formally defined as an ordering of specific alternatives. More concretely, the binary relationship between two alternatives can be one of strict preference (*a* is preferred to *b*), weak preference (an actor values *a* as much or more than *b*), or indifference (*a* is valued the same as *b*). Preferences between two alternatives also can be undefined.[16] If an issue is unrelated to the party agenda, for example, even on salient measures the relevant leadership may not develop a preference ordering between the main alternatives. And ordinary constituents often lack the interest or information necessary to order the alternatives under consideration in the lawmaking process.

Members of Congress develop preference orderings of this form as they make decisions about legislation and other matters. When a House member inserts his or her identification card in a vote station on the floor and pushes the button for "yes," for instance, that member's choice reflects and reveals a preference ordering in which he or she values the proposal under consideration more than the alternative if the question fails. When Robin Hayes cast the dramatic deciding vote on Fast Track in December 2001, the act revealed a preference on his part in which passage of the measure was ranked more highly than the outcome associated with defeat. But where do these revealed preferences come from?

At the heart of the behavioral perspective is the concept of member goals, rather than member preferences. Members of Congress are viewed as rational actors who make decisions in a manner that promotes the achievement of some mix of three main goals: reelection, promulgating good public policy, and accumulating influence within the chamber (Fenno 1973). Other goals might include winning higher office or simply making a mark in the legislative process (Dodd 1985, Hall 1996). But reelection, policy, and power are the most important goals for members of Congress, and of the three, reelection is paramount because staying in office is necessary for pursing the others.

In the abstract, the whip organizations can help members achieve all three of their goals. First, the whips can create electoral benefits for individual members. On the majority side of the aisle, the whips help the leadership pass legislation that enhances the party's name brand among voters, which in turn enhances the electoral prospects of most rank-and-file members of that party. For the majority, it is particularly important that individual lawmakers coalesce on so-called performance issues and legislation—job promotion, economic growth, and foreign affairs. Moreover, each year much of the congressional agenda concerns the day-to-day functions of government—program reauthorizations, budget bills, the annual appropriations process and the like. If the majority party fails to pass such measures, the party's public reputation may suffer. The minority party's leaders and whips also serve the reelection interests of their members. On the minority side, lawmakers can clarify their own partisan message by maximizing internal unity and distancing their alternatives from the majority program. On performance issues, they can weaken the majority by "throwing tacks on the road"—by delaying or sidetracking such initiatives.

Whipping can also promote the policy goals of members. Simply taking positions on issues may be enough to build electoral support at home, but improving public policy requires that members act collectively to pass or block bills. In the contemporary House and Senate, there is considerable agreement within each party caucus about the proper direction of public policy. On matters related to governmental involvement in the economy, most Republicans favor less and most Democrats want more. This internal agreement is particularly pronounced for party activists, who provide much of the infrastructure and financial support in campaigns. Members generally have close personal ties with the activist base of their respective parties. Indeed, as first-time candidates for office they often emerge from that base and are likely to have personal views that reflect the preferences of party activists and the national policy program. On the majority side, effective whip operations can help produce legislative outcomes that members favor relative to existing law. On the minority side, whipping may help block majority party bills contrary to minority views, and perhaps enable the minority to coalesce with majority party moderates to pass cross-partisan alternatives that shift policy toward their own position.

Effective whip operations also promote the power goals of members. Especially in the House, members of the majority party have greater control over the legislative agenda, committee staff, and other resources that are the hallmarks of influence on Capitol Hill. Majority status is necessary for a member to secure a position as chair of a committee or subcommittee, and thus exert personal influence over some portion of the pre-floor legislative agenda. Similarly, the dozens of positions in the extended party leaderships of both parties are far more valuable to members when they are in the majority. And the quantity of committee and leadership staff resources conferred upon the majority party is more than twice that allocated to the minority. The personal power stakes associated with majority control can make even potential defectors from the party line willing if not eager to tolerate effective whipping by their leaders, especially when party margins are tight (Lee 2016). A unified party is better able to maintain a coherent name brand, build a reputation for legislative competence (or undermine the reputation of the opposition), pass the legislation necessary to convince key national constituencies to support party candidates at the polls, and thereby obtain or retain majority control of the chamber and the power that brings.

Whip activity, however, does not occur in the abstract. The value of the whips for goal promotion is not a legislative constant and will vary significantly by member and question. As an analytical device, member goals imply an audience to which the legislator must respond. By audience, I am referring to discernible subsets of the four nested constituencies described by Fenno, as well as the outside constituency of national pressures. Individual audiences can take the form of ordinary voters, issue publics of more informed citizens who care deeply about one or more policy areas, wealthy donors and other powerful individuals inside and outside the district, or interest groups with some degree of formal organizational structure. Party activists and party organization officials at home and in Washington may also serve as potential audiences for the purposes of member decision making, as may leaders and other colleagues within the legislature. *Importn l* (handwritten)

In practice, goals and audiences are functionally inseparable. Securing reelection, for example, means the member must be responsive to audiences that control electorally relevant resources, such as the folks back home (votes), interest groups (organization and donations), and parties (all of the above plus message and the party name brand). Similar observations hold for the goal of making good public policy. Members of Congress typically emerge from and reflect the values of the relevant base within their party. As a result, the audiences most relevant to the policy goal are generally some combination of party regulars, issue activists, and the member herself. Along those lines, promoting the power goal means satisfying congressional and Washington elites who control access to the resources and positions that can translate into influence. Goals, in short, reflect both desired aims and the audiences that must be assuaged to achieve those aims. Critically, the audiences actually or potentially activated by a question—and the associated mix of goals that are evoked—will vary in important ways by legislator, policy matter, and other features of the decision context (Hall 1996).

When faced with a pending policy or procedural question, the behavioral perspective implies that a member of Congress will form a position via something like the following decision calculus: First, survey the constituencies relevant to the member's goals and determine which audiences within those constituencies care or potentially could care about the matter at hand; second, gauge whether the relevant audiences would prefer a "yes" or a "no" or some other position; and third, choose a position based on the weighted average of these pressures, where the weights capture how much the relevant audiences care about the matter and the relative importance of each audience to the legislator's goals.[17]

Clearly, the limits and possibilities of leadership influence over this decision calculus will depend on the precise configuration of audiences associated with the question on the table. The importance of audience configuration can be clarified by considering four ideal types or scenarios that a lawmaker might confront. In practice, the configuration of audiences that a member actually faces on legislative questions in Congress will seldom mesh perfectly with any one of these categories. Indeed, on most issues aspects of several may be present to some degree, with the precise mix varying by issue and member. Still, exploring these ideal types can sharpen our thinking about the context-specific nature of the whip process. For convenience, I refer to the four scenarios as disinterest, consensus, generalized conflict, and cross pressure.

Four Scenarios

Begin with *disinterest*. With this scenario, the issue at hand does not resonate significantly with any of a member's audiences outside the leadership circle. Across the personal, primary, reelection, and geographic constituencies, the matter barely registers. Party leaders may have an interest and a position. Perhaps the question is of concern to congressional colleagues representing very different kinds of constituencies or having very different policy priorities. Alternatively, the question may relate to some mundane aspect of managing the party agenda in Congress. The presence of a leadership position may mobilize party activists within the member's primary constituency to some extent, but otherwise that lawmaker will confront no serious pressure or demands from audiences relevant to her goals. If the audience's considered by a lawmaker on an issue or question are mostly uninterested or indifferent, but the leadership declares the matter a party concern, the member can easily defer to the party position without suffering serious political costs. If the question is whipped, most likely the member will respond as "yes" to the whip check (in favor of the party position) and that will be the end of it. If, for some reason, the member responds as undecided or as leaning toward casting an unenthusiastic vote the other way, the leadership may be able to secure that lawmaker's support simply by signaling that the matter is a party vote. Under such circumstances, the activation of the whips is pivotal to this member's decision, but party loyalty comes at little or no cost and does not require much pressure from the leadership.

Of course, the more interesting scenarios all concern issues where one or more of a member's audiences care enough to form a position. One such scenario can be labeled *consensus*. Here, core elements of a lawmaker's personal, primary, and reelection constituencies are largely in agreement on the matter, or at least there are no major pockets of dissention. Presumably, the outside constituency will also be in alignment because of the close relationships between national party forces and the activist base at home. The implication is not that the member will perceive no dissension on the matter within his or her district. If this is a party matter, there probably will be audiences in opposition within the geographic constituency. But these audiences are likely viewed by the legislator as lost causes that in an election will almost certainly support candidates of the other party.

The consensus scenario, then, occurs when all or nearly all of the audiences that are important to a member's reelection share similar preferences about a pending floor question and, as a result, the weighing process is straightforward. Given the alignment between the primary and outside constituencies, it is highly likely that, if whipped, the leadership position will be consistent with the rest of the member's audiences and the result should be an easy party vote. Robin Hayes confronted something like this scenario on defense issues, where the audiences relevant to his goals and the leadership position were generally consistent. If for some reason party leaders in Congress want the member to vote contrary to the consensus perspective, the overwhelming audience pressure to do otherwise would almost certainly result in a vote against the leadership. Either way, the impact of the whips on members confronting the consensus scenario probably will be marginal.

Next is the audience configuration labeled *generalized conflict*. This scenario occurs when there are significantly different viewpoints about a matter throughout the district—within all four nested constituencies (personal,
primary, reelection, and geographic), and perhaps within the outside constituency as well. Under such conditions, electoral goals alone should generate
mixed motivations because of the heterogeneity of interests paying attention back home, and the introduction of a leadership position basically adds
to the mix. By weighing in on one side or the other, the whips may be able
to tip the balance in favor of the party position. Moreover, by signaling that
a position is a party concern, the leadership can mobilize party activists in
the primary and outside constituencies and perhaps increase the importance
of those audiences in the member's thinking. Indeed, when something like
this scenario obtains for a member, the leadership may work hand-in-hand
with interest group allies located in the legislator's district. And the diversity
of viewpoints at home can provide the member with the leeway necessary to
toe the party line, assuming that the position can be explained to audiences
on the losing side. This scenario resembles the strategic dilemma faced by
Robin Hayes on trade issues.

The *cross pressure* scenario, in contrast, is for situations where the conflict that exists primarily is between the party position, on the one hand,
and the shared preferences of other audiences important to a member, on
the other. It largely is the polar opposite of the consensus scenario. In the
case of cross pressure, the personal, primary, and outside constituencies are
on one side of the question, while audiences outside this base of primary
support—including important portions of the reelection constituency—
embrace different views. Presumably, if the leadership engages the whips
on such a matter, their position also will be in line with the activist base
at home because of shared partisan loyalties. The magnitude of the cross
pressure that results will vary, depending on the size of the primary constituency relative to the reelection constituency. If the lion's share of the
support that a member needs for reelection comes from co-partisans, or if
the opposing viewpoints that exist within the reelection constituency are
not intense, the degree of cross pressure may be manageable. Conversely,
if the primary constituency is small relative to the reelection constituency and the legislator relies on large numbers of independents or voters
friendly to the other party for electoral success, the resulting cross pressure
can be daunting.

Either way, the cross pressure scenario can be vexing for members
and leaders alike. For rank-and-file lawmakers, such dissonance creates

difficult choices between building support at home versus casting a party vote that is probably more in line with that member's own policy and power goals. On the margin, voting against the leadership may also undermine the party name brand, especially if the roll call is close and the member's vote could be pivotal to the outcome. For leaders, the aggressive whipping of a subset of cross-pressured members may be necessary for the achievement of collective party goals. But they also will be reluctant to pressure lawmakers to vote contrary to powerful constituencies in their district if doing so harms their reelection prospects. In cases of party-constituency cross pressure, the leadership will need to supplement more routine signaling and persuasive tactics with special favors, possible sanctions, and legislative concessions aimed at keeping potential defectors in line. There also will be incentives for them to accept "as needed" responses from cross-pressured colleagues, where members pledge to vote the party line if needed, and otherwise have permission to vote the other way.

The work of the whips, then, is scenario specific and depends on the configuration of audiences confronting individual members on a pending question. As a thought exercise, consider the distribution of scenarios on a matter within a caucus from the perspective of the leadership. If numerous members tend toward the disinterest scenario, then the whips themselves may determine the outcome by signaling a party position and bringing disinterested members on board. Little effort beyond the declaration of a party position is required. On the other hand, if most members of a caucus perceive consensus across their audiences, the direct impact of the leadership on their decisions will be small. Indirectly, they may be affected by the party's success or failure at dealing with the pockets of opposition that still exist elsewhere within the caucus. If the typical member confronts something approaching generalized conflict on a matter, engaging the whips could potentially tip the decision for some, especially if the preexisting balance of pressures is fairly even and party leaders in Washington can coordinate their coalition-building strategies with allies in the district. Finally, when large numbers of the rank and file face significant party-constituency cross pressure, we likely will observe the full leadership toolkit in action. For the majority party, major substantive changes in the underlying legislation may be necessary to grow the party vote. If the balance of the cross pressure is strongly against the party position for a large number of members, whipping the matter may be a lost cause and detrimental to party prospects at the polls.

Theme

So far, the emphasis has been on how the structure of conflict at the constituency and audience levels shapes the limits and possibilities of whip action. Now we consider the kinds of leverage available to leaders, if and when they are important factors in the coalition-building process. Of particular importance are agenda control, side payments and punishments, legislative concessions, the provision of information, logrolling, and explanation. Top party leaders, it should be emphasized, are selected by their rank-and-file colleagues by private ballot and must retain that support to hold onto their leadership positions. Rank-and-file members, in turn, expect their leaders to promote the electoral, policy, and power goals of the individual legislators in that caucus. As a result, the leverage points that party leaders can use as part of the whip process need to be considered through the lens of the aforementioned behavioral logic that shapes the preferences of ordinary members. Doing so leads us to prioritize the forms of leverage somewhat differently than is the case for the leading theories of party influence.

Begin with *agenda control*. Central to the party cartel model is the assumption that the majority leadership has complete control over which bills are considered on the House floor. If a majority of the majority caucus would oppose the anticipated final draft of a pending measure in the full chamber, the cartel prediction is that the leadership will block consideration, either by having the chair of the panel with jurisdiction bottle it up in committee, or by using the majority dominated Committee on Rules to close the gates and deny the measure a rule (the procedural vehicle through which most major bills are considered in the House). Conditional party government implies that the majority leadership can use its control over the Rules panel to block alternatives proposed by opponents of a majority-backed measure and thereby produce non-centrist outcomes more proximate to the majority party program. Either way, the leadership's agenda setting powers potentially affect the revealed preferences of rank-and-file lawmakers by narrowing the array of alternatives under consideration.

Agenda influence and other procedural prerogatives certainly matter, and in the next chapter we will explore certain implications for the allocation of whip attention. In the real world of congressional politics, however, the House leadership's control over the agenda is not complete, and the agenda setting powers of Senate majorities are even weaker. Behavioralism implies that member preferences about procedural questions will tend to reflect the views of these legislators about the associated substantive matters. Indeed, in the pages that follow we will find that procedural questions, including the special rules that govern floor consideration of major bills in the House, are often themselves the focus of whip action. Although agenda prerogatives do provide the majority leadership with considerable leverage in the legislative game, less emphasis is placed on them here than is the case for the cartel and conditional party government theories.

Along those lines, consider the relative importance of *side payments and sanctions* according to the behavioral perspective and the leading alternatives. The use of special favors and occasionally of sanctions or punishments to build coalitions is integral to congressional lore, and under the right conditions the tactic can be pivotal to the outcome (Evans 2004). Such favors/sanctions take the form of concrete benefits or penalties that may or may not relate to the policy matter under consideration, but fall short of being primarily substantive modifications to the main proposal. Examples include distributive benefits that solely affect the district of the targeted lawmaker, pledges to advance unrelated legislation important to the member's goals, various forms of institutional patronage such as valued committee assignments, traveling with congressional delegations to desired locations, and so on. On occasion, leaders make threats to promote party loyalty on votes. For instance, they might vow to impede a disloyal member's career prospects within the committee system or withdraw distributive benefits that the member already expects for the folks back home. Under extreme circumstance, the leadership may threaten to "primary" a member who votes contrary to the party program—to convince someone to mount a primary challenge against the targeted member during the next campaign.

The potential value of rewards and sanctions in the legislative process, however, should not be overstated. For one, they are more readily available to members of the partisan majority or the party of the incumbent president, assuming the matter is a White House priority, because the majority leadership and the executive branch have the leverage necessary to provide them. Moreover, the overt use of payoffs may be framed as a bribe in the media by the other party, which can undermine the public image of the beneficiary. Especially when the White House is controlled by the opposite party, attempts at vote buying can be met with similar efforts on the other side, potentially creating a bidding war for the support of pivotal members. Along those lines, interest groups lobbying the other side of a question also make campaign contributions and could countervail side payments from the leadership. The use of sanctions, on the other hand, may primarily serve to damage the reelection prospects of a marginal member, which runs contrary to the leadership's efforts to maintain or secure majority status.

And the best study of "primarying" as a party sanction indicates that media treatments of the tactic are overblown (Boatright 2014).

Most important, the behavioral theory implies that the main concern of a wavering member will be casting a vote that is explainable to the audiences that matter. As a result, the most effective side payments will relate directly to the substantive concerns that the member and her audiences have about the question being whipped. A lawmaker cannot credibly explain a vote contrary to the preferences of district audiences on a social issue, for example, by responding, "Hey, the leadership promised to fund a project for the district in exchange for my switch." In contrast, the benefits that the leadership and Bush White House pledged to Robin Hayes on Fast Track dealt directly with audience concerns about the economic consequences of free trade for the 8th District. Side payments that enhance explainability tend to relate directly to the substantive matter at hand, and here all legislative vehicles are not created equal. The tactic may be most useful in issue areas with significant distributive potential, such as appropriations bills, transportation measures, tax legislation, and trade agreements.

Third, *substantive legislative concessions* in the underlying text aimed at growing the vote are a regular and underappreciated feature of the whip process. Initial opponents of a leadership backed measure can explain a vote switch by simply declaring victory and claiming that the party caved to their demands. Indeed, a primary purpose of the whips is to provide the majority leadership with the intelligence and the venue necessary to craft bills capable of passing on the floor. The version of the Thomas bill that passed in December 2001, for example, differed in important ways from the initial draft polled earlier in the year. Hayes and other textile lawmakers secured significant concessions aimed at helping industry producers and workers in their districts. Such changes should be distinguished from side payments or special favors, because they constitute major modifications in the legislation under consideration. Significant modifications to the text of a whipped matter, we will see, are often a regular precondition for majority party success on the floor. They indicate the importance of the whip process for the substantive content of legislation, and are particularly necessary if many members face generalized conflict or party-district cross pressure.

Fourth, party leaders can make use of significant *informational advantages*. Members of Congress make roll call decisions within an environment of imperfect information, which complicates the balancing process and creates opportunities for leadership input. In part, this uncertainty concerns the substantive consequences of the specific legislative alternatives that are on the table (Arnold 1990, Krehbiel 1991). On an environmental matter, for example, a member may have a general preference for policies that would protect the environment over alternatives geared toward promoting particular industries or economic growth. But where a proposed regulation on pollution emissions falls on that implied continuum might not be clear-cut. The legislative proposal, in other words, may be more appropriately viewed as a probability distribution than as a point along one or more underlying dimensions of evaluation. Party leaders can function as a clearinghouse of sorts through which policy relevant information from the committees of jurisdiction and the advocacy community is channeled (Curry 2016). Not surprisingly, much of the communication that takes place between the whips and rank-and-file lawmakers concerns the substantive policy consequences of the alternatives under consideration. By funneling information in favor of the party position, leaders reduce the uncertainty about the policy impact and make party loyalty more palatable to risk-averse politicians.

Other forms of uncertainty, however, are more political than purely substantive (Cooper and Sieberer, 2005). The various audiences with a potential stake in the member's decision may not have formed preferences between alternatives early in the process and might themselves be waiting for the decisions of other political actors. Interest group leaders confront their own audiences and constituencies—the donors and dues paying members to whom the leaders of an organization must be responsive—and may hold back on articulating clear-cut positions. Even informed citizens may rely on signals from the media, group leaders, and the members themselves before developing policy preferences (Zaller 1992). For these reasons, the pressures that a member wants to weigh may not take full form until late in the legislative process, or perhaps even after the decision on the floor has been made. As we have argued, members of Congress need to weigh the potential preferences of constituents, groups, and issue publics, and not just the audience preferences that already are formed (Kingdon 1973, Arnold 1990). By staking out clear-cut positions early in the whip process, party leaders can provide other political actors—within and outside the chamber—with a frame of reference for sorting out the political consequences of their choices. Indeed, what comes to be viewed as liberal or conservative, pro-environment or pro-growth, and so on may depend on the policy positions embraced by party leaders. Here, the position of the president is particularly consequential (Lee 2009). The president generally functions as party leader in chief on Capitol Hill and the whips of that party usually promote the White House agenda. Presidential engagement on an issue can transform how members and their audiences perceive it and thereby transform otherwise non-partisan questions into decisions where party considerations dominate.

Fifth, *intensity differentials* also matter and can be managed by the leadership to promote party goals (Bawn 1998). Emergent member preferences will differ in their intensity, as well as their substantive content or direction. Robin Hayes cared more about trade issues than did legislators representing districts more insulated from international economic competition. If the underlying issue is especially relevant to the goals of a member and the associated audiences, the stakes for that lawmaker will be much higher than if these linkages are less pronounced. We particularly need to consider differences in intensities to understand the political meaning of indecision or indifference, which is a common member response to party whip counts and a major source of position fluidity. When intensities are low, a member may not deem the question sufficiently important to gather enough information to form a preference over outcomes, and may simply defer to the leadership position, or absent that to other colleagues with stronger views. But differential intensities also create opportunities for party leaders and whips to manage reciprocal trades between potentially opposing factions within a caucus. If one faction within a party supports program *a* and opposes program *b*, while the other faction supports *b* and opposes *a*, the party is divided internally. However, if for both programs the intensity of support exceeds the intensity of the opposition, leaders may be able to arrange bargains where each faction endorses the program associated with the other, producing constituency benefits for both coalitions and a unified party.

Finally, unlike the production decisions of firms or the purchasing choices of consumers, *explainability* is a crucial factor in legislative decision making. Rather than conceptualizing legislative preferences as exogenously predetermined, as ideal points arranged along one or more ideological dimensions, or as summary indexes of roll call ideology, we need to think about them first and foremost as strategies. And since member positions are strategies aimed at reconciling potentially competing demands, the explanation of a position to the relevant audiences is a central consideration. As mentioned, the roll call votes that members cast cannot be separated from the feasible explanatory language available for rationalizing these votes to constituents. When members like Robin Hayes make decisions on the floor, they tend to base them on what appears to be explainable.

Such explanations generally take narrative form and the relative availability of persuasive narratives can lead lawmakers to choose the alternative that is not most preferred on policy grounds alone (Cherepanov et al. 2013). Here, the procedural prerogatives of the majority leadership are especially important. By structuring the agenda and otherwise providing cover for members confronting party-constituency cross pressure or conflict within the district, leaders can make the party position more explainable to key constituencies (Calvert and Fenno 1994). Moreover, there is intriguing evidence that voters tend to disproportionately punish members who take positions they oppose when that position also happens to be contrary to the party program (Kelly and Van Houweling 2010). In other words, if a member casts a roll call vote contrary to the demands of a constituent audience, the decrement of support from that audience for that member may be larger if the vote also is inconsistent with the party position on the matter. It is as if such a vote comes as a surprise to audiences in the district and is more difficult to explain. The formation of a convincing narrative, in short, may be easier when a lawmaker votes with the party, which in turn will facilitate the work of the whips.

Behavioral Signposts

For the behavioral framework to be meaningful, it needs to do more than produce analytic narratives about particular cases, even legislative episodes as instructive as the Hayes vote on Fast Track. The argument also needs to generate broader expectations about partisan coalition building that can be juxtaposed with qualitative evidence from multiple cases, and ideally with quantitative indicators covering larger numbers of observations of the whips at work. For now, I summarize six general expectations, or thematic signposts, that we will return to repeatedly in the chapters that follow. These signposts will be fleshed out and evaluated with quantitative data covering House whip action from 1955 to 2002 (Chapters 3 and 4), and then with more extensive quantitative and qualitative evidence from four distinct periods in recent House history (Chapters 5–8).

Strategic engagement. Activist whips can help members achieve their goals, but when leaders decide when and what to whip, the collective benefits that the whip networks can create must be tempered by the costs. These costs take the form of member dissonance and leadership resources. Even with highly unified caucuses where members represent relatively similar audience arrays, the electoral and policy goals of some lawmakers will be out of step with the party mainstream. Most members may face something like the consensus scenario, but there will be sizable numbers confronting generalized conflict or cross pressure. The potential for such dissonance is greater with more heterogeneous congressional parties— parties where the mix of audiences that rank-and-file lawmakers confront on an issue varies significantly across the caucus. Especially when there are large differences in the reelection constituencies of party members, attempting to advance an aggressive party program in Washington may primarily serve to expose large numbers of them to politically damaging crosswinds at home.

Leaders also consider the opportunities forgone when they activate the whips. Although members tend to expand the size and organizational strength of their whip networks when the party is relatively homogeneous at the constituency level, the leadership still confronts binding time and resource constraints and cannot whip everything. During a busy week on the House floor the chamber may hold more than 50 roll call votes, and even with the extensive whip networks of the modern chamber, the leadership cannot whip more than three or four matters per week. It takes time to contact members and tabulate their views. Once the initial poll results are in, the leadership's clean-up operations may require systematic persuasive efforts, protracted negotiations about possible compromise language, the dispersal of side payments and other special favors, and intensive outreach to lobbyists and constituent groups that might influence wavering members. We also need to consider the demands on the time of the rank and file. Party members will not tolerate what they view as excessive monitoring from the leadership and may respond to hyperactive whipping by refusing to listen or respond.

As a result, in deciding how often and when to whip, leaders need to reconcile the pursuit of collective party benefits, the prospects for member dissonance, and the opportunity costs of activism. They can do so by primarily engaging the whips when (1) a question is important to the collective goals of party members, (2) a high degree of unity appears feasible, and (3) there is a significant chance that the collective goals will not be achieved without leadership intervention. Or phrased in more colloquial terms, the whips should focus on party priorities capable of uniting the rank and file that are still in play. Absent one or more of these conditions, we can expect the leadership to refrain from intensive whipping and instead allow members to make up their minds based on their personal goals and the configuration of audiences they confront.

Audiences over ideology. The behavioral approach emphasizes the balancing of audiences over ideological reasoning in the preference formation process.[18] When a lawmaker's audiences are in conflict about a matter, that member is more likely to be undecided or in opposition during the whip process. And the more a member's constituencies diverge from what is typical for lawmakers of that caucus, the more likely such a legislator will wander away from the party line. Certain district-specific characteristics— such as the partisan or ideological leanings within a district, or the region of the country for Democrats prior to the enfranchisement of black voters— should trigger defections across issues and congresses. Other factors will depend on the policy area. On trade issues, for example, constituency characteristics like the presence or absence of textile, manufacturing, orga- nized labor, or agricultural interests may determine member positioning during the whip process. While spatial logic implies that support for the party program on whip counts should be strongest among the ideolog- ical center of each caucus, albeit with the potential for some alienation at the extremes among disenchanted purists, the behavioral approach is more consistent with pockets of indecision or even opposition spread throughout the ideological spectrum.

We also need to consider the potential for systematic differences between Democrats and Republicans in the kinds of audiences that they consider. As Matt Grossmann and David Hopkins (2016) argue, there may be structural differences between the primary and reelection constituencies of Democrats and Republicans, and the kinds of policy demands members of each party face may be qualitatively different. The audiences of impor- tance to the typical Democrat, Grossmann and Hopkins claim, can be usefully viewed as a coalition of groups or blocs with disparate program- specific concerns about government. As a result, Democratic audiences may share a pragmatic outlook about public policy emphasizing the delivery of services, rather than an abstract ideological orientation toward liberalism or some other belief system. If this is accurate, the consistent roll call lib- eralism of contemporary Democrats is more a behavioral manifestation of their efforts to satisfy such program-specific demands, rather than a sign of ideological thinking. In contrast, the audiences of concern to the typical Republican member tend to share a generalized skepticism about govern- mental action and are more overtly ideological. Movement conservatives constitute an important audience for most Republican members, but there is no comparable ideological presence on the left that Democrats routinely weigh as they form positions. The mosaic of program-oriented audiences facing congressional Democrats may complicate preference formation for them, but the pragmatism of these audiences can also make them more willing to accept middle ground positions and outcomes. The shared phil- osophical moorings of GOP audiences, on the other hand, may simplify the decision process for Republican members, but also impede their efforts to find middle ground when there is within-district conflict or cross pressure.

Presidential context. The relationship between the president's program and the party agendas on Capitol Hill should strongly condition every stage of the whip process. Presidential position taking raises the stakes for both parties and thus the overall likelihood of whip activity, especially if the White House stance is consistent with the policy inclinations of the president's co-partisans and contrary to viewpoints on the other side of the aisle. Few things activate audiences inside and outside the district on a matter more than a presidential speech or other public action. Everything else the same, presidential position taking and the work of the whips should be closely related. Moreover, if the president is of the same party as a lawmaker and the leadership is whipping in favor of the White House position, then the prospects for support should be higher. And if, as occasionally does happen, the leadership is whipping against the position embraced by a same-party president, then the prospects for leadership support should drop off. For members who do not share the partisan affiliation of the president, the opposite pattern should occur. In other words, if their leaders are whipping against the position of an opposite-party president, the likelihood a member will stay with the party should be high. But if that leadership is actually whipping in favor of the position taken by an opposite-party president (which also occurs periodically) then the behavioral calculus we have posited implies lower levels of leadership support. There are other implications, such as the benefits and costs from whipping veto overrides, that we will explore later in this book, but the bottom line is that party whip activity on Capitol Hill should take on a presidential cast.

Party size. The size of a majority party is not a major ingredient of the cartel or conditional party government arguments, but for us it is critical (Cooper and Sieberer 2005, Smith 2007). Size affects the scope of whip activity because of the consequences for winability and the likelihood that questions will be in play. Everything else the same, the smaller the majority party, the more likely that party priorities will be under threat until the end of the floor legislative process. As we will see, the small Republican majorities of 1997–2002 created significant coalition-building challenges for majority party leaders of that era. Moreover, the consequences of party margins for the need to whip should be conditioned by the relative homogeneity of viewpoints within a party. Large majorities are especially likely to factionalize, and thus to be characterized by differences of opinion internally on Capitol Hill. The Democratic majorities of the 1970s were huge by historical standards, but the reelection constituencies of Democratic members differed significantly. The chapter in this book focusing on that period is entitled, "Coalitions Built in Sand," for a reason. Even if a partisan majority is large, significant issues may remain in play on the floor and whip activity may be a regular feature of chamber action. Along with the direct effects of party size and internal homogeneity, in other words, we also need to consider the interactions that can occur between the two variables (Binder 1997).

Partisan balance.[19] Behavioral theory is not a recipe for majority party domination of the legislative process. Within both parties, the net flow of the position movement that occurs during the whip process generally should be toward the leadership position. The number of members switching from opposing the leadership on a whip poll to supporting the leadership on the vote should generally exceed the number moving in the opposite direction. Party leaders also should pick up most of their undecideds. And the magnitude of this flow toward the leadership position within each party should increase as the importance placed on party name brands and the resources available to party leaders grew over time. Importantly, such patterns should hold for both parties and not just the majority. As part of the whip process, member positions should become more overtly partisan.

Heightened partisanship, however, does not necessarily mean majority party domination and we can expect a significant amount of balancing to occur. True, the majority party does have disproportionate control over the agenda and other procedures, and it has greater resources for rewarding or sanctioning members. But what separates the behavioral approach from more spatially grounded theories of congressional partisanship is the emphasis on audience satisfaction, as opposed to structural arrangements within the House or Senate. And there are important commonalities in the internal decision-making practices of members across the majority and minority. Members of both parties have goals and confront audiences. Leadership on both sides of the aisle can tip the mix of considerations one way or the other by engaging the whips. Majority and minority party leaders alike serve as information portals for their rank-and-file colleagues. The existence of a coherent party position can enhance explainability on both sides of the aisle. Behavioralism, in short, does not imply some overwhelming advantage for the majority over the minority when it comes to persuading individual members to stay loyal on important votes.

Indeed, when we take a closer look at the processes through which members actually make up their minds, leaders of the minority party may have certain comparative advantages. Regardless of whether Democrats or Republicans are in control, the vote-gathering challenges confronting party leaders are somewhat different across the majority and minority. The majority's task is to build a coalition in favor of passage, while the task for the minority usually is to derail that effort and contrast its program with the majority-backed proposal. Members of the minority can agree to oppose the majority for a range of reasons and need not be unified behind a single substantive alternative, which makes vote gathering potentially easier on the minority side of the aisle.

In addition, the behavioral logic we have outlined taps a diversity of potential considerations—organized audiences in the district and nation, issue publics and other concerned citizens, party activists, the views of the personal constituency and the member herself, the White House position, the practical logistics of explainability, and so on. Although party leaders within Congress play prominent roles as major floor votes near, they are not the only actors seeking to influence the emergent preferences of lawmakers. In addition to the whips, White House liaison, interest group representatives, and other actors will be lobbying members in Washington and seeking to mobilize grassroots pressure in the district. The minority party's disadvantages in terms of internal institutional prerogatives and resources may be countervailed by the lobbying and mobilization efforts of its allies in the interest group community and elsewhere. This particularly will be the case if the congressional minority and the president are of the same party.

Perhaps most important, the majority leadership activates its whips when their control over the outcome is in doubt. The subset of whipped items is not a random sample of floor decisions more generally, but instead disproportionately reflects that portion of the broader agenda where the majority program is under duress. Otherwise there would be no need to activate the whips. Based on the strategic selection of issues to whip, alone, we would expect the majority to lose a decent portion of the associated floor fights.

The measure of influence. Contrary to the standard spatial explanations of lawmaking, behavioralism prioritizes the endogenous formation of member positions and preferences as part of the legislative process. The relationship between the spatial location of the outcome and the preferences of ideological centrists within the chamber cannot capture the impact of the whips, party leaders or any other factor that influences how lawmakers make up their minds. For our purposes, the distinction between party effects and preference effects that has become so central to legislative scholarship makes little sense. But if non-centrist outcomes, measured spatially, cannot serve as the benchmark for identifying whip operations that are consequential, where should we look?

Several more appropriate benchmarks come to mind, including the relative abilities of the majority and minority leaderships to retain and convert potential defectors, the extent to which substantive compromises are necessary to grow the party vote, and the incidence of majority as opposed to minority party success on outcomes. Importantly, these alternative benchmarks can be evaluated with systematic evidence from the whip process over time and across different configurations of partisan control. Along those lines, the default outcome for the legislative process—that is, what occurs absent effective coalition leadership by the majority party—should not be the ideal point of the chamber median or some other measure of exogenously determined centrist viewpoints. What constitutes the position of the ideological median may not even exist prior to leadership lobbying and thus cannot serve as a baseline for determining whether that lobbying matters. Behavioralism highlights the inherent difficulty of building floor majorities in Congress under even the most favorable of circumstances. Rather than the floor median position or some other measure of centrist preferences, the default outcome in the real world of Capitol Hill is probably no bill at all.

The behavioral theory of the whip process, it should now be clear, highlights the limits of leadership as much as the possibilities. For the majority party, the purpose of the whips is to compensate for weaknesses inherent to majority coalitions and the daunting challenges associated with passing legislation in Congress. The primary impact of the whips should be tactical, and exerted through the balance of considerations that structures the decision-making process for rank-and-file members. A large percentage of apparent majority leadership victories on the floor should result from commonalities in the constituencies represented by the members of that party, as well as significant substantive concessions made to opponents of a measure. Although outcomes should reflect the majority party position more often than not, the behavioral perspective does not imply anything approaching majority party domination of the legislative process. Like the media accounts of Tom DeLay's hammer, scholarly references to "party government" distort the real challenges of legislating on Capitol Hill.

Behavior Theory: Whip Process

THREE

When to Whip

According to the behavioral perspective, the dissonance that whipping can create for rank-and-file members, in conjunction with the opportunity costs of whip effort for the leadership, means that the decisions party leaders make about when to engage their whip networks will be selective and strategic. More concretely, leaders should whip their colleagues on matters that are important to the party program, where a high degree of internal unity appears feasible, and the outcome is not a forgone conclusion. Of course, context matters if we are to understand how these three conditions translate into actual decisions about whip engagement, and the period-specific treatments of Chapters 5–8 will provide rich portraits of such decisions at particular points in congressional history. But first we need to provide a firmer foundation for the more detailed narratives to come and consider aggregate patterns across the entire time span covered by this book. For the most part, you will see, these aggregate patterns comport with the behavioral arguments of the previous chapter.

This chapter proceeds via six sections. The first explores whether the broad trends we have observed in aggregate House whip activity still hold after controlling for changes in the size of the chamber workload and the relative significance of the underlying matter. Next is an examination of the relationship between the contents of the presidential agenda and party whip activity. Our attention then turns to the allocation of whip attention across different junctures in the legislative process, such as procedural motions, amendments, and questions on final passage. The focus of the fourth section is the expected association between whip action and fiscal management issues like spending bills, budget legislation, and debt limit increases. Following that, we examine whether the bivariate patterns we have found hold up in a multivariate treatment in which the separate factors are considered together. Finally, this chapter closes with an exploration of the margins of victory and defeat on majority whipped items and the implications for the behavioral perspective on party coalition building.

Workload Effects and Major Votes

From Table 1.3, we already know that whip activity for the House majority party increased substantially from the 1950s through the late 1990s. There also was a noticeable spike in floor whipping for the majority Democrats during the late 1970s. And based on the years where whip evidence is available for House minorities (always Republicans in these data), the minority generally whipped less often than the majority.

Such trends reflect changes over time in the composition of member districts and audiences. From the 1950s to the 2000s, the home constituencies of Democratic lawmakers became more alike, the districts represented by Republican members grew more similar, and the differences between the kinds of constituencies associated with Democrats and Republicans became starker (Rohde 1991; Sinclair 2006). A major reason for the heightened intra-party homogeneity and inter-party difference was passage of landmark civil rights legislation during the 1960s, which enfranchised black voters throughout the American south. The result was a regional realignment of sorts in which southern conservatives switched loyalties from the Democrats to the GOP and the primary constituencies represented by the remaining southern Democrats featured large numbers of African Americans (Rohde 1991). Civil rights and race, however, were not the only factors behind increased differentiation in the kinds of districts represented by Democrats and Republicans. The partisan polarization of member constituencies also occurred outside the south, largely because of tighter connections over time between socio-economic factors and political behavior, as well as other changes in the national political economy (McCarty, Poole, and Rosenthal 2006; Theriault 2008).

Still, to evaluate whether the observable changes in total whip activity are consistent with expectations, we need to go further. After all, the aggregate trends summarized in Table 1.3 may mostly reflect ebbs and flows in the congressional workload, rather than altered partisan audiences at home. From the 1950s to the 2000s, the congressional parties became more polarized at the constituency level, but the size of the congressional agenda also grew over that time stretch. Were the temporal increases we have observed in whip activity caused by changes in the makeup of the two parties, or were they simply a result of the growth in floor activity that also occurred around the same time? To address the question, we need a workable measure of the size of the floor agenda so that we can control for it, and the workload indicator most relevant to the whip process is the number of roll call votes per Congress occurring on the floor.

Figure 3.1 portrays the size of the whipped agenda for the House majority party as a percentage of floor roll calls, 1955–2002.[1] The missing data point is for the 100th Congress (1987–88) where systematic archival evidence is unavailable. For now, the focus is on the majority party— Democrats during 1955–94 and Republicans in 1995–2002. The percentages reported in the figure are calculated using three different workload "denominators": all roll call votes, just nonunanimous votes (fewer than 90 percent of members voted the same way), and only party-line votes (a majority of one party voted differently from a majority of the other). Given that partisan conflict and the whip process are so intertwined, it comes as no surprise that the proportion of the roll call record that was whipped increases when we move from all to nonunanimous to party-line votes. Regardless of the denominator, however, the upward trend over time in whip activity is still apparent, even after controlling for the number of floor votes. The percentage of whipped votes increases from the 1970s and early 1980s to the late 1980s and 1990s, which corresponds with the rise of party polarization in Congress. And as was the case when only the number of counts was considered, the percentage of votes that were whipped was very high during 1977–78, and also during the GOP majorities of the mid-1990s.

However, there also are some noteworthy differences when we switch from the number of whipped items to whip activity as a share of the floor agenda. For one, after controlling for the number of floor votes, the level of whipping that took place in the 1950 and 1960s appears much more consequential. Although the number of questions whipped by the House majority parties of that era was significantly lower than in succeeding decades, the fraction of the roll call record that was affected was not all that different from the years that followed. The main reason is that the number of roll call votes that occurred on the floor—the denominator for calculating the percentages of Figure 3.1—was much smaller before the 1970s. The early 1970s advent of recorded voting during the amendment process,

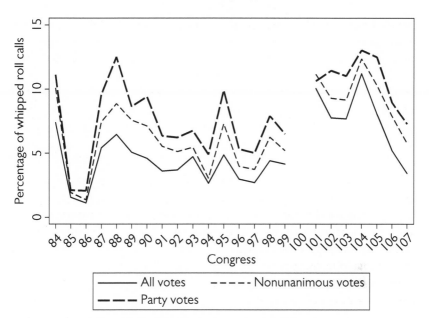

Figure 3.1. Percentage of House roll calls with majority whip counts

you will recall, more than tripled the size of the roll call record, from an average per congress of just 329 votes during 1955–72 to an average of over 1,000 for 1975–2002. As a result, the relatively modest number of whipped questions during the 1950s and 1960s actually constitutes a significant level of whip activity if we also take into account the much lower levels of roll call activity at the time.

This finding does not mesh very well with the standard view among congressional scholars that parties and leaders were relatively inactive during the 1950s and 1960s. However, as Mayhew (1966) demonstrated, partisan configurations were actually fairly common in certain issue areas during these decades. Froman and Ripley (1965) likewise argued that congressional party leaders of the era could be highly consequential under the right conditions. The role played by leaders and whips during the 1950s and 1960s is the focus of Chapter 5 and we will explore such questions in more detail there. For now, even after controlling for workload changes, the hypothesized relationship between constituency-level polarization and majority party whip activity appears consistent with the evidence.

Figure 3.1 also shows that only a limited portion of floor roll calls were directly whipped across the 1955–2002 time span—about 5 percent for all votes, 7 percent for nonunanimous votes, and 9 percent for party-line matters. Even when we focus on party-line roll calls—the most polarized subset of the floor agenda—the fraction of whipped votes per congress never exceeded 14 percent, and for most congresses it fell in the 5–10 percent range. The roll call record, of course, includes large numbers of relatively minor decisions, and the behavioral theory implies that the whips will mostly target significant items. The opportunity costs of activating the whips create incentives for leaders to focus on major questions and to forego allocating scarce political capital to mundane matters. The parties also form their agendas to market themselves before valued audiences at home, and major votes and bills are more likely to be on the constituency radar screen. Perhaps the relatively small portion of questions and bills singled out for whipping will appear more consequential if we focus on the more significant matters before Congress.

Indeed, the evidence supports that expectation. Every year, *Congressional Quarterly Weekly Report* (*CQ*), a respected news magazine that specializes in American national politics, singles out 16 or so roll calls in the House and Senate that its editors and reporters view as the "key votes" of that session.[2] For 1955–2002, *CQ* identified a total of 667 roll calls in the House as key votes. If we drop the stretches of time for which archival evidence about majority whip activity is unavailable, we are left with nearly 600 key votes that can be juxtaposed with the whipped agenda. Of these key roll calls, just over 30 percent were directly the subject of majority whip activity. So the scope of the whipped agenda is much greater if the focus is on more significant votes and measures. During the 84th Congress (1955–56), for example, nearly 40 percent of key votes were whipped. That percentage dropped in the late 1950s and then generally increased over the next 40 years. In 1995–96, nearly half of the *CQ* key votes were whipped. Interestingly, while overall whip activity dipped sharply for the 107th Congress (2001–02), the percentage of *CQ* key votes that were targeted during that two-year period was relative high at 40 percent. Especially here, party leaders targeted the questions that mattered.

Also keep in mind that *CQ* characterizes relatively few roll call votes as major. As a result, there may be instances where the majority whips do not ask their rank-and-file colleagues precisely about the vote that *CQ* singled out as "key" and focus instead on related questions about the same underlying legislation. For instance, *CQ* might identify as "key" the vote on final passage of a measure, while the whips focused their attention on a significant amendment or a related procedural matter. The effective reach of the whips may extend beyond the precise question subjected to formal canvassing, and touch on other aspects of the targeted legislation. If we consider *CQ* major votes that were part of legislation that was whipped in some manner—either on the key vote itself, or on another question related to the same measure—the proportion of directly or indirectly whipped items is nearly 50 percent for 1955–2002, and over 80 percent in 1995–96, the first two years of GOP control. Again, although only a fraction of House roll calls is whipped, the items that are targeted tend to address the most significant issues before the body.

The Presidential Context

The behavioral perspective also implies a strong association between whipped agendas and legislative initiatives important to the White House. Public attitudes about the president's party are shaped by citizen perceptions of his or her governing competence. Within the House and Senate, there often are incentives for members of the other party to oppose presidential initiatives in order to distinguish their own policy program from that of the president's party. And as the most visible and prominent office holder in the nation, the president's association with a proposal or policy position elevates its importance in the mind of the voter. Whip activity, then, should be especially likely for items included in the White House legislative agenda. Indeed, we can push this behavioral argument a few steps further. On presidential priorities, the precise alignment between the positions embraced by a president and congressional party should also matter, albeit in different ways depending on whether or not the caucus/conference and the chief executive are co-partisans.

Let's begin with situations where a congressional party (either majority or minority—for now the distinction does not matter) is interacting with a same-party president. Examples would include Republican whip decisions during 2001–02 when GOP president George W. Bush was in the White House, or Democratic whip activities during 1961–62 when fellow Democrat John Kennedy was president. For the president's co-partisans on Capitol Hill, the behavioral perspective implies that the whips will be disproportionately engaged when the position the White House takes on a matter is the same as the one taken by most rank-and-file members of the caucus. In contrast, when the positions of the same-party president and most members of the congressional party diverge, whip activity should be less frequent. In such instances, the leadership may not believe it possible to identify and build support for a consensus position capable of unifying the party and, as a result, will choose not to whip.

Now consider situations where a congressional party is interacting with a president from the opposite party. Examples would include House Republicans during the Clinton administration, or Democrats during the Nixon-Ford years. Under such conditions, we can expect the opposite relationship to arise between inter-branch position congruence and whip action. More concretely, the congressional party's ability to forge a consensus position capable of distinguishing it from the opposition should be greater when most rank-and-file members disagree with the opposite-party president. So when views within a House party diverge from the preferences of an opposite-party chief executive, whip engagement by that party within the legislature should be frequent. On the other hand, when most party members actually agree with an opposite-party president on a question, the potential for building a distinct party message or for undermining the White House program will fall, which of course implies less need to unleash the whips.

In short, behavioralism suggests that whip activity for both parties should be higher on presidential priorities. When the congressional party and the president are of the same party, the increase should be especially marked when the House contingent and the chief executive are in agreement, and much less so when there is discord between the congressional and presidential wings of the party. In contrast, when the caucus/conference and the president are of different parties, whip activity should be highest when the congressional party mostly disagrees with the White House position, and much lower when they are on the same side of the matter.

To address whether these expectations are consistent with evidence, we need a workable measure of the subset of issues and votes important to the White House.[3] Fortunately, for 1955–2002 *CQ* also identified the roll call votes for which the president took a public position and whether that position was "yes" or "no" on the relevant vote. If we exclude the time stretches for which archival evidence about majority party whip activity is unavailable, *CQ* was able to identify a presidential position for about 23 percent of the roll calls that took place on the House floor. For the more limited time stretches where archival evidence about minority party whip activities is available, about 17 percent of House roll calls can be associated with presidential positions.

Table 3.1 denotes the percentage of House votes that were whipped across the different presidential contexts. Only nonunanimous roll calls are included. The first column of the table is for the three different inter-branch configurations: *All presidents*—all votes regardless of the partisan configuration between the relevant caucus and the White House; *Own party president*—votes from congresses when the relevant caucus also controlled the White House; and *Other party president*—votes from congresses where the caucus and the White House were of different parties. Within each of these inter-branch configurations, the table further categorizes individual roll calls depending on the congruence between the votes of most party members and the position on the matter taken by the president. As indicated by the second column, entitled "Presidential position on vote," here we distinguish between: *Same*—votes where most party members and the president took the same position; *Opposite*—votes where most party members and the president took opposing positions; and *None*—votes where no presidential position was discernible. The third column shows the percentage of votes falling in each of the aforementioned categories that were whipped by majority parties (Democrats for 1955–1994, Republicans for 1995–2002), while the fourth column shows analogous percentages for minority parties where the necessary evidence is available (Republicans for 1975–80 and 1989–93).

Consistent with the behavioral logic, the cells of Table 3.1 indicate a strong association between whip activity and presidential position taking. No matter the inter-branch configuration, the votes where the president did not take a formal position are much less likely to be the subject of whip attention, and this holds for both majority and minority parties. There also is considerable support for the supplementary hypotheses that break down votes by party-presidential configuration and position congruence. As Table 3.1 shows, when the relevant congressional party and president are of the same party, whip activity is more prevalent when most party members and the White House agree, and considerably less prevalent when they do

TABLE 3.1. Percentage of votes whipped by party configuration and presidential position

Party-presidential configuration	Presidential position on vote	Majority parties (1955–2002)	Minority parties (1975–80, 1989–93)
All presidents	Same	13.7	22.3
	Opposite	18.7	11.0
	None	4.5	1.7
Own party president	Same	16.1	27.5
	Opposite	5.6	15.5
	None	4.0	2.1
Other party president	Same	8.9	7.2
	Opposite	20.1	10.1
	None	4.8	1.3

Note: Only nonunanimous votes included.

not. Conversely, when the relevant caucus or conference and the president were from opposite parties, the table indicates that whip activity was more likely when the positions of most party members diverged from that of the president, and less likely when there was position congruence. These patterns also hold for both the majority and minority parties. In short, the strong presidential context that we expected for party whip activity is fully apparent in the evidence of Table 3.1.

Junctures

If the three conditions for whip engagement hold, there also should be certain patterns over time and across parties in the specific junctures of the legislative process that are targeted for attention. By juncture, I mean the kind of question that is under consideration. To simplify matters, let's focus on six broad categories of question type. First are questions that pertain to entire bills or general policy matters. These questions ask members to take positions about entire measures or proposals, which of course may include certain portions that a lawmaker favors and other portions that he or she opposes. The second category pertains to conference matters, including motions to adopt the compromise language on bills produced by bicameral negotiations between the House and Senate, as well as motions by members to instruct conferees when such negotiations are underway. The third category is for amendments and other proposals that would modify discrete parts of legislation. Fourth is a category for procedural questions, which is largely comprised of special rules for the consideration of legislation and previous question motions related to these rules. Special rules, you will recall, are the procedures that the majority party uses to structure the floor agenda, and the previous question motions on these rules provide the minority party with a potential opportunity to seize control of that agenda (if the motion fails, the minority party can offer an alternative rule). We also need a separate category for motions to recommit, with and without amendatory "instructions." The motion to recommit provides the minority party with a chance to kill legislation procedurally, immediately prior to a vote on final passage, and if instructions are included as part of the motion, the minority can use them to force a vote on substantive modifications to the majority-backed bill. The final question category is for attempts to override a presidential veto.

Table 3.2 summarizes the distribution of whipped items across the different question types in two ways. First, we look at whipped questions, regardless of whether they actually came to a vote on the House floor, and calculate the percentage of the total that relate to final passage, conference matters, amendments, procedure, and so forth. Such percentages shed light on the composition of the whipped agenda over time, and are provided in columns 2 (for the majority party) and 4 (for the minority). To properly evaluate whether party leaders are disproportionately likely to target certain question categories over others, however, we also need to consider the prevalence of these questions in the broader floor agenda. The proportion of whipped items that are final passage motions, for example, might be quite high, but the reason could be that such motions are particularly likely to come to a vote, and not that they are especially important to the whips. For this reason, Table 3.2 also provides the percentage of roll calls within each question type that were targeted for whip activity (column 3 for the majority and column 5 for the minority, only nonunanimous votes included).[4] Once again, the evidence for the majority covers 1955–2002, while the evidence for the minority is for 1975–80 and 1989–93 combined.[5]

As you can see, just over half of the questions put to members by the majority leadership dealt with entire measures or general policy matters. Another 7 percent dealt with conference issues broadly construed. About 22 percent pertained to amendments or other discrete substantive modifications to legislation. Roughly 13 percent touched on procedural strategy. And relatively low percentages obtain for the motion to recommit (2.2) and veto overrides (2.0). When whip activity is considered as a percentage of roll calls in the relevant question category, however, a somewhat different pattern emerges. At nearly 15 percent, the percentage of final

TABLE 3.2. Types of questions targeted for whip activity

Question type	Majority parties Percentage of whipped questions	Majority parties Percentage of votes whipped	Minority parties Percentage of whipped questions	Minority parties Percentage of votes whipped
Bills, general policy	53.2	14.6	40.7	7.7
Conference matters	7.1	7.8	7.6	4.6
Amendments, parts of bills	22.4	4.0	36.5	4.3
Procedure, strategy	13.2	4.8	4.6	1.7
Motion to recommit	2.2	9.0	.9	2.3
Veto overrides	2.0	26.7	9.7	63.6

Note: Only nonunanimous votes included.

passage votes that were whipped by the majority party is still relatively high (at least in comparison with the other categories). But the percentage for motions to recommit is now fairly large, reflecting the challenge that these motions can create for the majority party coalition on the floor. Although whip counts on veto overrides constitute a small portion of all whip activity for the majority party, the percentage of overrides votes that were whipped is quite high (over 25 percent). Override votes are infrequent, but are particularly likely to be whipped when they occur. Vetoes and override attempts often touch on highly visible issues important to one or both party agendas. Moreover, the two-thirds threshold for success on overrides is higher than the simple majority required for final passage and amendment votes, necessitating near-perfect unity within the majority party to prevail.

Now consider aggregate whip activity by question type for the minority party. For the Republican minorities of 1975–80 and 1989–93, a smaller share of whip activity was allocated to entire measures and final passage motions and a larger fraction targeted amendments, which is entirely consistent with expectations outlined in Chapter 2. Minorities routinely attempt to undermine the majority coalition by targeting vulnerable portions of larger bills. The elevation of amendments over final passage votes is also apparent when we consider minority whip activity as a percentage of all roll calls in each category. Compared to the majority, Table 3.2 also indicates that the minority party placed less emphasis on rules and other procedural questions. As expected, control over the structure of the floor agenda is more important to the majority leadership than it is to the minority. Compared to the majority, the minority party also allocates less whip attention to the motion to recommit, even though it is one of the few minority party prerogatives guaranteed in chamber rules. Apparently, expectations of party loyalty within the minority party on such motions are sufficiently high that whipping is unnecessary, while these questions can be threatening enough to the majority coalition that its leadership has to whip.

Perhaps the most striking differences between the majority and minority sides of Table 3.2 concern veto overrides. As mentioned, the importance of these motions and votes to the party name brand creates incentives for whipping by the majority party. But such incentives were even stronger for the Republican minorities of 1975–80 and 1989–93. For the earlier period, the GOP minority conducted 20 whip counts on overrides, 19 of which occurred during a single congress (1975–76) when Republican president Gerald Ford confronted large Democratic majorities on Capitol Hill. For 1989–93, 12 minority whip counts on overrides occurred during the presidency of George H. W. Bush, where a GOP White House like-wise faced large Democratic majorities in Congress. Both presidents made regular use of the veto and relied on nearly unanimous support from congressional Republicans to defeat override attempts, which in turn resulted in high levels of minority whip activity on these matters. Once again, the presidential context strongly conditions party tactics within the legislature.

Unfortunately, we lack systematic evidence for the whip operations of Democratic minorities. To what extent, then, might the majority–minority distinctions we observe in Table 3.2 actually result from enduring differences between the Democratic and Republican parties, regardless of whether or not they are in the majority or minority? Although evidence for Democratic minorities is unavailable, we can shed some light here by comparing minority GOP whip activities during 1989–93 with the party's allocation of whip attention in 1995–2002 when it was in the majority. Does the allocation of GOP whip attention shift across the two periods in a manner consistent with our expectations about majority and minority party status?

For the most part, the answer is yes. First, as reported in Table 1.3 and Figure 3.1, when Republicans became the majority party the overall quantity of GOP whip activity increased, reflecting the party's newfound responsibilities for managing the floor agenda. Second, Republicans were also far more likely to whip procedural matters when they were in the majority. In 1989–93, a little over 1 percent of minority Republican whip activity concerned procedural matters, while for the majority GOP of 1995–2002 that proportion increased to 14 percent and was similar to the percentages for previous Democratic majorities. Third, GOP whip activity on the motion to recommit increased markedly when the party transitioned from minority to majority status, which likewise mirrored the practices of previous Democratic majorities. Indeed, the percentage of recommital votes that were whipped by Republican leaders increased four-fold between the two periods. As a House majority, the Republicans also placed greater emphasis on whipping final passage questions and less on whipping amendments than had been the case for the party's years in the minority. In 1989–93, roughly 44 percent of GOP whip counts concerned entire bills and slightly less than 40 percent targeted amendments, while for 1995–2002 nearly 55 percent of the now majority Republican counts dealt with entire measures and the proportion for amendments dropped to about 21 percent. The whip priorities of the majority Republicans, in short, more closely resembled the practices of previous Democratic majorities than they did GOP whip activities when the party was in the minority. As a result, we can infer that the differences between the two sides of Table 3.2 probably reflect majority versus minority status, rather than enduring differences between Republicans and Democrats.

Temporal Patterns

The behavioral argument also implies certain changes over time in the allocation of whip attention by question type, and the evidence again is generally supportive. For instance, we expect that the early 1970s rule changes that helped produce sharp increases in floor amendments should result in an increased percentage of the whipped agenda for amendments and a somewhat smaller percentage for final passage motions. Indeed, the portion of majority whip counts that targeted amendments increased after 1972 (from 14 percent in 1955–72 to about 24 percent during 1973–2002), and the portion targeting final passage motions and entire bills dropped substantially (from 72 percent in 1955–1972 to about half during 1973– 2002). Importantly, the percentage of floor votes on amendments that were targeted for majority whip activity was basically unchanged after 1955– 72—the over-time shift toward amendments and away from final passage motions primarily resulted from changes in the underlying floor agenda, rather than some alteration in the behavioral calculus of the leadership.

Second, the proportion of majority whip attention allocated to procedural matters also increased over time in interesting ways. Yet another consequence of the rise in floor amendments during the 1970s was increased reliance by the majority leadership on restrictive amendment procedures to reduce uncertainty and manage the floor agenda (Bach and Smith 1988). Faced with an avalanche of amendments, House Democratic leaders responded with increasingly restrictive procedures to maintain their grip over the floor agenda. While in the minority, the Republicans pledged to return the chamber to open amendment rules if and when they became the majority party, but as the new majority in 1995 their enthusiasm for open procedures dimmed abruptly. Like their Democratic predecessors, the GOP majority leadership viewed restrictive procedures as essential for holding their small majorities together on the floor, and the proportion of restrictive procedures was in the 60–75 percent range throughout 1995–2002. As expected, the portion of majority whip activity targeting procedural strategy increased markedly over time, from less than 4 percent during 1955–72 to nearly 15 percent for 1973–2002. The percentage of roll calls relating to special rules (the rules themselves and associated motions on the previous question) that were whipped by the majority did not change much over time. Like the heightened whip focus on amendments, the over-time increase in majority whip attention on procedural matters primarily reflects changes in the composition of the roll call record.

Still, the prevalence of whip activity on special rules and other procedural matters raises important questions about the foundations of majority party power in the House. If the majority's grasp over the instruments of agenda control are as firm as some scholars suggest, then why does the leadership need to whip votes on special rules so frequently? During 1995–2002, for example, the Republican majority whipped special rules on 56 separate occasions, apparently because they believed the outcomes of these votes were in play. The prevalence of whip activity on special rules implies that the influence of the House majority leadership does not derive from monopoly control over the process of agenda setting *a la* the cartel model. If it did, why would the majority party need to rely on the whips to avoid getting rolled on procedural matters? Majority party influence, it appears, is rooted in the party's ability to prevail during floor fights— on both substantive matters and procedure. The majority's grasp over the floor agenda ultimately rests on the effectiveness of the whips, rather than the cartelization of procedure.

Over-time changes in the minority's prioritization of procedural matters are also instructive. The inclination of the GOP minority to whip special rules dropped between the 1970s and the early 1990s (from nearly 10 percent of all Republican whip activity during 1975–80 to less than 2 percent during 1989–93). The more important floor procedure became as a majority party instrument for agenda control, in other words, the less the minority GOP whipped on rules-related motions. Apparently, the minority Republicans could count on extensive party loyalty on these matters without activating the whips. But as previously mentioned, when the Republicans transitioned to majority status in 1995 the share of their whip activity allocated to procedural matters grew to roughly the same level as had characterized previous Democratic majorities.

The final example of noteworthy over-time differences in whip activity concerns veto overrides in the Republican House. During 1995–2000, when Republican majorities regularly squared off against the Democratic administration of Bill Clinton, not a single one of the several hundred counts conducted by GOP Whip Tom DeLay dealt with a veto override. The reason was not a lack of veto activity. During his two terms as president, Clinton issued 36 vetoes, and between 1995 and 2000 there were 12 recorded votes in the House on override attempts. Why was the DeLay whip network completely inactive on these questions, while prior Democratic majorities periodically whipped override attempts when confronted by vetoes from GOP administrations? Once again, we need to revisit the three conditions. For the most part, the Clinton vetoes were on major bills important to the parties, and within the majority Republican Conference the prospects for high levels of internal unity on override attempts were good (conditions 1 and 2 were met). However, these overrides were seldom in play (condition 3) because of the small size of the Republican majorities and the likelihood of unified opposition from Democrats. DeLay and other Republican leaders were reluctant to waste their time and political capital whipping override attempts that almost certainly would fail. Prior Democratic majorities, in contrast, were often large, and cross-partisan coalitions were more common, making the successful override of a presidential veto potentially attainable. The gist of Table 3.2? The junctures in the legislative process targeted for whipping—including key differences by party and over time—are largely consistent with the behavioral logic introduced in Chapter 2.

Fiscal Management Issues

The behavioral argument also highlights fiscal management issues as potential whip targets. Handling the annual appropriations and congressional budget processes are core responsibilities of the majority leadership, and failure to pass spending bills or to effectively coordinate the budget can generate negative media coverage for the majority party and weaken that party's prospects at the polls. Along those lines, if the minority party can derail the majority's efforts to pass spending and budgetary legislation, the party can further its efforts to win more seats and gain majority control. For these reasons, whip attention should disproportionately target appropriations and budget measures.

We also expect heightened whip attention for a third form of fiscal management—legislation affecting the federal debt limit. The Public Debt Limit Acts of 1939 and 1941 established a statutory ceiling on the size of the federal debt. As a result, as the size of the debt has grown with increases in the scope of governmental activity, the Congress periodically has had to enact increases in the ceiling. Prior to the 1960s, these measures were seldom controversial. But as fiscal policy became more politicized in the 1960s and 1970s, and then increasingly partisan in the 1980s and 1990s, legislation to raise the debt limit has sharply divided members by party. For lawmakers, casting a vote in favor of more debt is seldom a popular act. On the other hand, a failure to cover US financial obligations would be highly detrimental to the national economy and global financial system. Consequentially, debt limit bills are generally viewed as must-pass legislation, especially by the White House. On Capitol Hill, members of the party of the incumbent president typically support the passage of such legislation. Members of the other party are inclined to oppose these proposals—but only if there are already enough "yes" votes to ensure passage and avoid an economic catastrophe. Debt limit votes, in short, are superb vehicles for partisan gamesmanship and name-brand politics, and are thus prime candidates for whip attention.[6]

The importance of fiscal management items to the whipped agenda is summarized in Table 3.3. Once again, the evidence is presented in two ways. The second column denotes the percentage of majority whip counts targeting appropriations bills, budget measures, and debt limit increases, with analogous information provided for the minority in column 4. The third column of Table 3.3 shows the percentage of House roll calls in each topic area that can be directly associated with majority whip activity, and the fifth column provides this information for the minority. "Appropriations" includes the annual spending measures, continuing appropriations (used when all of the annual bills are not enacted by the deadline), and supplemental appropriations measures (to cover allegedly unexpected spending needs). The "budget" category includes questions that relate to budget resolutions, reconciliation bills, and other general budgetary matters. And the "debt limit" category is for proposals to raise the ceiling on the federal debt.

As predicted, appropriations measures constitute a large share of the whipped agenda for both parties. For the majority party, nearly 20 percent of polled items relate to spending bills. Moreover, there also are instructive differences over time. Until the early 1980s, the portion of majority party

TABLE 3.3. Fiscal management and whip activity

Issue area	Majority parties Percentage of whipped questions	Majority parties Percentage of votes whipped	Minority parties Percentage of whipped questions	Minority parties Percentage of votes whipped
Appropriations	19.6	5.9	10.6	2.6
Budget	7.5	13.9	8.2	7.4
Debt Limit	2.2	15.4	1.2	3.5
Other	70.6	7.1	80.0	5.5

Note: Only nonunanimous votes included.

whip counts targeting spending bills was just 5 or 6 percent. In 1983–94 that portion increased to over 18 percent. And for the GOP majorities of 1995–2002, over one-third of all whip activity centered on appropriations. In contrast to the increases for amendments and procedural matters, heightened majority whipping on appropriations did not derive from changes in the number of appropriations roll calls. The portion of appropriations votes subject to majority whipping also grew from less than 2 percent during 1955–72 to over 10 percent during 1995–2002.

Why the change? For one, the importance of the appropriations process as a vehicle for policy change increased relative to the authorizations process in the 1980s and 1990s.[7] During those years, the House majority party generally confronted a White House controlled by the other party, and divided partisan control complicated the majority leadership's ability to move party priorities to passage. Moreover, during the 1980s and 1990s, the Congress also grew more polarized along partisan lines, reinforcing the aforementioned difficulties of altering policy via authorizations legislation. Appropriations bills, in contrast, must be enacted each year—either individually or as part of omnibus packages—or portions of the federal government will close. Not surprisingly, as the partisan political hurdles in the authorizations process became more daunting, House leaders relied more and more on the annual appropriations process to advance their priorities, and this in turn led to enhanced whipping on appropriations bills.

Also, consistent with expectations, Table 3.3 indicates that budget measures are regular targets of whip activity. The contemporary budget process was established by the Budget Act of 1974. Prior to the mid-1970s, there were few general budget questions before the body simply because the main budgetary vehicles—the budget resolution and reconciliation bills—had not been created. But from that point onward, nearly 9 percent of overall whip activity targeted budget questions. The number of counts is less than for appropriations bills because there are so many more discrete spending questions before the chamber. When we control for the number of relevant roll calls, party emphasis on budgetary matters becomes apparent. During 1983–2002, for both the majority and the minority, almost 19 percent of budget votes were subject to whip activity.

The number of whipped items that dealt with debt limit hikes was also relatively low for both parties, and their proportion of the whipped agenda was small. Again, the main reason is the relative paucity of roll calls. Debt limit votes are not a day-to-day feature of the House legislative process. When we consider the portion of debt limit votes that were whipped, their importance to the leadership becomes apparent. As Table 3.3 shows, the majority party targeted about 15 percent of these votes for whipping. The somewhat lower percentage of debt limit votes whipped by the minority is due to a complete absence of such activity for the GOP minorities of 1975–80. During 1989–93, the percentage for the minority Republicans was about the same as for the Democratic majorities of that period.

Bringing the Pieces Together

Consistent with expectations, then, there are strong bivariate relationships between the incidence of whip activity, on the one hand, and factors like legislative importance, presidential prioritization, question type, and fiscal management, on the other. These explanatory factors, however, also are related to one another. Substantively important motions are more likely to be presidential priorities; fiscal management issues like debt limit hikes are often singled out as *CQ* major votes; and so on. To gauge whether the behavioral perspective is consistent with evidence about whip attention over time, we also need to explore whether the causal factors have an impact on the allocation of whip activity, controlling for alternative explanations.

Table 3.4 summarizes the results of two probit regressions; one for the majority and one for the minority. The units of observation are roll call votes on the House floor that occurred during time stretches where evidence about whip activity is available for the relevant party. As was the case with the other tables in this chapter, our focus is on nonunanimous votes where fewer than 90 percent of members voted the same way. The dependent variables are dichotomous indicators that take on the value of one if a vote was directly whipped by the relevant leadership and otherwise are zero. There are eight independent variables. Like the dependent variable, six of the explanatory variables also are dichotomous and take on values of zero or one. *Major* captures whether or not *CQ* categorized a roll call as a key vote for the session. *President* captures whether or not *CQ* reported a White House position for the matter. *Passage*, *Procedure*, and *Veto* measure, respectively, whether or not the underlying motion related to final passage or an entire measure, a procedural question of some form, or an attempted veto override. To simplify matters, here we group motions to pass conference reports along with the final passage questions, and motions to recommit are included in the procedural category. *Fiscal* reflects whether or not a vote relates to an appropriation, general budget, or debt limit measure.

The last two explanatory variables—*Maj. cohesion* and *Min. cohesion*—are an attempt to incorporate baseline expectations for the underlying distribution of member views about a question. Recall that the second and third conditions for whip attention are that a high degree of internal unity within the party appears feasible and that the matter remains in play. To tap these conditions, ideally we would have direct measures of the leanings of members of both parties on a question immediately prior to leadership decisions about whether or not to whip. Unfortunately, such measures are unavailable. The results of whip counts may seem like a possibility, of course, but the positions they reveal are taken after the leadership has decided to whip, and in any event this intelligence is unavailable for the vast majority of roll calls that are not directly targeted for whip action. As a result, in Table 3.4 we rely on internal party cohesion for non-whipped votes in the relevant issue area during the relevant time stretch.[8] If a roll call dealt with health policy, for example, the *Maj. cohesion* variable is the cohesion of members of that party on health roll calls during the time period—excluding all votes that were whipped. Cohesion, in turn, is the proportion of party members voting together. If all Democrats voted yes

TABLE 3.4. Leadership decisions about whether to whip a vote

Variables	Majority party 1955–2002	Marginal effects	Minority party 1975–80, 1989–93	Marginal effects
Major	0.89*** (0.08)	.16	1.06*** (0.15)	.14
President	0.57*** (0.04)	.07	0.92*** (0.15)	.09
Passage	0.74*** (0.10)	.09	0.27** (0.11)	.02
Procedure	0.42*** (0.07)	.02	–0.18 (0.21)	–.01
Veto	0.56* (0.30)	.04	1.30*** (0.45)	.20
Fiscal	0.13 (0.09)	.01	–0.06 (0.13)	–.003
Maj cohesion	1.80** (0.74)	.05	2.56*** (0.94)	.05
Min cohesion	4.68*** (0.96)	.12	4.62*** (0.99)	.05
Constant	–7.33*** (0.72)		–7.91*** (1.01)	
Observations	12,081		4,643	
McKelvey-Zavoina R²	.22		.27	

*** p<0.01, ** p<0.05, * p<0.1

Note: Only nonunanimous votes included, standard errors in parentheses and clustered by Congress.

or no, the cohesion value is 1.0. If the party is evenly divided between "yes" and "no" votes, the cohesion value is zero, and for immediate values of internal agreement cohesion falls somewhere in between. The cohesion scores, then, vary by party, time period, and issue area. Needless to say, they constitute an imperfect measure of the underlying distribution of viewpoints, but are still a serviceable alternative for our purposes here. The parameter estimates reported in Table 3.4 are accompanied by marginal effects to facilitate inferences about substantive significance. For the dichotomous explanatory variables, the marginal effects are changes in the probability that a vote will be whipped resulting from a change in the relevant factor from zero to one.[9] For the two cohesion measures, the marginal changes result from shifting the relevant variable from its minimum to its maximum.

For the most part, the bivariate relationships already uncovered stand up to a multivariate treatment. For the majority party, whip attention is more likely on major votes and presidential priorities. Final passage votes are disproportionately likely to be whipped. Vetoes likewise are important whip targets. As expected, procedural votes are more likely to be whipped by the majority. Indeed, when the evidence is broken down by period that relationship is especially strong from 1983 onward as the House transitioned to increasingly restrictive amendment rules. Overall, fiscal management status does not appear to make much of a difference. However, if we focus exclusively on the years of Republican control, 1995–2002, the impact of this factor on whip activities is positive and significant.

Both majority and minority cohesion in the relevant issue area and time period are associated with enhanced whip activity by the majority party, but notice that the effects are much stronger for the minority cohesion measure. That's right—majority party decisions about when to whip, controlling for other factors, appear to be more responsive to the base-line cohesion of the minority party than to cohesion within the majority itself. At first blush, this result may seem counterintuitive, but it actually makes sense in light of conditions 2 and 3. Recall that the hypothesized relationship between internal unity and leadership decisions about when to whip is not linear. As initial unity rises, the prospects for intra-party consensus grow, but past a certain point the outcome may no longer be in doubt, mitigating the need to whip. This may dampen any direct relationship between majority party cohesion and majority party whip activity. On the other hand, the more cohesive the minority party is, the less cross-over support the majority can expect and the more likely a vote will be in play. The disproportionate impact of minority party cohesion on majority party whip activity, in other words, does resonate with the hypothesized behavioral logic.

For the minority party, the results reported in Table 3.4 are somewhat mixed, perhaps because of the relative paucity of evidence and the reliance on shorter time spans. Still, the table indicates that the GOP minorities of 1975–80 and 1989–93 also tended to whip major votes and presidential priorities. Procedural votes, in contrast, were not significant candidates for minority party whip attention. Again, procedural matters are expected to be of primary importance to members of the partisan majority. For the minority party, both majority and minority party cohesion help predict which roll calls will be subject to whip activity, and here both cohesion measures appear to have around the same effect. Overall, then, the results of Table 3.4 are generally consistent with the behavioral perspective.

Victory Margins

Before turning to the dynamics of partisan coalition building in Chapter 4, we take a preliminary look at some outcome data because of the implications for the contents of the whipped agenda. Whip count results, the leadership response, and the fate of whipped legislation are all strongly conditioned by the strategic selection of questions upon which to whip, and this strategic selection can complicate efforts to identify instances of party influence. The next chapter will show, for example, that the flow of member positions during the whip process tends to be toward the position of the relevant leadership, and that the majority party usually prevails on whipped votes. Are such patterns indicative of leadership influence, or do they primarily reflect strategic choices by the leadership to mostly whip when the prospects for internal unity and a floor victory are good? The relationships that exist between leadership decisions about when to whip and key aspects of the coalition-building process will be explored in the chapters that follow. But for now, we can examine the size of the majority party's margins on whipped and non-whipped roll calls to see if they mesh with our expectations about whip engagement.

Figure 3.2 portrays the size of the majority's margin of victory (or defeat) for whipped and non-whipped roll calls across the 1955–2002 time span, with nonunanimous and party-line votes considered separately. Here, the focus is entirely on questions whipped or not by the partisan majority, so the evidence relates to Democrats for 1955–94 and Republicans for

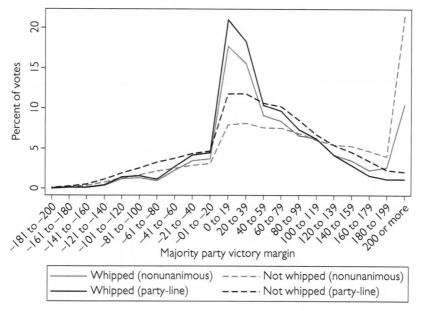

Figure 3.2. Majority party victory margins by whip status, nonunanimous and party votes (1955–2002)

1995–2002. The magnitude of a victory margin is denoted along the horizontal axis, and ranges from large losses (a margin of –181 to –200 votes) to large wins (vote margins of +200 or more). The interval near the center of the axis (from 0 to 19 votes) is for narrow wins by the majority party and the interval to the immediate left (–1 to –20) captures narrow losses. The vertical axis shows the percentage of the relevant roll calls falling in each of the victory margin intervals, and it ranges from a low of 0 to a high of nearly 20 percent.

A numerical example can clarify the contents of the figure. For each roll call, the position of the majority party is determined by the balance of the votes cast by members of that party. If most majority party members vote "yes," the party position is treated as affirmative, and if most vote "nay," the party position is taken as opposed.[10] For the purposes of illustration, assume that most majority party members vote "yes" on a question and the relevant motion passes by a single vote. Then the margin of victory is zero—there is no cushion of extra votes—and the roll call falls in the "0–19" category on the horizontal axis signifying a narrow victory. Alternatively, if most majority party members vote "no" and the motion still passes by a single vote, then the margin of victory is now -1. If the majority had been able to pick up just one more "no" vote, the outcome would have been a tie, resulting in defeat of the motion and a win for the majority party position. Some motions, of course, require super-majority support to pass the House (e.g., veto overrides, suspension of the rules) and thus present a more challenging threshold for adoption. Since vote margins for super-majority motions are not readily comparable to the lion's share of questions settled by a simple majority of voting members, they are excluded here.

As mentioned, the distribution of margins is shown separately for nonunanimous roll calls (90 percent or fewer members voted on one side) and party-line roll calls (50 percent or more of one party opposed 50 percent or more of the other). And within each of these subsets of the roll call record, votes are further distinguished by whether or not they were whipped by the partisan majority. The end result is the four curves in the figure. The distribution of majority victory margins for nonunanimous roll calls is in gray—solid for whipped votes and dashed for the rest—while the distributions for party-line roll calls are in black—once again, solid for whipped votes and dashed for the others.

For all four plots, there is a noticeable spike in outcomes for the "0–19" interval signifying a narrow victory. The percentage for narrow losses is always lower. When all nonunanimous roll calls are considered (the gray-colored curves), notice that there also is a spike for very large victories—here, outcome margins are disproportionately either narrow wins or lopsided victories for the majority party. If we focus just on party-line roll calls, in contrast, lopsided majority victories of 200 or more votes are very rare, and for obvious reasons. Unless the size of the majority caucus is extremely large (300 or more members), party-line outcomes with victory margins of 200 or more votes are not numerically feasible. For the party-line subset of the roll call record, there is only one spike, over majority party victories that are relatively close calls.

The spike for narrow victories and the relative paucity of narrow losses is consistent with prior research about vote margins in the House and may indicate the majority party's ability to pick up the necessary additional support when outcomes are close (King and Zeckhauser 2002). Alternatively, the pattern may surface because: (1) majority parties have more members by definition and (2) majority party sizes often are in the 20–40 seat range. In other words, if we assume that members will mostly vote with their parties and a roll call is close, the expectation might be for something like the spikes over narrow victories portrayed in the figure even without leadership intervention in the coalition-building process. What is different in Figure 3.2, however, is that the votes that the leadership targeted for whipping are distinguished from other roll call decisions. Does the distribution of victory margins look the same regardless of whether the whips are engaged, or are there perhaps some instructive distinctions?

Clearly the latter. For both the nonunanimous and party-line categories, the spike for narrow victories (and the associated drop-off for narrow defeats) is noticeably greater for the whipped votes than it is for the others. Whipped questions, in other words, are disproportionately likely to result in narrow victories for the majority party, which is exactly what we would expect if the leadership targeted questions where victory was possible but the outcome was still in doubt. This pattern is especially apparent for the party-line votes where we would most expect to see evidence of the hypothesized behavioral logic that drives whip engagement.

Interestingly, if we focus solely on the years of the GOP majority in the late 1990s and early 2000s, this pattern of many close wins and few close losses on whipped items is especially pronounced. During these years, the majority party was relatively small in size and the House was deeply polarized along partisan lines. Not surprisingly, party-line questions tended to produce very close votes. Indeed, nearly one-third of the outcomes during this period resulted in narrow victories for the majority party and there were very few losses of any magnitude. Moreover, the spike over narrow victories was nearly twice as high for the whipped votes than it was for non-whipped items. Particularly during the Republican majorities of 1995–2002, then, the strategic calculations of majority party leaders about when to whip are apparent in the outcome margins on votes. We will focus in more depth on the tactics of Tom DeLay and other leaders of the GOP majority in Chapter 8. But for now, our attention turns to the general patterns that exist in the process of party coalition building once the whips have been engaged.

FOUR

Growing the Vote

This chapter continues our exploration of whether the expectations implied by the behavioral theory presented in Chapter 2 conform with evidence about the main contours of the House whip process, 1955–2002. Now our focus is on what happens after the whips have been engaged—how rank-and-file members respond, the ability of party leaders to secure their support, and the prevalence of party success and failure on the floor. We proceed via five main sections. The first is an examination of the distribution of member responses over time. The second identifies general patterns and trends in the relationship between the positions members articulate during the whip process and the roll call votes they cast in the House. The third section considers the legislative outcomes of the whip process—who wins and who loses. The fourth is an analysis of "switcher behavior," which occurs when members change positions from opposition to support or from support to opposition between the whip count and the vote. The closing section is an examination of partisan "face-offs," which are occasions where both the majority and minority parties engage their whips and are taking opposing sides on the matter. Like the incidence of switching, these events are an illuminating vantage point for evaluating whether the majority party regularly dominates the partisan minority. Overall, the weight of the evidence in this chapter will indicate that leaders and whips matter. But it will not support broad claims about majority party dominance in the House legislative process, and will resonate instead with the behavioral logic advocated throughout this book.

How Members Respond

After leaders decide that a pending question should be whipped, members of the relevant whip network fan out, contact the subset of the rank and file they have been assigned, and ask these lawmakers for their positions about the question at hand. The precise mode of communication—member to member or through staff, in person or via the phone or even email—will vary by party and time period. But for more than 50 years, once leaders decide to whip, the next stage of the coalition-building process has been to systematically gauge the views of party colleagues.

Before examining the distribution of whipped responses over time, a few words of clarification are called for about how the tables and figures to come are structured. When presenting information about member views, roll calls, and whipped outcomes, we can sharpen the exposition by aggregating and otherwise reorganizing the evidence in five key ways.

First, data about the distribution of responses or votes usually will be organized by the four time periods that structure so much of the discussion in this book, rather than congress by congress or year by year. For certain years or congresses, there are significant evidentiary gaps, and routinely examining change on an annual or biennial basis may highlight data points that are distorted by the idiosyncrasies of particular whipped questions.[1] The first time span, you will recall, which we refer to as "period 1," covers 1955–72, when the Democratic majorities of the time were divided along regional lines. "Period 2" is for 1973–82, when the majority Democrats were large in number, but highly fragmented. "Period 3" is for 1983–94, the last decade of the Democrat's 40-year span as the House majority, when chamber decision making increasingly divided members by party. And "period 4" covers 1995–2002, the first eight years of the then new Republican majority, as the Congress grew still more polarized along partisan lines. Archival evidence about the House whip process, you will recall, is available for all four periods for the majority party, while evidence for the minority is available only for portions of periods 2 and 3.

Second, for some whipped items the counting process was either incomplete or significant portions of the results are absent from the archival record. To avoid having these cases bias our interpretation of the position configurations revealed by whip checks, the tables reported in this chapter only include information from completed whip counts, where a count is categorized as complete if the sum of nonresponders and missing observations does not exceed 25 percent of all party members.

Third, for a fairly small number of the whipped questions, no clear party position is discernible from materials in the archival record, or from scholarly or media coverage of the legislation. Perhaps the counting process was instigated at the request of a concerned committee chair, or the leadership took no position but needed whip intelligence to more efficiently manage scheduling logistics on the floor. Such items are excluded in the tables and figures that follow in order to provide a more accurate portrait of the coalition-building challenges confronting party leaders.

Fourth, in the tables and figures that follow, we generally will combine certain position categories to simplify the presentation. Recall that the whips in both parties classify the emergent positions of their colleagues via five main categories—"yes," "leaning yes," "undecided," "leaning no," and "no"—as well as certain residual categories that capture various forms of nonresponse ("absent for the vote," "no comment," "no answer," "ill or out of town," and so on). Here, we collapse these categories into four main groupings—yes or leaning yes (Y/LY), undecided, no or leaning no (N/LN), and other (for all the residual responses combined). Some information will be lost, of course, but not very much. Prior to the late 1970s, the leaner categories were used much less frequently, mostly because the whip networks were smaller and less developed, and because leaders were less concerned about distinguishing fine gradations of support or opposition. Indeed, the tabulation sheets and other whip materials leaders used during the 1950s and 1960s often did not include a column for leaners. In the 1970s, as party leaders sought more precise intelligence about member positions, more and more members were categorized as leaners, as opposed to unambiguously yes or no. To highlight general trends and comparisons, it helps to combine the categories for yes and leaning yes, and to do the same for no and leaning no. Indeed, the whips typically interpret the leaners in this fashion, anyway, and the roll call loyalty of the leaners more closely resembles that of the relevant polar response than it does the vote choices of undecideds.

Fifth, unless otherwise noted, whip count positions and roll call votes are always recoded so that a "yes" is the position of the relevant leadership. House Democrats almost always phrase their whipped questions so that an affirmative response reflects the party position. Republicans, however, traditionally have been more inclined to ask for a member's expected vote on a pending matter without rephrasing so that "yes" becomes the preferred response. In other words, whereas Democratic leaders might ask a colleague whether he or she will vote against an item the party opposes, the GOP would simply ask for that lawmaker's intended vote. To enable aggregation across whipped questions and comparisons across party lines, we need to present whip and vote information so that "yes" reflects the party position (assuming of course that such a position can be discerned).

Table 4.1 shows the percentage of responses per whipped question falling in the relevant category for each time period and with the majority and minority parties treated separately. Looking across the entire 1955–2002 time span, roughly two-thirds of members are recorded as in support of the party position or leaning that way, about 15 percent respond as undecided, 10 percent or so are no or leaning no, and depending on the party and time period about 10–13 percent fall in the residual category labeled "other." Interestingly, the percentages for the majority and minority parties are relatively similar. There also are some changes of note over time.[2]

Now consider the contents of Table 4.1 in more depth. It comes as no great surprise, of course, that the percentage of responses answering in support of the party position is generally high on both sides of the partisan aisle. After all, the decisions that leaders make about when to whip are based in part on the prospects for internal partisan unity. For the majority party, however, notice that the percentages for Y/LY in periods 1 and 2 are almost identical, and that the analogous percentages for periods 3 and 4 are likewise very similar. Between periods 2 and 3, however, there is a noticeable increase in the size of the leadership support base. In other words, the temporal increase in leadership support at the whip stage takes the form of an upward shift between the majorities of 1973–82 and 1983–94.[3] Importantly, the percentage of members answering yes or leaning yes for the Republican majorities of period 4 is also very similar to the rates for the Democratic majorities of period 3.

TABLE 4.1. Percentage of whip count responses, by party and period

Majority	All periods	Period 1 (Dem)	Period 2 (Dem)	Period 3 (Dem)	Period 4 (Rep)
Yes or leaning yes	65.8	58.7	58.6	69.2	73.7
Undecided	14.8	12.9	17.5	15.9	11.3
No or leaning no	10.0	12.6	12.0	8.2	8.6
Other	9.4	15.8	12.0	6.8	6.5

Minority	All periods	Period 2 (Rep)	Period 3 (Rep)
Yes or leaning yes	63.1	60.2	65.7
Undecided	15.8	17.2	14.6
No or leaning no	12.9	13.0	12.9
Other	8.1	9.6	6.8

Note: Included are all "completed" whip polls for which there was a clear leadership position.

Once again for the majority party, Table 4.1 also indicates that the percentages for "undecided" were greatest in periods 2 and 3, and somewhat lower in periods 1 and 4. Here, the inter-period differences are not very large, but member indecision appears to have been most prevalent during the transition from the relatively weak whip networks of the 1950s and 1960s to the more polarized Congresses of the 1990s.

Notice also that the percent of majority party members answering "no" or "leaning no" declined over time, with the change again occurring mostly between periods 2 and 3, mirroring in reverse the pattern for Y/LY. During the 1950s and 1960s, it was commonplace for 10–15 percent of the majority Democrats to report some degree of opposition to the leadership during whip checks, but by the late 1980s that portion had dropped to 8–9 percent. Overall, the cross-period movements between Y/LY, undecided, and N/LN are consistent with what we would expect for a legislature growing increasingly polarized along partisan lines.

As mentioned, the "other" category includes a variety of answers that do not fit cleanly into one of the main response categories, and here there was a substantial decline over time, especially when we compare the Democratic majorities of period 1 with both the majority and minority parties of periods 2–4. The steep decline for the "other" column derives in part from the 1970s expansion of the whip networks and the increased priority that party leaders placed on accurate intelligence about member positions. Leaders became less tolerant of ambiguity or nonresponse. For the Democrats, however, an important historical feature of their whip operation merits attention. During the 1960s, Democratic whip zones for certain states often refused to identify the positions taken by individual members and instead reported aggregate numbers to their leaders (e.g., nine yes, two no, three undecided). The whips, for their part, treated these aggregate tallies with skepticism. As a result, the zone aggregates are not incorporated into the percentages for the standard response categories in the table, and instead are added to the "other" category. The strategy of providing only position aggregates was mostly employed prior to the 1970s, and by southern zones comprised of party conservatives, which further explains why the percentages for the "other" category dropped over time.

For the minority Republicans of periods 2 and 3, Table 4.1 also indicates an over-time increase in the percentage of yes and leaning yes responders, and a decline for the "undecided" and "other" categories. The percentages for N/LN are basically the same across periods. What is most striking, though, is the relative similarity of the response distributions for the majority and minority parties during the two periods for which evidence is available for both parties. The factors that shape the response distributions in whip checks may have analogous effects on both sides of the partisan aisle. We can explore that conjecture more in the period-specific chapters that follow.

The contents of Table 4.1 are informative. But, to fully assess the magnitude of the vote-gathering challenges confronting party leaders, we also need to consider the *number* of supporters, not just their proportion of the full caucus or conference. The sizes of the two parties vary significantly from congress to congress and similar percentages at different points in time may mask large differences in the number of members in that response category. For this reason, Table 4.2 denotes the average number of members per whipped question in each response category, once again aggregated by time period and separated by party. For additional context, the table also has a row with the average size of the relevant party in that period across the completed whip polls where the leadership took a position.[4]

As Table 4.2 indicates, the average size of the majority leadership's base of support (the sum of yes and leaning yes responses) ranged from a low of about 150 votes in period 1 to a high of 179 votes in period 3, or about 166 across the four periods. Although the percentage of yes and leaning yes responders was highest for period 4 (the years

TABLE 4.2. Average number of whip count responses, by party and period

Majority	All periods	Period 1 (Dem)	Period 2 (Dem)	Period 3 (Dem)	Period 4 (Rep)
Yes or leaning yes	165.9	149.7	159.1	179.0	165.4
Undecided	37.4	33.0	47.4	41.1	25.3
No or leaning no	25.1	32.1	32.6	21.2	19.2
Other	23.6	40.4	32.4	17.5	14.5
Party Size	252.4	255.7	272.0	258.8	224.6

Minority	All periods		Period 2 (Rep)	Period 3 (Rep)	
Yes or leaning yes	101.6		88.8	115.1	
Undecided	25.5		25.4	25.5	
No or leaning no	20.8		19.1	22.6	
Other	13.1		14.2	11.9	
Party Size	161.1		147.8	175.1	

Note: Included are all "completed" whip polls for which there was a clear leadership position. The cell entries for the various positions do not sum perfectly to party size because of small numbers of responses that were illegible or for which archival data were lost.

of Republican House control), the number of majority party members who supported the leadership position typically was less than was the case for the Democratic majorities of period 3 because the GOP majorities were so thin.

The contents of Figure 4.2 underscore a critical, but under-acknowledged feature of floor decision making in Congress. As the whip process commences, the leadership typically lacks the votes necessary to prevail. Indeed, the criteria leaders consider in deciding when to whip almost guarantee this gap. Whipped matters, we have argued, tend to be party priorities with initial support levels that fall short. As a result, although there are major differences across periods in party sizes and internal makeup, the gap between the majority's initial base of support and the number of votes necessary to win is an enduring feature of the House legislative process. The causes and contours of the gap will vary, but the essential challenge remains.

For the two periods (2 and 3) where individual-level data are available for the minority Republicans, Table 4.2 shows the average number of leadership supporters on party whip counts increased from roughly 89 in 1975–80 to about 115 in 1989–93, while the numbers for the remaining position categories were fairly stable over time. In other words, the larger size of the GOP Conference in period 3 relative to period 2 mostly resulted in more members in the Y/LY column. Still, in both periods, from 45 to 50 members were wavering or opposed to the party position at some point during the whip process. One claim is that members of the minority may be more inclined to toe the partisan line on major votes because they are the party of opposition. Even if there are significant divisions within the minority party about public policy, there may be a broad consensus that the legislative alternatives advanced by the majority coalition should be defeated. Yet we do not observe significantly higher levels of leadership loyalty on the minority side of the aisle as the whip process begins. To the extent that they exist, the hypothesized advantages for the minority party at vote gathering must surface later in the game, as leaders seek to retain or convert individual members on the vote.

Question Types and Ideology

In Chapter 3, we observed major differences in whip attention across different question types (amendments versus final passage, procedure versus substance). Leaders tend to whip items that are important to the party program, have good prospects for internal unity, and are characterized by significant weaknesses in the party supporting coalition. As a result, they tend to prioritize certain question types over others in the whip process. But once the whips are engaged on a matter, the underlying strategic calculus about when to whip should produce significant continuities in the distribution of viewpoints across question types.

With a few exceptions, this conjecture is borne out when we break down the response evidence by question category. Start with the majority party. Across the four periods, leadership support among members of the majority was about 65 percent on entire bills, 64 percent on conference matters, and 63 percent on amendments, with the over-time changes mostly tracking the general shift toward greater leader support on whipped matters between periods 2 and 3.

In contrast, the distribution of responses was somewhat more favorable to the position of the majority leadership on veto overrides (about 79 percent Y/LY), procedural matters (about 70 percent Y/LY), and motions to recommit (also about 70 percent Y/LY). The whipped veto overrides were mostly from congresses in which a Democratic House majority faced a GOP-controlled White House and high leadership support on these questions reflects their importance to the party agendas. In addition, the two-thirds threshold required for a successful override created incentives for the leadership to only engage the whips when significant intra-party cohesion was feasible. The presence of undecideds was lowest for veto overrides (just 7 percent for the partisan majorities of period 1–4), in large part because the chamber already had acted on these matters at least once and individual lawmakers previously had taken public positions.

As mentioned, party support is also elevated somewhat on procedural questions. This category is mostly comprised of motions related to special rules that touch on the majority party's core prerogatives over the floor agenda. Since the 1975 decision to give the Speaker the power to nominate majority party members of the Rules Committee, as well as the 1980s increase in the use of restrictive amendment procedures, there has been significant pressure for rank-and-file members of the majority to toe the party line on rule votes, with little expectation of crossover support from the minority. Indeed, party support on whipped procedural matters grew substantially among the majority Democrats between periods 1 and 2 (from 39 to 64 percent Y/LY), and for the GOP majorities of period 4 the portion of members answering yes or leaning yes on procedure was nearly 79 percent. Support for the majority leadership was also somewhat elevated on motions to recommit (about 70 percent Y/LY and less than 7 percent N/LN). The number of whip counts per period was relatively low here and we should not infer too much from the evidence, but the motion to recommit also touches on the majority's control over the agenda and thus fosters incentives to stay loyal during the whip process.

Interestingly, when we consider variation by question type for the minority party, the results are mostly similar to what we observe on the majority side of the aisle. Indeed, there are few differences across question types that cannot be explained away by the low number of counts in the relevant category. The one noteworthy difference concerns veto overrides. For the GOP minorities of periods 2 and 3, the percentage of "yes" and "leaning yes" responders on these questions was about 51 and 68 percent, respectively. Especially during period 2, the minority leadership's initial base of support on veto overrides was fairly small, which is the opposite of what we observed for the majority party. The veto override counts for the minority party were from congresses where the Republicans controlled the presidency and GOP House leaders regularly sought to thwart efforts by Democratic leaders to override their co-partisan in the White House. As a result, the number of votes the minority leadership needed to mobilize against an override attempt was just one-third plus one, or roughly 145 lawmakers. Given this low vote-gathering bar, if the minority leadership needed to activate the whip process the likely reason was that significant defections were expected among the minority rank and file, which would explain the low percentages for leadership support on whipped override attempts for the GOP minorities.

Certain of the "behavioral signposts" hypothesized in Chapter 2 concerned the relationship between member positions during the whip process and the standard measures of member ideology derived from the roll call record. Spatial logic, you will recall, implies that there should be a strong and direct relationship between member ideology and leadership support during the whip process. For Democrats, yes or leaning yes responses should be positively associated with member liberalism, and for Republicans support for the party position should grow with ideological conservatism. Since members generally are whipped about their positions fairly close in time to the relevant floor vote, and the leading measures of member ideology are all calculated from the roll call record, it only makes sense that the same ideological structure be apparent in whip polls and votes.

The panels of Figure 4.1 summarize the relationship between member ideology and the whip count response by period and party. In each panel, the horizontal axis denotes ideological deciles within the chamber. More concretely, if a lawmaker's DW-NOMINATE score

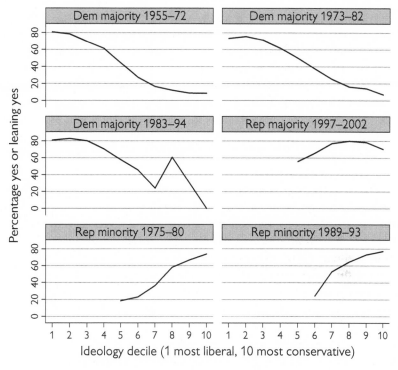

Figure 4.1. Member ideology and whip count responses

(dimension 1) is among the most liberal 10 percent for the House as a whole, then she falls in decile 1, while members with DW-NOMINATE values among the 10 percent most conservative in the chamber make up decile 10. Deciles 5 and 6 straddle the ideological median within the House. The vertical axes of each panel denote the percentage of members within each ideological decile that answered as yes or leaning yes during whip checks. To simplify matters, Figure 4.1 only includes trend curves for the members reporting yes or leaning yes—analogous curves for the other response categories all trend in the opposite direction and adding them would complicate the figure without adding much information. The gaps in certain of the panels are due to the lack of members in that particular ideological decile.

As expected, there is a strong and direct relationship between ideological liberalism or conservatism and support for the party position during the whip process. The relationship is generally downward sloping for Democrats (increased conservatism means less party support on whip counts) and upward sloping for the GOP (increased conservativism means more leadership support). With the Democratic majorities of period 1, for example, the proportion of party supporters within the most liberal ideological decile was roughly 80 percent, while in deciles 5 and 6 adjacent to the chamber median, the percentage for Y/LY is only half that level. As we move to the most conservative deciles, party support plummets to 10 percent or less. Analogous relationships exist between member DW-NOMINATE scores and party support in the majority whip process for periods 2 and 3 (the outlier for decile 8 in period 3 is due to the aberrant behavior of a single Democrat).

The pattern for the Republican majorities of period 4 also shows a strong ideological trend, albeit with increased conservatism now translating into higher percentages for Y/LY. As before, the percentage of party supporters is relatively low for the deciles adjacent to the chamber median (56 and 66 percent for deciles 5 and 6, respectively). For deciles 7, 8, and 9, where the party center and most GOP members were located, the support levels are substantially higher (about 80 percent). In the most conservative decile, though, support for the leadership during whip checks dropped back to around 70 percent. For the Republicans of period 4, the decline among the most conservative members was important tactically because of the party's small majorities. For the leaders of the GOP majority, the whip process revealed a significant potential for alienation at the extremes, and their most pressing challenges often came from the far right wing of their conference.

The last two panels of Figure 4.1 show the relationship between member ideology and whip count behavior for the minority Republicans of periods 2 and 3. Once again, we observe a strong and direct relationship between member conservatism and support for the leadership position on whipped matters. In contrast to the GOP majorities of period 4, though, there is little indication of alienation at the extremes when the Republicans were in the minority. During those years, the primary aim of the GOP leadership was to build opposition to the legislative program of the majority Democrats, and on occasion to muster the votes necessary to sustain vetoes by Republican presidents. The more conservative the lawmaker, the more likely that member would be opposed to the Democratic program on policy grounds and answer as "yes" on whip checks. Ideologically moderate members of the GOP Conference, in contrast, had viewpoints nearer to the Democratic position and were thus more likely to express opposition. The lack of extremist drop-off in the whip responses of minority party members further highlights the importance of audiences and "explainability" in the decision-making process. As the majority party in 1995–2002, the most conservative GOP legislators faced a higher explanatory burden than did their more mainstream conservative colleagues, and as a result were more likely to defect from the party position. While in the minority, though, there was no such distinction between the explanatory challenges faced by mainstream and extreme conservatives. Both Republican factions could endorse their leaders' positions against the Democratic agenda, albeit for different reasons, and thereby avoid serious blow-back from party audiences at home.

Interestingly, the relationship between member ideology and the whip count response also holds for an especially instructive subset of the whipped items: (1) final passage questions where there are (2) no intervening modifications in the legislation between the whip count and the vote and (3) the measure passed. Under these conditions, the whip count constitutes a "member opinion poll" of sorts about how the contents of a legislative outcome related to the "preferences" of individual lawmakers. If majority party members with ideal points located near the chamber median carry the day, as some scholars claim, then we would expect such members to be disproportionately Y/LY on the relevant whip count. Think about it. At the tail end of the legislative process on a major bill important to the party program, if the preformed views of chamber centrists determine the outcome and the bill that passes perfectly reflects their preferences, then why would they be ambivalent or opposed to their own most preferred language?

Again, for this thought experiment to make sense, we need to focus exclusively on questions about initial House passage where the bill passes without intervening alterations between the whip count and the vote.[5] Interestingly, when we follow this thought experiment to the letter and examine the relevant evidence, the majority legislators with preference estimates located near the chamber median (as measured by DW-NOMINATE scores) turn out to be substantially *less* likely to be party supporters, and substantially *more* likely to express indecision or outright opposition across all four periods. Indeed, graphical displays of the results are almost identical to Figure 4.1. Leadership support curves downward over the deciles where the median chamber viewpoint is located. Again, if the bills that pass most closely approximate the views of chamber centrists, why would these members be so inclined to be undecided or opposed? Clearly, they would not be. Leveraged in this manner, the whip evidence is not consistent with claims that exogenously determined, middle-ground preferences drive legislative outcomes in the US House, as predicted by spatial renditions of cartel theory, where party influence is exerted at the agenda setting stage and floor outcomes are expected to approximate the views of chamber moderates. The evidence is fully consistent with the behavioral perspective, however, where centrist viewpoints emerge endogenously as part of the whip process and moderates are especially likely to face cross pressure at home.

Retention and Conversion

As the whip process continues, leaders use the intelligence they gather about member positions to detect weak spots in their coalition, identify which members need to be retained or converted, and determine whether substantive changes are necessary in the party proposal to prevail on the floor. As the roll call nears, the number of undecided and nonresponsive legislators generally falls and member positions crystalize in the direction of yes or no. The roll call itself ends the floor whipping process, at least with regard to the targeted question. Overall, how successful have the majority and minority parties been at building their supporting coalitions between the whip count and the vote?

Table 4.3 summarizes leadership loyalty on whipped roll call votes by congress, with evidence presented separately for the majority and minority party. Cell entries are the percentage of the members in each category who voted the party position. Once again, the small subset of whipped questions without a clear party position are dropped, and counts deemed incomplete (more than 25 percent of members are nonresponders or missing) are excluded. Whip count positions and votes are recoded so that a "yes" is always the position of the relevant party leadership.[6] As you can see, for both parties roll call loyalty falls as we move from "yes" or "leaning yes," to "undecided," to "leaning no" or "no." Members falling in the "other" category tend to have loyalty scores on votes falling somewhere between the percentages for the "Y/LY" and "undecided" categories.

Clearly, the lion's share of majority party members who favored the party position during the whip process ended up voting that way on the associated roll calls. There is some variance by period, but 95 percent or more of the members responding as yes or leaning yes generally vote with the leadership. There is a small increase during the years of Republican control, but pro-leadership votes in this response category were nearly as common during Democratic majorities dating to the 1950s. To some extent, the high levels of leadership voting for Y/LY responders are simply an indicator of the basic accuracy of whip intelligence. But there also are significant incentives for members not to reverse themselves and break a pledge to support the leadership without a compelling rationale. Moreover, the default position for lawmakers often is to support the party unless there are pressing reasons to do otherwise, and the consistency between the whip stage and the roll call vote reflects that tendency.

In contrast, roll call loyalty among initially undecided members was usually 65–70 percent, at least until the Republican majorities of period 4, where party support in this category was over 80 percent. The likelihood of defection on votes was much higher for undecideds than it was for the Y/LY category. Still, with the exception of just one congress (1969–70), the portion of undecided lawmakers who stayed loyal on the vote always exceeded 50 percent.

Among members initially opposed to the leadership position or leaning that way (N/LN on the count), party support rates on the associated roll calls were much lower. During the 1950s and 1960s, the percentage of party supporters in this group was a little over 22 percent. As the parties became more polarized during the 1980s and 1990s, the majority leadership's ability to convert initial opponents grew to nearly 30 percent. And during the GOP majorities of the 1990s and 2000s, Republican Whip Tom DeLay was able to flip a remarkable 43 percent of the initial opponents to party support on the vote.

TABLE 4.3. Leadership loyalty on whipped votes, by party and period

Majority	Period 1 (Dem)	Period 2 (Dem)	Period 3 (Dem)	Period 4 (Rep)
Yes or leaning yes	96.4	93.9	95.3	97.8
Undecided	65.5	65.1	68.7	81.0
No or leaning no	22.2	24.3	29.9	43.4
Other	69.8	74.0	81.7	89.4
All	79.2	78.6	85.1	91.1

Minority	Period 2 (Rep)	Period 3 (Rep)
Yes or leaning yes	94.6	94.8
Undecided	60.6	66.5
No or leaning no	26.7	24.0
Other	67.2	74.7
All	77.2	80.5

Note: Cell entries are the percentage of members in the relevant category that voted with the leadership on a vote associated with a completed whip count upon which the leadership took a position.

For the "other" category, there also are clear trends over time. During the 1960s, you will recall, the category included large numbers of responses where entire Democratic whip zones, usually from the south, provided only aggregate results and the tactic attenuated the level of leadership support within the "other" category. But as the zone aggregate response became less common in the 1970s, roll call loyalty within the "other" category steadily increased, reaching nearly 90 percent during the years of Republican control. No matter the period, though, leadership opposition on votes was generally higher for the "other" responders than it was for the typical majority party legislator. Member decisions not to respond with one of the standard categories were far from random, in other words, and there are obvious signs of strategic behavior. Often, members who were disinclined to support the party simply refused to respond to leadership entreaties about their views, or otherwise were unwilling to take a clear position.

The cell entries for the minority GOP in the bottom half of Table 4.3 resemble what we found for the majority. Here, the proportion of roll call defectors in the "other" category is higher than the average for the Republican Conference as a whole, indicating that strategic nonresponse is also present on the minority side of the aisle. Perhaps because the time span covered by the minority party evidence is more limited (just periods 2 and 3), the increase in roll call support for the leadership over time is muted. Still, the percentages for the minority indicate high levels of leadership loyalty for members in the "yes" and "leaning yes" categories, and most of the initially "undecided" members also supported the party during votes.

Question Type and Ideology

As was the case with the distribution of member responses, it also is instructive to consider possible differences in leadership support on whipped votes by question type and member ideology. Beginning with question type, are there significant differences in roll call loyalty across the different kinds of motions that are whipped? Is the general increase in loyalty rates over time perhaps concentrated in particular question categories?

For the majority party, there are three noteworthy, question-specific differences in the "whip poll/roll call" nexus. First, on conference matters, members who answered "leaning no" or "no" during the whip process had relatively low conversion rates. This difference is not apparent during the GOP majorities of period 4, but for the Democratic majorities of periods

1–3, pro-leadership voting among N/LN responders was a full 10 percent lower on conference matters than was the case for the other question categories. The reason likely is that conference reports almost always are revised versions of legislation that already has passed the chamber. Since member votes on closely related policy questions are already public record, it is more difficult for them to switch from opposition to support. Not surprisingly, leadership conversion rates for these questions tend to be lower than is the case for other matters.

Roll call loyalty rates on procedural votes and motions to recommit also stand out, to some extent. Especially with these question categories, we need to be careful because the number of whipped items for certain congresses and periods can be low. Still, the over-time increase in leadership loyalty on whipped roll calls was particularly pronounced on procedural votes, which reflects the House majority's growing reliance on restrictive rules to win on the floor. If we juxtapose the Democratic majorities of period 1 with the GOP majorities of period 4, for example, roll call loyalty increased from 92 percent to 98 percent for Y/LY responders, 56 percent to 85 percent for undecideds, 21 percent to 48 percent for N/LN, and 32 percent to 95 percent in the "other" category. For the motion to recommit—a valued tactic for the minority opposition—support for the majority leadership within that party's rank and file is very high across all four time periods, but here as well there is a noticeable upward trend over time that reflects the majority leadership's increasingly aggressive posture over the floor agenda.

For the minority party, there also is limited variance in leadership support across the different question types. Party support rates on procedural votes are also particularly high on that side of the aisle. And consistent with behavioral claims that the amendment process in particular should be a major focus of the House minority party, the retention and conversion rates for the minority leadership are higher on amendments than on final passage questions for both periods where evidence is available. In period 2 on whipped amendments, the minority leadership was able to convert roughly 36 percent of N/LN responders into party supporters on the vote, while the analogous conversion rate for bills was just 24 percent. Similar differences in conversion rates between whipped amendments and passage motions also characterized the minority GOP in period 3.

Just as ideology helped structure the positions that members articulated during the whip process, there also is a strong ideological cast to leadership retention and conversion rates on the associated roll calls. Summary information about member ideology and leadership loyalty on whipped votes

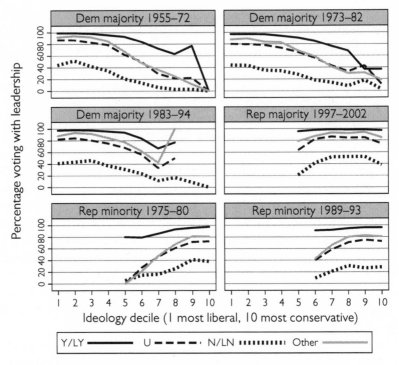

Figure 4.2. Member ideology and leadership loyalty on whipped votes

is provided by period and party in the panels of Figure 4.2. Once again, the ideological deciles denoted along the horizontal axes of each panel are for the entire House at the time of the vote. Here, there are instructive differences in loyalty by response category, so the figure includes separate curves for Y/LY, undecided, N/LN, and other. As you can see, across parties, periods, and ideological deciles, leadership support shifts downward as we move from Y/LY to undecided to N/LN, while the curves for the "other category" generally fall between the ones for Y/LY and undecided.

For the Democratic majorities of periods 1–3, as member conservatism grows leadership support on votes drops off significantly, with large decrements appearing around deciles 5 and 6 located near the median position in the chamber. This pattern makes sense. If legislation was moving public policy in a generally liberal direction during these periods, which seems reasonable given Democratic control, it follows that moderates and liberals alike should support the party position, with major drops in leadership support mostly occurring for lawmakers with views closer to the GOP minority.

For the Republican majorities of period 4, the strong ideological cast to member behavior is also apparent in Figure 4.2, with leadership support on votes generally increasing as members become more conservative (the position curves mostly slope upward). Especially in period 4, however, the relationship between member ideology and leadership support on votes is clearly non-linear. As was the case for previous Democratic majorities, ideological moderates were less likely to vote with the leadership on whipped votes, especially if they were undecided or opposed during the whip process. But we also see a similar drop-off among the most ideologically conservative members of the majority GOP Conference. Leadership support on whipped votes is lower in the 10th decile (for the most conservative members of the House) than it is in the 9th, and the decrease is particularly apparent for ideological conservatives who answered as undecided or no during whip checks. Once again, the inverted U-shaped relationship between member ideology and leadership support created significant challenges for GOP leaders during period 4, especially given their slim majorities. Moving legislation toward the center to pick up the support of Republican moderates meant the possible loss of votes among party conservatives. The roots of that tradeoff will be a central topic of Chapter 8.

For the minority party, Figure 4.2 likewise reveals a strong ideological structure in the transition from whip count positions to votes. Support for the minority leadership position increases significantly as we move toward the more conservative deciles in both periods for which evidence is available, and here there is little evidence of alienation at the extreme. The reason may be the time spans covered—there also was not much evidence of drop-off for extremist Democrats during these periods. But the fairly consistent leadership support of the most conservative elements of the GOP on whipped roll calls may reflect the party's minority status. Since the Democratic majorities of these years probably were mostly moving policy toward the ideological center and left, both mainstream and extremist conservatives would have felt inclined to articulate opposition during the whip process and then follow up with votes for the GOP position at the roll call stage.

Outcomes

After the votes are cast on whipped questions, the result is some gradation of victory or defeat for the two political parties. For the purpose of analysis, outcomes can be classified with five main categories: (1) unambiguous majority party wins; (2) majority party wins secured after major modifications in the underlying legislation; (3) the strategic removal of the targeted matter from the agenda; (4) majority party losses; and (5) a residual classification for outcomes that do not fit any of the other categories. Not surprisingly, there are some judgment calls in classifying the large number of whipped questions according to this scheme. Still, in making these calls, I was able to rely on ample evidence from the archival record, as well as information from the *CQ Almanac, CQ Weekly Report, Washington Post*, and other sources. When there were ambiguities, I consulted the relevant floor debate in the *Congressional Record*, including any discussion of special rules and other procedural preliminaries.

For the minority party, the stakes involved with the whip process are obviously different than are the stakes for the majority, and simply reversing the aforementioned five-point scale (with the win category now constituting victories for the minority, and so on down the scale) may impede efforts to draw comparisons across parties. As a result, I also categorized the outcomes for minority whipped items in terms of the consequences for the majority. For the minority whipped questions, then, a "win" continues to mean a victory for the majority party, major change is still a majority win accompanied by significant modifications, "pull" means the majority leadership removed the item from the agenda, and "loss" is for unambiguous defeats for the majority party.

Table 4.4 summarizes the outcomes for whipped questions by period and party using the aforementioned categorization scheme for questions with a clear party position. Outcomes for the majority whip activity are summarized in the top half of the table, while outcomes for the minority are provided in the bottom half. Included are the motions that could be directly linked to recorded votes and thus constituted the evidentiary base for most of the analysis reported in this chapter. But also included are hundreds of additional questions that were not the subject of roll call votes and for which outcome categories still can be assigned. Importantly, there are some differences across periods in the incidence of cases placed in the residual category. This category comprised about 3 percent of observations for 1955–72, but rose to 8–10 percent for each of the next three periods. The cause may be the higher percentage of final passage questions for period 1—such questions are less likely to be obviated by events. To simplify matters, the residual category is excluded in Table 4.4. The main cell entries in the table are the percentage of whipped outcomes falling within an outcome category for the designated time period, with the number of questions denoted below in parentheses.

Several patterns are discernable. First, although the strategic calculations of party leaders imply that whipped questions be "in play" and the outcome in doubt, across all four periods the majority party won most of these contests. Even with the fairly restrictive definition of party success employed here, the leadership unambiguously prevailed on almost three-quarters of the majority whipped questions. Still, if we combine the categories for major change, pulled items, and unambiguous losses, about 26 percent of the outcomes reflected something less than an outright win for the majority party. Although the majority leadership success rates are high, in other words, the party still tends to lose (to varying degrees) on a substantial portion of whipped matters.

Second, there are some noteworthy differences across periods. Most important, for the majority party the proportion of unambiguous losses declined substantially over time, from a high of 20 percent in periods 1 and 2 to just 8 percent in 1995–2002. The real distinction, however, is between the first two periods (taken together) and the latter two periods. Indeed, the outcome distributions for periods 1 and 2 are very similar, as are the distributions for periods 3 and 4, which reflects the temporal shift we observed for leadership support at the member level. For periods 3 and 4,

TABLE 4.4. Majority party success on whipped items

Majority whipped	All periods	Period 1 (Dem)	Period 2 (Dem)	Period 3 (Dem)	Period 4 (Rep)
Win	73.6	64.8	65.2	79.9	77.5
	(757)	(94)	(150)	(214)	(299)
Major change	6.9	7.6	9.1	3.7	7.5
	(71)	(11)	(21)	(10)	(29)
Pull	6.5	7.6	5.7	6.0	7.0
	(67)	(11)	(13)	(16)	(27)
Loss	13.0	20.0	20.0	10.5	8.0
	(134)	(29)	(46)	(28)	(31)

Minority whipped	All periods		Period 2 (Rep)	Period 3 (Rep)	
Win	68.8		54.6	76.8	
	(148)		(42)	(106)	
Major change	5.6		7.8	4.4	
	(12)		(6)	(6)	
Pull	8.4		13.0	5.8	
	(18)		(10)	(8)	
Loss	17.2		24.7	13.0	
	(37)		(19)	(18)	

Note: The main cell entries are the percentage of the whipped items for the relevant time period and party. The number of items in the relevant category is also included in parentheses.

the most prominent difference concerns the "major change" category, where Tom DeLay and his GOP colleagues of 1995–2002 were about twice as likely to be associated with major modifications in the content of party initiatives as had the Democratic whips of 1983–1994. The main reason is the relatively small size of the Republican majorities. When party size is controlled for in a multivariate analysis, any increases in the probability of major modifications for the DeLay years essentially disappear.[7]

Now consider the outcomes for questions whipped by the minority. As Table 4.4 indicates, the majority win rate for these items also increased between periods 2 and 3, reflecting heightened partisan polarization within the chamber. Not surprisingly, when we juxtapose the win rates for the majority and minority whipped agendas, the majority party does somewhat better for the former. Outright Democratic wins were more prevalent on the majority whipped items, and losses somewhat less prevalent. The most instructive takeaway, however, is that win rates for the majority increased over time on both sets of items and that the majority did very well across both whipped agendas.

In short, when we consider the distribution of whip count responses, the leadership's ability to retain and covert members at the time of the vote, and the incidence of majority party victories on whipped questions, there is considerable evidence that leaders matter within both parties and that the majority party generally prevails in the end. Yet, if we dig a little deeper and focus on position switching within each party and the flow of member support between the two parties, the case for unambiguous majority party power weakens considerably. We consider these caveats now.

Switchers

First up is position switching within the majority and minority parties. Here, our interest is in the behavior of members who take a position either against or in favor of the leadership during the whip process (they answer either N/LN or Y/LY on the count) and then vote the opposite way on the floor. Such "switcher" behavior is informative because it helps identify instances where leadership lobbying may have flipped votes toward the party position (Krehbiel 1998). Undecideds or members in the "other" category may be early in their decision-making processes, and for them movements toward party support may occur with or without leadership whipping as they gather information and make up their minds. Switchers, however, are members who were far enough along to take a stance, and their movements between the count and the vote can be attributed more directly to whip efficacy (or the lack thereof). On Fast Track in 2001, for example, Robin Hayes was a pro-leadership switcher and his decision-making process sheds considerable light on the work of the whips. On Fast Track, the number of Republicans who switched from opposition at the whip stage to support on the vote also exceeded the number that flipped the other way, which proved pivotal to the outcome. How common are pro-leadership switchers like Hayes and his colleagues?

At first blush, Table 4.3 seems to suggest the answer is "pretty common." Significant percentages of N/LN responders on whip checks switched sides and voted with the party on the roll call—over 40 percent for the Republican majorities of period 4. However, to put these percentages in perspective, we also need to consider members who initially responded as yes or leaning yes and then turned around and voted no. If position flips toward the party position are an indicator of leadership effectiveness, then switcher behavior in the opposite direction also needs to be taken into account. Moreover, because the number of members in the Y/LY category is so large, very low defection rates there may actually mask a lot of defecting lawmakers. And because the number of individuals in the N/LN categories is usually smaller, even high conversion rates there may mean that relatively few legislators switched from no to yes. To capture the real magnitude of switcher behavior toward and against the leadership, in other words, we need to focus on the number of members moving back and forth, not the percentages.

Define "net switching" as the number of members who flipped from N/LN on the whip count to yes on the vote, minus the number who flipped from Y/LY on the count to no on the vote. Figure 4.3 shows the average number of "net switchers" per whipped item by congress, with separate trend curves included for the majority and minority parties. The gaps are for congresses where archival evidence at the member level is absent. As usual, only questions with completed whip counts and a clear party position are included, and whip responses and votes are recoded so that "yes" is the position of the relevant leadership. In addition, for this portion of the analysis we drop whipped questions where the leadership made major adjustments in the content of the proposal between the whip count and the vote (i.e., the "major change" outcomes in Table 4.4). Otherwise, any net movement toward the leadership may have resulted from these substantive modifications, rather than the persuasive powers of the whips.

Interestingly, the panels of the figure provide yet another cautionary note against sweeping claims for majority party power. For the majority party,

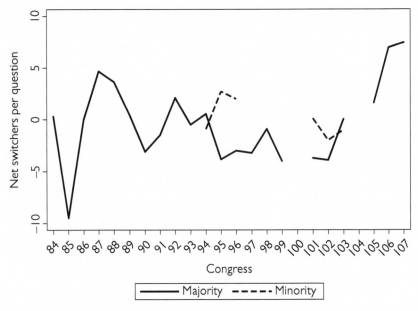

Figure 4.3. Net switchers toward the leadership position

there is considerable variance in net switching across the 84th to the 92nd Congresses, which corresponds with the years of period 1 (1955–72). The number of whipped items included in the calculations for certain of these congresses was low, however, and overall the average tends to hover around zero. In other words, for period 1 the incidence of pro- and anti-leadership switching was about the same. From the 93rd through the 103rd Congress, covering the Democratic majorities of periods 2 and 3 (1973–94), average net switching actually tilted somewhat negative—slightly more initial supporters chose to defect on the roll call than the number of initial opponents who converted to "yes" on the vote. Only during the Republican majorities of period 4 was net switching within the majority party disproportionately in the direction of the leadership stance. The curve for the GOP minorities of periods 2 and 3 falls near or slightly above the analogous curve for the majority, and for the most part reflects a rough parity between switching toward and away from that party's position. Figure 4.3 incorporates only a subset of the membership and is just one possible indicator of leadership or whip efficacy. Still, the clear implication is that we need to be very careful about inferring significant leadership power from the impressive rates of party support on whip counts and votes, or from the majority's high win rates on whipped outcomes.

Face-offs

Now consider another informative slice of the evidence—questions that are jointly whipped by both the majority and minority parties and in different directions. These floor fights can be called "partisan face-offs," for short, and they shed further light on the relative abilities of the majority and minority parties to whip their way to victory when the parties engage over the same terrain. Unfortunately, our ability to track the outcomes of face-offs is limited by the availability of evidence. Systematic data about whip engagement for both parties is only available for 1975–80 and 1989–93, and even here there are certain evidentiary time gaps.[8] Moreover, all of the face-offs for which comprehensive evidence is available are for congresses where the Democrats were the majority and the Republicans the minority. Still, even with these caveats, evidence is available about the outcomes of 63 face-off events, encompassing a wide range of domestic and foreign policy initiatives.

Our first task is to determine which party tended to win when Democrats and Republicans squared off in this manner. During 1975–80, it turns out, the outcomes were fairly mixed. The Democratic majorities of the time were large, but also divided, and the whip networks were expanded because roll call outcomes had become so unpredictable. Again, the majority leadership engages its whips when party control over outcomes is endangered. Together, these majority party divisions and the defensive posture of the leadership generally meant that the threat from the minority side of the aisle was very serious when the two whip networks faced off. There were 31 partisan face-offs during 1975–80, of which the majority Democrats won eighteen (about 58 percent) and the minority Republicans prevailed on 11 (about 35 percent). Two of the outcomes are best characterized as "split," where it is not possible to declare an unambiguous winner or loser (for instance, there were substantive concessions between the whip process and the vote and the parties appear to have split the difference).

That the majority prevailed or achieved a split decision on nearly two-thirds of the 1970s face-offs can be interpreted as evidence of efficacious whipping by that party. Moreover, three of the GOP wins were on Democratic attempts to override Ford administration vetoes, where the threshold for minority party success was just the "one-third plus one" necessary to block an override. Still, the Republican face-off victories were significant accomplishments, especially given the small size of the GOP contingents at the time. Moreover, the minority was able to prevail on major priorities of Democratic president Jimmy Carter, including three initiatives important to organized labor, an ambitious consumer protection measure, and the rule on a significant campaign finance reform bill. Many of the Democratic victories, it also should be noted, were by wide vote margins. For the closer votes, GOP successes were more common. Indeed, two attempted veto overrides, a common situs picketing measure, and the campaign finance rule all resulted in majority losses of less than 10 votes. If the whips were serving as the fulcrum for majority party government, would we expect so many narrow losses by the majority on face-offs?

The available evidence for the late 1980s and early 1990s paints a more favorable portrait of majority coalition building on face-offs. For this portion of the evidence, information about 32 face-offs is available. Of those events, 27 (about 84 percent) resulted in clear-cut wins for the majority party, three (about 9 percent) were victories for the minority GOP, and two (roughly 6 percent) are best categorized as split decisions. During 1989–93, then, the majority Democrats won outright or had a split decision on over 90 percent of the floor face-offs. The parties were more united internally during the late 1980s and early 1990s than they were during the 1970s, so some increase in majority party success on face-offs would be expected even without efficacious whipping. But keep in mind that party leaders target their whip efforts on floor fights where the outcome is in doubt. Face-off events, in particular, should arise when the majority's grasp over the outcome is endangered and there is considerable probability that the minority party might prevail. From this perspective, the majority party's win rate on face-offs during the latter period implies efficacious whipping and a degree of majority party influence.

A more nuanced understanding of these events, however, can be gleaned by turning our attention from legislative outcomes to the movement of individual member positions within each party toward and away from the majority party position. If the majority party prevails on the floor, but during the whip process most of the movement that occurs is actually toward the minority party position, then any claims about disproportionate influence by the majority need to be strongly qualified. To analyze position flow at the individual level, of course, we need to focus on the face-off events for which nearly complete evidence about individual member positions is available for both parties. Although we know that the parties faced off on over 60 items during 1975–80 and 1989–93, comprehensive information about member positions is only available for 46. That information is summarized in Table 4.5.

The first column of the table lists the face-offs with the necessary, member-specific evidence, ordered by congress and the magnitude of what

TABLE 4.5. Party face-offs: Net flow toward Democratic majority

	Winner	Dem flow	Rep flow	Net flow	Dem margin
94th Congress (1975–76)					
Override veto Health Rev Sharing	D	+36	+45	+81	+99
Override veto public works jobs bill	D	+12	+13	+25	+41
Override veto Agriculture Act	R	+13	–9	+4	–40
Override veto strip mining bill	R	+13	–10	+3	–3
Override veto of Labor/ HHS	D	+4	–7	–3	+28
Consumer Protection Act	Split	–11	+5	–6	+4
Override veto Emerg Employ Act	R	+5	–25	–20	–5
95th Congress (1977–78)					
Humphrey-Hawkins passage	Split	+41	+8	+49	+52
Black Lung bill	D	+28	+8	+36	+91
Natural gas substitute	D	+32	+1	+33	+14
Min wage: youth minimum	D	+33	–5	+28	+1
Labor bill	D	+16	+6	+22	+46
Prev Ques on rule, Financial Ethics	D	+25	–12	+13	+56
B1 bomber amendment	D	+17	–12	+5	+5
Consumer protection substitute	R	0	–3	–3	–20
Common Situs Picketing	R	+8	–1	7	–7
Min wage: indexing	R	+14	–26	–12	–15
ERA extension	D	–3	–22	–25	+21
Min wage: tip credit	R	–22	–4	–26	–52
FECA amendments—rule	R	–16	–15	–31	–6
Energy bill—prev question on rule	D	+7	–43	–36	0
Budget Resolution Conf Report	D	–20	–30	–50	+21
96th Congress (1979–80)					
Chrysler bailout	D	+54	+14	+68	+67
FEC—rule	D	+13	–14	–1	+22
Panama Canal	D	+2	–7	–5	+10
FEC—passage	D	–8	–8	–16	+9
Hospital Costs	R	+6	–39	–33	–34
Oil windfall profits	R	–4	–32	–36	–27
Revenue Sharing: Wydler amdt	R	–35	–10	–45	–69
101st Congress (1989–90)					
S&L bill—on budget financing	D	+92	–29	+63	+66
Airlines strike	D	+44	+5	+49	+42

(*Continued*)

TABLE 4.5. *(Continued)*

	Winner	Dem flow	Rep flow	Net flow	Dem margin
Defense Auth—procurement	D	+59	−22	+37	+67
Defense Auth—SDI	D	+8	+1	+9	+36
S&L bill—affordable housing	D	+23	−20	+3	+1
Min Wage—GOP substitute	D	+7	−5	+2	+10
Min Wage—Conference Report	D	+6	−8	−2	+37
Supp appropriations—rule	D	+9	−29	−20	+12
102nd Congress (1991–92)					
Legal Services Reauthorization	D	+4	−4	0	+49
NIH—Conference report	D	−7	−24	−31	+55
103rd Congress (1993–94)					
Reconciliation—rule	Split	+56	−1	+55	+20
Reconciliation—passage	Split	+46	−2	+44	+2
Budget Resolution	D	+23	−5	+18	+29
Motor Voter	D	+17	−11	+6	+49
Family Medical Leave	D	+1	+4	+5	+50
Hatch Act Suspension	R	+2	−4	−2	−3
Unemployment Compensation	D	−8	−14	−22	+46

can be termed "position flow." The second column identifies which party prevailed on each question. Information about the aforementioned flow measure is provided in columns 3–5, first for each party and then for the chamber as a whole. The final column denotes the margin of victory or defeat for the majority Democrats (negative numbers signify a majority party loss).

Now back to the flow concept. These indicators measure the shift toward the majority party position that occurs between the whip count and the vote. More precisely, flow is the number of votes cast *for* the majority Democratic position among members who were initially undecided or N/LN on the whip check, *minus* the number of votes cast *against* that position from members who were initially undecided or Y/LY. The concept is basically a generalization of the switcher behavior discussed earlier. But now, instead of focusing solely on movements out of the Y/LY and N/LN categories, we also take into account the roll call choices of initially undecided members and consider position shifts within both parties. Movements out of the "other" category are excluded because we lack systematic information about the initial leanings of these lawmakers. And because flow encompasses movements within both parties, whip count positions and votes are now recoded for members of *both* parties so that a "yes" is always the side taken by the majority Democratic leadership. If a Y/LY response on the Republican whip count was contrary to the majority stance, in other words, we treat that position as a N/LN in Table 4.5 to better capture movements across partisan lines.[9]

An example may clarify both the concept and the measure. Consider the entry for the attempt to override a Ford administration veto of the Health Revenue Sharing legislation at the top of the table. For the majority Democrats, the vote breakdown by position category on the whip check was 230-1 for Y/LY, 32-4 among the undecideds, and 9-2 for N/LN. Flow toward the majority position among Democrats, then, was negative one (the single defection among initial supporters) plus 32 minus four (the balance of pro-leadership votes among the undecideds) plus nine (the number of initial opponents who converted to leadership support on the vote), producing a total of plus 36. Notice that the 230 Y/LY Democrats who voted yes and the two N/LN Democrats who voted no are not incorporated into the flow calculation because the purpose of the measure is to capture movement and their positions did not change. On the GOP side of the aisle on this question, the vote breakdown by position category was 46-2 for Y/LY, 38-6 among the undecideds, and 15-25 for N/LN, which sums to a flow of plus 45 toward the majority stance. The column for "net flow" is simply the sum of the internal flows for both parties, or in this case a total of plus 81.

We begin consideration of the table contents with the face-offs that occurred during the 94th, 95th, and 96th Congresses (1975–80). For these items, net flow was toward the majority position on 13 of the 29 cases, and for the remainder (about 55 percent) the balance actually favored the minority side of the question. Also instructive is how often the flow that did occur turned out to be pivotal to the outcome. If net flow was toward the majority position, in other words, did that movement actually provide the leadership with its victory margin, or was the win primarily because the initial base of Y/LY supporters was very large in the first place? Of the majority party wins, positive net flow was pivotal to the outcome in just three instances: the natural gas substitute, the youth minimum amendment to the minimum wage bill, and the Chrysler bailout. The B1 bomber came close. There, net flow equaled the victory margin and the Democrats would have prevailed without the additional pickups, but with no room to spare. For the previous question on the rule for the energy bill, net flow was strongly away from the majority Democratic position, but the majority still won on the roll call because of its gain of seven new supporters from within the Democratic Caucus. In this case, within-party flow enabled the Democrats to stave off a loss and countervail particularly effective whipping by the opposition.

Of course, we also need to consider the other side of the victory margin coin; that is, the cases where the minority party won and the net flow toward that position was responsible for the outcome. These are instances where the whip process was likely determinative, but on the side of the minority. There are four clear examples here: the veto override of the emergency unemployment bill, the indexing amendment to the minimum wage bill, the rule for the FECA measure, and oil windfall profits. For each event, the minority side won, and net flow toward that position (and away from the majority) was pivotal. For the veto override on the strip mining bill, net flow was toward the majority side, but the GOP leadership's pickups within the Republican Conference determined the outcome. Similarly, even though net flow was less than the outcome margin for the hospital costs measure, the minority party's victory was due to large vote gains among Republicans.

Now consider the seventeen face-off events that occurred during 1989–93 where information is available about member positions at the whip stage.[10] On these items, net flow toward the majority Democrats was positive for 11 of the events, and for only six was the net flow zero or negative. Moreover, the flow that occurred was pivotal to the outcome in four instances: the airlines strike, the affordable housing amendment to the Savings and Loan (S&L) bill, and the rule and final passage questions for the reconciliation measure. The two reconciliation questions, it should be noted, resulted in split decisions rather than an unambiguous majority party win because major substantive concessions were necessary for the majority side to prevail. For the 1989–93 face-offs, the minority party only won on the Hatch Act question, and primarily because the proposal was considered under suspension of the rules, which requires a two-thirds supermajority for passage. Although the net flow toward the minority on this matter was less than its margin of victory, the four votes the GOP leadership picked up from among its own members were critical to the outcome, so effective minority party lobbying is probably what placed it in the minority win column.

The implications of the face-off analysis? Simply considering the incidence of majority party wins, the Democratic majorities of 1975–80 did fairly well and the Democratic majorities of 1989–93 did very well. But, as attention shifts from (1) majority party win rates to (2) net flow toward the party positions to (3) instances where movement between the whip count and the vote appears to have been determinative, the case for majority party dominance steadily weakens.

The standard arguments for majority party government imply a narrative about face-offs that might go something like this. The initial base of support for the majority is insufficient to guarantee victory prior to floor whipping. Once the whips are engaged, position movement within the majority caucus should be toward the majority leadership position, while movement within the minority contingent should go in the other direction (party effects are expected on that side of the aisle too). Since the majority party has important advantages (membership size and institutional leverage), net flow should mostly favor the majority party side of the question. Almost always, the majority should prevail. And for a nontrivial portion of cases, the majority-dominated flow should be pivotal to the outcome. As we have seen, however, most of the face-offs diverge from this narrative in important ways.

The bottom line? This chapter demonstrates that the broad contours of the vote-gathering process, including switcher behavior and the dynamics of partisan face-offs, are largely consistent with the behavioral perspective. There is significant position fluidity throughout the floor legislative process, which highlights the importance of position formation, rather than some distribution of exogenously determined preferences. On both sides of the aisle, leadership support at the beginning of the whip process is significant. Party leaders are generally able to grow their vote by retaining the support of initial backers, convincing most undecided members to stay loyal, and even converting initial opponents by the time of the roll call. The majority party usually prevails on whipped items. Party support and majority win rates increase over time as congressional Republicans and Democrats became more internally homogeneous and externally differentiated at the constituency level.

There is also a strong ideological cast to the distribution of responses on party whip counts and the relationship between initial positions and roll call choice. But the significant alienation at the extremes for the GOP majorities of period 4 underscores the importance of explanation, as opposed to roll call calculations based solely on spatial proximity. The pattern of member responses on successful House passage motions also suggests that legislative outcomes do not primarily reflect the predetermined preferences of centrist legislators *a la* the cartel model, which predicts that party influence occurs at the agenda setting stage and the legislation that gets passed should reflect the views of the floor median.

Yet, especially when we consider switcher behavior and partisan face-offs, the evidence of this chapter also fails to mesh with broader claims for majority power, such as the conditional party government argument. Except for the GOP majorities of period 4, within-party switching from initial opposition to roll call support is not substantially more prevalent than are position switches in the opposite direction. During face-offs, where the parties square off in opposition on the same question, there is still more evidence for partisan balance over majority party dominance. To be sure, these events tend to arise when the majority coalition is most endangered. Moreover, the degree of net movement toward the majority position does increase over time, along with constituency-level polarization. Especially during the late 1980s and early 1990s, the fluidity of member positions appears to advantage the majority party. But overall, the success rates for the majority are not all that consistent with the standard case for majority party government, while the more nuanced predictions of the behavioral approach are largely consistent with the evidence. In the next four chapters, we will look still closer at the dynamics of party coalition building by period, beginning with the cross-partisan congresses of the 1950s and 1960s.

FIVE

The Textbook Congress, 1955–72

This chapter explores in more depth the role of the House whips during period 1 (1955–72), the last two decades of what Shepsle (1987) has called the "textbook" Congress, and the first two decades of the Democrats' 40-year run as the House majority party. The period, you will see, is an illuminating vantage point for considering the whips and the behavioral perspective on partisan coalition building.

The concepts that contemporary scholars tend to rely on to understand party politics in the House (agenda-setting cartels, conditional party government, and the like) all emphasize the internal arrangements of the legislature in defining and explaining majority party power. Legislative outcomes, according to these accounts, primarily derive from the interplay of member views, on the one hand, and key structural and procedural features of the Congress, on the other. The contents of these views and the rules of the lawmaking game are conditioned by political winds outside the legislature, to be sure, but the spatial logic that undergirds most contemporary congressional scholarship tends to place primary emphasis on preferences and procedure.

By all accounts, major changes were implemented in the internal arrangements of the House during the 1970s, and the conditional party government thesis, in particular, claims that these structural reforms empowered the majority leadership and thereby promoted the occurrence of legislative outcomes that diverge from the preferences of centrist lawmakers in the chamber toward viewpoints more representative of the majority caucus. Not surprisingly, then, conventional accounts of the pre-reform textbook era play up the purported weakness of party leaders and the ineffectiveness of the whips. A closer examination of whip activity during the 1950s and 1960s, however, shows that even before the procedural empowerment of the leadership, leaders and whips regularly engaged in efficacious coalition building on the floor—at least when the circumstances were right. Indeed, the textbook era highlights precisely the constituent audiences, member goals, and decision-making processes that are at the heart of the behavioral tradition.

Contextual Considerations

Consider first the degree of overlap in the kinds of districts represented by Democratic and Republican House members during the 1950s and 1960s. Although there are no perfect summary measures of constituency composition, one serviceable indicator is presidential vote at the district level. Widely used by scholars, this measure taps the general partisan-electoral leanings of a constituency and allows us to draw certain inferences about the lawmakers most likely to be subject to party-constituency cross pressure. The most recent presidential vote within a House district reflects the relative strengths of the two parties in that area, the basic ideological tilt among voters, and a host of politically important district demographic characteristics, such as the presence of African Americans, the distribution of residents across cities, suburbs, and rural areas, the structure of the local economy, and so on.

During the 107th Congress (2001–02), for example, for districts with Democratic members in the House, the average vote for Al Gore in the 2000 presidential contest was close to 61 percent, while for districts represented by GOP members during that Congress, the average 2000 vote for Gore was 42.5 percent. This nearly 20-point deviation in average Gore support is an indicator of the very different constituencies represented in the House by members of the two political parties. Along those lines, when a member hails from a district where the presidential vote was closer to the average for the other party, that lawmaker is a prime candidate for party-constituency cross pressure during the whip process. And if a caucus includes large numbers of members from such "outlier" districts, the ability of party leaders to routinely and efficaciously engage the whips will be constrained.

Relative to later decades, we need to treat the district-level presidential vote with a little more care during period 1. Prior to the enactment of the Voting Rights Act of 1965, the American south was a largely Democratic stronghold and southerners disproportionately gave their votes to Democratic candidates for political office. Southern voters, however, were also generally opposed to racial integration, organized labor, and federal intervention in the internal operations of their states. Especially on legislation that touched on civil rights, education, or social policy, the southern Democrats in Congress tended to vote more like conservative Republicans than their co-partisans from other regions. As a result, presidential voting at the district level is not a particularly illuminating measure of the ideological leanings of southern constituencies during these years. Beginning with the enfranchisement of black citizens in the mid-1960s, the electoral politics of the region changed markedly, and from the mid-1970s onward district-level presidential voting became a better indicator of the degree of constituency-level polarization across the entire country. But for period 1, we can get a more accurate glimpse of the constituency composition of the two congressional parties by calculating the incidence of district outliers with southern districts excluded and treated as a separate category.

This information is provided in the two panels of Figure 5.1, and the basic constituency structure of the two congressional parties during 1955–72 is fully apparent.[1] The bars over "own" reflect the number of members from non-southern districts where presidential voting patterns were closer to the average for that member's own party. The bars over "other" show the number from districts where presidential voting more closely approximates the average for the other party. And the bars over "south" capture the number of southern lawmakers regardless of presidential voting at home. In the 84th Congress (1955–56), for instance, the Democrats had a narrow majority of 232 members. Of that number, less than half represented districts with unambiguously strong leanings toward their party based on the aforementioned measure. Another 30 or so were from outside the south, but hailed from districts that more closely resembled the constituencies represented by the typical Republican. The remainder—over 90 House Democrats—were from southern states and to varying extents reflected the distinct politics of the region. In the 89th Congress (1965–66), which passed the "Great Society" initiatives of President Lyndon Johnson, the House included 295 Democratic members. Over 70, however, hailed from districts that had supported Johnson in 1964 at rates closer to the average for Republican members. Another 80 of the Democratic members in that congress were

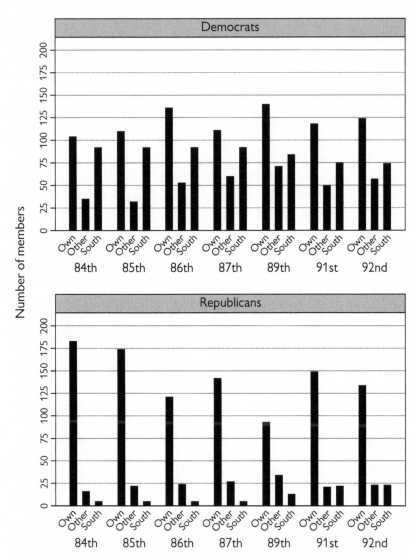

Figure 5.1. Partisan congruence of district-level presidential vote by congress, 1955–72

Note: Southern districts excluded from congruence calculations and treated as a separate category

from southern districts. In short, the Democratic leadership of period 1 worked within a caucus that was deeply divided, and these divisions structured the work of the whips. The number of cross-pressured Republicans, in contrast, was relatively low.

In addition to the outside environment of audiences and constituencies, contextual factors within the Congress also conditioned the work of the whips of period 1. Party leaders of that era had less impressive formal powers than their contemporary counterparts (Ripley 1967, Sinclair 1983). Throughout the 1950s and 1960s, the power to appoint members to committees was delegated to the Democratic contingent on the Ways and Means Committee, rather than to a leadership dominated committee on committees, which in turn limited the majority leadership's ability to use internal patronage as a bargaining chip for building coalitions. During 1955–72, the Rules Committee functioned with considerable autonomy from the majority leadership. Even after party liberals enlarged the panel in 1961 and added progressive members, ideological conservatives (Republicans and southern Democrats) were disproportionately represented. Not surprisingly, the majority leadership often had difficulties managing the floor agenda. As chronicled in Chapter 1, the whip networks of period 1 were small and informal, comprised of two dozen or fewer zone whips selected by rank-and-file Democrats, rather than the leadership. Prior to the institutional reforms of the mid-1970s, committees and committee chairs received substantial deference from party leaders and ordinary members alike (Deering and Smith, 1997).

Not surprisingly, other political actors often stepped in to fill the leadership gap. The deep sectional and ideological divisions that existed within the Democratic Caucus led to the establishment of the Democratic Study Group (DSG), a legislative service organization that functioned as an informational clearing house and lobbying organization for progressive members of the chamber. The DSG's elaborate whip organization often substituted for or complemented the formal party organs (Stevens, Miller, and Mann, 1974). The legislative liaison offices of the Kennedy and Johnson White Houses routinely lobbied members about presidential priorities and conducted hundreds of their own "head counts" before votes on the House and Senate floor. Indeed, Johnson himself was regularly and personally involved in party coalition building on Capitol Hill (Sullivan 1990a, 1990b). The whip priorities of House Democrats often were determined during meetings that Johnson and his legislative liaison staff conducted with members of the majority leadership. Although the interest-group community in Washington was less dense and influential during the 1950s and 1960s, certain peak organizations also lobbied lawmakers before major votes and kept track of emergent member positions. Organized labor, for example, worked hand-in-hand with the Democratic whips, the DSG, and White House liaison throughout period 1 (Sinclair, 1983).

A top aid to Democratic Whip Hale Boggs recalled the distinct atmo-sphere of the whip's office of period 1, especially during the Johnson years.[2]

Hale, McCormack (Speaker John McCormack) and Albert (Majority Leader Carl Albert) went to the White House for a morning break-fast every Tuesday, met with the president and his top aides, con-gressional liaison staff. The whip counts came out of those meetings. LBJ would ask how the education bill was going. Hale would come back and say, "do a count on the education bill." I would call my contacts in the offices of the assistant whips. They would call their own contacts in the relevant members' offices.

The whip's office in the Capitol served as a sort of headquarters for the White House people on the Hill. There were no cell phones then and they were welcome to use the whip's office to make phone calls, to check in. These guys were there every day, we had lunch with them. They would be looking over our shoulders as the whip count results came in. The White House people were swarming over the Hill.

The whip meetings were once a week and they occurred in Boggs' whip office with the chairs placed in a circle. Maybe 15 to 20 people would be there, the whip, majority leader, and assistant whips. The members were diverse, it was a discussion club. Boggs' wife Lindy (future Rep. Lindy Boggs, D-La.) would get up at 5 or 6 in the morn-ing and bake pastries for those meetings, the only reason some of the members attended. There was a pot of coffee and Lindy's pastries.

The absence of recorded voting in the Committee of the Whole, where amendments are considered, also affected the whip process and member decision making. For one, the greater proportion of floor decisions made without a formal record linking individual members to specific positions and roll calls enhanced the ability of leaders to convert potential opponents or perhaps convince them to simply "take a walk" and not vote (Froman, 1967). Indeed, the adoption of recorded voting was motivated in part by public frustration about not being able to hold members per-sonally accountable for their votes on amendments related to US military involvement in Vietnam (Ornstein and Rohde, 1974). These amendment votes typically were conducted by "teller," the procedure where members voting "aye" line up and march down the central aisle of the House chamber to be counted, and the "nays" file down an adjacent side aisle, also to be counted. No official record was kept of which members joined which line. In response, antiwar groups, the DSG, and other organizations placed "spotters" in the visitors' gallery above the floor to keep track of who walked where. Note taking is not permissible in the visitors' gallery, however, and these informal counts were often less than reliable. In short, the context within which the whips of period 1 worked was dramatically different from the deeply polarized, leadership driven, more transparent process of the contemporary House, and we need to evaluate whip impact with that in mind.

General Features

A common view is that the Congress was mired in gridlock for much of period 1 because of divided government (during the 1950s and 1969–72) and the regional divisions within the Democratic Caucus (especially in 1961–63, but during other years as well). Only after the landslide victory of Lyndon Johnson in 1964, and the election of an energized House majority of nearly 300 members in the 89th Congress, so the story goes, did the liberal logjam break. After large Republican pickups in the 1966 midterms, sectional divisions among Democrats and increases in GOP ranks once again constrained the majority leadership of the House. And with the 1968 election of Republican Richard Nixon and the return of divided partisan control, the legislation that passed had to be watered down to secure the necessary bipartisan support.

This view of the period 1 legislative process is incomplete. Certainly, the 89th Congress was a time of significant policy change. Among other laws, it produced the Voting Rights Act, Medicare, Medicaid, the Elementary and Secondary Education Act, and major new statutes associated with the Johnson administration's war on poverty. However, as Mayhew (2014) observed, there also were many major enactments during the 1950s and early 1960s, including trade bills, tax policy, and public works. Moreover, during Nixon's first term, several significant environmental statutes, campaign finance reform, revenue sharing, and other important measures became law. Above and beyond the 89th Congress, period 1 as a whole is best characterized as an era of significant legislative change. Not surprisingly, much of this legislative activity was the subject of whip attention.

The Whipped Agenda

Table 5.1 shows the prevalence of majority whip action during 1955–1972 by policy area, with summary information for all four periods provided as a comparison. To capture whip activity as a proportion of the broader floor agenda, the percentage of votes whipped by the majority within each issue area is also shown in the table, both for period 1 and for all four periods together. For the most part, the policy focus of the majority whips in period 1 resembled whip priorities for the four periods combined. Tax policy and the economy, for instance, was a major priority during period 1, just as it was for 1955–2002 in general. Along those lines, the first category—internal congressional matters and government organization—was a majority whip priority in period 1 and also across the entire 1955–2002 time stretch.

But, there also are some differences in the majority whip priorities of 1955–72. Civil rights, for example, was disproportionately important to the majority whips of period 1 (entirely post 1965—more on that later). And when we consider whip attention as a percentage of total votes in a policy area, education and especially health stand out. There were relatively few roll calls in these issue areas in the 1950s and 1960s, but the ones that occurred were especially likely to be whipped. Another take-away from the table is the relative paucity of whip activity on appropriations bills during the period. Although the annual spending measures touch on all the other

TABLE 5.1. Distribution of Democratic whip attention by issue area, 1955–72

Issue area	Whipped questions— 1955–1972	Whipped questions—All periods	Whipped votes— 1955–72	Whipped votes—All periods
Congress/Gov ops	15.3	14.1	4.5	5.7
Defense	.6	4.4	1.1	5.3
Foreign policy	6.5	7.0	7.2	7.1
Economy	17.7	18.4	13.2	12.1
Trade	4.7	2.9	11.7	9.0
Energy/Environment	8.8	6.4	4.4	4.9
Civil rights	6.5	1.7	7.3	6.1
Social welfare	6.5	4.7	7.4	8.1
Health	2.4	2.9	26.7	12.4
Education	6.5	3.0	10.5	8.9
Labor/Consumer	7.1	7.0	8.3	15.9
Appropriations	3.5	19.4	1.7	5.9
Other	14.1	8.2	5.4	5.7

Note: Cell entries are the percentage of whipped questions (columns 2 and 3), or of whipped votes within each issue category (columns 4 and 5, only nonunanimous votes used).

policy areas, they are treated as a separate category here because of the distinct politics of the appropriations process. During the 1950s and 1960s, spending decisions usually were made in an overtly bipartisan fashion, largely in the committee of jurisdiction, and with minimal involvement by party leaders (Fenno, 1966). Not surprisingly, party whip activity on appropriations questions was limited in period 1.

If we focus our attention on legislation where a *CQ* key vote occurred and there was at least one whipped question, it becomes clear that the whipped agenda featured many of the most consequential bills of 1955–1972, including the creation of Medicare and Medicaid, federal aid to education, open housing, US policy in Vietnam, and the admission of Alaska and Hawaii into the union. Interestingly, the *CQ* key vote bills that were whipped also included a number of major farm bills. Although agriculture is not generally viewed as partisan, especially during the 1950s it was the subject of intense party infighting over subsidies and the proper role of government in the farm economy.

Again, focusing on bills associated with a *CQ* key vote, there also are some glaring omissions from the list of whipped items, including the Civil Rights Act of 1964 and the Voting Rights Act of 1965. Arguably the two most consequential domestic policy enactments of the twentieth century, these measures were not formally whipped by House Democratic leaders because the issue of civil rights divided the Democratic Caucus by section and a broad-based consensus within the party was not viewed as feasible. Along those lines, whip activity on the Vietnam conflict did not occur during the Johnson administration. It was only after the election of Richard Nixon, and the transfer of responsibility for managing the war to a GOP president, that there was sufficient momentum within the Democratic Caucus to activate the whips.

As mentioned, comprehensive evidence about the whip activities of House Republicans is not available for period 1. Still, Robert Michel, R-Ill., was an assistant regional whip for the Republicans during the 1960s, responsible for networking with GOP members from Illinois. Included in Michel's congressional papers are records of the tallies he conducted for the party during 1962–65. It is possible from these whip sheets to identify which questions and measures were the subject of House Republican whip action over the four years, and the items are listed in Table 5.2.[3] As usual, the archival record needs to be interpreted with care. The information is for only part of a single region and there is no way to check against other sources, so the questions listed in the table may not encompass all of the whip activity undertaken by the House minority during that time stretch.

Still, the number and contents of the questions in Table 5.2 look about right. During period 1, GOP Whip Leslie Arends, R-Ill., largely served as an agent of the Republican Policy Committee, a leadership panel on which the whip participated as an ex-officio member. Decisions about party priorities on pending votes were made by the Policy Committee and the whip network largely focused on informing rank-and-file Republicans about these priorities and periodically tallying member positions (Jones, 1964). During the 1970s, the reinvigorated GOP whip organization led by Michel (who would replace Arends as whip in 1975) whipped roughly half the number of questions as did the majority Democrats. If something just short of that ratio characterized 1962–65, based on the number of questions we know were whipped by the Democrats, we would expect the Arends network to have been active on 15 to 20 items, and Table 5.2 lists 16.

Importantly, there is significant overlap between the GOP whipped items and the whipped agenda of the majority Democrats during 1962–65. Fully 12 of the 16 measures targeted by the House GOP for whip action were also targeted in some way by the majority Democrats. The others tended to be administration priorities that divided the Democratic Caucus, and where the White House took the lead in vote gathering for that side of the aisle. For example, House Republicans activated their whip networks in favor of the GOP substitute to the Voting Rights Act of 1965. While the underlying issue so divided House Democrats that the majority chose not to formally whip the matter, House Republicans believed they could mobilize most of their members behind a party substitute. Sponsored

TABLE 5.2. House Republican whip activity, 1962–65

Size of the Rules Committee (1962)*
Public Works (1962)*
Department of Urban Affairs (1962)*
Increasing size of the House (1962)*
Public Works acceleration (1963)*
Area Redevelopment Act (1963)*
Economic Opportunity Act (1964)
Mass Transit Act (1964)*
International Development Act (1964)
Food Stamps (1964)
Minimum Wage, rule (1965)*
Voting Rights Act, GOP substitute (1965)
Housing Bill, resent supplemental (1965)*
Medicare, motion to recommit (1965)*
Medicare passage (1965)*
Elementary and Secondary Education (1965)*

*Also subject of Democratic whip activity

by Minority Leader Gerald Ford, R-Mich., and William McCullough, R-Ohio, ranking Republican on the Judiciary Committee, the proposal was offered as the minority motion to recommit with instructions and was supported by Republicans on the floor by a margin of 114-21. The motion failed to pass, however, after southerners admitted it would not effectively enfranchise blacks and Democrats from other regions largely voted no.

Member Loyalty

Behavioral theory predicts that the decisions members make during the whip and roll call stages will be shaped by a complex combination of audience demands, explainability, national party imperatives, and the internal politics of the House. These explanatory factors will vary by issue area and member. Still, certain characteristics should be generally important. The distribution of whip count responses across six such characteristics is summarized in Table 5.3. Included are the region of the country from which a lawmaker hails, whether or not presidential voting within a member's district is closer to the average for other Democrats or for the Republicans,

TABLE 5.3. Distribution of majority whip responses, selected district and member characteristics, 1955–72

		Y/LY	U	N/LN	Other
	NE	73.3	8.4	5.5	12.8
	MW/Plains	73.4	10.2	7.4	9.0
Region	South	32.1	18.6	23.6	25.7
	Border	62.8	14.4	9.3	13.5
	West	74.1	9.8	7.5	8.6
District-level	Closer to R ave	66.1	13.6	8.7	11.7
pres vote*	Closer to D ave	71.6	10.0	6.4	12.0
Committee of	On	75.3	6.9	7.4	10.5
jurisdiction	Off	57.3	13.4	13.0	16.3
	Fresh	65.7	12.1	10.4	11.9
Seniority	2/5 terms	61.8	12.7	11.4	14.1
	>5 terms	53.5	13.4	14.4	18.7
Extended	Yes	62.2	11.4	10.0	16.4
leadership	No	58.2	13.1	12.9	15.8
Whip network	Yes	69.1	8.7	11.4	10.8
	No	57.8	13.3	12.7	16.2

*Excludes south

whether or not the lawmaker serves on the standing committee with jurisdiction over a whipped item, seniority within the chamber, participation in the extended party leadership, and formal involvement in the whip system.[4]

As mentioned, until the 1960s the Democrats were largely a southern party and there was a strong regional cast to congressional politics throughout period 1. Members from the south tended to face little GOP opposition in campaigns. Once elected, they often served for years and accumulated significant committee chairmanships and other positions of power within the House. Until passage of the Voting Rights Act, the political participation of African Americans was sharply circumscribed. Especially on issues that directly or indirectly touched on race, southern Democrats embraced policy positions that differed from their co-partisans from other regions. In period 1, then, we can expect significantly different responses from southern lawmakers during the whip process. The effects should be particularly strong for the states of the old confederacy, but also apparent for border states like Kentucky and Missouri. As shown in Table 5.3, support for the party position among southerners was less than half that of Democratic members from the northeast, midwest/plains states, and the west, and the percentages for the other response categories were much higher. Although the political consequences of racial segregation are also apparent in border states, these members still resembled the behavior of their non-southern counterparts more closely than they did representatives from the old south.

The table also summarizes the relationship between district-level presidential voting and the whip count response. Here, we only consider district presidential voting patterns in constituencies outside the south because the variable is not very instructive about constituency-level leanings below the Mason-Dixon line.[5] Even though presidential voting is a fairly general and blunt measure, the table shows that support for the party position is noticeably higher among members from districts that reflect the party average for the presidential vote. The constituencies that are partisan outliers in this regard are represented by members who are more likely to be in the undecided, opposed, or "other" response categories during the whip process. Still, for period 1, region dominates.

The next four explanatory factors relate to a member's place within the House hierarchy. The Congress of period 1 was more committee-centric than the contemporary chamber. Members generally served on a single committee and they gravitated toward jurisdictions of particular importance to their home constituencies. Within the House, committees tended to function as "little legislatures," with well-developed internal norms and powerful chairs and ranking minority members (Goodwin, 1970; Fenno, 1973). Bipartisan accommodation within committee was also more common then than now, and members not on the committee of jurisdiction were more inclined to defer to the originating panel during floor action on legislation. Indeed, the requests that the whips be engaged on a question often were made by the chair of the relevant committee. For these reasons, we would expect that support for the party position would be disproportionately high for the members of the originating panel. Indeed, as the table shows, there was an 18-point difference in party support between committee members and other Democrats during the whip process of period 1.

In the pre-1970s House, there was also substantially more fealty to the seniority norm. The selection of committee chairs and ranking minority members, for instance, was based almost entirely on years served on the relevant panel (Hinckley 1971). One possible implication is that more senior lawmakers will be more likely to defect on whipped matters because they have the internal clout and autonomy necessary to buck the leadership. Senior members also are more likely to have accumulated the informational expertise necessary to chart an independent course. On the other hand, more senior legislators may have a greater stake in protecting the existing power structure, and thus be more inclined to support the party on whipped matters. Overall, Table 5.3 suggests that the first set of considerations dominated. More senior members (those with five or more terms under their belts) are less supportive of the party position during the whip stage.

Yet another individual characteristic of potential importance is participation in the extended party leadership. The reference here is to members holding a formal leadership post, including the majority leader, the majority whip, the chair and vice chair of the Democratic Caucus, the party secretary, and the chief deputy whip. Speakers, by tradition, seldom vote on the floor or articulate positions during whip calls and are thus left off the list. The party infrastructure also includes certain leadership panels like the Democratic Steering and Policy Committee. The members of these panels are considered to be part of the extended party leadership and are treated as such here.[6] Interestingly, the table shows that during period 1 members of the extended leadership were only slightly more inclined to stay loyal during the whip process. The Democratic Caucuses of the pre-reform House were tolerant of ideological heterogeneity in their party hierarchy, and that tolerance is reflected in the whip responses reported in the table.

Finally, formal participation in the party whip network may increase leadership support during the whip process. The networks of period 1 were almost completely comprised of the two dozen or so zone representatives chosen by the Democratic members from the relevant geographic area. As a result, the primary loyalties of the assistant whips often were to their zone colleagues and to the audiences and constituencies that they shared. Still, many whipped items are not important to the home constituencies of all zone whips, and support for the party position may be higher among this group because of their role as leader-member conduits. Certainly, the zone whips should be less inclined to be unresponsive during whip calls. Indeed, the table indicates that zone whips were disproportionately likely to endorse the party position on whipped matters and substantially less inclined to be undecided, opposed, or nonresponsive.

The six explanatory factors are revisited in Table 5.4, but with the focus now on roll call loyalty within each whip response category. For each response category, the table shows percentage support for the party on the relevant roll call vote, assuming one occurred. For example, the table reveals that members

TABLE 5.4. Leadership support on votes by whip category, selected district and member characteristics, 1955–72

		Y/LY	U	N/LN	Other
Region	NE	98.6	82.9	46.3	91.3
	MW/Plains	98.0	80.4	36.9	87.0
	South	89.6	49.6	11.6	53.1
	Border	95.8	71.3	28.9	83.5
	West	98.2	86.0	42.2	89.3
District-level pres vote*	Closer to R ave	96.6	73.6	35.4	81.6
	Closer to D ave	98.5	85.2	43.7	89.7
Committee of jurisdiction	On	99.3	75.0	26.8	79.8
	Off	96.1	65.1	22.0	69.3
Seniority	Fresh	96.2	63.0	29.4	76.2
	2/5 terms	96.7	69.8	25.4	72.4
	>5 terms	96.2	62.2	18.0	66.7
Extended leadership	Yes	97.0	62.5	22.6	71.9
	No	96.3	65.8	22.1	69.5
Whip network	Yes	97.9	65.0	24.4	76.6
	No	96.3	65.5	22.0	69.5

*Excludes south

from the northeast who responded as "yes" on the whip count voted with the party on associated roll calls 98.6 percent of the time.

Consistent with our previous discussion, roll call loyalty overall is very high among initial party supporters, somewhat less high for the undecideds, and lower still for the members who signaled opposition to the whips. Party support on votes among the members classified in the "other" category fell between the Y/LY responders and the undecideds. Still, there are also significant and explainable differences across the aforementioned explanatory factors. Not only were southern members more likely to be undecided, opposed, or nonresponsive during the whip process, for instance, within each response category they also were less likely to end up voting with the leadership. While nearly half of the "no" responders on whip calls from the northeast decided to vote with the leadership anyway, less than 12 percent of the southerners who articulated initial opposition did so. Analogous voting differences hold for district-level presidential vote, committee status, seniority, involvement in the leadership, and whip role. The impact of these factors is not large for the "yes" responders. Loyalty rates for them were generally over 95 percent, regardless of any member-specific variance in the district or institutional context (south is an exception). But for the undecideds, initial opponents, and nonresponders on the count, the same factors that help explain differences in the whip count response also shed light on the differences in roll call loyalty that occur between members within each response category.

Ducking the Count

As mentioned, the strategy of nonresponse is particularly instructive for the Democratic majorities of period 1. Recall that southern whip zones often declined to report positions at the individual level for their members, and instead reported aggregate totals. In August 1961, for example, the Democratic leadership asked its members about their positions on passage of a federal aid to education measure that was a centerpiece of the domestic policy agenda of President John Kennedy. Federal aid to education was highly controversial in the American south, however, because of concerns in Dixie that federal monies would be denied to schools unless they desegregated. On the first version of the whip count, Paul Kitchin, D-N.C., the assistant whip for Zone 5, which included 19 members from North Carolina and Virginia, declined to inform the leadership about the preferences of individual members. Instead he reported that only four members supported passage, six were against, and nine were undecided. The tactic provided Democratic leaders with intelligence about the mood of the zone, to be sure, but not enough to target with precision individual lawmakers for lobbying and persuasion. Zone aggregate reports were a standard feature of the House Democratic whip process during the 1960s, and reflected the sense of separation and autonomy that existed within certain southern delegations.

When we break down the use of zone aggregates by state, the distinctly southern cast to the tactic is fully apparent. Georgia and South Carolina led the list with 31 separate questions each; followed by Texas (15); Virginia and North Carolina (13); the western states of Zone 17 (8–9); Illinois (5); Alabama, Arkansas, Florida, Kentucky, and Tennessee (3–4); and California (1).[7] Interestingly, with just two exceptions, reliance on the tactic by the large Texas delegation mostly occurred after the 1962 death of Speaker Sam Rayburn, who did not need formal whip counts to ascertain the policy preferences of his fellow Texans. During the Johnson administration, the delegation periodically declined to report individual positions in order to stave off intense pressure from the White House. Like Rayburn, of course, Johnson was from Texas and had his own lines of communication into the large and influential delegation.

The use of zone aggregates by the western zone (encompassing Democrats from Arizona, Colorado, Montana, Nevada, New Mexico, Oregon, and Washington) is another interesting case. The cause was a breach of security within the whip process the year before. In 1966, the Democratic leadership whipped their rank and file about a measure that would have permitted union picketing at construction sites. Although the legislation was strongly backed by the national party, there was solid opposition to it from southern right-to-work states, and considerable ambivalence in the western portions of the Democratic Caucus. Shortly after member positions were reported to the leadership, one opponent in Zone 17 was contacted by labor lobbyists attempting to change his position. The member inferred that someone—their zone whip, a member of the leadership—had leaked information about positions to the labor movement. If so, the leak was inconsistent with longstanding norms that whip intelligence could be shared with the White House, but not with interest-group representatives, the media, or the general public. The members of Zone 17 met and voted unanimously to only report zone aggregates, and threatened to respond to any retaliatory measures from House Democratic leaders by withdrawing entirely from the whip process. As a result, the western states were allowed to primarily report only aggregate totals until an accord could be reached with the leadership, at which point the westerners reverted to reporting individual member positions.[8]

Zone aggregates may seem like the ultimate of "inside baseball," but the tactic embodied the essential character of party leadership within the regionally divided Democratic Caucuses of period 1. It also complicated party coalition building on a range of significant bills championed by the national party. Among the targeted issues were federal aid to public schools, voting rights, the war on poverty, and the landmark open housing bill of 1968, which will be considered in depth later in this chapter. Importantly, with the election of a Republican president in 1968, the decline in size and importance of the southern faction within the Democratic Caucus, and the enervation of sectional divisions within the national Democratic party, the zone aggregate tactic fell into disuse during the 1970s.[9]

Outcomes

The discussion of whip outcomes in Chapter 4 indicated that Democratic leaders in period 1 unambiguously won about 65 percent of the time, were forced to accept major changes on about 8 percent of the whipped items, pulled nearly 8 percent from floor consideration, and suffered unambiguous losses on the remaining 20 percent. Overall, the majority whips of period 1 were about as successful as their counterparts during period 2, but significantly less so than the majority whips of periods 3 and 4. Although there were significant changes in the size of the majority Democratic Caucus over period 1, the percentage of outright victories was fairly high from 1961 until the period ended in 1972. In the 89th Congress (1965–66), which produced the domestic policy achievements of the Great Society, the whips won around 72 percent of the time. But their victory rates were about 78 percent during 1963–64 and 72 percent during 1969–70, the first two years of the Nixon administration. To be sure, the substantive importance of the bills passed in 1965–66 probably exceeded that of the other congresses. But in terms of the proportion of whipped measures that passed without major change, the majority leadership was fairly successful throughout the 1960s.

To better get at the roots of whip success, Table 5.5 breaks down the outcomes by issue area. Of course, the number of questions for certain of the policy areas is small and we need to be careful about inferring too much. Still, majority party wins clearly were more likely in certain policy areas than they were in others. A significant number of whipped questions dealt with the economy, for example, and the majority Democrats prevailed on nearly 80 percent of them. Success rates also were high for foreign policy, trade issues, health, and defense (with the caveat that only one whipped question fell in the defense category). The hodgepodge of topic areas included in the "other" category likewise provided solid win rates for the majority whips.

In contrast, gradations of majority party loss were more frequent in other policy areas, including Congress/government operations, energy/environment, civil rights, social welfare, education, labor/consumer, and appropriations.[10] Since most questions end with majority party wins, it is instructive to consider the smaller number of items that resulted in something else—major changes, withdrawal from the agenda, or an outright loss. The common thread is that these items generally evoked the sectional cleavages that bedeviled Democratic House leaders throughout period 1. Most obvious are the civil rights initiatives, where two questions (dealing with the Civil Rights Act of 1966 and a housing discrimination

TABLE 5.5. Majority whipped outcomes by issue area, 1955–72

Issue area	Win	Major change	Pull	Loss
Congress/Gov ops	13	3	3	6
	(52.0)	(12.0)	(12.0)	(24.0)
Defense	1	0	0	0
	(100.0)			
Foreign policy	8	1	0	1
	(80.00	(10.0)		(10.0)
Economy	21	2	2	2
	(77.8)	(7.4)	(7.4)	(7.4)
Trade	6	1	0	0
	(85.7)	(14.3)		
Energy/Environment	3	0	0	2
	(60.0)			(40.0)
Civil rights	5	2	0	3
	(50.0)	(20.0)		(30.0)
Social welfare	6	0	2	3
	(54.6)		(18.2)	(27.3)
Health	4	0	0	0
	(100.0)			
Education	5	1	0	4
	(50.0)	(10.0)		(40.0)
Labor/Consumer	5	0	3	2
	(50.0)		(30.0)	(20.0)
Appropriations	3	1	0	2
	(50.0)	(16.7)		(33.3)
Other	14	0	1	4
	(73.7)		(5.3)	(21.1)

Note: Cell entries are the number of items for the relevant issue-outcome category, with percentages by issue in parentheses.

measure whipped the same year) required major modifications, and three more resulted in unambiguous losses for the majority Democrats. During the 1950s and 1960s, education issues also were viewed in part through the lens of race, and here one proposal required major modifications (amendments to the Elementary and Secondary Education Act in 1966) and four produced unambiguous losses (school construction in 1956 and 1961 and revisions to the Education Act in 1967 and 1969).

Labor issues also divided the majority Democratic Caucus by section. Southern states were generally anti-union, and compared to their northern and midwestern co-partisans, Democratic legislators from the region were much less sympathetic of the policy agenda of the labor movement. Indeed, three labor initiatives were pulled from the agenda after Democratic leaders discerned that they lacked the votes to pass (a minimum wage hike in 1965 and picketing legislation in 1966 and 1967), and two more ended with outright losses for the majority party (dealing with the minimum wage and striker rights). When we consider the specific questions that ended with something less than a majority win in the Congress/government operations (12 distinct questions) and social welfare categories (five questions), the Democrats' sectional divisions were also on full display. Several of the government operations bills, for example, authorized the executive branch to make administrative reforms aimed at promoting civil rights. A proposal to create a federal department of urban affairs is one example. The losses that occurred within the social welfare category included anti-poverty proposals that likewise divided Democrats along sectional lines.

In short, the efficacy of the majority whips of period 1 was bifurcated. If an issue did not galvanize the sectional cleavage within the Democratic Caucus, then the leadership generally was successful in growing its vote and prevailed on the floor. But if an item did evoke the party's central divide, the likelihood of some form of loss was much higher. The pattern can be illustrated with a closer look at two issue areas: civil rights and agriculture.

Civil Rights

As mentioned, prior to enactment of the Voting Rights Act of 1965 the House Democratic leadership did not activate the party whip networks on civil rights measures.[11] From 1955 to 1965, as the movement for racial equality gained momentum, a number of related roll call votes occurred on the floor that were categorized as "key" by *CQ*. Included were motions to recommit for the Civil Rights Acts of 1956 and 1957, passage of measures barring court nullification of state law without congressional approval in 1958 and 1959, a voter registration amendment to the Civil Rights Act of 1960, passage of the Civil Rights Act of 1964, and of course, passage of the Voting Rights Act in 1965. Among the most important floor actions to occur in the history of the House, these votes were intensely whipped by various presidents and White House staff, the DSG and a wide range of outside advocacy coalitions. The House GOP leadership, we have seen, whipped in favor of a party substitute to the Voting Rights Act. But the majority Democrats chose not to formally whip any of them because the underlying issue divided them internally. Still, civil rights occasionally surfaced indirectly on the majority whipped agenda because of the linkages to other policy areas, especially education. In 1956, for example, the party whipped in favor of a school assistance bill that subsequently became embroiled in the sectional division over racial integration. The floor fight that ensued nicely illustrates the limits of whip efficacy in period 1 when these cleavages were evoked.

Between 1946 and 1955, the Senate periodically passed major legislation to extend federal assistance to elementary and secondary schools, but the measures repeatedly were bottled up in the House because of conflict over subsidizing religious schools, concerns about states rights, and (after the Supreme Court's 1954 decision in Brown v. Board of Education) disagreements about whether federal funds should be provided to segregated school systems. In 1955, the Eisenhower administration and Democratic leaders on Capitol Hill endorsed federal aid to elementary and secondary schools, with Democrats generally favoring higher levels of funding. The House Education and Labor Committee reported a school assistance bill in July 1955 after defeating an amendment from Adam Clayton Powell, D-N.Y., that would have denied funds to segregated schools. Proponents of the underlying bill argued that including the Powell amendment would cause southern Democrats to coalesce with most Republicans in opposition, effectively killing the measure. Committee deliberations over Powell's proposal were sufficiently tense that at one point Rep. Cleveland Bailey, D-W.Va., reached over and punched his New York colleague in the face.[12]

Even without the desegregation proviso, House Rules Committee Chair Howard Smith, D-Va., was still adamantly opposed to the committee-reported legislation, and the Rules panel failed to clear the education bill for floor action for an entire year. After much prodding from Speaker Sam Rayburn and other Democratic leaders, the committee finally reported a rule in June 1956. Prior to consideration by the full House, Democratic leaders publicly claimed that they had the votes to defeat the Powell amendment. On July 5, however, after days of heated debate and parliamentary maneuvering, the Powell amendment was adopted by a roll call of 225-192. Southern Democrats and many northerners (who believed passage of the amendment would kill the bill) voted "no." But other northern Democrats voted for the Powell amendment, largely because to do otherwise would have been difficult to explain to important constituency audiences. Republicans, many of whom also represented constituents sympathetic to desegregation, supported the amendment by a margin of three to one. Later that day, the bill as amended failed on a roll call of 194–224, with southern Democrats and a majority of Republicans voting "no" on final passage.

The roll calls on the Powell amendment and passage of the bill as modified have probably been the subject of systematic analysis by more prominent political scientists than any other votes in congressional history. In a series of now classic studies, Riker (1965, 1982) used the school construction fight as an illustration of a voting cycle and of sophisticated voting, both key concepts in the traditional canon of positive political theory.[13] Since the roll call record in 1956 demonstrates that a majority of members preferred the bill as amended to the clean education measure, and a majority also preferred existing law to the bill as amended, Riker concluded that there was a voting cycle: a clean education bill was majority-preferred to existing law, the bill with the Powell amendment beat the clean bill, and exiting law was majority-preferred to school construction with the Powell proviso. At various points, Riker also asserted that certain of the Republican votes in favor of the Powell amendment were sophisticated; they only supported the amendment because they knew it would kill the underlying bill. Over the years, Riker's interpretation of these events—including the consequences for leadership influence—has drawn criticism. Krehbiel and Rivers (1990) provide compelling evidence that the Republicans who voted for the Powell amendment but against the school construction bill on final passage did so for ideological reasons. Their votes were sincere, rather than sophisticated. Gilmour (2001) and Mackie (2004) also argue persuasively that the inferences Riker drew from the roll call record about the likely votes of Republican members absent the Powell amendment were flawed, and conclude that the unamended version likewise would have gone down in defeat.

Interestingly, the House Democratic leadership whipped its members about school construction on January 4, 1956, asking whether they favored the measure as reported by the Committee on Education and Labor (and thus without the Powell amendment). According to the whip count, 142

Democrats responded as "yes," including 29 of the 91 representatives from the deep south. Another 12 Democrats, including 9 southerners, were leaning yes. Even if we subtract Republican members who Gilmour and Mackie asserted would have preferred no bill at all to one without an anti-segregation rider, it appears that the unamended version of the Education and Labor measure would have passed on the floor, at least early in 1956. The whips clearly thought so and recognized that incorporation of the Powell language would fundamentally alter the positions of southern members. At the bottom of a chart summarizing the poll results by zone, Albert's staff wrote, "Adoption of the Powell amendment by the House would alter these figures materially because Southern Members would then vote against the bill."[14]

The whip process, in other words, lends support to Riker's assertion that the Powell amendment helped kill school construction, at least in 1956. The Democratic leadership was fully aware of the potential damage to their agenda from adoption of the proposal, but was unable to keep Powell from offering it on the floor, and also unable to convince northern Democratic supporters of the education bill to cast strategic votes against Powell. The problem they faced was explainability. Although casting a strategic vote against the Powell amendment may have produced an end result (passage of the school aid bill) that was spatially more proximate to their underlying views, many northern Democrats knew that such a vote would have caused them enormous difficulties with pro-desegregation audiences at home. The result was a major defeat for the majority leadership and the whips.

A decade later, enactment of the Voting Rights Act of 1965 was a turning point for the Democratic Caucus on civil rights. Indeed, House Majority Whip Hale Boggs, D-La., cast his first major vote in favor of civil rights on the measure. A charismatic politician and respected strategist, Boggs represented a New Orleans district that was over 30 percent African American in 1965 according to the US Census. Not surprisingly for a southern district, however, the white majority among his constituents largely opposed civil rights until at least the mid-1960s. For nearly two decades, Boggs had maintained constructive working relations with the black community in New Orleans and had relied on their support in close elections. But he generally downplayed those connections before white audiences and often was silent about major civil rights legislation before the Congress.[15] Although viewed accurately as a racial moderate among southerners, Boggs still signed the Southern Manifesto of 1956, which opposed racial integration in public places and was drafted by arch-segregationists like Strom Thurmond and Richard Russell, and until 1965 he voted with other southern members against civil rights measures on the House floor.

Casting votes in favor of civil rights, he believed, might cost him his seat in Congress. Indeed, for a time, the Louisianan's position in the House Democratic leadership created a classic example of cross pressure between national partisan imperatives, on the one hand, and constituency preferences, on the other. In 1962, for example, Boggs faced serious challenges from segregationist opponents in the primary and general elections, largely because of his association with the Democratic leadership and the Kennedy administration. After a difficult campaign, he eventually prevailed in the primary with 63.5 percent of the vote, and in November he won again in his solidly Democratic district against the Republican nominee, a political neophyte and future governor named David Treen. As a result of a state law mandating that the racial background of candidates be printed on official election ballots next to their names, in the general election voters were asked to choose between "Hale Boggs (Caucasian)" and "David Treen (Caucasian)."[16]

Boggs's personal ambition was to be Speaker of the House, however, and he recognized that to achieve the goal he would need to be consistent with the national party program on civil rights, if and when it emerged. In 1964, he considered supporting the Civil Rights Act, but ended up voting "no" after unsuccessfully attempting to amend the legislation to strike Title VI, which banned discrimination in programs funded by the federal government. In 1965, though, after asking several southern colleagues if a "yes" vote would "bother" them, Boggs voted in favor of the Voting Rights Act.[17] The final passage roll call was lopsided, 333-85, and he was joined by 32 of the 93 southern Democrats in the chamber. Importantly, polls of New Orleans voters indicated that by 1965 a clear majority of them favored voting rights in some form for African Americans.[18]

Following adoption of the Voting Rights Act of 1965, the House Democratic leadership periodically engaged its whip networks on civil rights issues. Of these measures, House action on open housing legislation in spring 1968 was especially instructive and dramatic. Discrimination in housing was among the most controversial of civil rights issues, and upon passage the 1968 measure became the first open housing bill enacted by Congress since 1866. The housing provision initially was added in the Senate as an amendment to a narrower House-passed bill aimed at protecting civil rights workers. Passage of the amended legislation in the Senate was highly difficult, however, and required significant modifications in the

housing language and four separate cloture votes. In the House, backers
of the legislation wanted to pass the Senate bill without change to avoid
conference committee deliberations and potential dilatory tactics from
Republicans and southern Democrats. There were two *CQ* key votes on
the measure on the House floor—one on a resolution to accede to the
Senate language (essentially passing the legislation), and the other on a
motion to end debate and preclude any modifications to that resolution.

Democratic leaders began whipping the matter shortly after Senate
passage in the second week of March 1968, asking rank-and-file members,
"Will you support the civil rights bill as passed by the Senate with all
amendments?"[19] The leadership and the Johnson administration attempted
to mobilize support behind the legislation throughout the month. By late
March, though, only 97 Democratic members had responded as "yes" or
"leaning yes," 14 were undecided, and 42 were overt opponents. Among the
opponents was Hale Boggs, who continued to walk a fine line on civil rights
issues because of evolving viewpoints within his New Orleans district. The
zone whips for South Carolina, Georgia, and several western states refused
to provide information about the leanings of individual members within
their zones. On March 19, over the objections of Democratic leaders, the
Rules Committee passed a GOP motion delaying any action on the bill until
April 9. With the expectation of significant opposition from Republicans
and a divided Democratic Caucus, the fate of the bill remained unclear.

Then, on Thursday, April 4, Martin Luther King was assassinated in
Memphis, Tennessee. Within hours, rioting erupted in cities across the
country, including the District of Columbia. The King assassination may
have been pivotal to House passage of the open housing bill just six days
later. According to a spokesperson for the real estate lobby, which opposed
the measure, there were 224 solid votes against the leadership's resolution
earlier in the day on April 4.[20] During floor debate on the open housing
measure, and with the Capitol Building under guard by armed marines,
William Colmer, D-Miss., chair of the Rules Committee and an implacable
foe of civil rights, claimed that, "On Thursday evening when I went home,
in my humble judgment as well as that of many others, we had the votes to
send the bill to conference. But now the situation is changed. Here we are
legislating in an atmosphere of hysteria, of threat, of arm twisting—an unsavory climate to legislate in."[21] Indeed, the whip counts conducted by House
Democratic leaders in April indicate a significant increase in Democratic
support for the party position, with the number of "yes" responses rising to
150 on the last iteration of the poll. Hale Boggs switched his position and
voted with the majority of his party on the previous question motion and

passage of the resolution, although over 80 percent of southern members and the rest of the Louisiana delegation all voted "no." In the end, the motion on the previous question, which turned out to be the critical vote, passed by a margin of 229-195, with support from 152 Democrats and 77 Republicans.

Table 5.6 summarizes coalition building dynamics on the whipped civil rights questions for which nearly complete information is available about the emergent positions of individual Democrats. To further simplify the "pickup" tables associated with the case studies here and in Chapters 6–9, only questions that can be assigned an outcome category are denoted. Included in Table 5.6 are the 1968 open housing legislation, an extension of the Voting Rights Act in 1970, and an equal employment measure from 1971. The table also includes vote gathering on the 1956 school aid question because of the centrality of civil rights to that measure. There are columns for the majority party's base of support (members answering "yes" and "leaning yes" on the count), as well as the number of members falling in the remaining response categories during the whip process. The column labeled "GOP support" is the number of Republican members who voted for the Democratic party position on the targeted roll call, assuming there was a vote. "Necessary pickup" is the number of additional supporters the majority leadership needed to accumulate on the roll call, above and beyond the initial base (as revealed by the whip count) and the number of crossover votes from among the minority Republicans (as revealed by the votes they cast on the floor). "Actual pickup" is the number of votes the majority leadership did add to its coalition, as indicated by the roll call result, and "Outcome" denotes whether or not the majority party prevailed in the end.

TABLE 5.6. Coalition-building success, civil rights

Item	Y/LY	U	N/LN	Other	Rep support	Necessary pickup	Actual pickup	Outcome
School construction, 1956	154	23	32	20	NA	NA	NA	Loss
Prev ques on anti-discrim bill, 1968	137	27	69	14	78	–2	14	Win
Senate amdt to Voting Rights Act, 1970	155	44	34	11	60	–11	9	Win
EEOC bill, GOP subst, 1971	107	21	26	100	29	64	61	Loss

The majority Democrats' record on whipped civil rights measures, you can see, was decidedly mixed. For the two majority party wins—the open housing bill and the 1970 extension of the Voting Rights Act—the majority party had the votes necessary to prevail based on its initial support on the whip count plus GOP votes as revealed by the floor roll call. In both cases, the minimum necessary pickup was slightly negative. Still, the margin of victory on the two items was tight and the substantial Republican cross-over votes occurred in part because of intense lobbying inside and outside of Congress. Especially on the open housing vote, the majority whips appear to have been consequential. For the other two whipped questions, the 1956 school aid bill and the GOP substitute to the EEOC bill in 1971, the Democratic leadership went down in defeat. Civil rights issues, in short, reflect the limits of Democratic majority leadership in the period 1 House. And when the party did prevail on these issues, one reason was ample crossover support from the minority side of the aisle.

Whipping Agriculture

Agricultural issues during the early years of period 1 provide a different perspective on the efficacy of the whips. According to the standard view, agriculture policy is a preeminent example of interest-group driven, distributive politics (Jones 1961). Farm policy derives from logrolls and mutual reciprocity across producer groups, most legislative decisions are made within the House and Senate Agriculture Committees in close consultation with the farm lobby, and most disagreements are not partisan. Periodically, however, significant differences arise between Democrats and Republicans about the broad contours of US agricultural policy, with GOP members generally seeking to make the program more flexible and reliant on market incentives and Democrats placing greater emphasis on the economic well-being of farmers. The 1995 "Freedom to Farm" act is one example of the intense partisanship that can erupt on agricultural matters (Hurwitz, Moiles, and Rohde, 2001). Partisan polarization was also fairly common on farm bills during the 1950s and early 1960s.

Following World War II, American agriculture was transformed by technological innovations, increased mechanization, and the more efficient use of fertilizers.[22] But because of the rigid price supports in place at the time, the consequences of this transformation also included plummeting crop prices and large surpluses. To alleviate the overproduction, President Eisenhower and the Republican-controlled Congress enacted legislation in 1954 that established more flexible price supports for five key commodities: wheat, corn, cotton, rice, and peanuts. Still, farm prices continued to drop. In 1955, the Democrats became the majority party in the House and Senate. Early in the year, the House Agriculture Committee reported legislation that would have shifted price supports back to 90 percent of parity for the major agricultural commodities and also increased price supports for dairy products. The measure sharply divided House members along party lines, with GOP Whip Leslie Arends asserting, "Political considerations, not economic, bring this [bill] before us.... We have here ... what may be called a political conspiracy simply for political power ... the farmer is the victim. The sole objective of this bill is to try to embarrass the Eisenhower Administration."[23]

Anticipating a tough floor fight and a close vote on passage, Democratic leaders whipped their members on two questions about the bill in mid-March: (1) "Will you vote for the legislation to support the basic agricultural commodities at 90% of parity as promised for in the Democratic platform?" (2) "Will you vote to increase the minimum support price on dairy products above the present minimum support price of 75% of parity?"[24] The results are summarized in Table 5.7. On the first question, 176 members supported the leadership position, while on question 2 there were 109 leadership loyalists. For both questions, there were only

TABLE 5.7. Coalition-building success, agriculture

Item	Y/LY	U	N/LN	Other	Rep support	Necessary pickup	Actual pickup	Outcome
Farm price supports (Gen), 1955	176	25	26	5	21*	7	9	Win
Farm price supports (Dairy), 1955	109	69	26	28	21*	74	76	Win
Soil bank, 1956	153	35	12	32	4	41	54	Win
Farm bill, 1962	123	57	42	40	1	86	81	Loss
Feed grains, 1963	116	43	16	82	1	85	91	Win
Cotton bill, 1963	132	60	55	9	34	34	50	Win

*Separate votes on the price support and dairy provisions did not occur, so the roll call data used for both items are from final passage on the entire package.

25 solid "no's" and one leaning that way. Still, the Democratic majority that Congress was not large (232 Democrats pitted against 203 Republicans) and the leadership needed to take steps to expand its supporting coalition.

On Friday morning, April 29, just days before floor action began, Majority Whip Carl Albert met with Speaker Rayburn, then deputy whip Hale Boggs, several of the zone whips, and Agriculture Committee Chair Harold Cooley, D-N.C., to discuss the impending floor fight. Participants emphasized the importance of the measure to the national Democratic Party. According to minutes from the session:

> Mr. Albert opened the meeting by saying that the Administration planned to try to beat [the farm bill] in a very political and partisan way and that it was very important that they get enough Democrats together to pass the bill and thereby offset the Republican polit-ical talk on the issue. Mr. Albert turned the meeting over to Mr. Cooley who reminded the group that the 90% program had been made a part of the Democratic platform at the 1952 Democratic Convention where he had been present. He went on to state that when Eisenhower was elected he said he would continue the price support program and that Mr. Halleck had come up with a com-promise by way of the 82-½% support program which passed the Congress last year....
>
> Mr. Benson [Secretary of Agriculture] favored a 75% program and didn't like the compromise.... The Speaker said that those who had voted for the flexible price support program last year had voted against the party and that the party was at stake this year on the bill coming before Congress next week.... The members suggested we get a list to the Speaker of those people whose votes were doubtful and that he contact them the early part of the week. Also suggested that Mr. McCormack meet with the New England group.[25]

Democratic leaders were particularly concerned about possible defec-tions from within Zone 1, the New England delegation, where members were worried about the impact of price supports on food costs. Of the 10 members of Zone 1, 4 were "no" on question one and 5 were "unde-cided." Only Majority Leader John McCormack, D-Mass., was a firm "yes." Following the Friday morning session, Albert did send McCormack a short memo: "Harold Cooley and the Speaker and I met on Friday with the Assistant Whips," he wrote, "and we thought you might be able to do some good if you got the New England group together and talked with them on the price support program."[26] Albert also gave Rayburn a list of 15 Democratic members (all from outside Zone 1) that "Harold [Agriculture Chair Cooley] and I think you could influence favorably on the 90% price support bill."[27] Seven of the members on Rayburn's list had answered "no" on the first question, one was "leaning no," six were "undecided," and one, James Delaney of New York, was "leaning yes." Anticipating close votes on the measure, Albert repeatedly contacted the zone whips, urging them to ensure that members supporting the leadership position would be present on the floor for the key roll calls.

After incorporating a minor committee amendment, the farm bill narrowly passed the House on May 5 by a margin of 206-201. Over 86 percent of Democrats voted for the measure while about 90 percent of Republicans were opposed. Of the 15 members on Speaker Rayburn's lobby list, 3 voted with the leadership, 12 voted against (including the notoriously unreliable Delaney), and Frances Walter of Pennsylvania, who answered "no" on the whip count, was the only Democrat (other than the Speaker, who seldom votes) not to participate in the roll call. Five of the Democrats on Rayburn's list voted with their party against the GOP motion to recommit (kill) the measure. As feared, every member of the New England delegation except the majority leader voted "no" on final passage, but McCormack was able to convince three of them, including zone whip Torbert Macdonald, D-Mass., to support the party on the motion to recommit. Since shifts of just three votes on final passage or seven on recommittal would have defeated the measure, it is likely that the collective efforts of the leadership were pivotal here. As Table 5.7 indicates (if we use the first whipped question as the benchmark), Democratic leaders needed to pick up seven additional Democratic votes to prevail on the floor. They secured nine.

The remaining rows of Table 5.7 indicate that leadership lobbying continued to be consequential, if not always successful, for the other agriculture items in our sample. An amended version of the 1955 price support measure cleared both chambers the following year, but was vetoed by President Eisenhower in April 1956. As a result, Democratic leaders crafted a scaled-back version that dropped major provisions opposed by the White House. Excluded from the new bill, however, was a key Eisenhower proposal to enable the Secretary of Agriculture to pay farmers in 1956 up to 50 percent of the amount they would receive from the Soil Bank program during 1957. Democratic leaders expected that the test vote on the floor would be a Republican attempt to add the Eisenhower language to the legislation. In the days before floor action, they whipped House Democrats about whether they favored the advance payment provision. As indicated in the table, 153 answered in support of the leadership position (against the amendment), 35 were undecided, and 12 were opposed or leaning that way, and 32 did not respond. On May 3, Albert Morano, R-Conn., moved to recommit the legislation with instructions that the advance payment provision be added to it. Democratic leaders prevailed on the roll call, 184–211. Only four Republicans voted with them against the motion to recommit, so with a base of just 153 supporters on the whip count, the Democratic leadership needed to pick up 41 votes to win. Their actual pickup was 54 members.

Compared to Eisenhower, the Kennedy administration's basic posture on agriculture placed less emphasis on market forces and more on federal management of the farm economy. Legislation embodying the Kennedy program, including severe new production controls for feed grains, was reported by the House Agriculture Committee on May 16, 1962. In additional to all GOP members of the panel, three southern Democrats voted "no," largely because they feared the new feed grains controls would increase costs for livestock, dairy, and poultry producers in their states. As ranking Republican Charles Hoeven, Iowa, observed, "This close vote simply means the bill is in for real trouble when it gets to the House floor."[28]

Democratic leaders conducted a whip count, asking members for their position on the bill, and the results are summarized in Table 5.7. As the process of end-game lobbying proceeded in earnest, they could count on an initial base of 123 supporters within the Caucus. Fifty-seven were undecided and 42 were opposed to the committee bill or leaning that way. The Secretary of Agriculture predicted that the outcome might depend on a single vote. The beginning of floor debate was pushed back a day to allow the leadership additional time to secure support. Minority Leader Charles Halleck, Ind., observed that Democratic leaders were exerting enormous pressure on rank-and-file members to support the administration. On the floor, Agriculture Chairman Cooley accepted a number of amendments to the feed grains section, attempting to broaden the supporting coalition. The key vote came on June 21, when the Republican motion to recommit passed, 215-205, effectively killing the bill. With only one Republican voting with them on the motion, the Kennedy administration and House leadership needed to pick up an additional 86 Democratic votes to win. They came close, securing 81, but still fell five votes short. A compromise bill was quickly drafted and passed the House in July and Kennedy signed an amended version of that legislation at the end of September.

The following year, congressional action on farm issues centered on the problems associated with particular commodities, especially cotton and feed grains. An administration-backed cotton bill cleared the House on December 4, 1963 on a 216-182 roll call. It was the first major measure passed by the chamber after the assassination of John Kennedy and Speaker John McCormack exerted significant pressure on wavering urban Democrats to toe the party line and vote "yes." Early in the year, the chamber had passed another bill, 208–195, largely along party lines, that provided the Secretary of Agriculture with enhanced discretion over managing the feed grains program. Both measures were subject to Democratic whip counts prior to floor action. As indicated in Table 5.7, there were 116 initial supporters on the feed grains measure and 132 on the cotton bill. Only one Republican voted with the Democrats on feed grains, the necessary pickup for the leadership was a full 85 votes, and they secured 91, drawing supporters about equally from the "undecided" and "other" columns. Interestingly, while the leadership lost the vote of just one Democrat who responded "yes" on the poll, half of the 12 members who were "no" switched positions and voted with their party on final passage. On the cotton measure, 34 Republicans supported the Democratic leadership position, so McCormack and his allies needed to pick up an additional 34 votes to carry the day on the floor. Even though the number of nonresponders on the count was low, they still managed to pick up 50 votes.

If the issue of civil rights illustrates the limits of leadership in the textbook House, then agricultural policy making illustrates the possibilities. For the six whipped questions in Table 5.7, all of the associated roll calls were highly partisan and the necessary pickup for the leadership ranged from 7 to 86 votes. Still, Democratic leaders prevailed on five of the six questions. On the one clear loss, the 1962 omnibus farm bill, the leadership still managed to grow its coalition by over 80 members following the whip count and fell just 5 votes short. What were the sources of leadership success in this issue area? For one, the transformation of the farm economy and the plight of producer groups created significant momentum on Capitol Hill to pass legislation throughout the 1950s and early 1960s. The serious differences that did emerge between competing constituent groups were more conducive to logrolling and compromise than were the deep sectional and ideological cleavages that characterized civil rights until the mid-1960s. On agriculture, the majority leadership was able to broker the necessary agreements, retain the support of wavering members, and otherwise manage the floor process so as to advance the party program through the House.

Closing Observations

The preponderance of the evidence indicates that the whips of period 1 were efficacious, especially when the sectional cleavage that divided House Democrats was not fully activated. After controlling for the smaller number of roll call votes during the 1950s and 1960s, the whips of this era were actively engaged in a wide range of policy areas. Compared to the 1955–2002 time stretch as a whole, civil rights, health, education, and other social welfare issues were particularly prominent on the whipped agendas of period 1. Perhaps not surprisingly, region was the strongest predictor of party support during the whip process, although there also were effects for district-level presidential vote, membership on the committee of jurisdiction, chamber seniority, and participation in the extended leadership or party whip network. Although roughly three-quarters of whipped questions resulted in a win for the majority party, there was significant variation by policy area. Policy categories like civil rights, labor/consumer, and other topics that evoked the party's sectional cleavage were particularly likely to produce outcomes short of a majority party win. Our explorations of whip activity on civil rights and agriculture reinforce all of these points. In the next chapter, we consider whether similar patterns occurred during period 2, 1973–82.

SIX

Coalitions Built in Sand,
1973–82

This chapter examines House whip activity during period 2 (1973–82), the transition years between the sectionally divided congresses of period 1 and the rise of partisan polarization during the 1980s.[1] The era provides yet another distinct vantage point for considering the role played by leaders and whips in the lawmaking process. In contrast to the sectional divisions of period 1, the large Democratic majorities of 1973–82 fragmented along regional, constituency, and generational lines, and by all accounts the floor decision-making process was far more fluid and unpredictable than had been the case during the textbook years. The expansion of the Speaker's control over the floor agenda that occurred during the 1970s empowered the majority leadership somewhat, but congressional scholarship about the period tends to emphasize the limits of leadership and the primacy of member individualism.[2] During the last two years of this period, House Democratic leaders confronted a popular and programmatically ambitious Republican president, Ronald Reagan, and on a number of major floor fights the White House carried the day.

Yet, on both sides of the aisle the whips of period 2 were often quite efficacious. Indeed, the independent impact of the whip process on coalition building was significant during the 1970s precisely because the majority program faced such steep challenges and the potential value added from effective leadership was especially large. As the behavioral perspective emphasizes, the importance of the leadership may be greater when there are significant weak spots in the party coalition. In exploring the whip process of the 1970s House, we will follow the same path as the previous chapter, advancing from contextual considerations to agenda contents to leadership support to outcomes. And once again, we will close with in-depth treatments of two issue areas. One key difference, however, is that for this chapter we have systematic whip evidence for both the majority Democrats and the minority Republicans.

Contextual Considerations

For the most part, the Democratic House majorities of 1973–82 were large by historical standards. Only 239 House members were Democrats in the 93rd Congress (1973–74). But following the Watergate scandal and Nixon's resignation from office, the Democratic Caucus was comprised of 291 members at the beginning of the 94th Congress, 292 members in the 95th, and 276 members in the 96th. After Reagan's presidential win in 1980, the size of the Democratic House majority fell back to 243 on opening day of the 97th Congress. Although generally large, the House majorities of period 2 were also divided by a myriad of cleavages rooted in constituency-level variance at the member level. As the relatively simple sectional divisions of period 1 receded, the multiplicity of constituency-level differences within the Democratic Caucus moved front and center and remained so until the gradual emergence of intense partisan cleavages during the 1980s and 1990s.

The complex cleavages lines of period 2 varied in importance by issue, depending on the specific audiences a policy activated at home. Still, presidential voting patterns at the district level can again provide a summary glimpse at the coalition-building challenges faced by party leaders. Figure 6.1 portrays the number of members from districts where the presidential vote was closer to the average for the other party, as well as the number that hailed from constituencies that were not partisan outliers according to this indicator. In contrast to the treatment of Chapter 5, here the party averages are based on results for the entire country, not just districts located outside the south. Although the south in many ways remained politically distinct, the national presidential vote within the region was beginning to reflect ideological and policy inclinations throughout the nation. Still, because the regional realignment was not yet complete and electoral politics continued to vary by region, in Figure 6.1 the prevalence of outlier versus mainstream districts is presented separately for the south for both parties (again, with the caveat that the baseline party averages are now for the country as a whole).

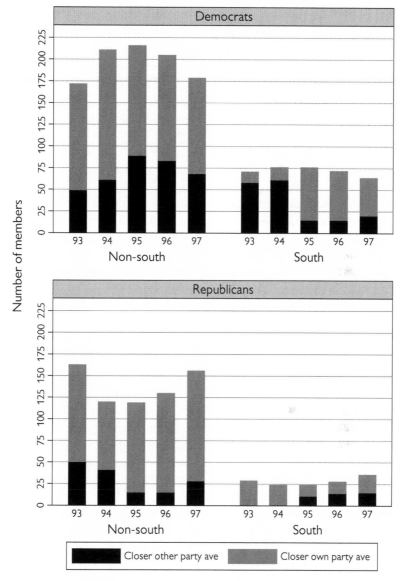

Figure 6.1. Partisan congruence of district-level presidential vote by congress, 1973–82

As you can see from the figure, a third or more of the non-southerners in the Democratic Caucuses of period 1 were from districts that based on the most recent presidential vote more closely resembled the constituencies represented by the typical Republican. For the 70 or so southern Democrats within each congress, President Jimmy Carter's strong electoral showing in his native region distorted the results somewhat for the 95th and 96th Congresses (1977–80), and to some extent probably the 97th (1981–82) as well. Still, during 1973–76 the vast majority of southern Democrats represented outlier districts. And because of the continued political distinctiveness of the region, the sheer size of the southern delegation itself remained an indicator of internal heterogeneity for the Democrats. On the GOP side of the aisle, the southern presence was still relatively small (that would change in the 1990s), and overall the incidence of outlier districts among Republicans was much lower than was the case for the majority Democrats.

District-level presidential votes, however, cannot do full justice to the unstable, and unwieldy coalitional structures that complicated life for the Democratic majorities of period 2. Barbara Sinclair, the most astute scholarly observer of the congressional parties, emphasized the remarkable fragmentation and fluidity of Democratic coalitions during that era (Sinclair 1983). On economic management issues, the concerns of district audiences in the south differed sharply from those of constituencies located elsewhere in the country. The configuration of constituency interests on social welfare issues was somewhat less heterogeneous by member, and on matters related to civil rights the impact of section likewise had grown less pronounced, but overall the diversity of constituency interests within the Democratic Caucus greatly complicated party coalition building.

The transformation of the national interest group environment that occurred during the 1970s was also a contributing factor. Organized advocacy coalitions had been an important feature of legislative work in Congress for many decades. During the 1970s, however, the scope of the Washington pressure community broadened and deepened. The heightened group activity largely resulted from the governmental and programmatic expansions of the Great Society and early Nixon years (Walker 1991). As the involvement of the federal government in day-to-day economic and social life grew, so did the policy-making stakes for individuals and groups across the country, and thus the incentives for them to mobilize and attempt to influence the legislative process. Both the number and diversity of these lobbying organizations increased markedly, as did the complexity of the advocacy group demands confronting Congress. Conversely, the organizational strength of the two political parties had grown weaker in period 2 because of the decline of patronage politics at the local level and the shift toward mass participation primaries for the selection of candidates for office (Polsby 1983). Sinclair aptly summarized the leadership challenges created by the constituency, group, and partisan changes that were sweeping the country:

[C]oalition building was more complex. The number of members the leadership had to contact and persuade had grown. Gauging the probability of winning was more difficult, and so was deciding how to spend scarce time and resources. The frequency with which the House leadership lost votes which it subsequently turned around is indicative.... In each case, the leadership's position prevailed on the second attempt—clear proof that a winning coalition could be fashioned. That a skillful and active leadership lost the first time shows how difficult it is to gauge what and how much needs to be done to win.[3]

The 1970s was also a decade of important institutional change and reform within the House. During the 1960s, the House Rules Committee had been enlarged to curtail the power of southern Democrats and conservative Republicans within the panel. Yet, as the 1970s began, the House legislative process was still characterized by strong committees and limited leadership control over the floor agenda. By the end of the decade, however, the internal operations of the House would become far less committee oriented and important new agenda setting powers would be extended to the majority leadership. Dozens of discrete reforms were adopted during the 1970s and some were critical for understanding the evolving role of the whips.[4]

In 1971, of course, the House adopted recorded voting during the floor amendment process, and electronic recordkeeping of these and other roll calls was implemented in 1973. As we have seen, one result was an avalanche of amending activity and heightened uncertainty in the legislative process. During the early 1970s, Democrats also took steps to increase the influence of the full caucus and of the leadership in the assignment of members to committees and in the selection of committee chairs (Deering and Smith, 1997). Although still a norm, seniority was no longer inviolate for choosing committee leaders. The operating autonomy of committee chairs was likewise curtailed. The Speaker was given the power to appoint majority party members to the Rules Committee, which transformed that panel from an independent actor into an arm of the majority leadership (Oppenheimer 1977). The GOP soon followed suit and gave its leaders the power to hire and fire Republican Rules members. Although not fully recognized at the time, perhaps the most far-reaching party building reform of the decade was adoption of the Budget and Impoundment Control Act of 1974, which for the first time provided members and their leaders with centralized tools for the formulation of fiscal and tax policy (Schick 1980). Some of the most heated whip battles of the 1980s and 1990s would concern budget resolutions and reconciliation bills, two legislative vehicles created by the 1974 Budget Act.

As discussed in Chapter 1, during the 1970s the party whip networks roughly doubled in size and became more organizationally complex and active in the House legislative process. Whip meetings on both sides of the aisle became more formal and more heavily attended. In short, although the coalition-building challenges the whips and other party leaders of period 2 faced were often serious, the organizational innovations of the era also provided the leadership with important new tools for meeting them.

General Features

The limits and possibilities of party leadership during period 2 fostered a mode of leadership that has been called "the strategy of inclusion" (Sinclair 1983). Especially during the speakership of Thomas P. "Tip" O'Neill, which began in 1977 and extended through 1986, the leadership used regular whip and caucus meetings to reach out to the diverse factions that comprised the full Democratic Caucus. The aim was to integrate potential opponents into the decision-making process as early as possible, accommodate their concerns where feasible, and thereby create buy-in for emergent party proposals. Persuasion was part of the whip role, to be sure, but also important was providing leaders with intelligence about the substantive and strategic modifications necessary to pass legislation. The measure of whip efficacy, in other words, was not a deviation of legislative outcomes from some pre-determined middle ground. Especially amid the large, unwieldy partisan majorities of period 2, the whip function primarily was to help discern and construct what could constitute middle ground in the first place.

The Whipped Agenda

The contents of the whipped agenda for period 2 are summarized by policy area in Table 6.1 for the majority Democrats and in Table 6.2 for the minority Republicans. As was the case in the previous chapter, cell entries in the second column denote the percentage of whipped questions that dealt with the relevant issue category, and for purposes of comparison the third column reproduces the percentages across periods. Since large percentages in these columns may primarily reflect a policy area's prominence in the broader floor agenda, the fourth column shows the percentage of the roll calls within a policy category that were targeted for whip attention, and the last column shows that percentage for all periods combined.

TABLE 6.1. Majority party, distribution of whip attention by issue area, 1973–82

Issue Area	% Whipped questions— 1973–82	% Whipped questions—All periods	% Votes whipped— 1973–82*	% Votes whipped— All periods*
Congress/Gov ops	18.4	14.1	6.1	5.7
Defense	1.9	4.4	2.1	5.3
Foreign policy	8.3	7.0	5.1	7.1
Economy	19.6	18.4	7.9	12.1
Trade	3.0	2.9	4.6	9.0
Energy/Environment	15.0	6.4	6.1	4.9
Civil rights	1.5	1.7	4.6	6.1
Social welfare	8.3	4.7	8.4	8.1
Health	2.3	2.9	7.7	12.4
Education	0	3.0	0	8.9
Labor/Consumer	8.3	7.0	10.8	15.9
Appropriations	5.6	19.4	1.4	5.9
Other	7.9	8.2	3.9	5.7

*Only nonunanimous votes used.

TABLE 6.2. Minority party, distribution of whip attention by issue area, 1975–80

Issue area	% Whipped questions— 1975–80	% Whipped questions—All periods	% Votes whipped— 1975–80*	% Votes whipped— All periods*
Congress/Gov ops	15.7	8.8	3.8	3.3
Defense	5.0	9.1	5.2	9.9
Foreign policy	7.4	6.4	2.1	4.4
Economy	12.4	20.9	2.4	7.1
Trade	.8	2.7	2.7	10.1
Energy/Environment	23.1	12.4	3.4	3.9
Civil rights	2.5	5.2	5.6	10.0
Social welfare	2.5	4.2	2.3	6.2
Health	2.5	1.8	2.8	4.9
Education	2.5	1.8	4.1	5.2
Labor/Consumer	10.7	8.5	9.1	13.3
Appropriations	5.8	10.6	1.2	2.6
Other	9.1	7.6	1.9	2.8

*Only nonunanimous votes used.

In the tables, the categories for Congress/Gov ops, the economy, and energy/environment clearly stand out. For the majority, about 18 percent of whipped questions during period 2 concerns the internal operating procedures of Congress and the federal government. The proportion of votes in that policy category targeted for whipping was not out of line with the percentage for the entire 1955–2002 time span, so the priority of these issues during period 2 largely reflects their heightened prominence on the congressional agendas of the time. Overall, the 1970s was a remarkable decade of institutional reform in American politics, the internal operations of Congress included. Major reforms to campaign finance laws were adopted; significant ethics reforms were considered and some enacted; and the internal administrative operations of the House were revamped. The Budget Act of 1974 was also repeatedly whipped. Interestingly, the committee and leadership reforms of the 1970s that set the stage for party coalition building were not formally whipped, mostly because major decisions about them were generally made within the House Democratic Caucus, rather than the chamber as a whole.

Throughout period 2, the US economy was wracked with inflationary recession and interest rates that were disturbingly high. Economic management, of course, can be critical to public perceptions of the governing competence of the party in power, so it comes as no surprise that these issues were front and center on the two party agendas during the 1970s and early 1980s. Moreover, the reformed budget process ushered in by the 1974 Act also created new challenges for party leaders. Now, the partisan majority was charged each year with shepherding to passage one or more budget resolutions that determined the framework for all the session's decisions about spending and taxing.[5] For these reasons, economic issues were regular targets for whip attention during the years of period 2. Indeed, among the policy areas in the table, the largest share dealt with these matters—nearly 20 percent of all majority whip activity.

Energy and environmental issues also were a whip priority on both sides of the partisan aisle. Fifteen percent of all majority party whip activity (or about one whipped question in six) touched on this policy area. As was the case for Congress/Gov ops and the economy, the portion of votes that were whipped was not substantially higher than for the four periods combined, so the increase in whip attention to energy/environment primarily reflects the heightened presence of these items on the broader agenda. Following the US decision to aid Israel during the Yom Kippur War of 1973, the Organization of Arab Petroleum Producing Countries (OPEC) declared an oil embargo that significantly increased domestic energy prices in the United States and caused widespread shortages across the country. Disturbing footage of long lines outside gas stations was a fixture on the evening television news, and energy reform was a major priority on Capitol Hill for the remainder of the decade.

The 1970s was also a critical juncture in the development of US environmental policy. Often labeled the "environmental decade," the list of conservation and anti-pollution statutes enacted during these years included the National Environmental Protection Act of 1970, the Water Pollution Control Act Amendments of 1972, the Endangered Species Act of 1973, the Safe Drinking Water Act of 1974, the Resources Conservation and Recovery Act of 1976, the Water Pollution Control Amendments of 1977 (often called the "Clean Water Act"), and the Comprehensive Environmental Response, Compensation, and Liability Act of 1980 (more commonly known as "Superfund"). Together, these eight statutes transformed US environmental policy. Yet the majority Democrats only whipped the 1972 and 1977 water pollution measures, and whip activity by the minority GOP was minimal to none. The reason is that the landmark environmental legislation of the 1970s was generally backed by large, bipartisan supermajorities. Indeed, on all eight measures more than 300 members voted "yes" on House passage. Since these roll calls were not viewed as in play, they were not regularly targeted by the whips.[6]

Although the majority Democrats placed somewhat heightened emphasis on social welfare matters during period 2, the temporal differences were not large. As was the case for period 1, appropriations measures were not a whip priority for 1973–82, largely because the spending process continued to be oriented around norms of cross-partisan accommodation. And overall, the whip priorities of the minority Republicans largely track the issues emphasized on the Democratic side of the aisle. As Table 6.2 indicates, the Republicans prioritized government process items for whipping in period 2, and like their majority counterparts they were much more active on energy policy.

For the most part, these general patterns are also apparent when we focus on the more significant measures—whipped bills and proposals associated with *CQ* major votes. Within this subset, energy policy continues to stand out. Six key vote measures dealing with energy and the environment were whipped by the majority Democrats, and a full nine were the subject of whip activity by the GOP. Among the *CQ* key vote bills, however, the largest share by far (17 separate measures) dealt with the economy. The minority Republicans, in contrast, were less likely to whip major economic votes, in large part because the electoral stakes for them were less severe. As we have argued, economic management issues are especially relevant to public perceptions about the partisan majority.

Member Loyalty

Now consider the member-specific factors introduced in Chapter 5 that, based on the behavioral perspective, should have an impact on the positions members take during the whip process and on the votes they eventually cast. For period 2, the relationship between these factors and the distribution of positions expressed during whip calls is summarized in Table 6.3 for the majority Democrats and in Table 6.4 for the minority GOP. Even though the regional realignment of conservative southerners toward the Republican Party was underway, the whip responses of southern and border state Democrats continued to differ markedly from those of their co-partisans in other regions. Southern Democrats remained significantly less likely to answer in favor of the party position, and significantly more likely to be undecided, opposed, or nonresponsive. Border state Democrats continued to fall between the southerners and the rest of the caucus in their fealty to the leadership position as reported to the whips.

Still, compared to analogous results for period 1, southerners were somewhat more likely to support the party position, and importantly, members from the northeast, midwest/plains states, and the west are now somewhat less likely to answer "yes" on party whip calls. Indeed, across all five regions the percentage of Democrats answering "undecided" was higher in period 2 than was the case in period 1. Again, party coalition building during the 1970s was remarkably fluid. Consistent with expectations, district-level presidential votes have a strong relationship with leadership support during the whip process. The partisan outliers are 7–8 percent less likely to endorse the leadership position on whip calls and more likely to be undecided or opposed. Although the presidential vote indicator is informative, the more significant constituency-level relationship remains the one that existed between region and the whip count response.

Interestingly, even though the gist of the internal reforms implemented during the 1970s was to curtail the operating autonomy of committees and committee chairs, members of the panel with jurisdiction over a whipped

TABLE 6.3. Majority party, distribution of whip responses, selected district and member characteristics, 1973–82

		Y/LY	U	N/LN	Other
	NE	69.8	12.3	6.5	11.3
	MW/Plains	68.1	15.5	9.1	7.4
Region	South	37.0	24.9	20.8	17.3
	Border	50.8	23.2	15.8	10.2
	West	67.2	13.0	8.2	11.6
District-level	Closer to R ave	53.8	19.8	14.1	12.2
pres vote	Closer to D ave	61.4	16.1	10.7	11.8
Committee of	On	71.5	10.1	9.7	8.8
jurisdiction	Off	57.2	18.3	12.3	12.3
	Fresh	56.9	19.6	12.0	11.5
Seniority	2/5 terms	59.1	18.0	13.0	9.9
	>5 terms	58.6	15.9	10.8	14.6
Extended	Yes	58.7	18.3	11.9	11.1
leadership	No	58.6	17.2	12.0	12.2
Whip network	Yes	65.2	15.6	12.7	6.5
	No	57.7	17.7	11.9	12.7

TABLE 6.4. Minority party, distribution of whip responses, selected district and member characteristics, 1975–80

		Y/LY	U	N/LN	Other
	NE	41.4	25.0	20.8	12.9
	MW/Plains	63.4	15.1	11.7	9.8
Region	South	70.4	13.0	8.7	7.9
	Border	63.8	16.6	12.3	7.4
	West	67.1	15.6	9.7	7.6
District-level	Closer to D ave	51.0	19.4	18.3	11.3
pres vote	Closer to R ave	62.9	15.6	11.4	9.1
Committee of	On	63.8	14.7	14.3	7.3
jurisdiction	Off	59.8	17.5	12.8	9.9
	Fresh	59.4	18.1	13.4	9.2
Seniority	2/5 terms	59.2	16.9	14.5	9.5
	>5 terms	62.1	17.3	10.5	10.1
Extended	Yes	61.7	16.6	12.4	9.4
leadership	No	57.4	18.0	15.0	9.6
Whip network	Yes	68.0	15.1	13.6	3.4
	No	59.3	17.5	12.9	10.4

question continue to be substantially more likely to stay loyal during the whip process. As the table shows, the difference for the Y/LY column is almost 15 percentage points. Committee members are significantly less likely to be undecided and also somewhat less likely to be opposed as compared with other members of the caucus.

In comparison to period 1, the association between chamber seniority and leadership support is less apparent in period 2. During period 1, the most junior lawmakers were 12 percentage points more likely to be leadership supporters during the whip process than were members with five or more terms under their belts. During period 2, that gap disappeared. The newly elected members of the House in the 1970s tended to be far more independent of parties and leaders than had been junior lawmakers in previous decades. The freshman members elected in 1974, for example, quickly became known as the "Watergate Babies" and were notorious on Capitol Hill for their independence. Among their first actions as a newly elected class was the dethroning of three longtime committee chairs that they viewed as out-of-touch or insufficiently responsive to the interests of younger Democrats (Rohde 1991). The heightened independence of junior Democrats in period 2 reflected the manner in which they were elected and the nature of their representational relationships with important constituent audiences. Within their districts, they tended to operate as independent contractors not beholden to local party organizations, and as Table 6.3 suggests, their independence at home was reflected in their strategic posture during the whip process.[7]

Being a member of the extended party leadership continued to have little association with the whip count response in period 2. Similar to the finding for the 1950s and 1960s, rank-and-file members were tolerant of considerable preference diversity at the leadership level. As Table 6.3 shows, for the majority Democrats participation in the whip process was associated with increased leadership support during the bargaining endgame on the floor. But also, notice that the difference appears to derive almost entirely from fewer nonresponses, rather than fewer reports in the undecided or N/LN columns. A key purpose of the expanded whip networks of period 2 was to establish conduits into the different factions that comprised the Democratic Caucus, which required a degree of preference heterogeneity among the whips even on major party priorities.

Based on Table 6.4, the regional challenges confronting leaders of the minority Republicans were very different. While Democratic leaders routinely faced opposition from within their southern delegation, the challenge for GOP leaders largely centered on the northeast. By period 2, the number of northeastern Republicans had dwindled, but the "Yankee Republicans" that remained were still disproportionately less likely to answer "yes" on party whip counts and significantly more likely to be undecided or opposed.[8] The cause, of course, lies in the greater ideological moderation of core GOP constituencies in the northeast. The regional differences among Republicans are also reflected in the presidential vote indicator. Here, the Republican outliers were nearly 12 percentage points less likely to endorse the leadership position during whip calls than were GOP lawmakers representing mainstream districts. For the remainder of the explanatory factors listed in the table, there is not much association with the whip count response on the minority side of the aisle, with the exception of membership in the party whip network (GOP whips were more likely to be Y/LY, somewhat less likely to be undecided, and a lot less likely to be nonresponsive).

Within each whip response category, the roll call loyalty of the relevant members is summarized in Tables 6.5 and 6.6. As was the case for period 1, the percentage of pro-leadership votes within each category largely tracks expectations. Leadership support generally declines as we shift from Y/LY

TABLE 6.5. Majority party, leadership support on votes by whip category, selected district and member characteristics, 1973–82

		Y/LY	U	N/LN	Other
Region	NE	95.2	75.2	34.9	84.8
	MW/Plains	95.5	72.2	30.1	82.1
	South	89.2	56.2	17.8	61.0
	Border	91.9	62.4	22.7	76.8
	West	94.7	69.1	30.9	81.3
District-level pres vote	Closer to R ave	92.8	62.0	21.0	71.0
	Closer to D ave	94.6	67.5	26.9	75.9
Committee of jurisdiction	On	95.9	63.3	20.8	72.2
	Off	93.7	65.3	24.6	73.9
Seniority	Fresh	93.2	64.7	24.9	72.5
	2/5 terms	93.1	64.7	25.2	76.0
	>5 terms	95.3	66.0	22.6	72.9
Extended leadership	Yes	93.9	66.2	23.5	69.4
	No	94.0	64.8	24.5	75.2
Whip network	Yes	94.4	59.2	21.2	78.1
	No	93.9	65.9	24.7	74.7

to undecided to N/LN. The likelihood of pro-leadership votes within the "other" category falls between the levels for Y/LY and undecided. Across response categories, the prevalence of pro-leadership voting is substantially lower for southern members, and to a less extent also for border state representatives. For district presidential vote, the differences in roll call loyalty between representatives from outlier districts and those reflecting the party mainstream are less pronounced than was the case for period 1. Compared to the 1950s and 1960s, the weak spots in the Democratic coalitions of period 2 were more broadly dispersed. Among undecideds and initial opponents, leadership support on votes is somewhat lower for participants in the majority party whip network. If a Democratic whip articulated some degree of opposition to the party program during the counting process, he or she was serious, and for them the likelihood of a flip-flop back toward the party position was lower.

The results for the minority GOP in Table 6.6 largely parallel what we found for the majority. Notice, though, that outside of the Y/LY category, support for the party position dropped off significantly for northeastern Republicans. While two-thirds of initially undecided southern Republicans ended up voting with the leadership, only half of the GOP

TABLE 6.6. Minority party, leadership support on votes by whip category, selected district and member characteristics, 1975–80

		Y/LY	U	N/LN	Other
Region	NE	91.1	50.1	19.5	54.8
	MW/Plains	94.3	65.7	31.5	73.2
	South	97.4	66.7	39.3	74.2
	Border	93.3	71.1	20.8	63.4
	West	95.8	63.4	27.2	73.1
District-level pres vote	Closer to D ave	92.3	49.3	19.5	57.9
	Closer to R ave	95.2	64.3	30.2	70.3
Committee of jurisdiction	On	96.0	59.2	18.7	73.2
	Off	94.5	60.7	27.7	66.6
Seniority	Fresh	94.9	60.8	27.8	62.4
	2/5 terms	94.5	60.2	26.8	62.5
	>5 terms	94.7	61.0	26.0	75.3
Extended leadership	Yes	95.1	59.8	28.5	68.6
	No	93.7	61.8	23.7	64.3
Whip network	Yes	93.1	58.0	24.7	75.0
	No	94.9	60.8	27.0	66.9

members from the northeast did so. Similarly, for GOP district outliers, roll call support for the leadership among undecideds was 15 percentage points lower for members from districts with presidential voting patterns closer to the Democratic average. Analogous differences are apparent for the N/LN and "other" categories. Especially on the minority Republican side of the aisle, then, constituency composition was central to member decision making during the whip process and on associated votes.

Outcomes

Our initial exploration of whip outcomes in Chapter 4, you will recall, indicated that a transition toward higher levels of majority party victories occurred between periods 2 and 3, and that the outcome distributions for periods 1 and 2 were fairly similar. For the Democratic majorities of period 2, about 65 percent of whipped questions resulted in clear-cut wins for the leadership, 9 percent required major substantive changes for the party to prevail, just under 6 percent were withdrawn from the agenda, and 20 percent were outright losses. For the questions whipped by the minority Republicans during this time span, a little over half resulted in majority party wins, about 8 percent were associated with major substantive changes in the underlying proposal, 13 percent were removed from the agenda, and nearly one-in-four resulted in an unambiguous majority party loss. Especially since whipped questions should be in play, these majority party win rates are fairly impressive, albeit less so than the majority victory rates of periods 3 and 4.

Relative to the 1950s and 1960s, the number of whipped questions was much higher during period 2, and the range of question types subject to whipping was broader. Moreover, the Democratic Caucuses of the 1970s and early 1980s were less balkanized along sectional lines. Why, then, are the majority win rates so similar between periods 1 and 2? To further address the question, Tables 6.7 and 6.8 break down the outcome distributions for period 2 by policy area, first for the majority Democrats and then for the minority GOP.

The number of majority whipped questions within certain of the policy areas is small, and to some extent outcomes for them may reflect idiosyncratic factors. In other policy categories, however, the incidence of whip activity is fairly high, and there clearly are noteworthy differences in majority party success and failure across these rows of the tables. For majority whipped questions dealing with the economy, for example, nearly one in three resulted in a loss for the Democrats. For the many energy

TABLE 6.7. Majority party, whipped outcomes by issue area, 1973–82

Issue area	Majority win	Major change	Pull	Majority loss
Congress/Gov ops	24	4	6	6
	(60.0)	(10.0)	(15.0)	(15.0)
Defense	4	0	1	0
	(80.0)		(20.0)	
Foreign policy	10	5	2	3
	(50.0)	(25.0)	(10.0)	(15.0)
Economy	30	1	0	15
	(65.2)	(2.2)		(32.6)
Trade	4	0	0	2
	(66.7)			(33.3)
Energy/Environment	28	2	1	4
	(80.0)	(5.7)	(2.9)	(11.4)
Civil rights	3	0	0	1
	(75.0)			(25.0)
Social welfare	11	4	2	4
	(52.4)	(19.1)	(9.5)	(19.1)
Health	5	0	0	1
	(83.3)			(16.7)
Education	0	0	0	0
Labor/Consumer	9	1	1	5
	(56.3)	(6.3)	(6.3)	(31.3)
Appropriations	12	0	0	1
	(92.3)			(7.7)
Other	10	4	0	4
	(55.6)	(22.2)		(22.2)

Note: Cell entries are the number of items for the relevant issue-outcome category, with percentages by issue in parentheses.

issues polled by the majority during period 2, in contrast, the party was much less likely to get rolled on the floor. The Democrats also did fairly well on appropriations bills, and somewhat less well on labor/consumer matters, social issues, and Congress/government operations. The outcome distributions for items whipped by the minority GOP largely track what we find for the Democrats, albeit with generally lower majority win rates across the board. But notice that Democratic leaders ended up pulling from the agenda nearly 40 percent of the energy proposals whipped by the minority. In short, there is considerable outcome variance to be explored within and across policy areas. To shed further light on the foundations of leadership success and failure, we can focus in more depth on two sets of issues where whip activity was abundant and there was considerable variance across outcome categories: budget politics and energy reform.

TABLE 6.8. Minority party, whipped outcomes by issue area, 1975–80

Issue area	Majority win	Major change	Pull	Majority loss
Congress/Gov ops	6	1	1	4
	(50.0)	(8.3)	(8.3)	(33.3)
Defense	4	0	0	0
	(100)			
Foreign policy	2	0	1	0
	(66.7)		(33.3)	
Economy	5	2	0	2
	(55.6)	(22.2)		(22.2)
Trade	1	0	0	0
	(100)			
Energy/Environment	8	0	6	2
	(50.0)		(37.5)	(12.5)
Civil rights	3	0	0	0
	(100)			
Social welfare	2	0	0	1
	(66.7)			(33.3)
Health	0	0	0	2
				(100)
Education	0	1	0	1
		(50.0)		(50.0)
Labor/Consumer	4	2	2	4
	(33.3)	(16.7)	(16.7)	(33.3)
Appropriations	6	0	0	1
	(85.7)			(14.3)
Other	1	0	0	2
	(33.3)			(66.7)

Note: Cell entries are the number of items for the relevant issue-outcome category, with percentages by issue in parentheses.

Budget, Taxes, and the Debt

Summary information about initial leadership support and pickup challenges for budgetary questions during period 2 is provided in Table 6.9, with Panel A reporting results for the majority Democrats and Panel B showing analogous information for the minority Republicans. Included are the items falling in the "economy" category in Table 6.7, excluding a few questions relating to domestic trade and securities regulation and two tax proposals that are better considered as part of the energy case study to follow. For each party, items are organized by outcome category and date. As the table shows, the vast majority of questions that produced a majority party win (18 out of 26) required pickups between the whip check and the vote. Typically, the majority's pickup challenge derived from a combination

TABLE 6.9. Coalition-building success, budgets, taxes, and the debt

	Panel A. Majority Democrats						
Question	Y/LY	U	N/LN	Other	Rep support	Min nec pickup	Actual pickup
Win							
Budget reform GOP amdt 1973	182	32	8	20	79	–60	34
Budget reform as reported 1973	129	43	15	55	180	–104	77
Budget resolution 1975	198	45	43	2	3	–2	–1
Budget resolution conference 1975	194	29	38	27	5	13	31
Tax Reform prev ques rule 1975	179	27	4	79	0	30	40
Budget Resolution (3rd) 1977	184	50	17	37	14	7	41
Tax Reduction prev ques rule 1977	179	31	7	71	1	15	28
Budget resolution (1st) 1977	163	64	34	28	7	27	43
Budget resolution conference (1st) 1977	200	32	27	29	29	–29	–8
Budget resolution (2nd) 1977	165	44	16	63	4	25	30
Debt limit 1977	187	29	49	23	19	2	7
Debt limit 1978	172	46	34	35	27	4	34
Budget resolution (1st) 1978	160	68	35	24	3	37	38
Debt limit 1978	166	40	72	8	9	29	30
GOP tax proposal prev ques rule 1978	167	53	27	39	136	–95	–19
GOP tax proposal M to R 1978	173	48	28	37	3	33	64
Budget resolution (2nd) 1978	182	43	25	36	2	14	33
Debt limit as reported 1979	187	30	38	20	3	14	22
Debt limit prev ques rule 1979	196	35	23	21	1	4	4
Debt limit 1979	166	27	32	50	5	38	48
Budget resolution motion 1979	148	43	20	63	0	50	57
Mortgage Subsidy cmte amdt 1980	145	61	19	47	147	–84	112
Mortgage Subsidy pass 1980	138	72	18	43	58	13	42
Debt limit 1981	119	57	17	14	150	–64	36
Tax cut rule 1981	166	60	4	10	132	–82	–18
Tax bill conference 1982	74	57	105	6	103	40	49

TABLE 6.9. (*Continued*)

	Panel A. Majority Democrats						
Question	Y/LY	U	N/LN	Other	Rep support	Min nec pickup	Actual pickup
Major change							
Humphrey-Hawkins passage 1978	177	56	40	14	25	3	55
Losses							
Budget resolution (1st) 1977	169	59	25	36			
Capital gains amdt 1978	120	81	47	38	1	87	46
Debt limit 1979	138	42	54	41	3	68	53
Oil windfall profits amdt 1979	139	39	41	56	10	61	34
Budget resolution (2nd) 1979	112	76	41	46	4	87	76
Budget resolution Dem 1981	140	63	36	2			
Budget resolution GOP 1981	145	60	34	2	1	69	30
Budget reconciliation prev ques/rule 1981	164	38	8	31	0	50	45
Budget Reconciliation pass 1981	172	23	14	32			
Tax cut Rep subst 1981	178	56	7	1	1	38	16
Budget resolution 1982	143	70	23	5	3	68	56

	Panel B. Minority Republicans						
Question	Y/LY	U	N/LN	Other	Dem support	Min nec pickup	Actual pickup
Majority wins							
Taxes conference 1975	58	26	45	15	45	103	22
Budget 1977	64	23	35	22	70	65	43
Plowback 1979	97	37	4	9	46	65	43
Major change							
Humphrey-Hawkins 1978	113	22	8	4	42	50	-3
Majority losses							
Windfall tax 1979	89	36	10	12	90	31	57

of internal divisions within the Democratic Caucus and a paucity of cross-over support from the GOP.[9]

Macroeconomic issues tend to divide the two parties, and GOP support on these votes often was fifteen or fewer members. These items also tend to be performance tests for the majority where legislation of some form must be enacted, and the impetus was squarely on the whips to assemble winning coalitions on the floor. Prior to 1981 and the emergence of a Republican White House, the majority whips were mostly successful at the task. Indeed, the major losses in this policy area during the Nixon, Ford, and Carter years were usually reversed later in the session, eventually producing wins for the majority party. Democratic whip performance on budget, tax and debt issues during 1981–82, in contrast, was less impressive.

The minority Republicans also whipped five items relating to budgets, taxes and the debt where comprehensive whip evidence is available and analogous pickup values can be calculated for them. Three of these questions resulted in wins for the majority Democrats; one in major modifications (the Humphrey-Hawkins face-off); and one clear majority party loss (windfall profits in 1979). In each case, the pickup challenge facing the Republican whips was substantial (ranging from 31 votes to 103), primarily due to internal GOP divisions. For them, cross-over support from the other side of the aisle was often substantial, and always exceeded 40 votes.

For purposes of illustration, we can juxtapose an example of majority party success on budgetary matters with the most significant of the majority party failures. The success concerned efforts during 1979 to raise the statutory limit on the debt, while the majority party failure concerned House consideration of the Reagan tax cuts during 1981. As previously discussed, the Congress periodically must pass legislation to raise the statutory limit on the federal debt; otherwise the government will default on its obligations and potentially wreak havoc on global financial markets. The politics of debt limit hikes had already fallen into a certain pattern by the late 1970s. Members of both parties, but especially the GOP, liked to vote against such increases to demonstrate to the folks back home that they were fiscally responsible. But prior to the deadline for enacting the necessary increase, and perhaps after one or two failed attempts that gave members the opportunity to cast politically advantageous "no" votes, the leadership would round up enough support to raise the limit before default occurred.

This pattern was fully apparent in 1979. That year, the federal government faced a possible breach in the spring, and the Carter White House and congressional Democrats sought to raise the limit.[10] On February 14, Democratic leaders whipped their colleagues in support of legislation that would have increased the debt limit through September 30 as proposed by the Committee on Ways and Means. That measure was defeated on the floor on February 28, with Democrats voting 191–73 in favor and all but a few of the Republicans opposed. The loss occurred even though O'Neill and other House leaders had pledged their support for deficit reduction and appointed a task force chaired by Rep. Richard Gephardt, D-Mo., to personally lobby Democrats new to the chamber. Still, their failed first attempt did allow Democratic budget hawks to take public positions in favor of reducing the deficit, at little political cost to the party. Plenty of time remained before the deadline.

Three weeks later, on March 8, Democratic leaders asked rank-and-file members to support a second version of the bill that would have extended the debt limit until the end of September 1979. They also whipped in favor of the motion on the previous question on an accompanying rule. By this point, the spring deadline for increasing the limit was getting closer, so the attempt was for real. The rule vote, in particular, was critical because the procedure was structured to block consideration of a Republican amendment linking the debt hike to requirements for a balanced budget. To stave off party defections, the leadership pledged to schedule a separate vote on the balanced budget issue within a few months. Rep. James Jones, D-Okla., a prominent advocate of deficit reduction, claimed that Democratic leaders were able to keep the support of 20–30 western lawmakers with their pledge.[11] In the end, Democrats voted 200–54 in favor of the previous question, and it passed even though just one Republican member voted aye. With votes against the motion still trickling in, O'Neill slammed down the gavel as soon as the required time period for roll calls had ended, locking in a narrow win for his party.[12] The underlying bill temporarily raising the debt limit was then adopted by a similar margin.

That legislation only put off the matter until the fall, however, and the House was forced to revisit the issue a few months later. First, on September 20 the House considered and rejected a proposal that would have increased the limit to $885 billion through the end of July 1980. The vote largely was for show, however, and was not the target of a whip count. Seventy Democrats broke with the party on the roll call and it went down in defeat. Party conservatives were able to strike yet another public pose against federal debt, while leaving sufficient time for the chamber to revisit the matter and pass a debt limit hike before the default deadline. Sure enough, a mere five days later the Democratic leadership whipped House passage on a revised proposal to increase the debt limit to $879 billion through May 31, 1980, and that measure passed with Democrats voting 214 to 52 in favor and all but five Republicans voting no.

If we consider just the debt hike proposals that were the subject of whip activity, only the February vote resulted in a clear-cut loss for the majority leadership, and that loss is best viewed as a nonevent because of the significant amount of time available for reconsideration before the deadline.

As Table 6.9 indicates, the other three whipped questions produced majority party wins. On all four of the associated roll calls, cross-over support from the GOP was five votes or less, and the minimum necessary pickup for the majority leadership ranged from 4 to 68 votes. In each case, then, the partisan vote gathering that occurred between the initial whip check and the roll call was consequential to the outcome. Chalk this one up for Tip O'Neill and the majority whips.

The landmark Reagan tax cuts of 1981, in contrast, produced a very different outcome for the House Democratic leadership. Following Ronald Reagan's failed but bracing campaign for the GOP presidential nomination in 1976, national Republicans coalesced behind an ideological agenda of across-the-board reductions in income tax rates. Indeed, supply-side economics was one of the defining issues of the 1980 presidential campaign, which Reagan handily won against the incumbent Democrat, Jimmy Carter. The passage of the core elements of the Reagan economic plan in 1981 was a signal achievement of his first term, helped define the essential differences between the two parties for decades to come, and in the short run fueled large increases in the federal budget deficit. Most of the major House votes were whipped by both party leaderships. Archival evidence for the minority Republicans is unavailable for these years. But as Table 6.9 shows, in 1981 the majority Democrats whipped the budget resolution backed by their party; the budget substitute proposed by GOP leaders; the rule and passage for the reconciliation measure that implemented Reagan's spending cuts; and the rule and Republican substitute for the measure that implemented the tax reductions. For the most part, even though Republicans were the partisan minority within the House, the GOP prevailed across the board. The essential elements of their success were apparent during House consideration of the tax cut package.

The critical action occurred on July 29, 1981, when the House voted to adopt a substitute amendment reducing individual tax rates by 25 percent over three years.[13] The proposal was the subject of extensive whipping by the Democratic leadership. On July 23, 1981, just six days prior to floor action, Majority Whip Thomas Foley, D-Wash., contacted the party zone representatives and directed them to conduct an attendance check for the following week and to poll their members on two questions: (1) "Will you support the rule as reported by the House Rules Committee?" (2) "Will you oppose the Republican substitute or block of amendments?"[14] Two days earlier, the Ways and Means Committee had reported a Democratic alternative to the Reagan-backed bill that would have provided $627 billion in tax relief as compared to the $730 billion price tag for the White

House initiative. To secure the support of party conservatives, Democratic leaders also added to their legislation sweeteners for the oil industry. Republicans responded by incorporating similar special interest provisions into their measure, which they planned to offer as a substitute for the Democratic legislation. The Reagan/GOP leadership vehicle quickly became known as the Conable-Hance substitute, after Barber Conable, R-N.Y., ranking Republican on the Ways and Means Committee, and Democrat Kent Hance, D-Tex., who was working across party lines with the Republicans.

The rule provided for consideration of both party packages, and thus passed by a large bipartisan majority. Instead, the key vote occurred on the GOP substitute, which aimed to reduce individual tax rates by 25 percent and provide for a range of business and investment tax credits. As the vote on the dueling party packages neared, the debate resembled a bidding war between the parties, but the magnitude of the cuts endorsed on both sides of the partisan aisle was an indicator of the extent to which the tax cut debate had shifted in the GOP direction. As Table 6.9 shows, the Democratic whip count indicated that 178 Democrats were supportive of the party position, only 7 were no or leaning that way, and one member was nonresponsive. Fifty-six members, however, were still undecided on what would prove to be one of the most important roll calls of the decade. Support for their party position on the GOP side of the aisle was nearly unanimous, with only James Jeffords, R-Vt., breaking ranks to vote with the Democrats. Indeed, GOP Whip Trent Lott and his top deputy, Rep. Tom Loeffler, R-Tex., spent most of their time lobbying sympathetic majority party members like Charles Stenholm, D-Tex., the titular head of the pivotal Boll Weevil Caucus of conservative Democrats.[15] As the table indicates, the minimum necessary pickup for House Democratic leaders to prevail over the Reagan administration was 38 votes, a significant but potentially manageable coalition-building challenge.

Still, after a week of furious lobbying by Democratic leaders and the White House, O'Neill and his colleagues only managed to pick up 16 votes, the White House carried the day, and the Reagan tax cuts were signed into law later in the year. The administration used a multi-pronged approach to rolling the majority leadership on the roll call, including extensive media buys in the districts of conservative Democrats.[16] Conservative interest groups also promised certain Democrats they would not oppose them in the 1982 midterms if they supported the president on the tax vote. Two days before the roll call, Reagan addressed the nation on television, urging the public to contact their representatives in support of the Conable-Hance substitute. Republican Whip Trent Lott commented, "I've got the best whip organization because Ronald Reagan is in it."[17] The president personally met with several dozen pivotal lawmakers. On July 24, Reagan spoke to the House Republican Conference to rally his troops in advance of the roll call.

The whip tally sheets indicate the softness in the Democratic coalition largely centered on southerners and members from districts where Reagan had performed particularly well during the 1980 campaign. Of the 65 southern Democrats who answered the party whip poll on the tax question, nearly half were undecided or opposed. Along those lines, mean support for Reagan in 1980 within the districts of "yes" responders was about 43 percent, while mean Reagan support across the districts of the undecided Democrats was 50 percent.

As Democratic leaders updated their poll results over the weekend before the vote, it became apparent that the undecideds were breaking toward the Republican position. The initial shifts across the first and second drafts of the count are instructive about the nature of the momentum. Of the initial "yes" responders, three Texans switched to opposition on round two: Kent Hance, Marvin Leath, and Charles Stenholm. The loss of Stenholm turned out to be critical. Of the initial undecideds, only three broke toward the leadership on draft two of the whip count and twelve mostly southerners shifted to "no" or "leaning no."

The hemorrhaging within the Democratic Caucus continued over the next few days. Consider the example of Charles Hatcher, a freshman moderate from an agricultural district in southwest Georgia. Hatcher's hold on his seat was tenuous. In 1982 he would survive a primary challenge with just 52 percent of the vote. A key concern of his constituents was maintaining the federal subsidy for peanuts, an important crop in the district. Although he responded as "undecided" on the whip count, Hatcher used his vote on the tax bill to leverage concessions from the administration for peanut farmers. As he commented at the time, "They were savvy enough to know that I would really appreciate [help on peanuts] and I'm smart enough to know that they would really appreciate my vote."[18] Hatcher voted for the Conable-Hance substitute and against his own leadership.

Indeed, whip counts reveal that 10 initial supporters of the leadership defected and voted with the Republicans. Eight were southerners, but also included was Dan Glickman of Kansas, who was inundated with 1,500 telephone calls about the issue in his Washington office following Reagan's speech.[19] Unlike Hatcher, Glickman did not extract any favors from the White House in exchange for his vote, but the Kansan was impressed by the grassroots support in his district for Reagan's proposal. Rep. William Boner of Tennessee switched positions after receiving a personal call from the president. "Assured him I will remember come election time," Reagan jotted down after that conversation.[20] Most important, 31 of the Democrats who were undecided at some point during the whip process ended up voting against their leaders. In the end, O'Neill's attempts to counter the Reagan tax agenda with a watered down alternative and appeals to party loyalty were swamped by the president's personal lobbying and his effective mobilization of constituent audiences important to Democratic members.

Energy

Energy issues provide still stronger evidence of efficacious whipping by both parties during period 2, especially for the majority Democrats. For each party, roughly half of the questions in the energy/environment category dealt with energy policy, and (for the items with sufficient response evidence) the coalition-building challenges are summarized in Table 6.10. Once again, Panel A is for the Democratic majority, while Panel B is for the Republican minority.[21] As the table indicates, most of the majority whipped questions in this issue area ended in wins for the Democrats. For four of the majority victories, the minimum necessary pickup was negative or zero, indicating that the party had the votes to prevail with its initial base of Y/LY supporters and cross-over support from the GOP. On these items, the vote-gathering challenge for the majority leadership during the floor endgame was not particularly daunting. But for other whipped items, large pickup challenges are apparent in the table, and there the outcomes are suggestive of meaningful whip activity. On the minority side of the aisle, the GOP leadership also was actively engaged. Indeed, the Democratic leadership pulled four of the minority whipped energy questions from the agenda, and it suffered an ambiguous loss on two more. In other words, while energy issues during period 2 are suggestive of whip efficacy, they are not suggestive of majority party dominance. The point is illustrated by House consideration of the Carter energy reform plan during 1977–78. Questions related to that landmark legislation are marked by an asterisk in the table.

President Jimmy Carter's initiative to reform US energy policy dominated the agenda of the 95th Congress (1977–78).[22] Indeed, more discrete whip activity occurred on energy reform than on any other bill included in the 50 years of archival evidence gathered for this book. In

TABLE 6.10. Coalition-building success, energy

Panel A: Majority Democrats							
Question	Y/LN	U	N/LN	Other	Rep support	Min nec pickup	Actual pickup
Wins							
Energy prev ques rule 1977*	210	22	16	40	5	–21	16
Energy ad hoc natural gas 1977*	141	63	29	55			
Energy subst natural gas 1977*	138	44	70	36	17	58	72
Energy ad hoc user taxes 1977*	114	85	28	61	9	87	98
Energy M to R 1977*	179	43	8	58	3	29	37
Jones Crude oil plowback amdt 1977*	131	69	54	34	15	65	77
Energy bill pass 1977*	219	23	27	19	13	–21	12
Natural Gas conference 1978*	128	64	57	36			
Energy package prev ques rule 1978*	184	23	72	7	8	15	15
Energy package rule 1978*	161	28	84	13			
Energy conservation pass 1979	180	48	22	26	32	0	51
Energy conservation conference 1979	179	35	18	42	71	–43	51
Energy discharge motion 1980	142	65	19	48	5	60	62
Major change							
Federal energy administration 1974	126	30	7	79	158	–92	69
Outer continental shelf as reported 1978	144	74	46	22	70	–22	77
Losses							
Gas tax ad hoc 1977*	77	61	97	53	2	133	–27
Howard gas tax amdt 1977*	65	60	123	40	6	140	11
Gas rationing 1979	93	86	56	40	7	103	59
Energy bill conference 1980	138	64	34	38	9	35	–16

Panel B: Minority Republicans							
Question	Y/LN	U	N/LN	Other	Dem support	Min nec pickup	Actual pickup
Majority wins							
President's oil plan 1975	92	27	18	8	56	67	19
President's revised oil plan 1975	107	17	12	9	71	31	11
Natural gas deregulation 1977*	121	13	8	3	72	21	6
Energy GOP subst 1977*	106	16	15	8	29	76	12
Natural gas separation 1978*	69	47	13	17	79	59	58

TABLE 6.10. (*Continued*)

Question	Y/LN	U	N/LN	Other	Dem support	Min nec pickup	Actual pickup
Panel B: Minority Republicans							
Pulled							
Debt/oil tax bill 1975	70	51	24	0			
Oil tariffs veto 1975	97	19	28	0			
Imported crude oil 1975	78	21	38	7			
Synthetic fuel as reported 1976	37	49	22	37			
Majority losses							
Synthetic pass 1976	52	37	29	27	111	30	29
Energy electric plant amdt 1977*	94	28	11	12	127	–12	36

*Part of House consideration of the Carter energy reform plan.

1977 alone, Carter spoke to the nation on television about energy reform on three occasions. Referencing rising energy costs and US dependence on foreign oil, he claimed that, "the energy crisis has not overwhelmed us, but it will if we do not act quickly."[23] On Capitol Hill, Speaker O'Neill likewise made adoption of some version of the Carter plan the central priority for his party. Mobilized against the plan, however, was the influential oil and gas lobby, which opposed more regulation. The automotive industry and other companies reliant on the availability of cheap energy likewise raised objections about portions of the Carter program. And because of the general importance of energy availability and pricing to the broader economy, a vast array of additional industries, from oil refineries to retail outlets, sought to influence aspects of the legislation. Conservation and environmental groups were also in the mix, as were individuals and organizations concerned about the implications of US dependence on foreign energy. The energy reform debate, in short, created complex cleavage lines that were multidimensional and overlapping. In December 1977, the Gallup organization found that 40 percent of Americans viewed the energy challenge as very serious, and another 42 percent characterized it as fairly serious.[24] Within the House, no districts were unaffected, and within most there was considerable disagreement about how to proceed. For Democratic leaders, the question was whether any substantively meaningful plan could muster the votes necessary to pass. Over the two-year fight on energy reform, House Democratic leaders whipped a dozen distinct questions, while the minority GOP whipped four.

During 1975–76, efforts to enact an energy bill had floundered in the House, largely because the decentralized committee system proved incapable of producing a coherent proposal that could win on the floor (Oppenheimer, 1980). As a result, early in 1977 Speaker O'Neill established a temporary Ad Hoc Committee on Energy and charged it with coordinating the activities of the standing committees with jurisdiction in the area. As part of its deliberations over the specific provisions produced by the standing committees, the ad hoc panel also accepted several amendments, which according to committee rules would require separate votes on the floor to be folded into the reform package.

In late July 1977, as floor action neared, Democratic leaders whipped seven questions, and within a week they followed up with several more. The first set of whipped items concerned the previous question on the rule, four likely amendments, and an expected GOP motion to recommit, as well as passage of the measure as reported by the ad hoc committee.[25] The whip questions for the week that followed included two more amendments (offered by Jones and Howard) and an updated count on final passage that took into account modifications that had occurred on the floor. For the most part, the majority leadership prevailed. The Democrats unambiguously won eight of the whipped items, and lost on two amendments.

Importantly, the majority party victories on energy reform often came in the face of significant pickup challenges for the leadership. Rep. James Jones, D-Okla., for example, offered a "plowback" amendment that would have reduced the tax burden on oil producers if they used the revenue to explore for additional resources. Members from oil producing states like Oklahoma and Louisiana strongly favored the proposal, while members from districts more oriented toward consumer interests tended to be opposed. Democratic leaders urged a "no" vote. Although the minimum necessary pickup as the vote neared was 65 members, the Democratic leadership secured 77 and prevailed.

The two amendments to raise the gasoline tax, in contrast, resulted in Democratic losses and GOP wins. In both cases, the table reveals, the majority leadership's base of support was under a hundred members and substantially less than the number of Democrats who answered as no or leaning no on the count. Another 60 or so Democrats were undecided, and cross-over support from Republicans was minimal. The gasoline tax proposals were unpopular across diverse factions of the Democratic Caucus—urban, rural, energy producers, and low-income consumers. As Massachusetts Democrat Paul Tsongas observed about the general unpopularity of gas taxes, "If you go out and talk to anybody in this country, they're not gonna say, 'Lay it on me baby.' "[26]

Throughout House consideration of the Carter energy plan, however, the pivotal floor fights concerned the natural gas provisions. In 1977, the ad hoc committee's amendment on natural gas was a compromise aimed at drawing support from members who favored some form of deregulation. Indeed, the panel's proposal had the support of a number of prominent Democrats from energy producing states, including Majority Leader Jim Wright of Texas. Still, pro-deregulation forces coalesced around a substitute amendment offered by Republicans that would have ended federal controls outright. Although the necessary pickup was substantial (87 votes) the Democrats won the floor fight in August. O'Neill and other Democratic leaders aggressively lobbied against the GOP substitute, with the Speaker himself closing debate on the floor as an indicator of the intensity of this commitment. After the decontrol substitute lost, the ad hoc committee amendment was accepted by voice vote. And following completion of the lengthy and heated amendment process, the legislation passed the House on August 5 by a 244-147 margin, largely along party lines. Only 13 Republicans voted with the Democrats, and 54 members of the majority party, mostly from producer areas, voted no on final passage.

After House passage, action on the energy package shifted to a House-Senate conference committee that was divided into multiple subconferences, each responsible for considering portions of the massive legislation. Over the next year, the conferees settled more than 1,400 differences between the House and Senate versions of the bill, but an impasse over the critical natural gas pricing section threatened to bring down the entire reform effort. After open meetings failed to produce progress, the Carter administration and Democratic congressional leaders orchestrated a series of closed-door private sessions between Energy Secretary James Schlesinger and selected members of the subconference panel. By conducting private sessions, the leadership believed, forging an agreement might be feasible amid opposition from a diverse coalition of pro-consumer liberals and lawmakers from producer states.[27]

Throughout, a key leader of the opposition was Democrat Toby Moffett of Connecticut. First elected as part of the Watergate Baby class of 1974, Moffett was former executive director of Connecticut Citizen Action Group, a pro-consumer lobbying organization. Within the House, he was a member of the energy subcommittee of the House Energy and Commerce Committee and a leading opponent to the deregulation of natural gas. Although he voted for initial House passage of the energy bill in 1977, he regularly broke with Democratic leaders over their efforts to forge a natural gas compromise. In April, Moffett engineered a test vote on the House floor aimed at blocking further private meetings about the natural gas impasse. He was joined in that effort by Rep. Robert Carr, D-Mich., who had authored a House rule at the beginning of the Congress requiring all conference deliberations be open unless the House votes otherwise.[28] Like Moffett, Carr was a Watergate Baby. He also generally opposed the deregulation of natural gas. But Carr's district was competitive between the parties and the automobile industry was a major employer. Whereas Moffett periodically answered "no" on natural gas whip counts and voted against the leadership, Carr was usually undecided. In the end, Carr's vote would prove pivotal to the outcome on energy reform.

Moffett's openness ploy was successful, but within a week a tentative agreement was struck among the conferees about the natural gas portion of the legislation, and the measure returned to the House floor in fall 1978 during the waning days of the 95th Congress. At this point, the key issue became procedural—whether or not to divide the package and consider the natural gas provisions separately from the remainder of the conference report. If the natural gas compromise was considered along with the other portions of the legislation, proponents believed it could pass. Considered separately, however, the likelihood of success was much lower. Democratic leaders favored one package and a single vote. Republicans wanted separate consideration and hoped to vote the natural gas compromise down.

The majority whipped the matter on October 4, 1978, asking for member positions on the previous question on the rule and on the rule, itself. The rule, of course, provided that the massive energy reform measure be considered as a single package, with the natural gas provisions included. Republicans had begun whipping against the strategy the week before, asking their members whether: (1) they would support an effort to bring down the proposed rule and thereby separate the package, and (2) they would then vote against the natural gas portions of the conference report.[29] The critical question turned out to be the previous question motion on the rule. Democratic leaders, the Carter administration, and pro-reform forces lobbied in favor of passage, while GOP leaders and producer interests lobbied against. Based on party whip counts, O'Neill believed that he could count on the support of 184 of his Democratic colleagues. Cross-partisan support from Republicans, he knew, would be minimal. Indeed, only 13 GOP members were initially listed as supporting the Democratic position on the Republican leadership's count, and on the roll call 8 of them voted with the majority.

The lobbying endgame on the matter continued right down to the wire, culminating in one of the most dramatic roll calls of the decade. The White House attempted to help convince wavering Democrats to support O'Neill on the rule but congressional liaison was never Jimmy Carter's strong suit and the vote-gathering burden primarily fell on House Democratic leaders. Thomas "Lud" Ashley, the Democratic chair of the Ad Hoc Committee on Energy, described his experience working with the president during the floor lobbying process.

> I called Carter on one occasion.... I said, "Mr. President,... I'm going to lose this natural gas bill unless I can get some guys to change their vote. And I have a list of ten people that we can work with but we got to get 'em and we got to get 'em today." He said, "It will be done. Thanks, Lud. Good-bye." So I went to Tip with the same list. I got back to my office and there was a call from the White House and it was the president. I said, "What is it, Mr. President?" He said, "There is a natural gas title that is being considered in the energy bill and I have got to have your vote on it." I said, "Does this sound familiar by any chance, Mr. President? For crissakes. I called you twenty-five minutes ago. How about crossing off the fellow at the top of the list and going from there? I think you got me."[30]

Fortunately for the Democrats, O'Neill and the whips were more effective. The day of the vote, as the roll call proceeded, the outcome clearly hung in the balance. With the roll call tied at 206-206 and time running out, the deciding vote was cast by Robert Carr, who earlier had answered as "undecided" on all of the relevant whip counts. On the floor, Moffett urged Carr to vote against the previous question motion and block the leadership strategy. But with O'Neill standing in the well of the House, watching him intently, Carr voted in favor of the motion, the Democrats prevailed on procedure, and the conference report was adopted.[31] By all accounts, the lobbying efforts of the House Democratic leadership were instrumental to the outcome.

Closing Observations

From the distributions of member positions and votes to the incidence of legislative modifications and the array of outcomes, the whip process of 1973–82 resembles that of 1955–72 in many ways. The context of partisan coalition building, however, was dramatically different. In period 1, House Democratic leaders often worked in conjunction with, or even subordinate to, the lobbying operations of co-partisans in the White House. During period 2, the majority leadership either faced a president of the opposite party, or had a Democrat in the White House (Jimmy Carter) who deferred extensively to them to build support for administration priorities. Whereas the majority leaderships of period 1 often confronted a caucus deeply divided along sectional lines, the majority parties of period 2 were larger, significantly more diverse, and much less predictable. On party priorities, member positions still varied by region, to be sure, but also along a myriad of crisscrossing cleavages rooted in a member's place in the institutional hierarchy, economic conditions at home, and a host of other factors. Such divisions also were apparent on the minority GOP side of the aisle, but were less severe.

Although there is significant issue-specific variation, the majority leadership generally prevailed during period 2. But the hallmark of a win was not some legislative deviation from centrist preferences toward the ideological viewpoints of most majority party members, which is the measure of party influence generally embraced by the cartel and conditional party government arguments. Instead, the central leadership challenge was whether any bill at all could muster majority support within the chamber, and for the most part Democratic leaders were up to the task. Indeed, the independent impact of the whip process—above and beyond other factors—was consequential precisely because the challenges confronting the majority were so large. Perhaps the main take-away from the 1970s whip process, then, is that weakness begets opportunity, which in turn can translate into consequential coalition building on the floor of the House.

SEVEN

The Turn to Partisanship, 1983–94

In November 1982, as a result of a weakening economy and the emergence of large budget deficits fostered by the sweeping tax cuts enacted the previous year, Democrats picked up 27 seats in the House. When the 98th Congress convened in January 1983, Tip O'Neill and other House leaders were committed to providing a more aggressive opposition to the Reagan White House and the GOP-controlled Senate. Indeed, the 98th Congress marked the beginning of a decade-long transition from the large, unwieldy House majorities of the 1970s to the more competitive, intensely polarized chambers of the mid-1990s and 2000s. The purpose of this chapter is to explore in greater depth the role of the House whips during this turn to partisanship during period 3, 1983–94. As was the case for the 1970s, relevant archival evidence is available for both the Democratic and Republican whips for portions of period 3, which facilitates our efforts to draw comparisons across the partisan aisle. As the House grew more polarized, you will see, the majority party became more successful on whipped questions. The end product, however, was not a form of party government in the House, but the reflection of evolving representational relationships at home as captured by the behavioral perspective on partisan coalition building.

Contextual Considerations

From 1983 until 1995, the last dozen years of the Democrats' four-decade stretch as the House majority party, the size of the Democratic Caucus continued to be relatively large by historical standards. The smallest was the 254 Democrats who organized the 99th Congress (1985–86), and the largest was the 269 that made up the partisan majority of the 98th (1983–84). Still, when the House convened in January 1983, the large Democratic majority reflected a diversity of constituencies. Figure 7.1 shows the incidence of constituency outliers by party, once again based on whether or not a member represented a district where the most recent presidential vote was closer to her own-party average or the average among members of the other party. As was the case in the previous chapter, because of the continuing political distinctiveness of the south the proportion of outlier districts is presented separately for that region.

Based on this measure, there is considerable stability over period 3 within both parties. Of the 180 to 190 Democrats not from southern states, the number of outlier districts declined from about 70 in 1983–84 to less than 50 in 1993–94. The number of southern Democrats in the House was in the 65 to 75 seat range throughout period 3, but the proportion from districts with presidential voting patterns closer to the GOP average roughly doubled over time. In other words, as southern voters increasingly came to identify with the GOP, for a time the southern presence in the House Democratic Caucus remained substantial, and the Democratic lawmakers most likely to confront significant cross pressure between the national party program and evolving district interests increasingly were from the party's southern and border state contingents. On the GOP side of the aisle, there were far fewer outlier districts, especially among the party's southern wing.

Once again, the prevalence of district outliers within the two party caucuses cannot fully capture certain broader changes in constituency-level polarization that occurred over the 1980s and early 1990s. While the likelihood that an individual member would represent a district that was out-of-step with her own party average may not have changed all that much, the districts represented by the typical Democrat and Republican grew substantially more distinct. In 1973–74, for example, the deviation between the two political parties in average district-level support for the most recent Democratic presidential candidate was less than 8 percent. By the 1980s, that difference had grown to more than 12 percent, and by the end of period 3 it approached 14 percent. As a result, for members

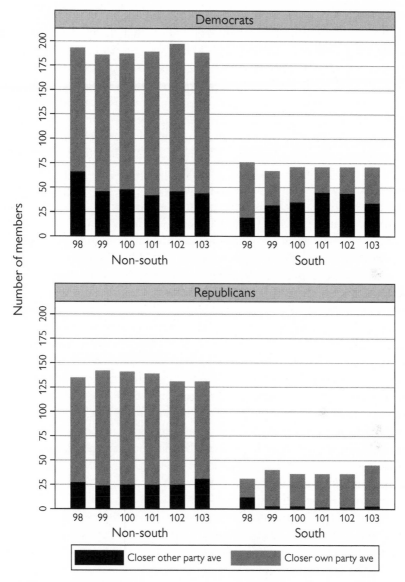

Figure 7.1. Partisan congruence of district-level presidential vote by congress, 1983–94

from districts that more closely resemble the constituencies represented by members on the other side of the aisle, the intensity of the cross pressure they experienced was greater during period 3, as the differences between the two parties at home and in Washington grew starker. The challenges of party coalition building may have become more structured and predictable than the shifting coalitional sands of period 2, but the magnitude of that challenge remained substantial.

Within the House, 1983–94 was not a period of major internal reform on Capitol Hill. Still, during period 3 the House leadership increasingly made use of highly restrictive procedures to structure chamber consideration of legislation, with consequences for the whips. Between 1981–82 and 1993–94, the use of restrictive amendment procedures roughly doubled from about 30 to 60 percent of all special rules (Smith 1989). As we have seen, there also were significant increases in the size and organizational complexity of the party whip networks during period 3. By the early 1990s, roughly a third of the House Democratic Caucus played some formal role in the party whip system. The GOP whip networks of period 3 also grew, but remained somewhat more streamlined than the majority networks.

For the majority Democrats, the weekly whip meetings, now scheduled like clockwork every Thursday morning the House was in session, evolved into an institutionalized, lively, and open-ended forum for airing member views. The whip meetings of period 1, you will recall, were conducted in a room in the majority whip's Capitol office suite. With a whip network largely comprised of just two dozen zone representatives, the meetings were small, private, and informal. As the size of the whip organizations expanded during period 2, the physical location of these sessions shifted to a larger meeting room located on the third floor of the Capitol. And by the end of period 3, the modern version of the old "sticky bun" fueled breakfasts of the Boggs era had fully emerged. Most important, there were scores more participants. Between 1983 and 1994, the number of whips for the Democrats jumped from 44 to 94, with the addition of multiple new layers of deputy and chief deputy whips; ad hoc whips representing the interests of African Americans, Latino lawmakers, women, southerners, and other factions; and dozens of interested and predominantly junior members of the Democratic Caucus. Now at the weekly whip breakfasts, top party leaders were arranged in a half-circle of chairs at the front of the room; the Speaker would make opening remarks; the majority leader would review the upcoming floor agenda; and the whip would highlight potential soft spots in the majority coalition on pending matters. The many dozens of zone and appointed whips would form an audience, pepper the leadership with questions, help clarify coalition-building challenges, and often simply vent.[1]

In the expanded majority whip process of period 3, initial head counts remained the primary responsibility of the elected zone representatives.

But refinements of the count, the persuasion of members—or what party leaders had come to call the "cleanup" process—became the purview of top leaders and bill-specific task forces. Speaker O'Neill had first relied on task forces in the late 1970s. On roughly 14 occasions during those years, O'Neill appointed Democrats to task forces charged with gathering votes on party priorities. During period 2, these groups had largely operated in tandem with the whips, and were not formally part of the whip network. In the 1980s, however, Majority Whip Thomas Foley fully integrated the leadership task forces into the whip system, and by the end of that decade the decision to whip a question was almost tantamount to the creation of an accompanying task force, largely comprised of appointed whips and Democratic members of the committee of jurisdiction. The task force members would work with the leadership to lobby potential defectors right up to the roll call on the floor.

Indeed, during major votes members of the whip operation often were positioned strategically in the well of the House, near all points of entry and exit on the Democratic side of the floor (located to the right of the center aisle), adjacent to electronic voting stations on the Democratic side, and even in the party cloakroom located at the rear of the chamber. During debates and votes of importance to the party, the whip participants positioned at these stations would speak with wavering members, offer information, and attempt to persuade them to vote with the leadership.[2] Potential defectors had to walk a leadership gauntlet before casting their votes. The basic division of labor that characterized the Democratic whip operations of period 3—zone whips conducting the initial counts, appointed bill-specific task forces working with the leadership to clean up the count and gather votes—was still in place two decades later during the 2000s.[3]

On the GOP side of the aisle, the whip networks also grew in size and organizational complexity during period 3, albeit at a slower pace befitting the party's minority status. In 1989, however, with the selection of Newt Gingrich as House Republican whip, steps were taken to invigorate the party network. Gingrich, in particular, sought to use the whips to enhance the minority's public relations efforts, and added multiple "strategy whips" to the GOP organization.[4] He also created an informal shadow whip system of Republicans with ties to Democrats for the purpose of lobbying members across the partisan aisle. The evolution of the House Republican whip system to its modern version would not be complete until the party assumed majority status, but like the Democrats, the GOP process also became more elaborate and active during period 3.

General Features

According to the best scholarship, the years of period 3 marked the emergence of activist party leaders in the US House (Rohde 1991, Sinclair 1995). Still, as Figure 7.1 shows, the potential for significant cross pressure remained within the home constituencies of members from both parties, especially the majority Democrats. Although the initial distribution of member viewpoints became more predictable, the majority leadership often lacked the votes necessary to prevail at the beginning of the whip process. Majority leadership success increased between periods 2 and 3, but much of that increase was concentrated in selected portions of the whipped agenda and legislative modifications aimed at building winning coalitions remained a key source of majority party success. During 1983–94, coalition building on the floor grew more overtly partisan, but the grasp of the whips remained tenuous and there was considerable counter balancing between the Democratic and Republican operations.

The Whipped Agenda

Along the lines of the treatments in previous chapters, Tables 7.1 and 7.2 summarize the incidence of whip activity across policy categories for the Democratic majorities and GOP minorities of period 3. For the Democrats, comprehensive evidence about what was whipped is available for 1983–86, all of 1989, and from September 1991 until the end of the 103rd Congress in fall 1994. For the GOP, unfortunately, archival evidence is unavailable for Trent Lott's many years as whip, 1981–88. For this reason, information about the whipped agendas of the Republicans during period 3 begins in 1989 and continues through early 1994, when reliable archival evidence for that party once again becomes unavailable. Cross-partisan comparisons would be enhanced if the years for which evidence was available for the two parties perfectly aligned. Still, the information we do have allows us to draw some noteworthy inferences. As with previous chapters, the allocation of whip activity is shown in two ways in Tables 7.1 and 7.2— the percentage of overall whip activity falling in each policy category, and the proportion of votes that occurred within each category that were subject to whip action.

For the Democratic majority, economic matters continued to be a whip priority. Energy and environmental issues, in contrast, were much less significant to the whips of period 3 than had been the case during period 2 when energy prices were a top domestic policy concern. The prevalence of whipped appropriations questions increased markedly during 1983–94. While such questions were seldom targeted during periods 1 and 2, nearly 20 percent of the whipped items in period 3 concerned the annual spending process. As noted in Chapter 3, prior to the 1980s the 13 spending bills that together funded the discretionary portions of the federal budget were generally completed on time in a

TABLE 7.1. Majority party, distribution of whip attention by issue area, 1983–94

Issue area	% Whipped questions— 1983–94	% Whipped questions— All periods	% Votes whipped— 1983–94*	% Votes whipped— All periods*
Congress/Gov ops	13.3	14.1	6.7	5.7
Defense	10.3	4.4	9.1	5.3
Foreign Policy	10.3	7.0	9.3	7.1
Economy	20.9	18.4	16.0	12.1
Trade	2.3	2.9	8.6	9.0
Energy/Environment	1.0	6.4	1.3	4.9
Civil rights	1.7	1.7	7.7	6.1
Social welfare	3.0	4.7	6.6	8.1
Health	1.7	2.9	4.9	12.4
Education	2.3	3.0	9.5	8.9
Labor/Consumer	8.0	7.0	26.8	15.9
Appropriations	18.3	19.4	5.4	5.9
Other	7.0	8.2	6.4	5.7

*Only nonunanimous votes used.

TABLE 7.2. Minority party, distribution of whip attention by issue area, 1989–93

Issue area	% Whipped questions— 1989–93	% Whipped questions— All periods	% Votes whipped— 1989–93*	% Votes whipped— All periods*
Congress/Gov ops	4.8	8.8	2.7	3.3
Defense	11.5	9.1	13.5	9.9
Foreign policy	5.7	6.4	9.2	4.4
Economy	25.8	20.9	15.4	7.1
Trade	3.8	2.7	16.7	10.1
Energy/Environment	6.2	12.4	5.8	3.9
Civil rights	6.7	5.2	16.7	10.0
Social welfare	5.3	4.2	14.8	6.2
Health	1.4	1.8	6.5	4.9
Education	1.4	1.8	7.1	5.2
Labor/Consumer	7.2	8.5	21.4	13.3
Appropriations	13.4	10.6	4.1	2.6
Other	6.7	7.6	4.7	2.8

*Only nonunanimous votes used.

bipartisan fashion. Key decisions were usually made within the subcommittee of the full appropriations panel that had jurisdiction. In the 1980s, as federal deficits swelled and congressional decision making became more partisan, all of this began to change. The new budget process established by the 1974 Budget Act was a contributing factor. By shifting fiscal responsibilities to the House and Senate Budget Committees, the 1974 reforms created incentives for appropriators to view themselves primarily as claimants for their constituents, rather than as guardians of the treasury (Schick 1980). Large deficits, partisan infighting, and enhanced parochialism within the committee combined to make successful passage of the freestanding spending measures more difficult. Within both parties, the whips began to regularly target questions related to appropriations, including supplementals and stop-gap continuing resolutions necessary to keep the government running.

On the GOP side of the aisle, the prominence of economic management issues on the whipped agenda increased substantially during period 3. In part, this may reflect the temporal skew in the available evidence. During 1989–93, efforts to reduce the federal budget deficit often dominated congressional politics, and intra-party disagreements within the House GOP during the Bush administration marked a critical juncture in party strategy. As Table 7.2 shows, appropriations also were a significant whip target for the Republican minority, but not to the same extent as for the majority Democrats. The difference reflects the importance of efficient management of the annual spending process to the public reputation of the majority party.

The issue emphasis of the whips appears somewhat different if we restrict our attention to major legislation. For appropriations measures associated with at least one *CQ* key vote, there is a significant increase in whip activity compared to analogous questions in periods 1 and 2. When the focus is on major legislation, defense, foreign policy, and the economy also stand out. During the Reagan and Bush years, the GOP administrations significantly increased defense spending and adopted a more aggressive posture toward the Soviet Union. As a result, foreign affairs and national security became regular partisan flashpoints and ripe targets for whip activity. Key votes about the economy and budget likewise remained an important feature of the whipped agendas of period 3. Reagan's 1981 tax cuts and the contemporaneous defense buildup helped create burgeoning budget deficits, which in turn led to significant concerns about deficits among important constituent audiences in both parties. We will revisit these policy areas in the case studies that close this chapter.

Member Loyalty

Recall that among majority Democrats both the prevalence of Y/LY responders on counts and the levels of party support on associated roll calls stepped up across periods 2 and 3. While the portion of Democrats answering as "yes" or "leaning yes" during periods 1 and 2 was about 59 percent, the analogous figure during period 3 was 69 percent, and there were compensating declines for the other response types. Within each whip response category, the incidence of pro-leadership votes also increased in period 3 relative to earlier decades. Still, these aggregate changes mask significant variance across constituency and member factors. Tables 7.3 and 7.4 (for the majority and minority parties, respectively) summarize the distribution of member responses during the whip process across the six district and personal characteristics that structured our discussions in Chapters 5 and 6. Tables 7.5 and 7.6 likewise report the percentage of pro-leadership votes across these same characteristics, once again separated by party.

Although the ongoing nationalization of party politics stepped up in period 3, the political distinctiveness of the south and border areas

TABLE 7.3. Majority party, distribution of whip responses, selected district and member characteristics, 1983–94

		Y/LY	U	N/LN	Other
Region	NE	78.2	10.7	4.6	6.6
	MW/Plains	73.6	13.2	6.9	6.3
	South	54.3	24.1	13.8	7.8
	Border	60.0	23.3	9.1	7.7
	West	79.6	9.7	5.3	5.5
District-level pres vote	Closer to R ave	59.6	22.0	12.1	6.3
	Closer to D ave	73.7	13.0	6.3	7.0
Committee of Jurisdiction	On	75.2	11.9	7.6	5.3
	Off	68.2	16.6	8.3	7.0
Seniority	Fresh	71.4	15.6	7.9	5.1
	2/5 terms	68.1	16.9	9.0	6.1
	>5 terms	69.5	15.0	7.4	8.0
Extended leadership	Yes	71.4	14.6	6.3	7.8
	No	68.5	16.3	8.8	6.4
Whip network	Yes	74.1	13.3	6.6	6.1
	No	66.9	17.1	8.9	7.1

TABLE 7.4. Minority party, distribution of whip responses, selected district and member characteristics, 1989–93

		Y/LY	U	N/LN	Other
	NE	50.5	19.2	22.5	7.9
	MW/Plains	68.2	15.1	10.5	6.2
Region	South	72.1	12.0	9.5	6.4
	Border	59.1	20.7	10.7	9.5
	West	73.5	10.4	10.1	6.1
District-level	Closer to D ave	53.8	18.3	20.2	7.7
pres vote	Closer to R ave	68.0	13.9	11.5	6.6
Committee of	On	69.0	12.1	12.1	6.9
jurisdiction	Off	65.2	15.0	13.1	6.8
	Fresh	65.9	16.3	12.6	5.2
Seniority	2/5 terms	68.1	12.8	13.1	5.9
	>5 terms	62.5	16.4	12.7	8.4
Extended	Yes	66.3	14.9	11.9	7.0
leadership	No	65.2	14.3	14.0	6.6
Whip network	Yes	73.2	10.9	11.8	4.2
	No	63.6	15.6	13.2	7.5

TABLE 7.5. Majority party, leadership support on votes by whip category, selected district and member characteristics, 1983–94

		Y/LY	U	N/LN	Other
	NE	96.7	78.4	37.6	85.8
	MW/Plains	95.9	70.0	30.0	85.5
Region	South	91.9	63.0	26.0	75.3
	Border	94.0	66.3	32.5	77.5
	West	96.9	76.9	35.4	86.4
District-level	Closer to R ave	93.0	63.2	26.1	72.5
pres vote	Closer to D ave	96.2	73.0	33.5	85.9
Committee of	On	96.8	69.4	31.1	84.6
jurisdiction	Off	95.0	68.6	29.7	81.3
	Fresh	95.4	72.8	31.6	83.5
Seniority	2/5 terms	94.9	65.6	28.9	80.0
	>5 terms	95.6	70.7	30.7	82.7
Extended	Yes	96.2	73.3	32.4	84.6
leadership	No	95.0	67.4	29.4	80.6
Whip network	Yes	96.5	72.9	33.2	83.4
	No	94.6	67.1	28.8	81.0

TABLE 7.6. Minority party, leadership support on votes by whip category, selected district and member characteristics, 1989–93

		Y/LY	U	N/LN	Other
Region	NE	93.0	56.4	19.1	64.8
	MW/Plains	94.0	66.6	30.2	69.2
	South	96.4	74.9	24.6	84.4
	Border	95.3	73.2	12.4	77.0
	West	95.2	72.9	30.3	80.3
District-level pres vote	Closer to D ave	93.4	54.2	17.6	63.6
	Closer to R ave	95.0	69.7	26.1	77.1
Committee of jurisdiction	On	95.5	61.7	22.5	86.0
	Off	94.7	67.2	24.2	72.6
Seniority	Fresh	94.5	62.7	22.3	74.3
	2/5 terms	94.7	68.5	23.5	74.6
	>5 terms	95.1	65.6	25.1	74.8
Extended leadership	Yes	95.5	69.2	23.8	72.6
	No	94.0	63.3	24.1	76.9
Whip network	Yes	95.8	72.2	23.6	75.7
	No	94.4	65.4	24.1	74.5

continued. As you can see, southern Democrats are significantly less likely to answer as "yes" or "leaning yes" during the whip process, and significantly more likely to be undecided or opposed. Overall, party support levels were higher across all regions, and the differences between the south and border areas, on the one hand, and regions like the northeast, on the other, were somewhat attenuated relative to the 1970s. But the Democrat's southern challenge in the coalition-building game remained. When we consider presidential voting patterns at the congressional district level, the differences between mainstream and outlier districts are if anything somewhat larger in period 3. For example, the Y/LY responses among members representing outlier districts are now about 14 percentage points lower than is the case for lawmakers from mainstream constituencies.

When our attention turns to personal characteristics of lawmakers, members of the committee of jurisdiction are more likely to be leadership supporters in 1983–94, but the differences relative to non-committee members are less significant than they were in period 2. Chamber seniority, which mattered a lot in the 1950s and 1960s, but not so much in period 2, is mostly a nonfactor for period 3. And the results for membership in the extended leadership and the party whip network are similar to the findings for period 2, even though the Democratic networks grew significantly in size and organizational complexity during the 1980s and early 1990s. Small differences in party support on whip counts are now apparent for members of the extended leadership, but the effect is small.

With regard to leadership support on votes, the observable patterns from period 2 are mostly apparent here, as well. The constituency and member-specific characteristics associated with enhanced leadership support at the whip stage are also connected with heightened loyalty on votes. But notice that the effects of district-level presidential voting, in particular, are stronger in period 3 for the majority Democrats than had been the case in period 2. While pro-leadership votes for the undecided or N/LN categories were about 5 percent lower for outlier districts in period 2, Table 7.5 indicates that the difference is nearly twice that magnitude in period 3. Not surprisingly, the impact of a district's partisan-electoral leanings on party support during the floor endgame increased during the 1980s and early 1990s.

For the minority GOP, the party's problems in the northeast, and to some extent the border states, continued in period 3. While the differences in Y/LY responses between the northeast and the south had been roughly 30 percentage points in period 2, that difference fell to a little over 20 percent in period 3. But the regional gap remained substantial, both during the whip process and on the associated roll calls. As was the case for the majority Democrats, the relationship between district-level presidential voting and leadership support stayed the same or increased for the GOP minorities of period 3. Interestingly, as was the case in period 2, the differences in leadership support between participants in the party whip network and other members were much more significant on the GOP side of the aisle during period 3. Recall that the GOP whips were all appointed by the centralized party leadership, and pro-leadership sentiments were thus more apparent among the Republican whips. There also may have been greater expectations that they toe the party line.

Although heightened polarization at the constituency level was associated with elevated levels of leadership support during the whip and roll call stages, the outcomes of the whip process were generally in play. For the majority Democrats, a party size of 250-270 members and Y/LY proportions as high as 75 percent still produced initial intra-party support of fewer than 200 votes, which is substantially less than the number necessary to prevail on contested roll calls on the floor. Again, the coalition-building challenges for the majority leadership were more predictable during period 3, but still significant.

Outcomes

As was the case for leadership support at the individual member level, the aggregate incidence of majority party wins during the whip process also stepped up across periods 2 and 3. While the incidence of clear-cut majority party victories was about 65 percent during periods 1 and 2, in period 3 it reached nearly 80 percent. For items whipped by the Republican minority, the prevalence of majority party victories likewise increased from about 55 percent during period 2 to nearly 77 percent in period 3. Given the continued intra-party heterogeneity at the constituency level, and the improved but still problematic levels of initial leadership support at the start of the whip stage, why were the majority whips of period 3 so successful? To begin addressing the question, Tables 7.7 and 7.8 break down the distribution of whip outcomes by policy area.

TABLE 7.7. Majority party, whipped outcomes by issue area, 1983–94

Issue area	Majority win	Major change	Pull	Majority loss
Congress/Gov ops	26	1	4	6
	(70.3)	(2.7)	(10.8)	(16.2)
Defense	20	0	1	4
	(80.0)		(4.0)	(16.0)
Foreign policy	17	3	1	4
	(68.0)	(12.0)	(4.0)	(16.0)
Economy	46	4	3	3
	(82.1)	(7.1)	(5.4)	(5.4)
Trade	5	0	0	1
	(83.3)			(16.7)
Energy/Environment	2	0	0	1
	(66.7)			(33.3)
Civil rights	3	0	1	1
	(60.0)		(20.0)	(20.0)
Social welfare	8	1	0	0
	(88.9)	(11.1)		
Health	3	0	1	0
	(75.0)		(25.0)	
Education	6	0	0	0
	(100.0)			
Labor/Consumer	16	0	3	3
	(72.7)		(13.6)	(13.6)
Appropriations	47	0	2	1
	(94.0)		(4.0)	(2.0)
Other	15	1	0	4
	(75.0)	(5.0)		(20.0)

Note: Cell entries are the number of items for the relevant issue-outcome category, with percentages by issue in parentheses.

For the majority Democrats, party wins are commonplace for economic management issues, just as they were in period 2. For the increased number of whipped items in the defense and foreign policy realms, the incidence of majority party wins is also impressive. Also, note the high Democratic win rates on appropriations questions, which by 1983–94 were emerging as regular leadership priorities on the floor. On appropriations, the omnibus character of the legislation, its overt distributive content, and the importance of the policy area for the core management responsibilities of the majority party provided leaders with considerable leverage. Appropriations bills can encompass thousands of discrete spending accounts that direct federal largesse to every congressional constituency in the nation. The context is ideal for splitting differences, targeting additional funds to pivotal members, and otherwise cutting the deals necessary to construct floor majorities. But perhaps the most significant reason for the Democratic

TABLE 7.8. Minority party, whipped outcomes by issue area, 1989–93

Issue area	Majority win	Major change	Pull	Majority loss
Congress/Gov ops	5 (71.4)	0	1 (14.3)	1 (14.3)
Defense	9 (69.2)	1 (7.7)	0	3 (23.1)
Foreign policy	11 (91.7)	0	0	1 (8.3)
Economy	29 (80.6)	2 (5.6)	0	5 (13.9)
Trade	3 (75.0)	0	0	1 (25.0)
Energy/Environment	3 (75.0)	0	0	1 (25.0)
Civil rights	5 (55.6)	2 (22.2)	2 (22.2)	0
Social welfare	7 (77.8)	1 (11.1)	0	1 (11.1)
Health	1 (100.0)	0	0	0
Education	2 (66.7)	0	1 (33.3)	0
Labor/Consumer	11 (84.6)	0	2 (15.4)	0
Appropriations	14 (77.8)	0	1 (5.6)	3 (16.7)
Other	6 (66.7)	0	1 (11.1)	2 (22.2)

Note: Cell entries are the number of items for the relevant issue-outcome category, with percentages by issue in parentheses.

majority's high win rate on appropriations was the simple expectation that the party organizing the chamber effectively manage the annual budget and spending process, and thereby keep the day-to-day wheels of government rolling. For items whipped by the minority GOP, Table 7.8 indicates that the majority party win rates were somewhat lower, but still largely consistent with the aforementioned patterns. Further perspective on whip success and failure in period 3 can be gained by focusing on two broad policy areas where the whips were highly active and the outcomes varied: foreign affairs and (once again) the economy.

Foreign Policy and Intelligence

As summarized in the outcome tables for this chapter, the whips were active on foreign policy issues throughout the 1980s and early 1990s. The majority Democrats, for example, whipped 25 foreign policy questions during that period and won nearly 70 percent. Yet, major modifications were required on three items, one had to be pulled from the agenda, and four resulted in unambiguous losses. Moreover, foreign policy making in the 1980s often took the form of highly partisan debates about the provision of covert assistance to governments and groups in Central America, and based on our issue categories such questions are often included under "defense." As a result, to gauge when and why the whips were efficacious on foreign affairs during period 3, it helps to consider foreign policy and intelligence questions together, itemized by question. This information is provided in panels A (for the majority Democrats) and B (for the minority GOP) of Table 7.9.[5]

For foreign policy and intelligence items with the necessary archival evidence, the table summarizes member positions during the whip process, crossover support from the other party on the vote (assuming one occurred), and the necessary and actual pickups at the roll call stage.[6] If we consider the majority party wins, about half were associated with negative pickup requirements, that is, the leadership's base of Y/LN supporters plus crossover votes from the GOP was enough to win. In these cases, the majority's coalition-building challenges were attenuated by the relatively firm support in place fairly early in the floor endgame. Still, a number of significant questions, especially items about the Reagan administration's policy toward the Nicaraguan "Contras," featured pickup requirements that were positive and substantial, and the majority leadership still prevailed.

TABLE 7.9. Coalition-building success, foreign policy and intelligence

	Panel A. Majority Democrats						
Question	Y/LY	U	N/LN	Other	Rep support	Min nec pickup	Actual pickup
Win							
Nuclear freeze rule 1983	226	22	8	9	22	−38	22
Intelligence authorization 1983*	159	77	20	10	18	35	51
Intelligence authorization "Contras" 1983*	201	19	46	0	18	−8	8
El Salvador 1984	219	30	11	6			
"Contra" funding resolution*	200	31	31	5	24	−14	17
Intelligence authorization "Contras" 1984*	208	22	25	11			
Nicaraguan "Contras" 1985*	195	19	35	2	40	−21	13
Nuclear testing pass 1986	179	26	11	36	49	−19	40
Nuclear testing subst 1986	156	46	12	36	37	15	65
Nicaraguan "Contras" 1986*	187	40	25	0	16	13	19
"Contras" supplemental 1986*	174	25	37	15	1	36	37
Anti-apartheid 1986	204	19	5	23			
SALT II 1986	200	33	7	11	37	−36	19
Military approps prev ques & rule 1986*	166	38	13	34	153	−105	−40
Nicaraguan "Contras" 1989*	132	32	43	52	156	−78	21
Foreign aid amdt 1989	133	89	21	13	167	−90	106
Foreign aid pass 1989	123	61	19	53	116	−31	75
October surprise subst 1991	196	27	3	41	0	8	53
October surprise pass 1991	215	40	10	2	0	−10	2
Nuclear testing amdt 1992	178	36	20	33	24	1	35
Major change							
Nuclear freeze pass 1983	202	21	38	5	60	−48	16

TABLE 7.9. (*Continued*)

			Panel A. Majority Democrats				
Question	Y/LY	U	N/LN	Other	Rep support	Min nec pickup	Actual pickup
IMF 1983	107	87	52	20	72	36	38
Foreign assistance 1985	94	119	23	16			
Pull							
Foreign assistance 1993	169	46	34	8			
Loss							
Foreign assistance subst 1984	190	44	29	4	8	12	10
Nicaraguan "Contras" subst 1986*	196	29	26	0	11	8	2
Angola amdt 1986	194	35	20	2	7	7	−15
Foreign assistance 1991	173	40	51	2	28	10	−42

			Panel B. Minority Republicans				
Question	Y/LY	U	N/LN	Other	Dem support	Min nec pickup	Actual pickup
Majority win							
FSX agreement 1989	44	67	41	22	211	−45	65
FSX pass 1989	99	39	31	6	38	68	31
FSX amdt 1989	121	32	20	2	26	62	8
Foreign assistance 1989	91	40	36	8	198	−81	25
El Salvador 1990	132	27	11	6	24	54	19
Angola 1990	145	22	4	5	52	10	9
Foreign assistance 1993	64	26	42	44			
Majority loss							
Foreign assistance amdt 1989	150	16	7	2	69	−10	14

*Part of House consideration of "Contra" aid.

Here, it helps to spotlight the questions that dealt with US support for the Contras, which are marked by an asterisk in the table. Early in his first term, President Reagan made American assistance to the right-wing guerilla insurrection against the socialist "Sandinista" government of Nicaragua a major foreign policy priority for the administration. There was considerable skepticism on Capitol Hill, however, and in 1982 Congress adopted the "Boland Amendment," prohibiting direct US military action aimed at overthrowing the Sandinistas or instigating armed conflict between Nicaragua and Honduras. In April 1983, five members of the House Intelligence Committee traveled to the region to investigate reports that US personnel were in violation of the Boland proviso. Upon their return, the Democratic members of the delegation alleged that they had uncovered such evidence, but the Republicans on the trip argued that no violations were occurring.[7] Later that month, Reagan spoke to a joint session of Congress and requested $600 million in assistance for anti-communist forces in Central America. In the House, Democratic leaders responded by drafting legislation aimed at ending covert US involvement in Nicaragua. The primary author of the measure was Edward Boland, D-Mass., Speaker O'Neill's closest personal friend in the chamber and a former roommate.[8] Boland's initiative produced the first legislative skirmish in what would become a multiyear effort during period 3 by House Democratic leaders to alter US foreign policy in Central America.

On July 19, Majority Whip Thomas Foley instructed the zone whips for the party to poll their members, asking if they would support Boland's Nicaragua bill as reported by the Intelligence and Foreign Affairs Committees. Within the next few days, 159 Democrats reported as yes or leaning yes. If we factor in the 18 GOP votes that eventually would be cast in favor of the measure, that still left a pickup requirement of 35 additional votes if the majority leadership was to prevail on the roll call. When the vote occurred the following week, O'Neill and the rest of the leadership picked up 51 additional votes from within the Democratic Caucus and won on the floor. The outcome was a major blow to administration plans for the region. What was behind this swing toward the leadership? On the aforementioned whip count, mean district support for Reagan in 1980 was higher the further a response category was from "yes," suggesting that some of the undecideds confronted party-constituency cross pressure on the matter. Similarly, district population in the military also increased as we move from "yes" to "undecided" to "no."[9] On the vote, the vast majority of Y/LY responders stayed with the party and most members in the N/LN column voted no. But through intensive member-to-member lobbying, O'Neill was able to pick up about two-thirds of the initially undecided.

For the remainder of the Reagan administration, the House revisited Contra aid every year via the intelligence reauthorization bill or on related appropriations measures. The basic politics of the issue remained the same. The White House sought to increase and broaden US assistance to anti-Sandinista forces; Democratic leaders wanted to limit overall aid and end or severely restrict covert operations; and Democrats from largely southern districts or constituencies with a significant military presence were caught in the crossfire. As Table 7.9 shows, major votes on Contra aid occurred later in 1983, and during 1984 and 1985, and in each case the pickup requirements were negative or the party prevailed without a vote. Legislative action on the matter in 1986, however, took a dramatically different turn. In February 1986, Reagan attempted "an all or nothing roll of the dice" and submitted a request to Congress for $100 million in assistance for the Contras and an end to all restrictions on US involvement in Nicaragua.[10] The request was viewed as an enormous risk to the administration's prestige because of the almost-certain opposition in the House. The White House did take some steps to dampen opposition in the chamber—if the legislation was enacted, for instance, Reagan promised to open direct discussions with the Sandinistas. Still, the initiative constituted a direct challenge to past legislative actions aimed at restricting US involvement in the region.

Although moderates from both parties urged the White House to seek middle ground on the matter, the intensity of the rhetoric on both sides ratcheted up as the March 20 roll call neared. In a March 5 meeting with Jewish leaders, Reagan claimed that Democrats in Congress were "courting disaster.... If we don't want to see the map of Central America covered in a sea of red, eventually lapping to our own borders, we must act now."[11] Speaker O'Neill personally lobbied Democrats to vote against the Reagan initiative. With the assistance of an outside coalition of conservative interest groups, the administration attempted to counter the leadership pressure. In the week leading up to the March 20 showdown on the House floor, Reagan worked full time on the issue and made daily speeches in support of his request. Several dozen House members received personal telephone calls from the president. One advocacy group, called "Citizens for Reagan," placed newspaper advertisements in the district of Buddy McKay, Fla., who unknown to the Republicans reported in favor of the leadership position throughout the whip process. The ads were titled, "Whose Buddy is He?.... Your Congressman & Communist Nicaragua."[12]

The strategic challenge confronting the majority leadership in 1986 is captured in the table. Compared to the 1983 roll call, the leadership's base of support was nearly 30 members larger, and the minimum necessary pickup was just 13 votes. Far fewer members were undecided because the issue was no longer new and lawmakers had developed positions. As was the case in 1983, the undecideds disproportionately were party moderates representing centrist, often rural constituencies. The average support for Reagan in the 1984 elections within their districts was about 60 percent, as opposed to a mean district support for Reagan of just over 50 percent in the districts of "yes" responders on the Democratic whip count. Compared to the leadership supporters, the military presence in the districts of undecided members also was substantially larger. Although the pickup requirements were relatively manageable, once again the intensity and effectiveness of Reagan's personal lobbying and his appeals for public support kept the outcome in play.[13] As is typical, almost all of the Y/LY responders voted with the leadership and all but one of the members who were N/LN on the poll voted with the administration. Compared with Contra aid in 1983, O'Neill was less successful in securing the support of undecided members, who split evenly between the Democratic and GOP sides on the roll call. Still, the additional support from the undecideds was sufficient for the majority party to carry the day and Reagan lost by just seven votes. Pivotal to the outcome was the personal lobbying of the Speaker and a pledge by the leadership to permit the consideration of middle-ground proposals for Contra aid the next month during House consideration of a supplemental appropriations bill. Reagan, for his part, publicly vowed to continue his efforts on behalf of insurgent forces in Nicaragua.

In April, the Democratic leadership allowed Dave McCurdy, D-Okla., to offer a scaled back version of Reagan's request as an amendment to the supplemental appropriations measure. House Republicans, however, caught the leadership by surprise by casting strategic votes in favor of a more liberal substitute offered by Lee Hamilton, D-Ind., that would have withheld all aid to the Contras.[14] The minority was concerned that McCurdy's amendment might pass, imperiling House adoption of the full Reagan request sometime down the line. Indeed, on April 14, the majority leadership whipped a question about whether members would support the McCurdy amendment, premised on the defeat of the Hamilton proposal. Over one hundred and seventy had been yes or leaning that way, so the prospects for a McCurdy win were strong.[15] With progressive Democrats also supporting the Hamilton substitute for substantive reasons, it won a majority, precluding a separate vote on the McCurdy amendment. Clearly outmaneuvered, the majority leadership decided not to consider Contra aid at all on the supplemental spending bill. Democratic Whip Foley claimed at the time that the minority had committed "parliamentary suicide."[16] But Republican leaders and the White House preferred to work for another direct vote on the Reagan request later in the year.

They got their vote in July. By early summer, most observers believed that a majority of the House (Republicans and conservative Democrats) supported some form of aid to the Contras. At issue were the level of assistance and whether arms would be included. As a result of pressure from moderate and conservative Democrats, O'Neill agreed to schedule another roll call on Reagan's request during chamber consideration of the military construction appropriations bill. The coalition-building challenges for the leadership on this measure are captured in Table 7.9, where the question is listed among the majority party losses. Only 11 Republican centrists would vote with the Democrats in opposition to Reagan's proposal, so the majority whips needed the support of 204 Democrats to win on the floor. The party base on the whip count was 196 votes, necessitating that they pick up an additional 8 before the roll call. They only managed to pick up 2 and the Reagan position prevailed. Coming just three months after the administration's March defeat on Contra aid, the outcome was a remarkable reversal and a significant personal defeat for Speaker O'Neill and Majority Leader Jim Wright, D-Tex.

What happened? The Democratic leadership used all the resources available to it in whipping against the GOP plan, which was offered as a floor amendment by Mickey Edwards, R-Okla.[17] At O'Neill's insistence, the Rules Committee drafted a "self-executing" rule that upon adoption automatically incorporated McCurdy's proposal into the legislation to be considered on the floor. The leadership wanted to avoid a repeat of the minority's embarrassing procedural coup of April. Interestingly, although the whip count on the rule continued to indicate significant divisions within the Democratic Caucus, 153 Republicans crossed over and it won handily on the floor. Clearly, the minority party believed it could win on substance.

Once again, Democratic leaders whipped strongly against the GOP proposal. When on June 23 Reagan requested the opportunity to address the House the next day, O'Neill refused permission.[18] The majority leadership's vote-gathering efforts were hindered, however, by disenchantment among party liberals about O'Neill's decision to coalesce behind the McCurdy proposal. In their view, Democratic leaders had already conceded too much ground to the conservatives. In building his floor majority, Reagan once again relied on a combination of personal meetings with undecided legislators, extensive telephone conversations with Republicans and Democrats, and a nationally televised speech. The GOP also modified the White House request and incorporated several aspects of the McCurdy initiative into their proposal. As indicated in Table 7.9, along with the 196 Democrats in the Y/LY column during the whip process, another 26 were opposed, and 29 were undecided. Unfortunately for O'Neill, the vast majority of the undecideds defected to the Republicans on the vote, giving them the win.

Consider, for example, the defection of Les Aspin, D-Wis., who that year was completing his first term as chair of the Armed Services Committee. Aspin, who would serve as President Bill Clinton's first Secretary of Defense, was a moderately liberal Democrat, but he represented a potentially competitive district near Milwaukee that in 1984 gave Ronald Reagan 54 percent of its votes. Initially, Aspin did not respond to the whip count on the Edwards amendment (the GOP/Reagan alternative), and then he reported as "undecided." On the roll call, Aspin voted with the Republicans. Afterward, O'Neill remarked that the defection "will give him a hard time the next time he runs for chairman."[19] Indeed, the Democratic Caucus passed a "no-confidence" motion against Aspin as chair the following year and he barely held onto the position. The next time that Contra aid was considered by the House, a chastened Aspin switched positions and voted with his party. Also of interest were the decisions of three Oklahoma Democrats who were personally close to McCurdy and did not cast their roll calls until it was clear the Republican proposal would carry the day and the leadership no longer needed their support.[20] Two of them, Glenn English and James Jones, had responded as "undecided" on the whip count. The third, Wes Watkins, reported in favor of the Democratic position. All three represented conservative districts in which 60 percent or more of voters cast ballots for Reagan in 1984. After it became obvious that McCurdy's proposal would be defeated by the GOP amendment, the three Oklahomans voted in favor of the more readily explainable Republican position.

For the foreign policy and intelligence items of period 3, then, the House majority generally prevailed. As the Contra aid battles illustrate, however, the enhanced role of the executive branch on national security matters and the aggressive foreign affairs and defense programs of the Reagan White House created significant challenges for the Democratic whips. Reagan's effectiveness at regularly marshalling grassroots support for his position within the districts of moderate Democrats attenuated intra-party support for the leadership within the Democratic Caucus. Even though the size of the majority party was generally large, the president won some important floor fights in this area, and the 1986 turnaround on Contra aid is a telling illustration of how such outcomes occurred. Especially on foreign affairs, the ability of a White House controlled by the other party to influence rank-and-file members via their representational relationships at home was an essential feature of the whip process.

Budget, Taxes, and the Debt Revisited

For whipped questions in period 3 dealing with budget politics—and where the archival evidence necessary to calculate required and actual pickup is available—Table 7.10 provides the standard information about party coalition building. As panel A of the table indicates, most of the outcomes were Democratic wins. Crossover support from the GOP was relatively limited, and about half the time the minimum necessary pickup for the Democrats was positive. The coalition-building summary for the minority GOP on economic issues is mostly the flip side of this pattern. As the table also shows, many of the whipped economic questions dealt with budget resolutions and reconciliation bills, the central legislative vehicles in the budget process created by the reforms of 1974. During the 1980s, budget resolutions emerged as an important legislative vehicle through which the majority party presented its policy agenda to the nation, and reconciliation bills became consequential legislative vehicles for implementing portions of that agenda. The major budget vehicles, in other words, were now significant party-defining measures on Capitol Hill. Not surprisingly, the standard rhythms we have come to associate with partisan floor fights were fully apparent. Two historic budget fights from period 3 are especially illuminating—House consideration of the budget resolution in 1990 and chamber action on reconciliation in 1993.

As mentioned, the size of the federal deficit increased markedly during the 1980s, and the public noticed. Throughout the decade, divided partisan control hindered efforts to get the deficit under control. In 1985, the Congress passed and Reagan signed the Gramm-Rudman-Hollings deficit law, which established statutory limits on the size of the debt and provided for required cuts, called "sequestration," if these limits were breached. But the sequestration procedure was not fully enforceable, and via accounting gimmicks and other maneuvers, political Washington was able to duck the mandated cuts.[21]

In early 1990, however, both the GOP White House, now led by George H. W. Bush, and Democratic leaders on Capitol Hill embraced deficit reduction, at least in the abstract.[22] The administration advocated spending cuts outside the defense area and opposed any new taxes. During the 1988 presidential contest, the widely publicized mantra of the Bush campaign had been, "No New Taxes." Congressional Democrats, in contrast, preferred that deficit reduction be accomplished with heavier cuts in defense and they were open to tax hikes. Recognizing the pending

TABLE 7.10. Coalition-building success, budget, taxes, and the debt

	Panel A. Majority Democrats						
Question	Y/LY	U	N/LN	Other	Rep support	Min nec pickup	Actual pickup
Win							
Budget resolution prev ques rule 1983	197	45	14	11	0	12	33
Budget resolution as reported 1983	178	33	28	28	4	31	47
Debt limit prev ques & rule 1983	188	60	4	13	1	22	60
Debt limit pass 1983	128	75	35	28			
Tax cut 1983	199	21	43	3	0	12	30
Tax reform prev ques rule 1983	171	55	19	22			
Pay-as-you-go amdt 1984	192	43	16	15	21	−3	37
Tax reform rule 1984	208	27	25	6			
Tax reform pass 1984	178	60	22	6	95	−65	45
Budget resolution 1985	167	25	5	54	1	46	74
Debt limit mot to conf 1985	177	32	16	27	119	−107	31
Tax reform rule 1985	179	30	15	28	70	−35	9
Tax reform GOP sub 1985	177	40	8	27	54	−17	63
Tax reform pass 1985	116	80	32	24			
Budget resolution 1986	184	55	7	5	17	12	44
Budget resolution pass 1989	150	78	29	2	105	−44	8
Budget resolution conf 1989	141	38	52	28	93	−20	7
Tax reform rule 1992	167	59	41	0	0	45	77
Budget resolution 1992	214	29	17	7	5	−11	5
Tax reform conf 1992	191	21	33	22	1	9	19
Rescissions prev ques rule 1992	195	35	10	27	8	7	37
Budget resolution 1993	212	35	5	2	0	2	31
Rescissions reform rule 1993	190	29	35	1	2	19	20
Reconciliation conf 1993	202	13	42	0	0	16	16
Budget resolution pass 1994	224	3	9	20	0	−24	−1
Budget resolution subst 1994	205	34	12	5	9	−12	24
Budget resolution mot to instr 1994	208	23	24	0	6	−5	2
Budget resolution conf pass 1994	208	14	4	29	0	−6	12

TABLE 7.10. *(Continued)*

		Panel A. Majority Democrats					
Question	Y/LY	U	N/LN	Other	Rep support	Min nec pickup	Actual pickup
Major change							
Reconciliation rule 1993	164	48	33	10	0	52	72
Reconciliation pass 1993	139	102	16	0	0	78	80
Loss							
Tax reform rule 1983	151	71	26	19	13	46	40
Budget process reform 1992	173	41	53	1	0	40	14

		Panel B. Minority Republicans					
Question	Y/LY	U	N/LN	Other	Dem support	Min nec pickup	Actual pickup
Majority win							
Budget resolution 1989	83	49	27	16	158	–30	22
Debt limit 1989	64	34	66	12	182	–37	–15
Budget resolution 1990	161	11	0	4	36	16	11
Balanced budget amdt 1990	123	28	18	7	37	55	24
Balanced budget pass 1990	158	8	5	5	112	–55	9
Budget resolution conf 1990	137	0	34	5	29	41	–2
Reconciliation amdt 1990	144	13	7	12	30	41	18
Budget resolution subst 1993	116	30	23	6	3	95	16
Budget resolution pass 1993	134	5	0	36	11	68	38
Debt limit 1993	152	9	2	12	12	43	13
Enhanced rescission reform 1993	73	61	28	13	71	64	13
Major change							
Reconciliation rule	146	1	0	29	19	50	29
Reconciliation pass	167	2	0	7	38	11	8
Majority loss							
Reconciliation capital gains 1989	156	17	3	0	66	–7	17
Budget resolution 1990	23	57	87	9	108	86	48

impasse, the White House proposed high level "summit" negotiations between administration officials and the bipartisan congressional leadership, and Democratic and Republican leaders on the Hill accepted the invitation. The talks continued throughout the summer months, often conducted in the officer's club of nearby Andrews Air Force Base. At first, negotiations stalled over the revenue issue, but at the end of June Bush agreed that a budget package would have to include some tax hikes. That concession pleased congressional Democrats and accommodation-minded Republicans in the House, but generated fervent opposition from GOP conservatives.

In July, over the objections of the Bush administration and Minority Leader Robert Michel, the House Republican Conference adopted a non-binding resolution opposing new taxes.[23] The pace of the private talks increased in September—without a deal the Gramm-Rudman law called for another round of across-the-board cuts spread across defense and domestic programs, to be implemented on October 1. On September 30, with just hours to spare, the negotiators announced a bipartisan agreement at a press conference in the Rose Garden of the White House.[24] If accepted, the accord would have reduced the deficit by $500 billion over five years through a combination of spending cuts and tax hikes. The agreement was quickly drafted as a budget resolution, and both House Democratic and Republican leaders whipped strongly in favor of passage. Archival evidence for the Democratic whip processes at that time is unavailable, but GOP records show that the Republican leadership began whipping on October 1, the day the plan was released.

As shown in panel B of Table 7.10, the whip count revealed an incipient revolt against the bipartisan agreement within the Republican Conference. On an historically important deficit reduction measure embraced by a president of their own party, only 23 Republicans were in the Y/LY category, 57 were undecided, and 87 were N/LN. Nine members declined to provide a position. Among members who had served five terms or fewer, over 55 percent took positions against the deal during the whip process. Interestingly, there was not much difference in district presidential voting in 1988 across members in the Y/LY, undecided, N/LN, and other categories. Instead, the potential defectors disproportionately were younger members who preferred the more confrontational stance associated with Newt Gingrich, R-Ga., who had been elected House Republican whip by a single vote the previous year.

The main sticking point, of course, was the new revenue at the heart of the agreement. Shortly after the accord was announced, Tom DeLay, R-Tex., a top lieutenant to Newt Gingrich in the party whip operation, and other party conservatives began sporting yellow, "Junk the Summit," buttons on their jacket lapels.[25] Gingrich, for his part, expressed deep concerns about the pending deal during the negotiations and declined to attend the Rose Garden announcement, but as the second ranking member of the leadership he initially held his fire in public. On the first drafts of the whip poll, Gingrich was nonresponsive, but soon reported in opposition to the deal. Minority Leader Michel, in contrast, fully endorsed the bipartisan package and led efforts within the GOP Conference to build support for House adoption. The results reported in the table, however, show clearly that party conservatives had the upper hand from the beginning. The gist of the intramural disagreement concerned party strategy. While Bush and Michel believed that the Republicans would be better served by working across the aisle with congressional Democrats, Gingrich and DeLay preferred opposition and potentially a short-term legislative loss for the party on the budget resolution. Instead, their hope was to turn the proposed tax hikes into a party-defining issue for future campaigns.

The day after the deal was announced, Minority Leader Michel conducted a rare Sunday meeting of the full Republican Conference, where he urged his colleagues to give the agreement serious consideration. John Sununu, the White House chief of staff, publicly threatened to make opposition to the budget resolution a campaign issue for Republican members who voted against the administration position. Sununu's threat appears to have been a factor in Gingrich's decision to go public with his opposition to the package. The Georgian's defection was a major strategic loss, in part because it meant the party could not fully depend on its whip operation to build support for the budget agreement. The administration attempted to fill the gap. In the days before the vote, Bush invited dozens of House Republicans to the White House for personal lobbying sessions, and he delivered a nationally televised address in support of passage. As the roll call neared, however, undecided Republicans broke fairly evenly toward and away from the Bush-Michel position. Although administration lobbying in favor of the package was intense, almost all of the initial GOP opponents stood firm.[26]

On the Democratic side of the aisle, support for the budget accord was always contingent upon a substantial number of "yes" votes from Republicans. If Bush and Michel could not deliver most of their own members, Democrats reasoned, why should they cast difficult votes in favor of benefit cuts and tax hikes. As the insurrection within the Republican Conference became apparent, support for the package within the Democratic Caucus crumbled. On October 5, 1990, the summit agreement went down in defeat, 179-254. Majorities within both parties voted no. On the roll call, Bush and Michel managed to retain their base of "yes" and "leaning yes" responders, and they even converted over a quarter of the members who had been "leaning no." But they were largely unsuccessful in flipping the "no" responders and 40 percent of the undecideds ended up voting with Gingrich.

Following the defeat, congressional leaders (minus House Republicans, of course) held a series of meetings to craft an alternative budget resolution, which passed the House early in the morning on Sunday, October 7 on a party-line vote of 250-164. This time, both Michel and Gingrich were in opposition. When the House considered a reconciliation bill implementing the budget resolution on October 16, Michel and Gingrich again voted no. After weeks of bicameral negotiations that also included the White House, the bipartisan congressional leadership agreed on a compromise measure, which the House passed on a party-line vote. Here, Michel and Gingrich differed, with the Minority leader supporting the Bush-backed deal and Gingrich voting "no." Importantly, 126 of the 173 House Republicans who cast votes on the measure sided with Gingrich and against Michel, reflecting a critical and enduring strategic shift for House Republicans, from the relatively cooperative approach of Michel to the more confrontational tactics embraced by Gingrich. In the end, the landmark budget votes of 1990 set the stage for Pat Buchanan's damaging (for Bush, anyway) primary challenges to the president in 1992 and Gingrich's emergence as the dominant GOP congressional leader in Washington.

Now fast-forward several years to House action on the 1993 reconciliation package. In part because of the fallout from the 1990 budget votes and economic recession during 1991–92, Democrat Bill Clinton was now in the White House and his party had large majorities in the House and Senate. After the demise of an economic stimulus package championed by the administration that spring, reconciliation became Clinton's central domestic priority for 1993, and the measure encompassed a wide range of discrete tax increases and spending cuts. As shown in Table 7.10 (panel A, under "major change"), the House Democratic leadership whipped both the rule and the passage motion in May 1993. Initial results on the count were not promising, and no GOP crossover support was expected (none was received). On the rule, only 164 Democrats were recorded as Y/LY, 48 were undecided, 33 were N/LN, and there were 10 nonresponders. The results for the whip count on passage were even less promising. Here, only 139 Democrats were in the Y/LY column, over 100 were undecided, and 16 were N/LN.

As floor action neared, Clinton personally called all of the "no" responders on the whip counts urging them to support the party. The president visited the Capitol on May 19 to speak with reluctant Democrats.[27] Cabinet members likewise contacted potential defectors. As it became clear the Democrats still lacked the support necessary to prevail, the administration and House leaders accepted significant modifications in the legislation. The day before the vote, Clinton agreed that if entitlement expenditures exceeded preset targets the executive branch would propose offsets and the Congress would be required to vote on the reductions. Charles Stenholm of Texas, and Timothy Penny, D-Minn., another prominent deficit hawk, came on board because of this concession, which was folded into the measure via a revised version of the rule. To pick up votes, the White House also agreed to roll back the proposed energy taxes in the measure if and when it was considered in the Senate. Among other energy state lawmakers, Jack Brooks of Texas switched from leaning no on the count to yes on the vote because of the concession.

Along with White House lobbying and vote-gathering efforts of the whips, considerable pressure on wavering members was exerted by the large class of newly elected Democrats. On May 27, the day the reconciliation package was brought to the floor, freshman Democrats led by Leslie Byrne of Virginia circulated a petition demanding that any committee or subcommittee chairs who voted against passage be stripped of their positions.[28] The freshmen felt that they were being pressured to cast a vote that would be hard to explain at home, while more senior members from safer districts were bucking the leadership. Among the committee chairs, eight were not in the "yes" column on the count, but all of them ended up voting with the leadership. In large part because of the last-minute substantive concessions, the majority Democrats prevailed on the rule and then won the passage roll call, 219-213. That said, 38 Democrats still voted no on passage and the leadership's victory margin was thin, heralding further challenges in the Senate and when the package returned to the House after conference deliberations.

Indeed, following an equally difficult vote-gathering process in the Senate, Vice President Al Gore broke what had been a 49–49 tie and a revised version of the reconciliation measure passed that chamber on July 25. Action then moved to a House-Senate conference committee for the purpose of integrating the two versions of the legislation. After conferees accepted the weaker Senate language regarding a tax hike on gasoline, the remaining differences were quickly resolved and the measure returned to the full House and Senate for one last up-or-down vote. The White House, the congressional parties, and coalitions of outside advocacy groups on both sides of the matter whipped the conference report. As indicated in Table 7.10 (panel A, under "majority wins"), prior to the vote 202 House Democrats were listed as Y/LY, 13 were undecided, and 42 were in the

N/LN column. No crossover support was expected or received from chamber Republicans. Based on the number of votes that would be cast, the minimum necessary pickup for the Democrats was 16 members. Once again, the outcome was a cliff-hanger.

Clinton gave yet another television speech about the reconciliation plan on August 3. Senate Minority Leader Robert Dole, R- Kans., followed the president with a televised statement against the package.[29] Over the next two days, member offices were deluged by phone calls urging votes against passage. In addition to the intense member-to-member lobbying, White House officials and congressional leaders reached out to media outlets in the home constituencies of lawmakers to generate additional pressure. Clinton pledged to send to the Congress a measure later in the year to further cut expenditures. House leaders, for their part, promised expedited consideration for that measure and ample opportunity for members to offer amendments.

In the House, the vote on the conference agreement occurred on August 5, and the outcome was a 218-216 win for the Clinton administration. House Democratic leaders picked up precisely the number of votes they needed to win. On the floor, as votes were being cast, members of the whip team hovered, reaching out to Democrats who voted no but might be convinced to switch.[30] John Conyers, D-Mich., for instance, was angry that Democratic leaders had not adequately consulted with him in the drafting of an omnibus crime package and he retaliated by voting against the reconciliation bill. Members of the whip team swarmed, convinced him that his concerns about the crime measure would be accommodated, and Conyers switched to yes. Elsewhere in the chamber, Matthew Martinez, D-Calif., also voted no, primarily because of his opposition to the new energy taxes. At the request of the whips, Clinton telephoned Martinez on the floor, made an unspecified promise, and Martinez changed to yes. Appropriations Chair Jamie Witten, D-Miss., also initially voted no, but switched to yes after conversations with members of the whip team.

When the normal period for the roll call ended, the vote was stuck at 216-215, and the attention of the chamber focused on three Democrats: Marjorie Margolies-Mezvinsky, Penn., Pat Williams, Mont., and Ray Thornton, Ark. What unfolded was one of the most famous roll call decisions in recent memory—the choice by Margolies-Mezvinsky to cast the pivotal vote that produced a dramatic win for her party. Scholars and journalists alike routinely point to it as perhaps the classic case of leadership arm-twisting, or of so-called "vote buying," where presidents or other party leaders induce a lawmaker to act contrary to her pre-formed preferences in exchange for special favors of some kind.[31] If accurate, this narrative would be a superb illustration of party govern-ment at work. The archival evidence, however, tells a more complicated story more in line with the behavioral perspective on partisan coalition building.

On the August whip count, Margolies-Mezvinsky was clearly recorded as "no," and she had voted against the measure during initial House con-sideration in May. First elected in 1992, Margolies-Mezvinsky was the first Democrat to represent her suburban Philadelphia district in 76 years. Living in the wealthiest district in Pennsylvania, her voters were dispro-portionately Republican and Margolies-Mezvinsky was rightly viewed as one of the more endangered House Democrats nationally. Yet, her district also had supported Clinton over Bush by a 44-40 percent margin in 2002, with the remaining 16 percent going to independent Ross Perot. As a former television reporter and best-selling author, she had substan-tial name recognition at home. To be sure, the most straightforward vote for Margolies-Mezvinsky on the reconciliation conference report would have been "no," but properly framed a yes vote may have been explainable. Indeed, the measure presented her with precisely the kind of represen-tational challenge that regularly confronts cross-pressured lawmakers on both sides of the aisle. Although listed as opposed on Democratic whip counts, whip records also indicate that she promised party leaders to be with them if her vote was needed for passage.

Williams, in contrast, was undecided throughout the whip process. A pragmatic liberal serving his 8th term in the House, he became the sole representative for Montana after the state lost its second district in the reap-portionment that followed the 1990 census. The addition of thousands of conservative voters from eastern Montana into his constituency reinforced incentives for Williams to demonstrate independence in Washington. Like Bill Clinton, Thornton hailed from Arkansas. He had voted in favor of ini-tial House passage of reconciliation in May, and as the whip process began on the conference report was recorded as a party supporter.

Of the three members, two would need to support passage for the measure to clear the House. Thornton flat-out refused to vote for the bill. Under intense pressure from Democratic leaders and the Clinton White House, Williams agreed to vote aye. At that point, Margolies-Mezvinsky walked up to the Speaker's dais and cast the deciding vote in favor of passage. The *New York Times* described the bedlam on the House floor that evening as the roll call came to a close.

As the voting went on, Ms. Margolies-Mezvinsky stood by the leadership desk, rubbing her arms nervously and hoping against hope that she could vote no, to keep her skeptical constituents happy.... At the last moment, the whips gave her the word that she was needed, and she walked down the aisle. One Democrat after another hugged her, patted her on the back and touched her as if she were Joan of Arc. As she finally voted aye, her Democratic colleagues cheered as the Republicans jeered, "Goodbye Marjorie."[32]

The GOP taunts that night proved to be accurate. Margolies-Mezvinsky lost her seat in the 1994 midterm elections and her turnaround on reconciliation was an issue in the campaign. The day after the dramatic House roll call, Vice President Gore broke yet another tie in the Senate, the measure passed 51–50, and it was quickly signed by the president. For Clinton and Democratic congressional leaders, the outcome was widely viewed as their most significant legislative accomplishment of the year.

As mentioned, the Margolies-Mezvinsky vote is often treated as a paradigmatic example of arm-twisting, vote buying, and leadership influence during the whip process. Although the roll call certainly presented her with difficult political challenges, under the right conditions a "yes" vote could have been framed to minimize the resulting political damage. Conservative icon Alan Greenspan and many business organizations had endorsed the Clinton plan. Perhaps the main reason why the decision hurt her so much at home was a widely publicized story in the *Philadelphia Inquirer* the day before the roll call announcing her intention to vote no.[33] Presumably, Democratic leaders believed that her vote would not be needed and she felt free to take a public position against passage. In making the case for vote buying, scholars mention the pledge that Margolies-Mezvinsky secured in exchange that Clinton would show up at a conference in her district about deficit reduction. That's right—no appropriations favors, highway projects, legislative concessions, or other concrete benefits for her Philadelphia mainline constituents, just an event appearance that could only serve to prime constituent dissatisfaction with her reconciliation vote. Clearly, the orchestration of her decision was badly bungled.

Indeed, if the goal is to shed light on the inner workings of the congressional whip process, the more telling roll call cast that night was the "no" vote from Ray Thornton that made the Margolies-Mezvinsky debacle necessary in the first place. Simply put, Democratic leaders had counted on Thornton's support. Elected in 1990 to represent the second district of Arkansas, Thornton was from Little Rock, a reliable Democratic stronghold.[34] His constituents included a mixture of professionals, university staff and students, a significant labor presence, and a major Air Force installation. Nearly 20 percent were African American. But this was actually Thornton's second stretch as a House member. During 1973–78, he had represented Arkansas 4, which at the time reached across the southern portion of the state and was primarily known for poultry production. In his first House career, Thornton had presented himself as a national Democrat with a moderately liberal voting record. He was perhaps best known at the time for his effectiveness during televised hearings in the House Judiciary Committee about the impeachment of Richard Nixon. After a failed bid for the Senate, he spent a decade working for Arkansas universities before returning to the House as the member for Little Rock.

Importantly, while Thornton had stressed national concerns during his first House incarnation, during his second stint in the chamber he embraced a very different representational style. Thornton 2 focused primarily on constituency service and the economic needs of his state. Rather than the Judiciary panel, he secured a seat on the Appropriations Committee, from which he attempted to channel large quantities of federal largesse to his constituents and otherwise promote agricultural interests in Arkansas. Although Thornton voted for reconciliation in May, he was especially sensitive to the grassroots mobilization breaking out against the conference report as the House vote neared. The whips clearly detected his movement away from the party line. In the hours before the roll call, Thornton's position shifted from yes to no to leaning no. His constituents, Thornton warned Democratic leaders, had swung strongly against passage.[35] On the floor, he voted no, and the whips were forced to turn to Margolies-Mezvinsky. Vote-buying models and journalistic analogies to the "Maid of Orleans" largely miss what happened here. Instead of arm-twisting or the provision of special favors, the outcome mostly derived from the complex interface of partisan imperatives and member representational relationships at home at the heart of the behavioral perspective.

Closing Observations

Period 3, in short, was characterized by a House legislative process that was consistently and predictably more partisan than the shifting floor majorities of 1973–82. The size of the leadership's base of support increased somewhat, crossover votes from the minority declined, and the majority party win rate grew. Still, for a nontrivial portion of the whipped agenda, the majority was forced to accept major changes, to remove items from the agenda, or suffer an unambiguous loss. As discussed in Chapter 4, when the majority and minority parties "faced off"—when they simultaneously whipped the same question in opposite directions—the Democratic majorities of period 3 usually prevailed, but there was still substantial movement of members in both directions. Although the floor decision-making process became more overtly partisan during the years of period 3, in other words, it did not resemble anything like "party government." And as the case analysis of this chapter illustrates, the work of the whips was integrally related to member relationships with important audiences at home.

On the minority GOP side of the aisle, the ability of the leadership to win outright victories on the House floor declined across periods 2 and 3. The portion of Y/LY responders on party whip counts grew, as did the percent of undecided Republicans who broke toward the party position on votes. Yet, while the majority Democrats won only about 55 percent of the questions whipped by the minority during the 1970s, by the late 1980s and early 1990s that figure increased to nearly 77 percent. As illustrated by the 1990 budget fight, the purpose of the minority whip process increasingly was to distinguish the GOP program from the Democratic position, respond to important audiences outside the chamber, and build the case for Republican electoral gains in the voting booth. On Election Day in November, 1994, that strategy paid off, and after four long decades in the minority wilderness the party achieved majority status in the House, as well as the Senate.

EIGHT

The Republican House, 1995–2002

This chapter explores whip action in period 4, the Republican-controlled Houses of 1995–2002. By the mid-1990s, the decades-long trend toward heightened partisanship and activist leadership on Capitol Hill was fully realized. Scholarly accounts of the era emphasize the centralization of power in the hands of Speaker Newt Gingrich and other House leaders. Tom DeLay, the House Republican whip during these years, was widely portrayed as a highly aggressive coalition builder willing to do what was necessary to eke out party victories. With the White House in the hands of Democrat Bill Clinton, legislative gridlock was commonplace during 1995–2000. But during 2001–02, with fellow Republican George W. Bush now serving as president, the House GOP leadership was able to shepherd through many significant enactments, including major tax cuts, the "No Child Left Behind" education reforms, Fast Track trade authority, creation of a new Department of Homeland Security, and the authorization to use force against Iraq, among other measures. Not surprisingly, the period often is singled out as an illustration of party government within the House (Rohde 2013). Indeed, the contents of this chapter will buttress claims that DeLay was the most influential and successful party whip since at least the 1950s. As was the case for the whips of previous Democratic majorities, however, the DeLay vote-gathering operation was firmly rooted in the representational relationships of individual legislators at home. His whip process resembled a top-down version of Tip O'Neill's "strategy of inclusion," with more precision and a much harder edge.

Contextual Considerations

The defining characteristic of the Houses of period 4 was the small size of the majority party. At the beginning of the 104th Congress (1995–96), the House was comprised of 230 Republicans and 204 Democrats. With 218 votes constituting half the chamber, unless crossover support was available from the minority, GOP leaders could only lose a dozen or so of their members and still win on the floor. Moreover, the Republican margins of 1995–96 were actually the largest of period 4. Majority party sizes were 227 at the start of the 105th Congress, 223 in the 106th, and just 221 at the beginning of the 107th. That last congress, 2001–02, marked the first two years of the newly elected Bush administration, and House Republicans had essentially no cushion for building floor majorities.

Scholarship of the era often refers to House majorities that were thin, but also unified. Such generalizations are usually rooted in "preference" distributions derived from the roll call record, party voting scores, and other outcome-based measures, and they fail to capture the heterogeneity of interests and viewpoints that actually confronted leaders within both congressional parties. Once again, patterns of presidential voting at the congressional district level can provide a rough, but still instructive glimpse at the constituency-level differences that existed within the Republican Conference and the Democratic Caucus. Analogous to the other period-specific treatments, Figure 8.1 shows the prevalence of districts within each party where the percentage of the votes cast for the Democratic candidate in the most recent presidential contest was closer to the average for the opposite party. To promote comparisons across periods, we once again present the results separately for southern states.

As you can see, for both parties the prevalence of district outliers is much lower in period 4, and there continues to be significantly more constituency-level homogenization on the GOP side of the aisle. Within the Republican's growing southern wing, just a handful of members were from districts with presidential voting patterns closer to the Democratic average. For the remainder of the Republican Conference, roughly two dozen fell in that category. Still, given the small sizes of the GOP majorities, having 25–30 members with districts that in important ways look more like the constituencies represented by the typical Democrat created problems for the leadership. On the Democratic side of the aisle, a

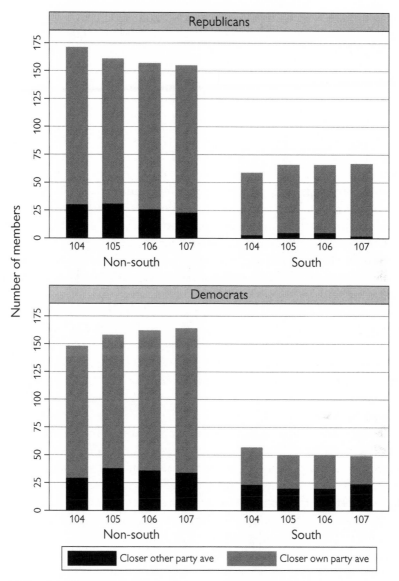

Figure 8.1. Partisan congruence of district-level presidential vote by congress, 1995–2002

larger proportion of the membership hailed from districts with presidential voting patterns closer to the average for the partisan opposition, and the prevalence of these outliers was particularly marked within the party's attenuated, but still important, southern wing. Roughly half of all southern Democrats during period 4 were from districts that looked more like the typical GOP constituency according to the presidential vote measure. Outside the south, another 30–35 Democrats faced analogous cross pressure. Although the Democratic Caucuses of period 4 were large relative to most House minorities, in other words, Whip David Bonior and other party leaders still had to deal with considerable heterogeneity at the constituency level. On both sides of the aisle, then, high levels of party loyalty on major votes were not a forgone conclusion.

The context for whip operations during period 4 also featured important changes to House organization and operations.[1] In 1995, Speaker Newt Gingrich and the new GOP majority took steps to empower the central party leadership. Among other changes, the Republicans restricted chairs to six-year term limits, increased the role of the leadership in the chair selection and committee assignment processes, and required that the chairs of the influential Appropriations subcommittees pledge fealty to the party program. Largely at the incoming Speaker's instigation, senior members of three standing committees were bypassed, and leadership loyalists instead were given the relevant chairmanships. In 1994, GOP candidates for the House had coalesced behind a Gingrich-inspired campaign manifesto, called the "Contract with America." Along with a Republican pledge to substantially roll back the federal budget deficit, the Contract items for a time structured the congressional agenda and promoted high levels of party unity on the floor.

Perhaps most important, in the months before the 104th Congress convened, House Republicans selected Tom Delay as their new whip. Then in his seventh term, DeLay was a former owner of Alpo Pest Control in suburban Houston, a movement conservative and devout evangelical Christian. Elected to the House in 1984, he quickly was appointed to the party's "committee on committees," and during his second term won appointment to the Appropriations Committee. During his third term, then whip Richard Cheney asked him to serve as a top deputy. A few months later, the Texan helped manage Rep. Edward Madigan's, R-Ill., losing race against Gingrich to replace Cheney as whip, and he had to restart his climb to power. Within a few years, however, DeLay was at the helm of the Republican Study Committee, an influential group of party conservatives. When the GOP won majority status in the 1994 midterm elections, he combined persuasive ability, highly active fundraising for his colleagues, and above all a driving tenacity to win the role of whip. DeLay himself once captured his signature strengths as a political leader.

I have often acquired power simply by taking the time to learn a
process thoroughly. This is a key to understanding who I am....
My gift is ... constancy. Once I determine my goals, I orchestrate
the hours of my day to achieve them. I spend my time getting better
at whatever skill I need to achieve them. This requires the fine art
of self-education. I take a long look at the mechanisms in place—in
politics, pest control, or life in general—and then I read and ask
questions until I know the details of the process.... This is my brand
of leadership, a brand not based on looks or charm or brilliance, but
on hard work, mastery of details, and constancy of purpose.[2]

Never close to Gingrich, in summer 1997 he participated in a failed coup
to remove the Georgian as Speaker. And once Gingrich announced his resignation after the party's poor performance in the 1998 midterm elections,
DeLay orchestrated the selection of his chief deputy whip, Dennis Hastert,
R-Ill., to be the new Speaker.

From the start, DeLay maintained a highly-disciplined vote-gathering
operation that was almost machine-like in its efficiency. Over his eight
years in the position, he whipped over 400 distinct questions, with the
canvassing process often beginning early in the legislative game and
continuing right up to the vote. What many pundits came to call "DeLay
Incorporated," however, was an organization and not just an individual. In
2001–02, for example, the Texan led an elaborate network consisting of a
chief deputy whip, Roy Blunt, 17 deputy whips, and 49 assistant whips.[3] Of
the 68 legislators in the organization that year, 47 were formally designed
as "counters," and as such were responsible for regularly canvassing the
views of four to six of their colleagues that had been assigned to their
group. For the most part, the groupings were based on geography, with
members drawn from the same state or general area.

The distinction between the deputy and assistant whips mattered.
DeLay mostly relied on the deputies for tactical advice and to assist the
leadership in following up on the initial canvassing that was conducted by
the group leaders, who disproportionately were assistant whips. Still, there
was a lot of functional overlap in the roles and activities of the deputy and
assistant whips, reflecting the tactical flexibility necessary to gather votes
in the House. Eleven of the 17 deputy whips, for example, also served as
counters. In 2001–02, 36 of the 49 assistant whips (about three-quarters)
had group counting responsibilities. The rest of the assistants helped
DeLay and Blunt with the follow up that occurred after the initial counting

took place and otherwise served as conduits between the leadership and the Republican Conference. Interestingly, several of the assistant whips that year were freshman members, including Eric Cantor, Va., who was the counter for a four-member group covering Virginia and portions of South Carolina. When Blunt succeeded DeLay as whip in 2003, he appointed Cantor chief deputy, and in 2009 Cantor succeeded him as the GOP whip. There is archival evidence that DeLay and the leadership kept close tabs on the votes cast by members of the whip organization on roll calls important to the party.[4] But ideologically, the deputies, assistants, and counters in the GOP whip operation were representative of the Republican Conference as a whole.[5]

Once the top leadership decided to engage the whips on an issue or vote, DeLay and his aides would inform other members of the whip system, especially the counters. Together, the deputy and assistant whips with group responsibilities would conduct the initial canvassing, primarily focusing on the members of their respective groups.[6] DeLay distinguished between full whip checks and whip surveys. The "checks" relied on the group structure and the counters generally made the initial contacts with their members. Whip surveys, in contrast, often focused on a subset of the Republican Conferences that might be in play or otherwise unpredictable on the matter. In conducting the surveys, DeLay typically relied on a combination of deputy and assistant whips, as well as GOP members not in the formal whip organization, but who had expertise or a strong interest in the issue.

After the leadership settled on the wording of the question, staff to the whip would print out cards that the counters would use to record the positions of their members. The cards also included a brief explanation of the issue and often a rationale for the leadership's stance. While the Democrats usually phrased their whip questions so that a "yes" response was always the position of the leadership, the GOP tended to word their questions in a more neutral manner. The Republican whip cards generally included boxes to be checked for the full range of responses—yes, leaning yes, undecided, leaning no, and no—but fairly often DeLay would drop the leaning categories or perhaps the box for undecideds to help push ambivalent members off the fence. At the beginning of the whip process, DeLay's counters would pick up the cards for their groups on a leadership table near the House chamber, usually while roll calls on other matters were underway and they needed to be on the floor anyway. If multiple questions were being whipped simultaneously, the DeLay staff would try to print the cards out on different colored paper to help the whips and their staffers associate member responses with the appropriate issue. Also included on the whip cards was a deadline for returning the results back to the whip's office, usually later the same day, or perhaps, "after the next series of votes." When needed, the second, "cleanup" stage of whipping would usually commence a day or two after the initial results arrived in the whip's office. Here, DeLay would use a grid of deputy whips and assign to them members who had been nonresponsive or were insufficiently supportive of the leadership during the initial count. For the cleanup stage, DeLay and Blunt made the whip-to-member assignments based on their judgments about who among the deputy and assistant whips would be most likely to keep a wavering Republican on board.

Like past Democratic majority whips, the DeLay operation also conducted several member meetings every week the House was in session. DeLay and Blunt met with the deputy whips, usually on Thursday mornings at 10:00, to discuss party strategy and the floor agenda. Typically, attendance at the meeting was about 15 members, who sat around a central table. Staffers were in chairs arrayed along the walls. Meetings of the entire whip organization also took place each week, generally on the day following the first day with votes. If the first roll calls of the week occurred on Monday afternoon or evening, then the whip meeting would take place on Tuesday morning. If the first votes occurred on Tuesday, then the whip meeting was held on Wednesday. The meetings took place in a large, windowless room located in the terrace level of the Capitol Building. A dozen or so tables would be arranged in an open rectangle, with seats placed around the tables and along the perimeter of the room to accommodate the participation of dozens of members and staff.

The agendas for the weekly whip meetings usually included the three or four most significant measures or political challenges facing the party that week (or the week after). The first whip meeting in 2001, for example, occurred on Wednesday, February 7 at 11:00.[7] DeLay began the session by introducing new members of the whip organization. Next, he and Blunt reviewed the responsibilities of the whips. DeLay then discussed plans for the leadership to conduct a series of "listening sessions" with rank-and-file Republicans about the budget resolution and proposed tax reductions that were part of the Bush economic program. That was followed by a discussion of GOP ideas for putting the trust funds for Social Security and Medicare into a "lockbox," led by Pete Sessions, R-Tex., a prominent advocate within the Republican Conference for the lockbox approach. Indeed, it was fairly standard for the members with primary institutional responsibility for a bill or issue, especially the chairs of the committee or subcommittee of jurisdiction, to attend the whip meeting and lead the discussion when a matter relevant to their panels was on the agenda. Periodically, legislative liaison staff to the Bush White House would lead discussions of the president's agenda on Capitol Hill. Although the exchanges between participants were extensive and often lively at the whip and deputy whip meetings, steps were taken to keep the proceedings private. At the end of these sessions, DeLay's staff would gather all agendas, handouts, and other sensitive material from the room and place them in a burn bag to be returned to the whip's office. According to an office manual, these bags were to be picked up every other Friday for disposal at the Pentagon.[8]

In addition to the formal party whip system, DeLay and his staff orchestrated an informal whip network comprised of lobbyists, interest group officials, and representatives of the business community. This outside network took shape early in 1995, when DeLay and other Republican leaders urged trade associations and industry groups to hire only Republicans to staff their Washington operations (Evans and Oleszek, 1997). At weekly sessions conducted away from the Capitol, DeLay, top aides to the leadership, and the private sector attendees would share intelligence about soft spots in the party coalition and make plans to activate potential allies in the districts of wavering Republicans. As long had been the practice on both sides of the aisle, experts in the advocacy community were regularly consulted in the drafting of legislation important to the party. Through his fundraising committee, Americans for a Republican Majority (or ARMPAC, for short), DeLay funneled campaign assistance to members who stayed loyal on key votes. Such campaign largesse was not enough, alone, to influence an election outcome, but it helped signal to GOP campaign donors nationally that the recipient was worthy of their assistance (Jenkins and Monroe, 2012). Most important, DeLay developed an extensive understanding of the districts represented by his Republican colleagues, and through his connections nationally in the advocacy community, and locally with party elites around the country, he was able to identify the special favors and district-level pressure points necessary to retain the support of potential defectors on votes. All of these tactics, it should be emphasized, had been employed by Democratic whips in previous congresses, but DeLay used them more systematically.[9] And like certain other top congressional leaders, his integration of partisan coalition building with extensive fundraising and other outside political work were the backdrop for a succession of ethics challenges, as well as the legal actions that eventually would drive him from office.[10]

On the minority side of the aisle, the Democratic whip networks of period 4 were also organizationally complex and highly active. In 2001–02, for instance, David Bonior and his successor as whip, Nancy Pelosi, led an organization even larger than the GOP network comprised of 113 members, including six chief deputy whips, 12 deputy whips, 70 at-large whips, and 24 regional whips.[11] The Democratic Caucus was now divided into 12 zones and the members within each zone selected two of their colleagues to serve as their regional whips; conducting whip counts and otherwise interfacing with the leadership on their behalf. The rest of the whips—the 88 chief deputy, deputy, and at-large whips—were appointed by the leadership to help mobilize support for the party program and to serve as informational conduits for them with the full Democratic Caucus. As in period 3, much of the vote gathering continued to be conducted by bill-specific task forces. Democratic leaders were careful to ensure that the appointed whips were representative of the Caucus in terms of ideology, region, ethnicity, and gender. Like the Republicans, the Democratic whips also conducted regular whip polls as major bills were scheduled for floor action, but they tended to rely more on staff-to-staff communication during the counting process and were more likely to use email as the mode of communication.

General Features

As mentioned in the opening pages of this book, journalists nicknamed DeLay "The Hammer" early in his term as whip, an image that the Texan embraced because the reputation might enhance his effectiveness in the job. The evidence shows that DeLay's win rates were historically high, and especially striking given the party's narrow margins. Still, the evidence also indicates that GOP leaders occasionally lost during 1995–2002, major modifications were often necessary to pass legislation, and now and then items were removed from the agenda because of insufficient support. Relative to his Democratic predecessors, DeLay was more inclined to whip early in the legislative game, and legislative content was adjusted throughout the lawmaking process based on intelligence from the whips. Then, as roll calls commenced and the leadership was still a few commitments short, DeLay would call in the chits. Often, he would have a half dozen or so pledges from members to support the party if their votes were needed. These members would wait in or near the front row of seats on the GOP side of the chamber, immediately adjacent to the well. When it became clear how many additional votes the party needed to prevail, DeLay would select roughly that number from among the "as needed" members and release the others to vote otherwise. According to knowledgeable staff, he did not rely on the same members to cast "as needed" votes, and he weighed the intensity of their concerns and the potential political costs to them from a pro-leadership vote.

The Whipped Agenda

The contents of the whipped agenda for the Republican majorities of period 4 are summarized in Table 8.1. Once again, the distribution of whip attention across policy categories is shown in two ways: The percentage of whipped items associated with each issue area, and the percentage of roll calls within each policy category that were directly whipped. Analogous percentages for partisan majorities across all four periods are also provided for purposes of comparison. Unfortunately, systematic archival evidence about the whip activities of the minority Democrats is not available for period 4. Wherever feasible, however, information about coalition building on that side of the aisle will be incorporated to provide a fuller portrait of the whip processes of the period.

Although the shift to GOP control in 1995 resulted in dramatic changes to the congressional agenda, the majority leadership's whip priorities were mostly in line with the distribution of attention across the four periods

TABLE 8.1. Distribution of Republican whip attention by issue area, 1995–2002

Issue area	% Whipped questions— 1995–2002	% Whipped questions— All periods	% Votes whipped— 1995–2002*	% Votes whipped— All periods*
Congress/Gov ops	11.7	14.1	5.4	5.7
Defense	3.4	4.4	5.5	5.3
Foreign policy	4.3	7.0	7.4	7.1
Economy	16.2	18.4	14.0	12.1
Trade	2.5	2.9	11.9	9.0
Energy/Environment	3.8	6.4	7.2	4.9
Civil rights	0	1.7	0	6.1
Social welfare	2.9	4.7	10.2	8.1
Health	4.3	2.9	18.0	12.4
Education	3.8	3.0	13.1	8.9
Labor/Consumer	5.6	7.0	25.9	15.9
Appropriations	34.5	19.4	10.6	5.9
Other	7.0	8.2	8.2	5.7

*Only nonunanimous votes used.

combined. A little over 10 percent of whipped questions, for instance, dealt with government operations and the internal processes of Congress. In period 4, that would include a number of questions about campaign finance reform, lobbying rules, and the regulatory process. Once again, economic management issues were a regular whip priority, especially budget resolutions and reconciliation bills.

Notice, however, that over the eight years covered in the table the GOP majority did not whip a single item in the category for civil rights. The absence of whip activity here is a departure from previous Democratic majorities, and also from the Republican minorities of period 3, which occasionally whipped civil rights matters like the application of Title IX restrictions to private universities. The reason is that initiatives in the policy area primarily are of interest to core Democratic constituencies. For the Republican majorities of period 4, free-standing civil rights questions failed to satisfy the three conditions associated with whip engagement (part of the party program, capable of uniting the rank and file, action still in doubt).

Notice also the high levels of GOP whip activity on appropriations matters during period 4. As noted in Chapter 7, the prioritization of the annual spending bills for whip attention began under the Democratic majorities of the 1980s and early 1990s. When the GOP assumed majority status in 1995, however, the appropriations process moved to the forefront as an arena for partisan dispute (Aldrich and Rohde, 2000). The Republicans had committed to rolling back federal spending, especially for programs of primary interest to Democratic constituencies. Moreover, the party had accumulated a vast backlog of preferred policy changes during its many decades in the minority, and advancing all or even most of these proposals through Congress and securing the signature of an opposite-party president was a daunting task. Consequently, Gingrich and his leadership allies chose to draft many of these proposals as legislative add-ons, called "riders," to appropriations bills. Typically, these riders took the form of floor amendments that prohibited spending for certain programs or purposes opposed by the GOP, such as publicly funded abortions or certain environmental regulations. Importantly, the Republicans also adopted a rule change at the beginning of the 104th Congress giving their leadership, rather than Appropriations subcommittee chairs, the authority to cut off consideration of such amendments on the floor. As a longtime appropriator, DeLay served as the leadership's point person for implementing the party's appropriations strategy. The centrality of appropriations to the Republican program continued during the 105th and 106th Congresses, as GOP leaders sought to use the must-pass legislation to leverage policy concessions from the Clinton administration. Not surprisingly, over a third of the party's whip activity in period 4 concerned the annual spending process.

If we focus solely on major legislation associated with one or more key votes as identified by *CQ*, the list of whipped items includes all of the major partisan flashpoints of the era—the GOP "Contract with America," welfare reform, deficit reduction, partial-birth abortion, health insurance regulation, various trade agreements, tax reduction, the "No Child Left Behind" education reforms, and the profoundly important Iraq resolution. Although DeLay led efforts within the House to adopt articles of impeachment against President Bill Clinton in 1998, which of course produced a *CQ* key vote, that issue was viewed as a matter of conscience by the leadership and was not formally whipped by the party. Compared to analogous compilations for previous periods, the list of major whipped measures during period 4 had a decidedly Republican cast.

Member Loyalty

During period 4, the relationships that existed between various district- and member-specific characteristics, on the one hand, and leadership support on whip counts and votes, on the other, mostly follow the patterns that surfaced during prior periods. Table 8.2 summarizes these relationships for the whip count stage. The archival record includes a list of the questions whipped during the 104th Congress (1995–96), but lacks comprehensive evidence about member responses. For this reason, Table 8.2 only covers 1997–2002.

The most important takeaway from the table is the generally higher leadership support rates across all of the rows relative to prior periods. From Chapter 4, recall that the proportion of Y/LY responders stepped up between periods 2 and 3, and that the percentages of leadership supporters during the whip stage were fairly similar between periods 1 and 2, on the one hand, and between periods 3 and 4, on the other. Still, the proportion of Y/LY responders for the GOP majorities of period 4 was nearly 5 percent higher than had been the case for the Democrats of period 3, and also 8 percent higher than had been the case for the minority Republicans of 1989–93. There are also differences by region, the partisan-electoral leanings of a lawmaker's district, and other member-specific factors. Although region still matters, the differences here are smaller than they were for prior periods. As was the case when Republicans were in the minority, leadership support at the whip stage is strongest for southern

Republicans, with the midwest/plains, western, and border state areas also exhibiting high levels. The lowest levels continue to be for northeastern Republicans, but the magnitude of the difference is only about half as large as we observed for the Republican minorities of 1989–93. Either because of the continuing nationalization of American politics, or the party's shift to majority status, the regional differences in leadership support at the whip stage narrowed considerably between periods 3 and 4.

Further perspective on the constituency foundations of whip support can be gleaned by juxtaposing outlier and mainstream districts based on the presidential voting measure. The proportion of Y/LY responses for members representing districts closer to the GOP average is 9 percent higher than the proportion for members from districts with presidential voting patterns closer to the Democratic average. Yet, as was the case for region, the differences associated with divergent presidential voting patterns at the district level are not as large here as they were for the GOP minorities of period 3.

The other four characteristics summarized in the table likewise resemble findings for the 1980s and early 1990s. Members of the committee with

TABLE 8.2. Distribution of majority whip responses, selected district and member characteristics, House Republicans, 1997–2002

		Y/LY	U	N/LN	Other
Region	NE	64.0	17.5	10.7	7.9
	MW/Plains	74.3	11.5	9.0	5.2
	South	77.6	9.1	7.3	6.0
	Border	73.0	12.3	9.3	5.3
	West	74.8	9.3	7.9	8.0
District-level pres vote	Closer to D ave	66.0	15.3	11.3	7.5
	Closer to R ave	75.0	10.6	8.1	6.3
Committee of jurisdiction	On	78.7	7.9	7.5	6.0
	Off	72.7	12.0	8.8	6.6
Seniority	Fresh	79.9	9.9	6.3	3.9
	2/5 terms	72.8	11.8	9.0	6.4
	>5 terms	73.0	10.9	8.5	7.5
Extended leadership	Yes	75.9	10.3	7.3	6.5
	No	72.6	11.8	9.2	6.4
Whip network	Yes	77.8	9.9	7.6	4.7
	No	72.1	11.9	8.9	7.2

jurisdiction over a whipped matter are more likely to be in the Y/LY column, but the difference appears to derive almost entirely from the lower incidence of undecideds. Members of the relevant standing committee probably have already articulated positions on the questions subjected to floor whipping, and thus are less likely to report indecision at that stage of the process. Freshman lawmakers register higher levels of support for the leadership on whip calls than do more senior members, and the magnitude of the difference is higher here than for either party in periods 2 or 3. Apparently, senior members were more inclined (or better able) to buck the leadership during the DeLay years. Members of the extended leadership (elected party leaders plus members of various party committees) are somewhat more likely to answer as Y/LY during the whip stage, but once again the differences are not large. Not surprisingly, members of the whip operation exhibit higher loyalty rates during the floor canvassing process, but a nontrivial minority still reported as undecided or opposed. Although the leadership appointed members of the GOP whip team, steps were taken to make the network representative of viewpoints within the Republican Conference as a whole.

Analogous inferences can be drawn concerning leadership support at the roll call stage on whipped items. Overall, leadership support on whipped roll calls increased from about 85 percent for the Democratic majorities of period 3 to over 91 percent for the Republican majorities of period 4. The Republican minorities of period 3, you will recall, had loyalty rates on votes that resembled those of the Democrats. So, the heightened support scores on whipped votes during 1997–2002 appear to be largely a phenomenon of the GOP as the partisan majority, rather than enduring differences between the two parties.

Not surprisingly, the overall rise in pro-leadership voting on whipped roll calls during period 4 primarily derived from the response categories traditionally associated with attenuated support. For instance, roll call support within the Y/LY category was only 2.5 percent higher for the GOP in period 4 than it had been for the Democratic majorities of period 3. When party support scores are already in the 95 percent range, large increases are not feasible. But inter-period differences for the remaining categories were substantial. From the Democratic majorities of period 3 to the Republican majorities of period 4, roll call support for the leadership position increased from about 69 percent to 81 percent for the undecideds, from about 30 percent to over 43 percent for the N/LN category, and from almost 82 percent to over 89 percent in the "other" category. Clearly, DeLay's ability to convert initial opponents to the party position was striking in comparison with his majority whip predecessors.

Table 8.3 breaks down these broader patterns in roll call loyalty according to the standard member and district characteristics. Once again, controlling for the response category, there were noticeable differences in party loyalty on whipped votes by region, district partisan makeup, and so on. Among members answering N/LN, for instance, western Republicans were about 10 percent more likely to vote with the leadership than were the initial opponents from the northeast. Within the undecided and N/LN categories, members from outlier districts were substantially less likely to cast pro-leadership votes than were their colleagues representing districts closer to the party mainstream. There also are noteworthy differences in the expected direction for membership on the committee of jurisdiction and participation in the whip system.

To identify precisely which subsets of the Republican Conference were most affected by the transition to majority status, it is instructive to consider the changes that occurred within each cell of the table for the GOP majorities of period 4 relative to the GOP minorities of period 3.

TABLE 8.3. Leadership support on votes by whip category, selected district and member characteristics, House Republicans, 1997–2002

		Y/LY	U	N/LN	Other
Region	NE	97.6	80.3	38.3	84.7
	MW/Plains	97.9	79.5	45.5	88.0
	South	98.1	82.1	42.7	90.8
	Border	97.6	81.7	39.7	92.0
	West	97.4	82.0	47.9	92.0
District-level pres vote	Closer to D ave	97.3	74.8	33.4	85.4
	Closer to R ave	97.9	82.5	45.7	90.3
Committee of jurisdiction	On	98.7	79.6	47.9	91.5
	Off	97.6	81.1	42.8	89.1
Seniority	Fresh	97.7	81.7	42.5	96.2
	2/5 terms	97.7	81.4	44.4	87.9
	>5 terms	98.0	79.8	41.8	90.4
Extended leadership	Yes	98.2	82.5	49.3	92.0
	No	97.6	80.3	41.3	88.2
Whip network	Yes	98.3	83.9	49.5	88.7
	No	97.5	80.0	41.3	89.6

As reported in the previous chapter, during 1989–93 undecided Republicans from the northeast voted with the party about 56 percent of the time. In period 4, roll call support rates for this subgroup were over 80 percent, or an increase of about 24 percent. Among Republican southerners in the undecided column, in contrast, voting support for the leadership only increased about 7 percent between periods 3 and 4. Along those lines, for GOP undecideds from outlier districts, leadership support on votes grew over 20 percent across the two periods, while for mainstream districts the increase was only about 13 percent. Overall, then, it appears that the rising tide of party voting did require particularly large behavioral changes from certain subsets of the Republican Conference, especially northeasterners and members from districts with a heavy Democratic presence. It was not easy being a moderate Republican in the GOP controlled House.

Constance Morella, R-Md., is an illustration. First elected to the chamber in 1986, Morella represented the 8th district of Maryland, which encompassed most of suburban Montgomery County, adjacent to the D.C. border. Within the 8th district, Democratic presidential candidates typically outpaced their GOP competitors by nearly 20 percentage points, making it one of the most liberal constituencies to elect a Republican to Congress. Home to major federal installations and large numbers of government employees, the district was also one of the wealthiest and highly educated in the nation. Further from the D.C. line, north and west of Gaithersburg, the voters were more conservative and increasing in number, but the makeup of the district routinely created serious cross pressure for Morella on party votes.[12] Based on her DW-NOMINATE scores, she was one of the most liberal Republicans in the House throughout the 1980s and 1990s, especially on social issues. But as the House Republican Conference became more conservative, her attempts to balance district interests and the party call grew more tenuous. Morella's response was to vote with the party when such positions could be explained at home, maintain a pervasive physical presence in the district, and focus intensely on promoting the material needs of her constituents. Asked how she held the district, Morella responded, "All the work I've done for constituents. I'm accessible. I'm independent. I'm open-minded. I know my district. Like someone said, I'll go to the opening of an envelope. They call me Connie. I get around the district like a cheap suit."[13]

Morella was also close to Tom DeLay, with whom she worked to reform the D.C. family court system, and during period 4 she had to function within an increasingly conservative GOP Conference with narrow majorities and an ambitious legislative program. During 1989–93, her responses to party whip counts were about 15.5 percent Y/LY, 31 percent undecided, 42 percent N/LN, and 11 percent "other." With only a few exceptions, when Morella was Y/LY or N/LN during the whip stage of period 3, she also voted that way on the floor, and when she was in the "undecided" or "other" categories her votes split fairly evenly between party support and opposition. Now fast-forward to 1997–2002, and a Republican-controlled House with DeLay as whip. Here, her responses to party whip counts were about 45 percent Y/LY, 22 percent undecided, 31 percent N/LN, and just 3 percent for "other." Once again, if she took a position during the whip process for or against, she disproportionately voted that way on the floor. But within the "undecided" category, her percentage of pro-leadership votes increased to 62.5 percent during period 4. In other words, at both the whip stage and the translation of poll positions into votes, Morella's party support levels increased substantially during the Republican majorities of period 4. Not surprisingly, Democrats in her district repeatedly charged that a vote for Morella was a vote for Tom DeLay.[14] And following reapportionment of the 8th district in 2002, Morella narrowly lost her seat to Democrat Chris Van Hollen.

Outcomes

As we have seen, the majority party is disproportionately successful on whipped questions across the entire 1955–2002 time span, albeit somewhat less so when the minority whips are engaged. Moreover, there was a significant increase in majority win rates between periods 2 and 3. The proportion of unambiguous majority party victories on questions whipped by that party was about 65 percent in periods 1 and 2, 80 percent in period 3, and 77.5 percent in period 4. Overall, then, the aggregate win rates for the Republican majorities of 1995–2002 were fairly similar to the outcome distributions of the Democratic majorities of period 3. But when the much smaller sizes of the GOP majorities are factored in, the remarkable effectiveness of the DeLay operation becomes apparent.

Consistent with the other period-specific chapters, Table 8.4 shows the outcome distribution by policy area, and there are meaningful differences by issue. In the "Congress/Gov ops" category, for instance, there were 12 GOP losses and three cases where the leadership removed an item from consideration. Such questions related to member pay or committee funding, or to campaign finance reforms opposed by the leadership and where large numbers of Republicans believed that voting the other way would be easier to explain at home. Campaign finance reform, in particular, evoked cross-partisan coalitions comprised of Democrats and moderate Republicans. The GOP leadership generally tried to keep these initiatives off the agenda. When such efforts failed (perhaps because of successful attempts to circumvent the majority's control over the schedule), substitute proposals backed by Republican leaders occasionally went down in defeat. There also were a number of pulled items and leadership losses in the appropriations category, but here the party's failures were dwarfed by the large number of wins.

Unfortunately, we lack systematic information about the questions whipped by the minority Democrats during period 4. But it is feasible to identify certain effects from counter lobbying by the minority by integrating additional information about the partisan configurations associated with questions whipped by the majority. Three broad configurations are relevant here: (1) questions where the GOP and Democratic leaderships

TABLE 8.4. Majority whipped outcomes by issue area, 1995–2002

Issue area	Majority win	Major change	Pull	Majority loss
Congress/Gov ops	26	0	3	12
	(63.4)		(7.3)	(29.3)
Defense	13	0	1	0
	(92.9)		(7.1)	
Foreign policy	15	2	1	0
	(83.3)	(11.1)	(5.6)	
Economy	52	4	3	2
	(85.3)	(6.6)	(4.9)	(3.3)
Trade	5	0	2	1
	(62.5)		(25.0)	(12.5)
Energy/Environment	8	5	0	2
	(53.3)	(33.3)		(13.3)
Civil rights	0	0	0	0
Social welfare	12	0	0	0
	(100)			
Health	12	1	0	1
	(85.7)	(7.1)		(7.1)
Education	9	0	2	3
	(64.3)		(14.3)	(21.4)
Labor/Consumer	15	0	3	1
	(79.0)		(15.8)	(5.3)
Appropriations	113	14	8	7
	(79.6)	(9.9)	(5.6)	(4.9)
Other	19	3	4	2
	(67.9)	(10.7)	(14.3)	(7.1)

Note: Cell entries are the number of items for the relevant issue-outcome category, with percentages by issue in parentheses.

clearly took opposing positions, (2) questions where they were on the same side of the matter, and (3) questions where there was a discernible Republican position, but not one for the Democrats.[15] The assignment of questions to configuration categories is primarily based on legislative history, rather than the presence or absence of party unity on associated roll calls.[16] For period 4, there were nine cases where the underlying configuration was asymmetric (a GOP position, but no position for the Democrats), 66 where both leaderships were active and on the same side, and 311 where the parties were in opposition.[17] Interestingly, the win rate for the last category, partisan opposition, was 74 percent and somewhat lower than was the case for the bipartisan (92.4 percent) and asymmetric (88.9 percent) configurations. There are indications, then, that coalition building efforts on the minority side of the aisle created serious challenges for the partisan majority and drew down majority victory rates in the Republican House. Bipartisan and asymmetric configurations, it should be emphasized, are more prevalent in the issue categories for defense and foreign policy, which may be partially responsible for the elevated majority win rates in these areas. For further insight into the sources of party success and failure during the whip process of period 4, we consider in more depth the many whipped appropriations questions, and also the items prioritized during the historically important 107th Congress (2001–02).

Appropriations

Table 8.5 provides a summary glimpse at party coalition building on the more than one hundred appropriations questions whipped by GOP leaders during period 4. Only items from 1997–2002 are included because the necessary individual level response evidence is not available for 1995–96. For the appropriations areas where there are five or more whipped questions (an "area" of appropriations is one of the annual appropriations bills), average response and pickup information is provided in a separate row of the table. For them, the averages probably were not distorted by the idiosyncrasies of just one or two questions. Information for the other appropriations areas, where four or fewer questions were whipped (and have the necessary data), is combined in the category labeled "other subcommittees." And since omnibus, continuing, and supplemental appropriations transcend the different appropriations areas and subcommittee jurisdictions, they also are treated as a separate group ("Omnibus") in the table.

For each appropriations area, Table 8.5 denotes the average number of members per question who fell into the standard response categories. For the questions related to Commerce-Justice-State appropriations, for example, the average number of members reporting as yes or leaning yes per question was about 179. The column in the table for Democratic support is the average number of minority party members who voted with the GOP leadership on the associated votes. And the minimum necessary and actual pickup figures are likewise averages that encompass the questions included in the relevant appropriations category.

As you can see from the averages, the minimum necessary pickups on whipped appropriations questions often were negative. Across all the appropriations questions, the required pickup ranged from a low of –151 to a high of 67, with a mean of –11.7. For just over half of the questions with the required evidence, the minimum necessary pickups were zero or less. The pickup requirements for questions related to transportation spending, for example, tended to be strongly negative. Transportation bills are especially likely to feature particularistic projects that benefit specific constituencies and geographic areas, and because of their overtly distributive content tend to draw wide, bipartisan support. For such items, strongly negative pickup requirements imply that the majority's vote-gathering challenges were not especially difficult.

On the other hand, the pickup requirements for the Commerce-Justice-State area and for omnibus measures tend to be positive and large. For Commerce-Justice-State, only one of the 11 whipped questions had a negative pickup requirement, and even there the margin was tight (only eight votes). These questions largely dealt with final passage, so the challenges the leadership faced did not relate to particular amendments or procedural motions. The annual Commerce-Justice-State bill includes

TABLE 8.5. Coalition-building success, appropriations

Measure	Y/LY	U	N/LN	Other	Dem support	Min nec pickup	Actual pickup
Commerce/Justice/State	179.4	19.3	16.2	9.7	19.2	11.7	19.8
Interior	175.9	21.3	17.9	10.1	47.0	–11.0	29.7
Labor/HHS	150.2	36.9	21.7	16.8	84.0	–33.5	34.0
Legislative branch	182.3	21.9	11.9	8.3	35.3	–14.7	21.5
Transportation	146.6	20.6	23.6	33.8	170.0	–122.0	35.5
Treasury	159.7	18.9	28.5	15.9	74.5	–21.9	16.0
Other subcommittee	171.1	21.2	19.1	12.7	67.8	–28.3	32.1
Omnibus	154.8	25.9	24.5	18.7	39.4	19.5	42.1

funding for the United Nations and various foreign policy initiatives, crime control, border security, and the Census. This last item, in particular, generated intense partisan infighting during the 1990s because of the implications for reapportionment and congressional elections. In addition, Commerce-Justice-State was often one of the last spending bills considered by the House each session. As the chamber repeatedly breached the spending caps for other appropriations measures, House leaders were forced to compensate with particularly draconian cuts there. In 1999, David Obey, D-Wis., ranking Democratic on the full Appropriations Committee, asserted on the floor that the "Wizard of Oz" could not implement the Commerce-Justice-State bill that year. Bill Young, R-Fla., chair of the panel, responded, "I don't know if I'm the Wizard of Oz or the Wicked Witch of the West, [but] I can guarantee you I am going to click my heels three times and we are going to move on."[18]

For the vast majority of the omnibus appropriations measures, the pickup requirements likewise were positive, ranging from a low of four additional votes needed on the conference report for the 1998 emergency supplemental to 66 on a supplemental considered the following year. Omnibus appropriations measures touch on diverse portions of the legislative agenda and often create strong partisan cleavages in the House. Overall, crossover votes from the minority Democrats averaged less than 40 on these questions, and on five of the items were less than 15. What is especially striking here, however, is the relative softness of the initial support within the Republican Conference itself. Indeed, across all of the categories in the table, the number of Republicans in the Y/LY column routinely was in the 170 to 180 range, with as many as 50 members signaling indecision, likely opposition, or nonresponse. Given the importance of competently managing the annual spending process to the majority party name brand, as well as the considerable crossover support available from the minority, why were so many members of the Republican majority not behind the leadership position?

The ranks of GOP members most likely to answer as N/LN on whipped appropriations questions points to an answer. As you might expect, there are some prominent cross-pressured moderates on the list, including Constance Morella, Sherwood Boehlert, R-N.Y., and Jack Quinn, R-N.Y. But also striking is the presence of highly conservative Republicans from safe GOP areas, such as the quasi-libertarian, Ron Paul, R-Tex., Philip Crane, R-Ill., and Tom Coburn, R-Okla. Especially on appropriations bills, the ideological composition of leadership support at the whip stage was shaped like an upside-down "U," with opposition to the leadership position emanating from both the moderate and the most conservative wings of the party.

In spring 1999, for example, Coburn led a revolt by conservative Republicans against the GOP leadership's management of the annual spending process. The strategy of the dissidents was to offer large numbers of amendments on the floor—appropriations typically are considered subject to open amendment procedures—aimed at freezing or significantly cutting most domestic policy programs. On May 25, for example, Coburn circulated a "Dear Republican Colleague" letter pledging to offer 115 different amendments to the agricultural appropriations bill on the floor, all aimed at cutting expenditures.[19] After two days of contentious floor action on the amendments, the Republican leadership was forced to pull the bill from the schedule. On spending measures, in short, GOP leaders often were able to pick up crossover support from Democrats because of the programmatic benefits for their constituents, but that meant potentially losing support on their right flank.

"Earmarked" expenditures, it should be emphasized, were also a central part of GOP coalition building during the appropriations process, as well as on unrelated legislation important to the leadership. Earmarks are discrete provisions added to appropriations measures that target funding to a particular project or group of projects, and they create opportunities for credit claiming by the House members and Senators representing the affected geographic area. The number of earmarks included in appropriations bills had increased somewhat during the Democratic majorities of period 3, but under the Republican majorities of period 4 the practice exploded in use. According to the Congressional Research Service, the presence of earmarks in the Commerce-Justice-State bill increased from 171 in 1996 to over 1,100 in 2002, and on the massive Labor/HHS appropriations bill the number increased from just seven in 1996 to over 1,600 in 2002.[20] In part, the remarkable growth of appropriations earmarks reflected GOP efforts to impose their spending priorities on an executive branch controlled by the other party.[21] But the increase also reflected efforts to construct floor majorities behind the party program. Targeted expenditures helped the GOP leadership "grease the wheels" and pick up the votes of wavering members.[22]

In short, DeLay's ability to successfully whip the scores of appropriations questions prioritized by the GOP majorities of period 4 rested on four related strategies. First, cut spending where possible, but also fund the bills to levels that were satisfactory to GOP constituent audiences with stakes in the relevant programs. Second, make the adjustments necessary to secure modest crossover support for the must-pass legislation from House Democrats, and perhaps after protracted veto bargaining, from the Democrat in the White House during 1995–2000. Third, provide the more conservative elements of the GOP with ample opportunity to offer targeted reduction amendments and otherwise take public positions in favor of cuts. And fourth, use earmarked expenditures and other special favors to put the Republican vote tallies over the top.[23]

The 107th Congress

For further illustration of the DeLay whip networks in action, consider the remarkable string of victories during the 107th Congress (2001–02), the first two years of the George W. Bush presidency. The legislative agenda of the new Republican White House was broad and the party's House majorities were slim. Over the two years, DeLay and his colleagues whipped 43 distinct questions where the leadership took a clear position and the standard response format was employed. Of this number, 25 were full counts with positions reported for most members and 18 were partial efforts where only a subset of the membership (ranging from just 13 to nearly 80) was targeted. The whip's office referred to the comprehensive efforts as "whip counts," and to the augmented efforts as "whip surveys." However, many of the items that staff denoted as surveys included nearly comprehensive position information, and certain of the items they referred to as whip counts only targeted subsets of the membership. For the purpose of analysis, I refer to the complete or nearly complete canvassing efforts using the standard response categories as "whip counts," and to the others as "spot checks," or "partial counts."[24] Several additional canvassing efforts during the 107th Congress took the form of open-ended questionnaires (e.g., regarding the use of force in Iraq) or were clearly incomplete. In Table 8.6, the comprehensive whip counts conducted during 2001–02 are listed, along with the summary information about member positions, crossover support, and necessary and actual pickups.[25]

   Before considering the contents of the table, however, a few words about the spot checks are called for. By the 107th Congress, internal unity within the House Republican Conference had reached levels where comprehensive head counts were not always necessary. For many questions, DeLay knew precisely which members were likely to be in play, and he focused whip attention there. Indeed, even with the spot checks, the total number of whipped questions in 2001–02 was less than half that of the previous

Congress, even though a fellow Republican was now in the White House and the party agenda was expansive. According to knowledgeable staff, the reason was not complementary lobbying by White House legislative liaison, *a la* the Johnson or Reagan years. The Bush administration relied heavily on the DeLay whip operation. Instead, the Texan's understanding of member positions within the GOP Conference had become so refined

TABLE 8.6. Coalition-building success, 107th Congress, 2001–02

Question	Y/LY	U	N/LN	Other	Dem support	Min nec pickup	Actual pickup
Win							
Tax cuts 2001	211	8	0	2	10	–6	10
Committee funding resolution 2001	172	13	6	30	155	–117	30
Budget resolution 2001	180	30	1	9	3	32	40
No Child Left Behind 2001	132	32	49	7	198	–114	55
Community Solutions Act 2001	195	18	8	1	15	7	24
Human Cloning 2001	173	27	14	8	64	–22	29
Arctic National Wildlife Refuge amdt 2001	156	25	38	3	36	23	32
CAFÉ amdt 2001	139	43	31	9	86	–10	44
Airline Security as reported 2001	171	24	15	9	74	–31	42
Economic Recovery Act 2001	182	27	6	4	3	31	32
Airline Security subst 2001	183	19	13	6	6	28	30
Fast Track 2001	142	27	41	9	21	53	53
Budget resolution 2002	184	12	25	2	1	31	36
Welfare reform 2002	194	15	10	3	14	6	22
Welfare reform amdt 2002	98	50	35	39			
Supplemental appropriations rule 2002	166	24	30	2	1	46	49
Medicare prescription drugs 2002	159	34	25	4	8	48	54
Treasury approps rule prev ques (pay) 2002	139	21	56	6	130	–61	–11
Treasury approps rule 2002	200	11	9	2	29	–22	–5
Fast Track conf 2002	163	17	35	7	25	27	28
Health care liability 2002	184	16	10	12	14	13	20
Pull							
Fast Track June 2001	162	27	32	0			
Tax breaks for educational expenses 2002	186	12	7	17			

that comprehensive canvassing was often unnecessary. For the most part, the partials posed general questions about member views, concerned specific amendments where relatively few votes were in doubt, or were cases where there was insufficient time to conduct a comprehensive whip effort. Four spot checks in February 2002, for instance, dealt with amendments to a pending campaign finance reform measure. As mentioned in the introduction, the party partially whipped a question about Fast Track in March 2001 to gauge the mood of the conference on trade issues.

In general, the members singled out by the partial whip efforts were not a random sample of the Republican Conference. On these questions, the proportion of members from districts with presidential voting patterns closer to the Democratic average was over a quarter, whereas for the members who were not contacted the percentage was less than nine. In terms of region, while northeastern Republicans comprised less than 16 percent of all reported positions during the 107th Congress, they accounted for nearly a third of all positions recorded on partial counts. DeLay also focused on newer members without extensive prior voting records. While first term members made up less than 15 percent of reported whip positions overall in 2001–02, they accounted for over a fifth of the position reports on spot checks. Relative to the position distributions for all counts combined, the responses on the partials were also about 10 percent less likely to be in the Y/LY category, with compensating increases in N/LN and "other." For leadership support on roll calls, if and when a vote occurred, the loyalty rates were also somewhat lower here, especially for the undecided and N/LN columns. The spot checks, in short, mostly targeted the subsets of the Conference that were most problematic for the leadership.

Still, the bulk of DeLay's whip activity during 2001–02 is reflected in the list of questions subjected to comprehensive canvassing in Table 8.6. On that list, there was not a single unambiguous loss. For the two items that were removed from the agenda, note that the first dealt with the preliminary subcommittee draft of Fast Track. That version soon was replaced by a revised measure constructed by Ways and Means Chair Bill Thomas, R-Calif., and therefore reflects a tactical move more than a party loss. The second "pulled" measure, which touched on school vouchers, was not considered by the leadership until the waning days of the 107th Congress, and most likely the Republicans simply ran out of time. Of the 21 unambiguous wins on the list, only three were overtly bipartisan initiatives (the committee funding resolution, the final version of "No Child Left Behind," and a procedural motion to protect a federal pay hike). All of the others were contested, and for just over half the minimum necessary pickup was positive. These items were very much in play right up to the vote. Indeed, several of the roll calls were squeakers associated with substantial pickup challenges. Each time, with a very small majority, considerable ambivalence or outright opposition within the GOP Conference, and minority party crossover votes in the single digits, DeLay was able to cobble together the floor majorities necessary to prevail. Across the two dozen congresses covered in this book, DeLay's pickup and win rates during the 107th Congress clearly stand out.

The story of House action in 2001 on Fast Track trade authority—summarized in the introduction and used to motivate the conceptual arguments of Chapter 2—epitomized the DeLay method in important ways. As indicated in Table 8.6, however, work on the measure did not end when Robin Hayes cast his pivotal vote in favor of initial House passage that December. If anything, the plot thickened when the Senate began consideration the following year. With that chamber now under Democratic "management," Majority Leader Thomas Daschle, D-S.Dak. put the measure on hold for a time because of opposition from organized labor and protectionist forces within the states of many members. Only after dramatically expanding trade adjustment assistance for displaced workers, and adopting other changes, were free-traders within the chamber able to secure passage. The next step was conference negotiations to reconcile the House and Senate versions. On June 26, 2002, House Republican leaders conducted a spot check, asking members whether they would support a procedural motion allowing the House to participate in the conference committee, and explicitly making the language the House endorsed the previous December (as well as other House passed trade provisions) within scope for conference discussions.[26] The Senate had crafted its fast track provisions onto a different vehicle, and House Republicans were concerned their own language might not receive full consideration without the binding motion.

The aforementioned spot check targeted 56 members, or about a quarter of the GOP Conference. Included were lawmakers with district concerns about free trade or who otherwise had signaled they might break with the party on the procedural motion. Thirty-four of the targeted members responded as yes or leaning yes, nine were undecided, eight were no or leaning no, one was formally recorded as "if needed" (Howard Coble, R-N.C.), and four were nonresponsive. The notes that the counters reported back about reservations of individual members ranged from major substantive concerns about free trade to unrelated projects important to their districts.[27] Edward Whitfield, R-Ky., for instance, had an appropriations project backed by the committee, but not by leadership. Whitfield was listed as "leaning no" on the spot check, but voted yes on the floor. Robin Hayes and James DeMint, two members with significant textile interests in their districts, and who had played major roles the previous December, continued to raise concerns about domestic producers. Still, both were recorded as "yes" on the procedural spot check. The leadership made plans to bring the motion to the floor in mid-June, but pulled back because of a lack of votes. Whipping on both sides stepped up, with significant participation from the White House, as well as a myriad of interest groups. DeLay personally took responsibility for whipping six members, five leaning no and one undecided. In the end, 11 pro-business Democrats broke with their own leadership and voted for the GOP motion, and the leadership prevailed, 216–215. Of the six DeLay whip targets, all but two switched to yes. Importantly, the crossover votes from the minority enabled DeLay to release some of his supporters to cast "no" votes that would play well within their districts. On the roll call, Coble, Hayes, and DeMint all voted no.

Following successful passage of the House motion, the conference committee began work. After protracted negotiations, an agreement between the chambers was announced in late July, and the final version of the measure returned to the House for one last, up-or-down vote. Once again, the whip operations on both sides engaged. On July 27, the DeLay team asked Republican members if they would vote for the conference report. The results were troubling to GOP leaders and the Bush White House. After nearly two years of repeated whip activity, numerous visits and phone calls from the White House, one cliff hanger vote after another, and extensive outside lobbying on both sides, only 163 Republicans were Y/LY on the conference report, 17 were undecided, 33 were N/LN, and 7 were nonresponsive. Two members were recorded as "if needed" and are included in the N/LN category of Table 8.6 because of their substantive concerns about the measure.

Once again, the comments that DeLay's deputies reported back ran the gamut from broad policy concerns to parochial needs at home.[28] Appropriations Chair Bill Young, R-Fla., complained that the trade adjustment assistance added to the bill had not been considered by his panel, and a number of appropriators signaled opposition because of concerns about their jurisdiction. Other members mentioned the consequences for poultry producers, sugar, canned pears, the steel industry, and of course textile. Several were worried about the Ecuadorian tuna industry. Yet another lawmaker mentioned a pending appropriations project. Jo Ann Davis, R-Va., opposed the conference report, but signaled to the whips that she would vote yes if needed. During the roll call, the plan was to have her sit next to Eric Cantor, a DeLay protégé in the whip operation (and himself a future whip and majority leader).

The result was a classic full-court press from the DeLay team, the Bush White House, and their allies in the business community, with Democrats and their coalition partners pushing hard the other way. Appropriations Chair Young backed off. After voting against the rule, he switched to "yes" on passage and the appropriators fell into line. Bush met with House Republicans in the Capitol on July 26 to plead for support. Adam Putnam, R-Fla., and Mark Foley, R-Fla., had been no and leaning no, respectively, but switched to yes on the vote because of commitments from the White House to promote citrus and sugar interests in their districts.[29] When the roll call was gaveled to a close at 3:00 a.m. on Saturday, July 27, the conference agreement passed, 215–212. Importantly, administration and industry lobbying brought six more pro-business Democrats to yes, and the crossover support from the minority grew to 25 votes, once again enabling DeLay to release GOP members to vote no and thus curry favor with constituent audiences at home.

Overall, 161 of the Y/LY responders voted yes, none voted no, and two did not vote. Nearly 90 percent of the undecideds voted with the leadership. Jo Ann Davis was able to vote no. DeMint switched from undecided to yes. Over time, the textile interests within his South Carolina district had become less uniformly opposed to trade pacts, and the simultaneous growth of the manufacturing sector at home likewise made pro-trade votes more explainable.[30] No position had been reported for Robin Hayes during the whip process on the conference report. On the roll call, he voted no, and during his campaign for reelection that year he used the action to countervail the political damage inflicted by his pivotal vote in favor of initial House passage the year before. Although seldom as dramatic as Fast Track, the essential ingredients of the DeLay whip operation were also on exhibit during House consideration of the other items listed in Table 8.6.

Closing Observations

Period 4, in short, is the culmination of a decades-long trend toward intense partisan polarization within the hallways of Congress. The House Republican majorities were generally unified about the contents of the party program, and the positions of most Democrats often were striking different. After the 1994 elections, incoming Speaker Newt Gingrich and other GOP leaders helped shepherd through institutional changes and new practices that further centralized power at the leadership level— essentially reinforcing and extending changes in the congressional process implemented by previous Democratic majorities during the 1970s and 1980s.

Yet, the evidence of this chapter also indicates that there were significant disagreements among House Republicans during 1995–2002. Pockets of opposition existed among party moderates, often from northeastern states or representing districts with large numbers of Democratic voters. But there also was skepticism about party proposals among the most conservative elements of the House Republican Conference, especially on appropriations where the majority's need to manage the decision-making process often conflicted with the desires of individual members to demonstrate ideological purity before important constituent audiences. DeLay and other GOP leaders were able to stitch together winning coalitions by making aggressive use of the full tactical toolkit employed by party whips for more than a generation—persuasive appeals rooted in knowledge about member districts, substantive changes to party legislation, calls to loyalty based on collective interests in promoting the party name brand, special favors such as appropriations earmarks, the integration of outside advocacy groups into the floor lobbying process, and—yes—occasionally threats or other heavy-handed measures.

What perhaps was most different in 1995–2002 was the intensity and especially the scope of whip activity. In influential research, Layman and Carsey (2002) demonstrate that American party politics since the 1970s has undergone a form of "conflict extension," where the range of policy areas that polarize Democrats and Republicans at the mass level has broadened considerably. While Democratic and GOP identifiers once disagreed primarily about economic issues and the proper role of government, now they also are at loggerheads about racial issues, cultural matters—indeed, about much of what constitutes the policy agenda of contemporary American politics. On Capitol Hill, the partisan issue extension that was occurring among voters and advocacy groups was associated with a major expansion in the size of the whipped agendas. From 1995 to 2002, you will recall, DeLay and his GOP colleagues whipped more than 400 distinct questions, encompassing the vast majority of significant legislative items considered on Capitol Hill. Essential ingredients of the whip machinery of period 4 had been in place for some time, in other words, but the range of affected legislation was much broader.

One final point before we move on to the Senate. In Chapter 4, we found that for period 4 there was an upside-down "U" shape to the relationship between member ideology, on the one hand, and party support on whip polls and the associated roll calls, on the other. At both the whip and roll call stages, the majority Republican leadership often confronted the prospects for serious alienation at both ideological extremes of their conference. Not surprisingly, when we explored party support on the many appropriations questions whipped by the DeLay team during 1995–2002, we found that the most significant challenges confronting the leadership emanated from the most conservative elements of the House Republican Conference, not primarily party moderates. All of this raises a question. In the relatively few cases where DeLay and the leadership lost, was the culprit primarily defections from the centrists or from conservatives?

We can address this question by dividing the full Republican Conference into five equally-sized quintiles based on DW-NOMINATE scores and then calculating the percentage of votes cast against the leadership position from within each quintile. Does the distribution of party defections on votes vary, depending on whether the outcome was a party win, major modifications, or a party loss? Once again, we need to focus only on whipped questions where there is complete or nearly complete whip poll information at the individual level and an associated roll call vote occurred, which narrows the evidentiary base somewhat. Moreover, the number of majority party losses during the DeLay era was not large. Still, examining the ideological sources of party defection under the different outcome scenarios can inform our understanding of the coalition building process on whipped matters.

Interestingly, there are instructive differences by outcome category. For the majority party wins, votes against the leadership are especially prevalent in the most ideologically moderate (e.g., Morella) and the most ideologically conservative quintiles (e.g., Coburn) within the Republican Conference, with the incidence of defections about 5 percent higher on the far right (compared to the moderates). For the whipped questions with major changes, roll call defections again were significantly higher for the moderate and extreme conservative quintile, but the drop-off in leadership support within the most conservative quintile is now substantially larger (about 14 percent higher than the defection percent for the moderates). Apparently, the aforementioned modifications moved legislation toward the center, perhaps enabling the leadership to pick up support from moderate Republicans and Democrats, but at the cost of votes on their right flank. And finally, for the rare whipped votes that

DeLay and his team actually lost? For these items, the upside-down "U" shape essentially disappears. Here, roll call defections are highest for the moderate quintile (nearly 40 percent) and decline steadily as we move through the more conservative quintiles, with only a slight uptick at the far right. Although DeLay confronted challenges at both ideological ends of his conference, in other words, when he lost the main reason was party moderates who voted with the Democrats. As mentioned, this conundrum surfaced on a number of campaign finance votes during period 4, and it underscores the potential role played by chamber centrists, even within houses that provide the strongest case for majority party control. How could it be otherwise? DeLay needed their votes to win.

NINE

Whips in the Senate

This chapter considers the role played by party whips in the US Senate. Although the formal definition of the position resembles the range of functions fulfilled by House whips, the internal operations and impact of the Senate whip process diverge from the analogous House systems in important ways. For one, the majority leadership of the Senate has far less institutional clout than does the majority leadership of the House. In the Senate, there is nothing like the position of Speaker. The constitution does provide that the vice president will serve as "president of the Senate," but in practice that means casting an occasional tie-breaking vote and little else. The nation's founding document also stipulates that the Senate choose from among its members a president pro tem to preside when the vice president is otherwise disposed. In practice, however, that function is delegated to rank-and-file members of the majority party and likewise conveys little formal power. To the extent that organized partisan leadership exists in the Senate, it is concentrated in the hands of the majority and minority leaders, the two party whips, and various party committees. But the coalition leadership that occurs within the body is structured and constrained by the remarkably different institutional context on that side of the Capitol.

For both Democrats and Republicans, the leader and whip positions were formally established during 1913–15. As the 63rd Congress (1913–14) commenced, Democrat Woodrow Wilson was the newly elected president and Democrats likewise had majority control of the House and Senate. The party's Senate majority was thin, however (just 51 of 96 seats), and there were concerns that the minority Republicans might derail the majority agenda. Senate Democrats created the positions of leader and whip in 1913 to enable their party to counter such tactics. Senate Republicans likewise formalized the role of floor leader on their side of the aisle in 1913, and then created the position of GOP whip two years later. Smith and Gamm (2002) make a strong case that organizational innovations within the Senate parties have generally occurred "at moments of weakness," especially when there is "near parity in party strength."[1] Their claim is fully consistent with why and when the whip positions were established. Rather than a byproduct of polarized policy preferences within the chamber *a la* conditional party government, in other words, the motivations for formalizing and institutionalizing the leader and whip roles resonate more with the behavioral logic advanced here—the majority party had an ambitious legislative program and there were solid prospects for internal partisan unity, but floor outcomes were in play because of the small size of the majority caucus. In the Senate, as in the House, leadership activity is as much a response to majority party weakness, as it is an indicator of majority party strength.

Although the positions were formally established decades earlier, the modern role of Senate party leader mostly took form in the 1930s, in large part because of precedent established at the time that gave the majority leader the right of priority recognition on the floor. The privilege of first recognition enabled the majority leadership to structure the legislative agenda to promote alternatives backed by the party. Still, in comparison with the Speaker's control over the House Rules Committee, the agenda-setting powers of the Senate majority leadership remained limited.

While structural arrangements within the Senate provide a relative paucity of formal power to the majority leadership, chamber rules and precedent extend significant leverage to leaders of the partisan minority. The absence of a motion on the previous question in Senate rules makes possible filibustering and other obstructionist tactics that determined minorities can use to bring the chamber to a grinding halt (Binder 1995). Although the Senate has restricted such obstructionism via Rule 22, which in its modern manifestation enables majorities to end extended debate if 60 members vote to invoke cloture, and also by recent decisions to disallow filibusters on the confirmation of executive branch and court nominees, the practice still provides determined minorities with enormous leverage in the legislative process. Senate obstructionism increased markedly during the 1970s and 1980s, as individual members of both parties used such tactics to promote their policy goals and secure parochial benefits for their constituents (Sinclair 1989). Then, beginning in the 1990s, the obstructionist potential in Senate rules increasingly was used by the minority party to delay or derail policy proposals backed by the partisan majority (Smith 2014). In the Senate, the ready availability of efficacious tactics for obstruction empowers the minority whips relative to their counterparts in the House.

That said, from the 1970s to the 2000s, the Senate like the House grew significantly more polarized along partisan lines. Indeed, based on the standard measures, the levels of partisan polarization in the two chambers are about the same (Theriault 2008). Over time, party organizations within the Senate, including the two whip operations, have also increased in size, internal complexity, and overall activity. As you will see, decision making on the Senate floor is even more fluid than is the case on the House side. Campbell, Cox, and McCubbins (2002) show that Senate majorities, like their House counterparts, seldom lose final passage roll calls. Lawrence, Maltzman, and Smith (2006) consider Senate "roll rates" at the member level, and find that members of the partisan majority are much less likely to be on the losing end of votes than are members of the minority. And Den Hartog and Monroe (2011) marshal considerable evidence that the limited procedural prerogatives of the Senate majority leadership can translate into enhanced leverage in the bargaining game, and thus a degree of power over outcomes. So, amid the conventional wisdom about weak party leaders, there is also a case to be made for at least the possibility of majority party influence within the chamber.

This chapter will show that party whip operations in the Senate have come to resemble their House counterparts in important ways, albeit smaller in size, somewhat less active, and leaving a more modest footprint on floor decision making. Yet, a close examination of majority whip operations in the Senate during 1997–2002—roughly the same period when Tom DeLay managed the majority whip network in the House— also indicates that the impact of the whips was very different across the two chambers. Whereas House majorities use the whips offensively to advance the party program through the chamber, Senate majority whips play a more overtly defensive game. In the Senate, the majority leadership relies on the whips to counter the obstructionist and other tactics of the partisan minority, which in turn are made possible by the unique procedural context within that body.

Senate Whip Organizations and Operations

As mentioned, in the Senate the positions of majority and minority party whip date from the second decade of the twentieth century, and early on their main responsibilities concerned monitoring attendance on the floor and ensuring that rank-and-file members were present for votes. The specific duties of Senate whips, however, have varied substantially over time, depending on the operating style of the relevant majority or minority leader. In the early 1970s, both parties changed the title of the position from whip to assistant floor leader in part because of the fluid nature of the job.

The less institutionalized nature of Senate party whip operations is especially apparent in the size and composition of the broader whip networks.[2] Prior to the 1960s, there were no deputy or assistant whips for the Democrats. In 1966, because of concerns that Majority Leader Mike Mansfield, D-Mont., had about the performance of the then Democratic Whip Russell Long, D-La., the party established four deputy whips. In 1977, when Alan Cranston, D-Calif, became the Democratic whip, the number of deputies was increased to nine, each with regional responsibilities. During Cranston's 14-year stretch in the position, he earned a reputation as one of the best "nose counters" in the chamber, and routinely managed whip count and canvassing operations on as many as two dozen questions a year. When Cranston was replaced in the position by Wendell Ford, D-Ky., in 1991, the number of deputies was cut in half, and the Democratic whip system was comprised of Ford, a chief deputy, and four deputy whips with regional responsibilities.

As Democratic leader from 1989–95, George Mitchell often relied on the secretary to the majority, a top party staffer, to conduct position counts for the leadership. An aide to Mitchell described this more personalized approach as a useful supplement to the whip process, consistent with the less-structured coalition building that takes place on the Senate side of the Capitol. "When an issue is elevated in importance [by formal whip action]," the staffer observed, "Senators' bargaining positions as well the price to be paid on big votes also intensify. It is better to avoid stirring things up [until] you figure out how to operate."[3] During the 2000s, after Ford was succeeded as whip by Harry Reid, D-Nev., the number of deputies in the Democratic system was increased to nearly a dozen, with each selected to cover a different geographic portion of the country.

On the GOP side of the aisle, the party first expanded its whip network in the 1970s with the appointment of six deputy whips with regional responsibilities. In 1981, the new Republican leader, Howard Baker, R-Tenn., abolished the deputy whip positions, choosing to rely on his own staff and President Reagan's legislative liaison team to canvass for votes. Baker's successor as Senate Republican leader, Robert Dole, R-Kan., reestablished the deputy whip positions in 1987 following the party's return to minority status. Until the selection of Trent Lott, R-Miss., as whip in 1995, however, the Republican leader retained responsibility for tracking the evolving positions of GOP members on major party priorities.[4] Lott had been Republican whip during his prior service in the House, and in fall 1994, just six years after his election to the Senate, he challenged the long-time GOP whip, Alan Simpson, R-Wyo., for the position. In his contest with Simpson, Lott argued that the party would need a whip system in the Senate that was more like the House operation to advance the Republican policy agenda through the landmark 104th Congress.[5] Lott defeated Simpson for the position, and over the next 18 months he transformed the whip role. Beginning with Lott, and continuing with his successors, Don Nickles, R-Okla., Mitch McConnell, R-Ky., John Kyle, R-Ariz., and John Cornyn, R-Tex., the Senate GOP whips have conducted as many as 25 formal whip counts per year before major floor fights.

As in the House, during formal canvassing efforts Senate whips query rank-and-file members about their emergent positions, and categorize them as "yes," "leaning yes," "undecided," "leaning no," "no," or in some way nonresponsive. Usually the decision about when to engage the whip system is made by the party leader in consultation with the whip and other members of the relevant leadership. In addition to conducting counts of member positions, Senate whips help party leaders keep members informed about the agenda, assist the leadership with parliamentary duties on the floor, and when necessary help persuade undecided or waving members to toe the party line. On occasion, they also serve as spokespersons for the party for interviews and other media events, and they periodically organize and run meetings of the party's whip network.

The primary focus of this chapter is on the whip operations of the majority GOP during the late 1990s and early 2000s. In part, this focus is for practical reasons—extensive archival evidence about Senate whip activities of the sort that made possible our analysis of the House is only available for the Senate Republican majorities of 1997–2002. But fortunately, that period happens to align with Tom DeLay's stretch as whip for the majority Republicans on the other side of the Capitol, which creates a useful point of contrast for generalizing about inter-chamber differences in the party whip process.

For purposes of illustration, consider the organizational makeup of the Senate GOP whip network for the 105th Congress (1997–98). The whip was Don Nickles of Oklahoma, who held the position throughout the time span under focus in this chapter. Judd Gregg, R-N.H., served as chief deputy whip, as he had under Lott. Gregg's duties were ill-defined, however, and according to close observers his appointment was largely a reward for supporting Lott during his contests for whip and party leader. Serving as "counsel" was Olympia Snowe of Maine, a moderate Republican who had been close to Lott during their prior service in the House. Nickles also appointed ten deputy whips, each responsible for tracking the preferences of four or five colleagues on party priorities. The assignment of rank-and-file members to deputy whips was only loosely based on region, in sharp contrast to practices within the Senate Democratic network and whip operations in the House. For example, John Kyl, Ariz., was responsible for canvassing five southern Senators, and Dan Coats, Ind., was mostly assigned members from the midwest. But the main intention was to make assignments based on who the deputies would be comfortable working with on a regular basis. James Jeffords, a moderate from Vermont who would bolt from the party in 2001, for instance, was assigned to Deputy Whip John Ashcroft, Mo., even though they were from different regions and had divergent political views, in part because both were part of a barbershop group called "The Singing Senators" that periodically practiced in Trent Lott's hideaway office. Dirk Kempthorne of Idaho was from the west and far more conservative than John Chafee of Rhode Island, who often broke with his party on major roll calls. But both men were also active members of the Committee on Environment and Public Works, so Chafee's deputy whip was Kempthorne. The more ad hoc and flexible structure of the Republican whip system resonates with the greater emphasis placed on personal relationships in the Senate as compared to the House.

As in the House, the Senate Republican whip process of this era generally began with a decision by the leadership that an issue or roll call was important to the party, substantial unity appeared feasible, and the outcome was not a forgone conclusion. During the 105th–107th Congresses, the size of the Republican Conference never exceeded 55 senators and thus fell short of the 60 votes needed to invoke cloture without Democratic support. As a result, the GOP whip system was fairly active throughout the period. The number of distinct questions put to Republican members is one indicator. There were 28 whip counts in 1997, 23 in 1998, 20 in 1999, 16 in 2000, 22 in 2001, and 18 in 2002, for an average of about 21 per year.[6] Certain of the questions asked members about nonlegislative matters, such as whether they would cosponsor a party bill or attend a May 2002 press conference protesting Senate inaction on Bush judicial nominees. But the vast majority (over 95 percent) dealt with bills, treaties, and nominations. Across the three Congresses, just under half of the whip counts concerned amendments (Will you oppose the Daschle substitute, will you support the leadership and vote to table the Kennedy amendment, and so on). About 20 percent dealt with cloture, either on the motion to proceed or on bills or amendments. Roughly 14 percent of the polled questions were about entire measures, treaties, or nominations. Five percent concerned requests for budget waivers, and there was one whip count about a possible veto override (a May 1998 question about a possible Clinton veto of the Nuclear Waste Policy Act, which was pulled from the schedule because the count was weak). Almost always, questions were phrased so that a "yes" reflected the position of the leadership. Often, the question wording explicitly referenced the leadership's stance on the matter.

After the decision to "whip" a question was made, Nickles, directly or through staff, would inform the deputy whips, who in turn were provided with four-by-eight inch cards that included the question being polled, the date, the names of the members in the deputy whip's "zone," and often the day and time by which results needed to be submitted to the whip's office. Often, the reverse side of the card included talking points the whips could use when speaking with their colleagues. As the cards were returned to the whip's office, Nickles's staff would compile the results on tally sheets. Lott, Nickles, and other members of the leadership would then use the tallies to evaluate whether the party position could prevail, if and when the matter should be brought up on the floor, and which members were in need of follow-up lobbying. Often, strategic adjustments were made in the party's stance as a result of intelligence from whip counts. Many of the tally sheets also featured the names of individuals—Lott, Nickles, the relevant committee chair, perhaps executive branch officials during the Bush administration—who were charged with lobbying the wavering members. On occasion, it was clear that certain members had asked not to be contacted about the whipped matter and as a result were left alone. The whip's office kept careful track of which members failed to respond to whip counts and whether the roll calls that followed matched the responses on the cards. Particular attention was paid to the roll call loyalty of the deputy whips on targeted items. In many ways, then, the Senate whip process mirrored whip operations in the larger, more regimented House.

If possible, the deputy whips tried to speak directly with their assigned members about whipped matters. The weekly lunches held by the Republican Policy Committee on Tuesday afternoons provided a useful forum for the whips to touch base with their colleagues.[7] A staple of Senate life since the 1950s, these lunches (both parties now conduct them in separate rooms in the Capitol) take place every week the chamber is in session, and are used to discuss the upcoming agenda and formulate party strategy. For both parties, the policy lunches are closed and private. The only staff in attendance at the GOP lunches were two or three aides to the Republican leader, a whip staffer or two, the Secretary for the Republican Conference, and an aide to the chair of the policy committee. During the Bush administration, Vice President Cheney often attended the Republican lunches, as did top congressional affairs staff from the White House.

The sessions usually began with short presentations about the legislative agenda for the week by the chair of the policy committee and the Republican leader, followed by discussion among the GOP lawmakers about strategy. Typically, attendance was almost perfect. As the sessions proceeded, the deputy whips often would circulate among the tables, asking their assigned colleagues about their positions for pending whip counts. Indeed, it was fairly common for the whip cards to be handed out at the beginning of a party lunch, with instructions that results were due by the end of the meeting. If a deputy whip was unable to speak with a member in his or her "zone" during the lunch, follow-up contacts might be made at the staff level later in the afternoon. But if at all possible, positions were not recorded for members unless the question at some point was directly put to the Senator. On occasion, the completed whip cards referenced a position for a Senator, but with the caveat that the response had come "from staff."

Another forum for member-to-member whipping is the Senate floor itself, which one veteran staffer likened to "a huge political marketplace ... with a mix of people milling around, occasionally separating like a chemical reaction on partisan votes."[8] When roll calls occur in the full chamber, members often stay on the floor, speaking with colleagues for a few moments before returning to committee meetings or appointments in their offices. During floor votes, the whips and other Senate leaders know they may have the opportunity to talk briefly with colleagues about other pending matters, including the subjects of party whip counts. Much has been made of the heightened individualism and increased partisan polarization of the modern Senate (e.g., Sinclair, 1989, 2006). Neither chamber of Congress any longer resembles the "cocoon of good feeling" described by then Congressman Clem Miller during the early 1960s.[9] But the relatively small size of the Senate membership means that personal interactions at the member level can matter a great deal, and this is apparent in the internal operations of the whip system.

Before proceeding, a few comments are in order about the working relationship that existed between the Republican leader, Trent Lott, and Don Nickles, the party whip, during the three congresses under focus in this chapter. Both Lott and Nickles were ideological conservatives. But by most accounts, Trent Lott as leader was also a pragmatist who generally sought to cut the deals necessary to move legislation through the chamber. Nickles, by his own account, was primarily interested in policy and thus was less drawn to the bargaining and compromise that was Lott's great strength.[10] Throughout 1997–2002, there was periodic speculation that Nickles might challenge Lott for the position of Republican leader. Although the agendas of the two individuals may have diverged on occasion, there typically was broad agreement within the leadership about which issues and strategic concerns were party priorities, and thus fodder for whip activity. When it came to collecting information about member preferences, staff interviews and the archival record indicate that Nickles and his aides were team players. For purposes of analysis, we can treat the whips as agents for the Senate leadership and the Republican Conference as whole.

General Features

Senators, of course, represent states rather than congressional districts, and states generally are larger and more diverse than are the constituencies represented by members of the House. As a result, a larger percentage of Senators tend to hail from constituencies where presidential voting patterns are more proximate to the typical member of the opposite party than is the case for House members. Since the constituencies of Senators vary in size, and typically are much larger than are House districts, particular care must be taken in juxtaposing representational challenges within the Senate based on the presidential voting indicator. Still, it is instructive to calculate the average Democratic presidential vote within states represented by GOP and Democratic Senators, respectively, and determine whether a member is closer to her own party average or to the average for members of the other party. For Republican Senators during 1997–2002, a little over 37 percent were from states where presidential voting patterns more closely resembled the average for Democrats than for their fellow Republicans. That percentage is nearly triple the proportion of so-called outlier districts that we found for GOP House members during this period. For Senate Democrats, a little over 31 percent were from constituency outliers, which is slightly higher than what we found for their partisan counterparts in the House. Although the measure is rough, it does suggest that the potential for party-constituency cross pressure was more pronounced in the Senate, especially for members of the Republican majority.

Table 9.1 lists the GOP Senators during 1997–2002 who hailed from states where voting patterns in the most recent presidential contest more closely resembled the average for Democratic members than for their Republican colleagues. Not surprisingly, states from the northeast, the traditional bastion for centrist Republicanism, are disproportionately present, including Maine, New Hampshire, New York, Pennsylvania, Rhode Island, and Vermont. Also present are GOP Senators from midwestern and plains states where Democrats traditionally have done well, including Illinois, Iowa, Michigan, Minnesota, Missouri, and to some extent, Ohio. The presence of Senators from Arkansas in 1997–2000 and Tennessee in 2001–02 is probably an artifact of elevated Democratic presidential votes due to the presence of a favorite son at the top of the relevant ticket (Clinton of Arkansas in 1996 and Gore of Tennessee in 2000). But overall, the lists identify GOP Senators representing states that are out of step with the partisan-ideological leanings of most of their co-partisans in the chamber. Few of the states featured on the lists, you will notice, were represented by

TABLE 9.1. Partisan congruence of state-level presidential vote, Republican Senators closer to the other party average

105th Congress (1997–98)	106th Congress (1999–2000)	107th Congress (2001–02)
Abraham, Michigan	Abraham, Michigan	Bond, Missouri
Ashcroft, Missouri	Ashcroft, Missouri	Chafee, Rhode Island
Bond, Missouri	Bond, Missouri	Collins, Maine
Chafee, Rhode Island	Chafee, J., Rhode Island	Dewine, Ohio
Collins, Maine	Chafee, L., Rhode Island	Domenici, New Mexico
D'Amato, New York	Collins, Maine	Ensign, Nevada
Dewine, Ohio	Dewine, Ohio	Fitzgerald, Illinois
Domenici, New Mexico	Domenici, New Mexico	Frist, Tennessee
Gorton, Washington	Fitzgerald, Illinois	Grassley, Iowa
Grams, Minnesota	Gorton, Washington	Gregg, New Hampshire
Grassley, Iowa	Grams, Minnesota	Jeffords, Vermont
Gregg, New Hampshire	Grassley, Iowa	Santorum, Pennsylvania
Hutchinson, Arkansas	Gregg, New Hampshire	Smith, G., Oregon
Jeffords, Vermont	Hutchinson, Arkansas	Smith, R., New Hampshire
Roth, Delaware	Jeffords, Vermont	Snowe, Maine
Santorum, Pennsylvania	Roth, Delaware	Specter, Pennsylvania
Smith, G., Oregon	Santorum, Pennsylvania	Thompson, Tennessee
Smith, R., New Hampshire	Smith, G., Oregon	Voinovich, Ohio
Snowe, Maine	Smith, R., New Hampshire	
Specter, Pennsylvania	Snowe, Maine	
	Specter, Pennsylvania	
	Voinovich, Ohio	

two Republican Senators, which reflects the presence of important constituent audiences that tilt toward the Democrats. Along with the less favorable
procedural context that the majority leadership of the Senate confronts,
then, Senate GOP leaders also had to contend with greater proportions
of potentially cross-pressured members than did their counterparts on the
other side of the Capitol.

The Whipped Agenda

Bicameral differences in the context of whip action are also apparent in
the distribution of whip attention across policy categories. Table 9.2 shows
the incidence of Senate whip activity for the majority GOP across the 12
issue areas that structured our analysis of whip priorities in the House.[11]
Also featured is the portion of roll call votes within each category that
were directly targeted by the Senate majority whips. The calculus of whip
engagement implied by the behavioral approach should capture leadership
decision making in both chambers, not just the House. On both sides of
the Capitol, then, the whips should be activated on party priorities where
internal consensus is feasible and the outcome is in play. As a result, there
should be similarities in the issues targeted by Republican whips across the
Senate and House.

Indeed, the percentages reported in Table 9.2 do resemble what we
found for the House Republican majorities of period 4 in many ways. For
example, economic issues were often whipped by the GOP majorities in
both chambers during the late 1990s and early 2000s. Budget resolutions,
reconciliation bills, and related items are disproportionately important
to the majority party name brand on both sides of the Capitol. As in the
House, Congress/Govt ops, foreign policy, energy/environment, and
labor/consumer were also periodically targeted by GOP whip teams in the
Senate, but accounted for a lower proportion of overall whip activity than
did economic matters. In neither chamber did the GOP whips target a
single civil rights question for whipping during this time period. Whether
in the Senate or in the House, civil rights issues during the late 1990s and
early 2000s were primarily of importance to Democratic audiences.

Still, there are also significant differences between Republican whip
activity in the Senate and House. For one, although appropriations questions comprised nearly 35 percent of the whipped agenda for the House
Republicans of period 4, less than 12 percent of the questions whipped by
Senate Republican leaders were in that category. Moreover, while Chapter 8
reported that only about 4 percent of the questions whipped by Tom

DeLay's networks targeted health matters, that policy category accounted for about one-fifth of the whipped agenda for Senate Republicans of the period. And while less than 4 percent of the questions whipped by House Republican leaders dealt with education, on the Senate side of the Capitol GOP leaders allocated about 12 percent of their whip attention there.

These differences are fully consistent with the behavioral argument if we consider the bicameral context. First, the much higher fraction of cross-pressured moderates and other members from Democrat-leaning states within the Senate Republican Conferences of 1997–2002 shaped appropriations politics within the chamber in important ways. Although conservative Republicans also pushed for spending reductions in the Senate, within that chamber there was nothing like the deficit hawk revolt led by then-Representative Tom Coburn in the House. Traditionally, the Senate has functioned as an "appeals court" of sorts, where the constituencies denied requested funding during the House appropriations process are able to secure additional monies for their priorities during Senate consideration of the annual spending measures (Fenno 1966). Although party polarization increased in both the Senate and the House during these years, the Senate appropriations process remained somewhat less partisan than its House counterpart. As a result, Senate Republican leaders did not need to prioritize appropriations questions for whipping to the same extent as did the DeLay operation.

The heightened emphasis Senate Republican leaders placed on health policy, as well as education matters, also derived from contextual differences between the chambers. In the House, the majority leadership's enhanced

TABLE 9.2. Distribution of whip attention by issue area, Senate Republicans, 1997–2002

Issue area	% Whipped Questions	% Votes Whipped*
Congress/Gov ops	7.1	5.8
Defense	1.6	1.5
Foreign policy	6.3	9.1
Economy	13.4	5.0
Trade	5.5	14.3
Energy/Environment	4.7	5.1
Civil rights	0	0
Social welfare	2.4	7.3
Health	18.9	11.1
Education	11.8	11.3
Labor/Consumer	6.3	8.3
Appropriations	11.8	3.2
Other	10.2	7.5

*Only nonunanimous votes used.

powers over the floor agenda reduce the ability of the minority party to unravel majority coalitions with strategically crafted amendments. Again, although priority recognition and related tactics can provide the Senate majority leadership with a degree of leverage over the floor agenda, there is nothing analogous to the House Rules Committee on the Senate side of the Capitol. Germaneness rules (or the lack thereof) also matter here. In the House, only amendments that are substantively relevant to the bill under consideration are in order unless the special rule for the measure stipulates otherwise. Senate rules do not include a general germaneness requirement for the amendment process. Often, the chamber agrees by unanimous consent to only consider amendments that are substantively relevant to the underlying text. But absent unanimity about the floor agenda, individual members are remarkably free to offer nongermane alternatives and essentially change the policy subject on the floor for a time.

As the Congress grew more polarized along partisan lines during the 1990s, members of the Senate minority party made increasing use of nongermane floor amendments to advance their own legislative priorities—a tactic that was not available to minority leaderships in the House (Smith 2014). During 1997–2002, the public was concerned about the quality and availability of health insurance, and by wide margins had more confidence in the ability of Democrats, as opposed to Republicans, to handle the associated policy challenges (Evans 2001). As a result, prominent Democrats, especially Edward Kennedy, D-Mass., ranking member on the committee with primary jurisdiction over health, regularly attempted to use the Senate amendment process to advance and publicize party initiatives in that area. The majority Republicans, for their part, produced GOP alternatives to the minority backed proposals, but their internal divisions made them vulnerable to Democratic substitutes and second-degree amendments on the floor. To be sure, health insurance issues, Medicare prescription drug benefits, and other health items also created problems for GOP leaders in the House, but their greater control over the agenda gave them leverage unavailable to Trent Lott, Don Nickles, and other Republican leaders on the Senate side. For these reasons, Senate GOP leaders regularly needed to whip health care items.

Similar dynamics characterized education policy. Like health proposals, education issues traditionally had been a Democratic message priority, where most citizens tended to view that party as more capable of providing leadership. In the late 1990s, however, Senate Republicans decided their party potentially could compete with the Democrats on education matters, and they developed an alternative program that featured increased flexibility in how states could allocate federal education funds, along with heightened accountability for achieving outcome targets stipulated by the federal government (Evans and Oleszek 2000). Such initiatives began with the "education flexibility" legislation passed during 1999–2000 and signed by President Clinton, and culminated in the "No Child Left Behind" law that cleared Congress during 2001–02 and was signed by President Bush. As was the case with health policy, the enhanced ability of Democrats to secure Senate consideration of their education amendments created the need for more GOP whip attention in that chamber. The distinctive procedural context of the Senate, in other words, make it more likely that health and education items would be in play on the Senate floor (condition 3 for whip engagement), and the result was the elevated whip percentages in Table 9.2.

Member Loyalty

Overall, the distribution of whip count responses for Senate Republicans during 1997–2002 resembles what we found for GOP members on whipped matters in the House during those years. For Senate Republicans, about three-quarters of the responses were Y/LY, 9.7 percent were undecided, 8.4 percent were N/LN, and 7.1 percent entailed some portion of nonresponse. For House Republicans during this period, the analogous proportions were 73.7 percent, 11.3 percent, 8.6 percent, and 6.5 percent. When we consider the legislative agenda as a whole, the same general array of constituent audiences shape position taking within the Republican Conferences of the two chambers, so broad similarities in the distribution of whip count responses come as no surprise. Still, the aggregate tallies underscore the significant vote-gathering challenges facing majority party leaders in the Senate. With partisan majorities of 55 in the 105th Congress, 54 in the 106th Congress, and just 50 during the opening months of the 107th Congress, Trent Lott and Don Nickles typically had around 40 co-partisans in the Y/LY column on party whip counts. The number was far short of a majority, and even further from the 60 votes necessary to overcome a filibuster by the minority party. Especially in the Senate, position fluidity during the final stages of the floor decision-making process was critical to legislative outcomes, and the challenges such fluidity signaled for the majority leadership often were substantial.

Our juxtaposition of whip activity in the Senate and the House continues in Table 9.3, which summarizes the distribution of positions taken by individual Senate Republicans during the whip process, 1997–2002. The table

denotes the incidence of the standard response categories, overall, and is
also broken down by the constituency and member characteristics that
structured our treatment of whip responses in the House. Only questions
with a clear GOP position and complete or nearly complete results (25 percent or less of the Republican Conference is missing) are included.

As the table indicates, Senate GOP leaders faced their own version
of the "northeastern problem" confronted by DeLay in the House.
Republican Senators from the northeast were substantially less likely (by
a full 20 percent) to report as Y/LY during the whip process, and significantly more likely to be in the undecided, N/LN, or "other" columns.
Across the other four regions, there are no clear differences. The reason
for the attenuated party support numbers in the northeast largely derives
from the greater prevalence of Democrat-leaning states in that part of the
country. For Republican members from states where presidential voting

TABLE 9.3. Distribution of majority whip responses, selected state and member characteristics,
Senate Republicans, 1997–2002

		Y/LY	U	N/LN	Other
Overall		74.8	9.7	8.4	7.1
Region	NE	55.8	16.2	16.2	11.9
	MW/Plains	76.2	9.6	8.9	5.2
	South	79.3	7.7	5.3	7.7
	Border	81.0	5.6	4.6	8.8
	West	78.9	9.2	7.4	4.5
State-level pres vote	Closer to D ave	65.2	12.9	12.9	9.1
	Closer to R ave	80.4	7.9	5.8	5.9
Committee of jurisdiction	On	75.6	7.8	8.7	7.9
	Off	74.6	10.3	8.3	6.9
Seniority	First term	75.5	9.3	9.8	5.4
	Second term	78.5	8.6	6.0	6.9
	Third term or more	71.8	11.0	8.0	9.3
Extended leadership	Yes	75.2	9.4	7.2	8.1
	No	74.2	10.1	10.1	5.6
Whip network	Yes	78.5	8.6	8.6	4.2
	No	73.8	10.0	8.3	7.8
In cycle	Yes	71.3	10.5	10.0	8.3
	No	76.3	9.4	7.7	6.6

more closely resembled the average for Democratic Senators than the average for their GOP colleagues, the prevalence of Y/LY responses is much lower than it was for Republicans representing constituencies closer to the party mainstream.[12]

Notice that membership on the committee with jurisdiction over a whipped item does not appear to have much of an effect on whip count responses. Unlike their House counterparts, Senators often serve on three or more panels, Senate committees receive limited deference on the floor, and the ability to offer nongermane floor amendments provides all members with the chance to meaningfully participate on legislation regardless of whether they are on the committee of jurisdiction. Moreover, the personal staffs of rank-and-file Senators are relatively large and members of the chamber are more likely to have access to the expert assistance necessary to form positions independent of the leadership regardless of whether they serve on the relevant committee. Not surprisingly, the prevalence of undecided members is somewhat smaller among committee members. Membership on the panel of jurisdiction means that such lawmakers often must make up their minds and articulate positions earlier in the legislative game. But overall, the Senate is less committee oriented than is the House and this is apparent in the table.

As in the House, the most senior members of the chamber appear to be less inclined to support the leadership position during the whip process. More senior Republicans may have the stature within the chamber necessary to signal independence from the party hierarchy. Inclusion in the extended leadership (a formal leadership position or a position on a major party committee) is associated with slightly higher levels of leadership support during the whip process, but the differences are not very large. Similarly, participation in the whip network as a deputy whip is associated with modest increases in leadership support, but the difference largely derives from fewer nonresponses, which we would expect given that these are the lawmakers doing the counting.

For the Senate, we also need to consider whether or not a member is up for reelection at the end of the relevant Congress. Within the chamber, distinctions often are drawn between Senators who are "in cycle" and other members who are not. A member is in cycle if she is in the final two years of the six-year term and is expected to run for reelection. The claim often is made that constituency pressures are somewhat less pronounced for Senators immediately following their election or reelection, and then step up as the next campaign becomes more temporally proximate. As a result, pro-leadership position taking during the whip process may be lower for Senators who are in cycle. Indeed, as reported in Table 9.3 Senators entering the campaign phase are somewhat less likely to answer as Y/LY on party whip checks and somewhat more likely to fall into one of the other response categories.

The relationship between the positions Senators took during the whip process and the roll call votes they cast (assuming a vote could be directly linked to a whipped question) are summarized in Table 9.4. Once again, the table setup resembles the approach we adopted for the House in previous chapters, with the addition of reelection proximity as a potential factor. As was the case for the House, nearly all of the Y/LY responders supported the party on associated votes, party support dropped off as we move from undecided to N/LN, and leadership loyalty within the "other" category falls between the percentage of pro-leadership votes within the Y/LY and undecided columns.

TABLE 9.4. Leadership support on votes by whip category, selected state and member characteristics, Senate Republicans, 1997–2002

		Y/LY	U	N/LN	Other
Overall		97.6	74.4	27.4	81.7
Region	NE	97.7	69.8	21.4	69.0
	MW/Plains	96.3	79.7	32.4	65.0
	South	97.7	76.6	21.7	89.1
	Border	96.8	77.3	56.3	97.1
	West	98.6	73.2	29.2	94.1
State-level pres vote	Closer to D ave	97.2	73.8	26.3	70.6
	Closer to R ave	97.8	75.0	29.0	90.6
Committee of jurisdiction	On	98.2	70.4	29.3	84.5
	Off	97.4	75.2	26.8	80.8
Seniority	First term	97.2	77.5	28.3	67.6
	Second term	98.4	63.8	19.6	84.8
	Third term or more	97.6	76.6	29.5	90.7
Extended leadership	Yes	97.8	72.9	31.4	86.8
	No	97.3	76.6	23.0	71.8
Whip network	Yes	98.5	71.9	23.6	67.7
	No	97.3	74.9	28.4	84.2
In cycle	Yes	97.7	74.8	30.9	78.4
	No	97.5	74.3	25.7	83.3

When we attempt to break down such patterns by the explanatory factors included in the table, the various constituency and member
characteristics do not appear to make much of a difference. There are some
notable differences for the various forms of nonresponse. Among members
in the "other" column during the whip process, for example, leadership
support on votes is substantially lower for members from states with presidential voting patterns closer to the Democratic average or who are in
cycle. Similarly, within the "other" column leadership support levels on
votes are also lower for members serving their first terms in the chamber,
are part of the whip network, or are not included in the extended leadership. Compared to the House, however, the actual number of nonresponses
is relatively small, and we should not infer all that much from such a limited subset of the evidence. Overall, the impact of the various constituency
and member characteristics appears to be primarily felt during the whip
stage, when members stake out initial positions, rather than the processes
through which such positions translate into votes. Why the lack of strong
associations here, when such relationships were apparent on the House
Republican side for period 4? Compared to the much larger House, the
number of Senators who are seriously "in play" on major votes may be as
few as a dozen or less, and the factors that determine their choices tend to
be idiosyncratic, typically varying by member and question. This is why
Trent Lott often likened coalition building within the chamber to "herding
cats."[13]

Before proceeding to an analysis of the outcomes of the Senate whip
process, we should briefly consider the relationship between whip count
responses and roll call loyalty, on the one hand, and member ideology
on the other. Recall that for the Republican House majorities of period
4, the level of leadership support on whip counts increased markedly
with member conservatism, but then dropped off somewhat for the
most rightward leaning elements of the GOP Conference. Similarly,
when we considered party loyalty on the associate roll calls, within each
whip response category the prevalence of pro-party voting generally
increased with ideological conservatism, but also dropped off for the
extreme right.

Interestingly, a nearly identical relationship between member ideology and leadership loyalty at the whip and roll call stages is apparent
for Senate Republicans during these years. If we divide the entire Senate
into 10 equally sized deciles based on their DW-NOMINATE scores for
the relevant Congress, Senate Republicans like their House counterparts
are entirely clustered in the six most conservative deciles and none fall

in the four most liberal. Based on the standard measures of roll call ideology, almost complete partisan polarization characterized both chambers by 1997–2002. In addition, the prevalence of Y/LY responders during the Senate GOP whip process increased with member conservatism. While about 47 percent of Republicans in the most moderate decile answered as yes or leaning yes on party whip checks, the portion of leadership supporters among members in decile 8, located near the party median, was nearly 80 percent, with analogous reductions for the other response categories. For the two most ideologically conservative deciles (nine and ten), however, the portion answering Y/LY fell to about 75 percent.

When we consider the prevalence of pro-leadership voting within each response category, there is still more evidence for alienation at the ideological extremes. Not surprisingly, for members answering Y/LY, votes were overwhelming cast for the leadership position (> 95 percent) across the entire ideological spectrum. Among the initially undecided, the portion of pro-leadership votes overall was about 74 percent, but for the most ideologically moderate decile and for the most conservative decile there is a drop-off of about 5 percent. Similarly, among members who were initially no or leaning that way, about one-third of the members near the median ideological position within the party ended up voting with the leadership on whipped roll calls, but for the most moderate and conservative deciles these levels were about 19 and 17 percent, respectively. Like Tom DeLay in the House, in other words, Senate Republican Whip Don Nickles confronted coalition-building challenges that arose in part from both ends of the ideological spectrum. Adjusting legislation to the right risked the votes of party moderates, while tacking toward the center meant possibly losing the support of party conservatives.

Outcomes

Now consider the aggregate outcomes of the floor whipping process in the Senate. Categorizing whip outcomes is more complicated in the Senate than is the case for the House. In the House, the majority leadership has effective control over the structure of the floor agenda, albeit subject to the support of a majority of voting members when a special rule is in place. As a result, there is considerable predictability about which alternatives will be considered by the chamber, the terms of consideration, and so on. The positions of individual members may be in flux and the legislative outcomes in play, but the contents and structure of the floor agenda tend to be known by the whips ahead of time.

Agenda setting in the Senate is very different. Most agenda decisions are made via unanimous consent agreements (UCAs), which are binding orders of the chamber and only have force if no Senator objects. Typically, floor action on major measures requires dozens of discrete UCAs, which are adopted sequentially in a piecemeal fashion, with each covering some segment or juncture of the floor decision-making process. As often is the case, one or more members will signal opposition to a proposed UCA, and negotiations will ensue between the objectors and backers of the legislation about possible substantive modifications, or alterations to the terms of debate. If an agreement can be struck, the objections are lifted, the UCA is adopted, and floor consideration proceeds. If not, backers of the measure may need to file for cloture. Assuming the requisite 60 votes can be secured to invoke cloture, legislative action on the underlying question commences subject to the restrictions stipulated in Senate Rule 22. If not, floor consideration of the targeted question is effectively blocked unless the negotiators can arrive at some sort of bargain. On important or controversial matters, portions of the debate may be structured by UCAs, while cloture is necessary elsewhere on the agenda. And of course, if the motion to proceed to consideration draws objections and cloture cannot be invoked, floor action on the entire measure may be stymied from the beginning.

Compared to the House, then, agenda setting in the Senate is more a byproduct of ongoing bargaining between interested members than it is the exercise of a formal prerogative by the majority leadership (Den Hartog and Monroe 2011). Decisions about the structure of the agenda and the contents of the proposals included on that agenda are functionally inseparable, and as floor action nears there often is not much advance notice about timing or contents. The distinctions that we draw between outright party wins and losses in our analysis of House whip outcomes are also clear-cut in the Senate. Often, the Senate whips ask their members whether or not they will vote for an amendment or in favor of the passage of legislation, roll calls are cast, and the party position either wins or loses. Similarly, it also is fairly straightforward to identify instances where major changes in a whipped proposal are made during the coalition-building process on the floor. On the Senate side, however, the functional inseparability of agenda setting and legislative construction complicates somewhat distinctions between cases where the leadership pulls an item from the agenda and situations where chamber consideration is obviated by events. Indeed, while this last category was seldom necessary in the House analysis, it is more prevalent in the Senate evidence. For these reasons, we can once again rely on the four-point scale used in the House chapters, where whipped outcomes were classified as party wins, major change, pulled from the agenda, or an unambiguous loss. But here we also need to report results for the "other" category that includes items that could not be readily placed in one of the main classifications. Table 9.5 reports the outcomes for the GOP leadership on the questions that were the subject of whip counts, 1997–2002.

As you can see, there are certain additional differences between the Senate outcome table and analogous tables reported for the House. As mentioned, the GOP had clear (but small) majorities in the Senate during the 105th and 106th Congress. In 2000, however, the voters produced a Senate that was equally divided between the parties. With the 50–50 split, then Vice President Richard Cheney cast the deciding organizational

TABLE 9.5. Senate Republican success on whipped questions by vote threshold, 1997–2002

	Win	Major change	Pull	Loss	Other
105th/106th Congress (1997–2000) Republican Majority					
One-third plus one	1	0	0	0	0
	(100)				
41	2	0	0	1	0
	(66.7)			(33.3)	
Plurality	43	0	4	4	6
	(75.4)		(7.0)	(7.0)	(10.5)
60	5	2	3	4	2
	(31.3)	(12.5)	(18.8)	(25.0)	(12.5)
Two-thirds	1	0	0	0	1
	(50.0)				(50.0)
NA	2	0	0	0	2
	(50.0)				(50.0)
Totals	54	2	7	9	11
	(65.1)	(2.4)	(8.4)	(10.8)	(13.3)
107th Congress I (1/20/01–6/5/01) Republican majority					
Plurality	4	0	0	3	0
	(57.1)			(42.9)	
107th Congress II (6/6/01–10/5/02) Democratic majority					
41	9	0	0	2	0
	(81.8)			(18.2)	
Plurality	9	0	1	5	3
	(50.0)		(5.6)	(27.8)	(16.7)
60	1	0	0	3	0
	(25.0)			(75.0)	
Total	19	0	1	10	3
	(57.6)		(3.0)	(30.3)	(9.1)

Note: Cell entries are the number of items, with percentages in parentheses.

vote in favor of the Republicans, so the GOP continued to function as the majority party for a time. In June 2001, however, James Jeffords, R-Vt., switched his partisan affiliation from Republican to Independent and opted to vote with the Democrats on organizational matters, which effectively flipped majority control to the other party. For this reason, in presenting information about whipped outcomes, we need to distinguish between the different gradations of majority and minority status. In the table, outcome results are first presented for the 105th and 106th Congresses where the GOP had continuous majority party status, and then for the 107th Congress, with the periods of Republican and Democratic party organization treated separately.

Especially in the Senate, we also need to consider the vote threshold necessary for a party to prevail (Krehbiel, 1997). The opportunity to filibuster and other non-majoritarian features of Senate procedure create considerable variance in the height of the vote-gathering bar a Senate party must clear to prevail. On partisan issues, it can be relatively easy for leaders to marshal the 41 votes necessary to defeat cloture and thereby block changes to the status quo opposed by the party. In contrast, gathering enough support to reach the 60 votes necessary to overcome a filibuster can be difficult for even the most cohesive of majority parties. As a result, we need to consider how the vote threshold affected the coalition-building efficacy of Republican leaders. Indeed, these thresholds themselves are often a reflection of party strategy, as leaders selectively choose which motions to whip based in part on their ability to muster the required number of votes. Again, the behavioral theory predicts that leaders will engage the whips on matters where the outcome is in play, so clearly they should consider the threshold for victory when making such judgments.

For this reason, Table 9.5 also reports outcome results based on five vote thresholds. For attempts to block treaties or veto overrides, the relevant threshold is relatively low—just one-third plus one of voting members. For questions that directly or indirectly required Republican members to defeat a cloture motion or a motion to waive budget rules, the threshold is signified as "41" (of course, fewer may have been required if all Senators were not present and voting). Most questions—amendments, motions to table amendments, and often final passage of measures and nominations— required a plurality of members present and voting. Still other whipped matters (for example, motions to invoke cloture or to waive budget procedures) required that the party muster 60 votes to prevail. Treaties and veto overrides require a two-thirds super-majority. If a threshold did not surface in the evidence for a particular period of time, that threshold is omitted in the relevant portion of Table 9.5. And during 1997–2000, four whipped questions could not be meaningfully assigned a vote threshold and are simply denoted as NA for "not applicable."[14]

Overall, the Nickles whip operation won 62.6 percent of the questions it targeted; under two percent were instances of major change; 6.5 percent of the proposals were pulled from the agenda; 7.9 percent resulted in unambiguous losses; and 11.4 percent could not be classified. During the House majorities of period 4, you will recall, the DeLay operations won 75.5 percent of the questions it whipped, prevailed with major modifications on 7.5 percent, pulled the item on 7 percent, and experienced a clear-cut loss on 8 percent. At first blush, the prevalence of GOP wins appears higher on the House side. But keep in mind that the Senate was equally divided between the parties during 2001–02, and that for much of the 107th Congress the Republicans were formally the partisan minority. As Table 9.5 reports, the Nickles victory rate for 1997–2000 when the GOP had continuous majority status was over 65 percent. And if we omit items where outcomes could not be classified, which are prevalent in the Senate evidence, the outcome percentages for the Nickles team were actually very similar to what we found for the House.

Notice also that the vote thresholds make a difference. During 1997–2000, the GOP win rates were substantially larger for questions decided by a plurality vote (or less). Only seven whipped questions were settled during the opening months of Republican control in 2001, and each was a plurality matter. But after organizational control shifted to the Democrats in June, sharp differences in GOP success by decision threshold again become apparent. While the Republicans won over 80 percent of items where their vote-gathering bar was 41, their win rates dropped significantly for plurality items and matters where they needed 60 votes to prevail. Interestingly, the success rates for the Nickles whip team did not change all that much across the periods of Republican and Democratic organization during the 107th Congress. The percentages for outright wins were nearly identical and the fraction for outright losses actually declined after the Jeffords defection.

The reason, of course, is that GOP leaders chose a very different mix of motions over which to fight when they were in the minority. Although their success rate on whipped questions remained high, fully half of these victories were successful attempts to block cloture or forestall efforts to waive the Budget Act where the vote-gathering bar was relatively low. Rather than contest the Democrats on amendment votes, for instance, they opted for motions with the lower threshold requirement of just 41 votes. Nine other GOP victories occurred on matters settled by a plurality and it is important not to overgeneralize. Still, Republican leaders clearly altered their mix of strategies to leverage their considerable blocking power under chamber rules. Precisely because the membership of the Senate was unchanged from the period of Republican control in early 2001, the magnitude of the GOP leadership's strategic adjustments is indicative of the importance of formal party control, even within the freewheeling procedural context of the contemporary Senate. Yet, the efficacy of the GOP whip operation after the Democrats gained majority status is also indicative of the enhanced leverage available to Senate minorities relative to their counterparts in the House.

Once again, it also is instructive to break down party win rates on whipped questions by issue content. Given the smaller population of whipped items relative to the four House periods, we need to be especially careful not to infer too much from issue categories containing only a few items. But certain of the policy areas, such as the economy, health, education, and appropriations, include 15 or more questions each, and 5 more (Congress/Gov ops, foreign policy, trade, energy/environment, and labor/consumer) include 6 to 8 whipped questions. There is considerable variation in GOP success across the policy areas with ample evidence, ranging from a low of just one-third for energy/environment to a high of nearly 87 percent on education matters. Other Senate Republican win rates include 85.7 percent for trade and economic issues, 73.3 percent on appropriations, 70.6 percent on economic matters, 62.5 percent on labor/consumer, 57.1 percent on foreign policy, and about 43 percent on Congress/Gov ops (campaign finance reform also bedeviled GOP leaders in the Senate). For health issues, which constituted the most heavily whipped policy area for Senate Republicans during 1997–2002, the party clearly won about half of the whipped questions. Why did the party prevail on certain whipped matters, and suffer some gradation of party loss on the others? To gain further insight on the sources of party success and failure in the Senate, we can consider the health questions in more detail.

Healthcare

During 1997–2002, Senate GOP leaders whipped 19 distinct questions classified as healthcare issues and for which complete or nearly complete information is available about the positions taken by rank-and-file members. These items, along with the standard summary information about party coalition building, are denoted in Table 9.6. Two whipped

TABLE 9.6. Coalition-building success, health policy

Question	Y/LY	U	N/LN	Other	Dem support	Min nec pickup	Actual pickup
GOP win							
Health expenditures amdt 1997	37	7	2	9	18	–4	8
Medical savings accounts amdt 1997	39	4	0	12			
Tobacco revenue bud point of order 1998	39	5	0	11	1	1	14
Cloture tobacco cmte sub 1998	36	4	14	1	2	2	4
Patients' bill of rights 1998	50	4	1	0			
Dem patients' rights amdt to agric approps 1999	49	0	2	4	0	2	4
GOP patients' rights amdt to agric approps 1999	49	0	2	4	0	1	6
Patients' rights to sue amdt 1999	46	6	1	2	0	5	7
Patient's rights medical necessity amdt 1999	50	3	1	1	0	1	2
Rx Daschle-Kennedy amdt point of order 2002	42	1	0	6	0	–2	5
Rx Graham-Smith amdt point of order 2002	35	5	2	7	6	–1	9
Pull							
Medical savings accounts expansion amdt 1997	36	5	3	11			
GOP health care proposal 1998	47	5	1	2			
Cloture pain relief prevention 2000	42	11	1	1			
Loss							
Patients' rights state deference amdt 2001	43	2	1	3	1	5	0
Bipartisan patients' rights bill 2001	35	2	8	4	1	12	0
Other							
Patients' right to sue amdt 1998	51	2	1	1			
Medical savings account amdt to strike 1998	53	1	0	1			
Patients' rights state preemption amdt 1998	54	0	0	1			

questions initially were categorized as appropriations issues using the classification scheme employed in this book, but are more properly viewed as part of chamber action on managed care reform, perhaps the central health policy issue of the 105th and 106th Congresses. Both related to Democratic attempts to force managed care reform onto the Senate agenda via amendments to the agricultural appropriations bill, and they are also included in Table 9.6 because of the tie-in to health.

As you can see, Senate Republicans were fairly successful on whipped healthcare questions. For this slice of the evidence, there were just two outright losses, both relating to managed care and occurring just weeks after the Democrats assumed majority control of the chamber in June 2001. Three items were pulled from the agenda and three more fell in the "other" category—for these questions the Senate failed to take action. The remaining 11 were unambiguous GOP wins. With the sole exception of the health expenditures amendment in 1997, crossover support from Democrats was slim to none, the minimum necessary pickups were generally positive, and Senate leaders prevailed in each case, often narrowly. The impression left by the table, then, is one of consequential and mostly effective partisan coalition building by Trent Lott and Don Nickles on health legislation. Since the bulk of the questions dealt with managed care reform, it is instructive to look still closer at leadership tactics there.

Following defeat of the Clinton administration's proposal for comprehensive healthcare reform in 1994, the House and Senate shifted toward more incremental proposals, including initiatives to increase protections for customers of managed care organizations.[15] These health plans, many critics argued, were routinely denying patients medically necessary services in order to hold down costs. The major proponents of managed care reform included consumer organizations, patients' rights groups, and a broad coalition of physician and non-physician providers. Lobbying against the proposals were many employers, managed care providers, and the health insurance industry. Although there were differences of opinion within each congressional party, Democrats generally favored major reforms, while Republicans were in outright opposition or preferred a more limited approach. During the late 1990s, the issue was highly salient with the public, and the Clinton administration and congressional Democrats made it a central message priority. Republicans sought to counter the Democratic proposals with their own, more market-oriented alternatives and to otherwise limit the political damage.

On the House side of the Capitol, GOP leaders could rely on their enhanced agenda prerogatives to contain the momentum for managed care reform (with only limited success, it should be emphasized). But within the Senate, the open-ended nature of the agenda setting process provided Democrats with numerous opportunities to secure votes on party-backed alternatives. Within the chamber, the leading Democratic proposal for managed care reform, often called "The Patients' Bill of Rights," was sponsored by Edward Kennedy. In April of 1998, Kennedy forced a test vote on his proposal during chamber consideration of the annual budget resolution. The proposal was defeated via a 51-47 party-line vote, but it marked the opening salvo in what would be a three-year partisan struggle. Sensing that they needed to do more than simply vote no, Republican leaders crafted their own managed care proposal that involved less federal intervention into the healthcare marketplace and a more limited expansion of patient guarantees. As part of their effort to "inoculate" themselves on the issue, Senate Republicans also took to calling their proposal, "The Patients' Bill of Rights."[16] Majority Whip Don Nickles was the key player for Senate Republicans here, and he led an informal task force aimed at crafting managed care alternatives acceptable to the party. A product of nearly 18 months of private meetings, the Senate GOP alternative was formally released in June 1998 and was not considered in committee, yet another indicator of its importance to the party program.

With two dramatically different and dueling versions of the "Patients' Bill of Rights," Senators recognized that a key tactical question would be the choice of vehicle for amendment. At first, the expectation was that the GOP version would be the base bill, and Democrats responded by demanding ample opportunities to offer amendments to that package on the floor. Nickles and Lott, in contrast, preferred just two up-or-down votes, one on the Republican measure and the other on the Democratic substitute. As a result of this disagreement over process, the Senate was unable to act on either proposal during summer and fall of 1998 and managed care legislation failed to clear the chamber during the 105th Congress. As shown in Table 9.6, Senate Republican leaders whipped five questions related to managed care during 1998. For four of them, the procedural snarl resulted in no action (one pulled and three in the "other" category), and thus an ambiguous outcome for the parties. The sole GOP win that year pertained to a July 9th question that asked rank-and-file members whether they would vote against the Kennedy version of the legislation. Since the party was opposed and the Democratic initiative did not pass in any form, this question is classified as a win for the GOP. Interestingly, although there was considerable support among moderate Republicans for some version of managed care reform, only five members were not included in the Y/LN column on that question: Alphonse D'Amato, R-N.Y., Olympia Snowe, R-Maine, Ben Nighthorse Campbell, R-Colo., and Larry Craig, R-Idaho, were undecided, and Arlen Specter, R-Penn., was recorded as no. Three of the five were from states with presidential voting patterns closer to the average Democrat, and thus had to explain their positions to constituent audiences more friendly to the Democratic approach on health issues. Although Lott and Nickles were able to contain the Democratic momentum, neither party viewed the overall outcome in 1998 as a clear-cut victory and both recognized the subject would be prominent on the Senate agenda the next year.

Indeed, both chambers devoted considerable attention to managed care reform during the 106th Congress. Clearly under pressure from the Clinton administration and Senate Democrats, as well as a coalition of outside groups lobbying for reform, Senate Republicans marked up their leadership's market-oriented approach to managed care in the Committee on Health, Education, Labor, and Pensions in early spring 1999. During committee deliberations, Democrats offered 18 amendments, all of which were defeated on party-line votes.[17] The measure was reported to the full chamber on March 18, also along party lines. At that point, the focus once again turned to procedure, with Democrats pushing for multiple opportunities to offer amendments on the floor and the Republican leadership attempting to restrict the amendment process. The negotiations over process dragged on through May.

Frustrated by the inaction, Democratic leaders in June attempted to force chamber consideration of the issue by offering the Kennedy bill as a nongermane amendment to the year's appropriations bill for agriculture.[18] In response, Lott and Nickles offered their own proposal as a second-degree amendment to the Kennedy initiative. On June 22, the leadership asked rank-and-file members whether they would vote to table the Democratic amendment, and also whether they would vote against tabling the second-degree GOP proposal to be offered by Lott. As Table 9.6 indicates, 49 members responded as Y/LY, two were N/LN, and four were nonresponsive. No crossover votes from Democrats were expected and none were received.[19] On both whip counts, the "no" responses were from Peter Fitzgerald, R- Ill., and Arlen Specter, both ideological moderates from states that often voted Democratic. The members without a formal response included Lott and Nickles, and they were left off because their positions were obvious. No position also was recorded for Judd Gregg, chief deputy whip for the Senate GOP, and he likewise was almost certainly left blank because his support for the leadership position was never in

question. The final member in the "other" category, though, was Olympia
Snowe, who like Fitzgerald and Specter was a moderate from a Democrat-
leaning state and still in play on the questions. On the associated roll calls,
all of these members supported the party position not to table the Lott
second-degree amendment, but two of them—Fitzgerald and Specter—
also voted contrary to the party and against tabling the Democratic alternative. Neither defection was pivotal to the outcome, however, and were
much easier for the two members to explain back home than would have
been pro-leadership votes.

In response, Democrats used the dilatory potential of chamber rules to
shut down the Senate agenda for nearly a week. Work on appropriations bills
and other must-pass measures ground to a halt.[20] To end the embarrassing
impasse, Lott and Minority Leader Thomas Daschle, D-S.Dak., struck
a bargain about the terms for considering managed care reform on the
Senate floor. In exchange for an absence of limits on the number of
amendments to be considered, Lott secured a commitment for a vote on
passage by July 15, and also the right to offer the final amendment himself. Interestingly, there was open disagreement between Lott and Nickles
about how to proceed with negotiations over the managed care agenda.
Nickles opposed granting the minority unlimited amending opportunities
because he believed Democrats would use the amendment process to force
cross-pressured Republicans like Fitzgerald and Specter to cast repeated
votes contrary to the preferences of important constituent groups in their
states. However, frustrated by the logjam on the floor, Lott went ahead and
cut the deal with Daschle anyway, and legislative work on the Senate floor
began again.

When floor action on managed care reform commenced in early
July 1999, Lott attempted to preempt the avalanche of Democratic
amendments by using the Kennedy proposal as the base bill on the floor,
rather than the revised Nickles measure that was the main GOP alternative.[21] By starting with the Democratic proposal, Lott reasoned, there
would be less material for them to use as amendment fodder in the days
ahead. Then, relying on his right to offer the final alternative, the majority
leader could offer the Nickles measure as the last amendment, thereby
replacing the Democratic language, and secure a final up-down vote on the
Republican proposal. As a result, Lott reintroduced the Daschle-Kennedy
patients' rights measure under a new bill number and brought it up on the
floor. Clearly outflanked, the Democrats attempted to respond in an analogous fashion by themselves reintroducing the Republican version of the
legislation, with an eye toward using that language as the base vehicle for

offering their amendments. But here, the contents of the bargain over the agenda and the majority leader's priority recognition rights gave the GOP the upper hand and their strategy prevailed.

When the full chamber took up the issue in mid-July 1999, both bills were considered simultaneously, with the Republicans offering multiple amendments to the Democratic package, and the Democrats doing the same vis-à-vis the GOP proposal. Over the four-day floor fight, Lott and Nickles were able to defeat a succession of Democratic amendments, all by near party-line votes. For many of the Democratic proposals, GOP leaders orchestrated the drafting and consideration of so-called mirror amendments that took the form of Republican substitutes or second-degree proposals.[22] When Democrat Charles Robb, D-Va., offered an amendment to expand healthcare coverage for women, for instance, GOP leaders saw to it that Olympia Snowe offered similar language expanding coverage for mastectomies that was acceptable to rank-and-file Republicans. They could cast votes in favor of women's healthcare, while still voting against Robb and sticking with the party. The Snowe proposal prevailed with the support of every Republican Senator except moderate John Chafee of Rhode Island. As the final amendment, Lott offered a package containing the Republican-backed managed care initiatives, plus a related tax measure. The amendment passed and the GOP leadership won on the floor.

On July 12, as part of the preparation for floor action, Senate GOP leaders had whipped two questions relevant to the pending fight. More concretely, they asked rank-and-file Republicans whether they would support the Nickles task force and vote to strike from the Democratic bill a provision granting patients the right to sue managed care companies in court. In addition, they asked fellow Republicans to support the task force by voting to strike a Kennedy-Daschle proposal establishing a new federal definition of "medical necessity." As denoted in the table, the minimum necessary pickup on the liability amendment was five votes, and for the medical necessity amendment the pickup requirement was one. Once again, crossover support on the proposals from Democrats was not anticipated, and on the roll calls no members of the minority broke with their party. As a result, Nickles and Lott focused on the handful of Republicans who were undecided, opposed, or who failed to report a position.

On the pivotal liability amendment, there were six undecided members, one N/LN, and two in the "other" column. The undecideds included Spencer Abraham, R-Mich., John Ashcroft, R-Mo., Chafee, Thad Cochran, R-Miss., Craig, and Specter. All but Specter supported the leadership on the vote. Peter Fitzgerald was listed as leaning no and he likewise defected on the roll call. The two nonresponders were Charles Grassley, R-Iowa, and John Warner, R-Va., and both cast pro-leadership votes. As the table indicates, for the medical necessity amendment there were three undecideds and one each in the N/LN and "other" columns. The undecideds included Abraham, Chafee, and Specter. Fitzgerald was once again leaning against the party, and no position was denoted for Warner. On this amendment, Specter cast a pro-leadership vote, while Abraham, Chafee, and Fitzgerald all voted with the Democrats. Warner, as before, voted with Lott.

Peter Fitzgerald, in particular, illustrates the cross pressure confronted by GOP Senators from centrist states on domestic policy priorities important to the party program. First elected to the Senate from Illinois in 1998 at the age of 38, Fitzgerald in many ways was a traditional conservative. A strong advocate of tax reduction and market-oriented reform, he also was a devout Roman Catholic and fervent opponent of abortion rights. Still, in 1996 Clinton outpaced Dole in Illinois by a margin of 54–37 percent (the remaining 8 percent went for independent Ross Perot), and in 1998 Fitzgerald himself had only defeated incumbent Carolyn Moseley Braun by about three points to win his seat in the Senate. On many domestic policy issues, he confronted considerable pressure from constituent audiences in his state to defect from the party line. Managed care reform was an example. A top aide to Fitzgerald described the strategic dilemma the senator confronted on the issue during summer 1999. "This was a hard issue. When the first motion to table was up, Fitzgerald said he was committed to supporting the liability impositions in insurance plans. We can get into shouting matches with business lobbyists on the issue.... There was a two-hour discussion with Fitzgerald and staff about the issue the evening before the tabling vote.... We played out the different scenarios for him."[23]

Asked if there was pressure from the leadership, the staffer responded, "Yes, and no. There was a lot of pressure at the staff level. We heard from Lott and Nickles's people. Initially there was pressure, but when they saw we were sticking to our position, they backed off. The message from the leadership was you can have a pass on the liability vote, but we want you on other stuff. It was an evolving dance." GOP leaders, in other words, balanced the need to pick up enough support to win on the floor against the electoral needs and policy commitments of wavering lawmakers. If they could prevail without the vote of a cross-pressured colleague, there was tolerance of defection from the party position, albeit with the understanding that such lawmakers would stay with the party when possible, especially when their votes might be pivotal to the outcome.

After passage of the Lott amendment and the legislation as modified, congressional action on managed care reform largely focused on the House. There, a compromise version that resembled the Kennedy plan passed the chamber on October 6 over the objections of Republican leaders.[24] Conferees were appointed to reconcile the two different versions of the legislation, but partisan differences precluded a compromise acceptable to congressional Republicans, the Clinton White House, and Democrats on Capitol Hill. The next year, in June 2000, Kennedy attempted to amend the defense authorization bill with the House-passed version of managed care reform, but the chamber voted 51-48 to table his proposal. Later that month, Senate Republican leaders changed their position on the right of patents to take managed care providers to court—a key sticking point in the ongoing negotiations.[25] Although Nickles and Kennedy made considerable progress toward a comprehensive deal, in the end they were unable to strike a bargain and the legislation once again died at the end of the 106th Congress. Overall, the issue illustrates the possibilities, but also the limits, of party whipping in the US Senate.

Concluding Observations

Even in the Senate, where leadership prerogatives are so restricted in comparison to the House, and where chamber rules create ample incentive to legislate across the aisle, the process of end-game bargaining needs to be viewed through the lens of party. Party support during the whip process was generally high for the Senate Republicans of 1997–2002, as it was among GOP members on the other side of the Capitol. Especially in the Senate, however, claims for party government, or for systematic legislative deviations away from the views of chamber centrists toward preferences within the majority party, do not resonate with the evidence. Decisions to create and expand the whip networks, for instance, have been rooted in challenges to majority party control, rather than an indicator of majority party strength. On the Senate side of the Capitol, there also is evidence of alienation at the extremes among Republicans, with moderates and the far right most likely to bolt the party during the whip process. In the Senate, chamber moderates are also disproportionately likely to be undecided in the days or hours before major votes, and it is difficult to see how their "preferences" can serve as a benchmark for establishing the presence or absence of party power.

As we have seen, Senate Republican leaders won more often than they lost on whipped questions, but they still lost fairly often. Moreover, the questions they chose to whip reflect the overtly defensive posture of the majority party whips within the chamber. While House majorities engage their whip operations to advance the party program through the chamber, especially in the Senate majorities rely on the whips to counter minority party tactics made possible by chamber rules. Perhaps most telling, during the 107th Congress the win rates of the Senate GOP whips did not change all that much when the chamber reverted to Democratic control following the Jeffords switch, and there was actually a noteworthy drop in outright losses. The reason was not some ascendant coalition-building prowess exhibited by the new Senate minority. Instead, the strategic terrain shifted for the Republican whips, away from defending their own initiatives and toward defeating the program of the majority Democrats via cloture motions and budget points of order where the threshold for victory was lower. Especially in the Senate, it is easier to block the proposals of the other party than it is to advance the initiatives of your own, and the challenges that confront the whips are fundamentally different on the majority and minority sides of the aisle.

TEN

Epilogue and Implications

A lot has happened in American politics since 2002, the end of the time span emphasized in this book. Wars in Afghanistan and Iraq, the Great Recession of 2007–12, and the emergence of angry populist upheavals within both political parties, but especially the GOP—the list could go on. Indeed, as the first year of the Donald J. Trump presidency came to a close, many informed observers questioned whether partisan majorities on Capitol Hill had become too fractious to whip. During 2017, even though they were at the helm on both ends of Pennsylvania Avenue, Republicans periodically failed to build majorities around major portions of their party's legislative program. Increasingly, it seemed, energized activists and well-heeled donors were using social media and other tools to mobilize public sentiment prior to major roll calls and otherwise insert themselves into the vote-gathering process on Capitol Hill. New restrictions on the use of appropriations earmarks adopted by House Republicans during the 114th Congress also complicated the work of the whips.[1] Not surprisingly, many pundits claimed that House Speaker Paul Ryan and Senate Majority Leader Mitch McConnell were historically weak, forced by political conditions to operate somewhere between a rock and a hard place.

Yet, if we look beyond the atmospherics and the day-to-day twists of legislative influence and focus instead on the fundamentals of party coalition building as identified in this book, it is clear that the behavioral logic advanced here is still informative and that the whip process is still at the heart of congressional politics.

The Whips—An Enduring Role

Since the end of 2002, the long-term trend toward increased homogeneity within each congressional party at the constituency level continued to unfold. By 2011, within the House, the gap between the parties in district-level support for the most recent Democratic presidential nominee (Barack Obama in 2008) had grown to more than 20 percentage points. Among the majority Republicans, only about a dozen members represented districts with presidential voting patterns closer to the average for the other party, and for the minority Democrats roughly two dozen members were from districts where the 2008 Obama vote was closer to the average for Republicans. Remarkably, the presence of such outlier districts had fallen to a little over 5 percent for the GOP and just under 13 percent for the Democrats. On the Senate side of the Capitol that year, a dozen members of each party represented states where presidential voting patterns were closer to the average for the partisan opposition, or about 22 percent for the Democrats and 25 percent for the GOP. Overall, the prevalence of constituency outliers remained somewhat higher for the Democrats relative to the Republicans, and for both Senate delegations relative to their House counterparts. But over time and in both chambers, the parties continued to grow more internally homogeneous in the kinds of constituencies they represented, and the size of the gap between them increased.

When we consider majority control, party margins, and the presence or absence of unified government, the story since 2002 is more volatile. Majority status within the House remained in GOP hands until 2007, shifted to the Democrats from 2007 to 2010, and then reverted back to the Republicans in 2011, where it stood until at least the end of 2018. On the Senate side, GOP control also continued until 2007, but here the Democrats were in the majority from 2007 to 2015, when Republicans regained organizational control. Since 2002, majorities in the House have ranged in size from 229 to 257 members, while in the Senate the size of the majority party has varied from a low of 51 to a high of 60 (if we include two independents who also caucused with the majority Democrats that year). With Republican George W. Bush continuing as president until 2009, Democrat Barack Obama in the White House during 2009–17, and Donald Trump as president following the 2016 elections, the result was unified GOP control of Washington during 2003–06 and 2017–18, unified Democratic control during 2009–10, and various forms of divided partisan government in between.

And yet, even with the aforementioned increases in intra-party homogeneity at the constituency level, and amid all this variation in majority status, party sizes, and unified or divided government, party leaders in the House and Senate still confronted substantial position fluidity on the floor and cliffhanger votes and sustained leadership lobbying continued to be staples of the legislative process. Here are just a few examples.

In the wee hours of November 22, 2003, House Republican leaders held the roll call on passage of the conference report for a landmark Medicare prescription drug measure open for more than three hours because they lacked the votes to prevail on what was the Bush administration's top legislative priority of the session. Via intense pressure that purportedly left one GOP moderate crouching on the Democratic side of the floor to avoid eye contact with her own leaders, as well as the provision of special favors, Speaker Dennis Hastert and now Majority Leader Tom DeLay were able to convince two initial no votes to switch to yes, producing a party win at 5:15 in the morning.[2] Later, DeLay would be admonished by the House Ethics Committee for promising campaign support that night to the son of retiring Rep. Nick Smith, R-Mich., in exchange for his vote on the bill.

In summer 2005, the House passed the Central American Free Trade Act (CAFTA) by a single vote, with Robin Hayes again switching his position at the last minute under enormous leadership pressure to secure a dramatic win. And once again, the outcome turned on a full court press of White House lobbying, grassroots mobilization, and a combination of promised rewards and threats by House leaders. Virgil Goode, R-Va., who voted against CAFTA for district reasons, recalled, "The next morning we looked through [a pending] transportation bill and saw that my projects had been cut 76 percent—and that's all I know."[3]

In March 2007, with the Congress now controlled by Democrats, Nancy Pelosi serving as Speaker, and James Clyburn, D-S.C., the majority whip, the outcome on major legislation dealing with U.S. intervention in Iraq was "hanging by a thread" just days before the scheduled roll call. With only 15 votes to spare, a wall of GOP opposition, and a threatened veto from President Bush, whip counts indicated that 10 or more Democrats were leaning against passage and three dozen more were undecided. Using what we now recognize as the full range of whip tactics, Pelosi and Clyburn eked out a victory. Democratic liberals had formed a pact agreeing to stand in lockstep against the measure, but they caved just before the vote. "We have released people who have been pained by all this," Maxine Waters, D-Calif., observed: "We don't want to be in a position of undermining Nancy's speakership."[4]

In March 2010, after a protracted partisan battle, the House and Senate passed the Affordable Care Act, or "Obamacare" for short, the top legislative priority of the Obama administration and arguably the most consequential domestic policy enactment since the Voting Rights Act. In both chambers, effective last-minute whipping was integral to the outcome.[5] As a result of whip intelligence, House leaders backed away from a "public option" for health insurance championed by party liberals, and in both chambers last-minute concessions were made to win the support of pro-choice Democrats who otherwise would have voted no. By most accounts, the member-to-member lobbying of Speaker Pelosi was instrumental to the outcome in the House. But the historic roll call helped mobilize the grassroots Tea Party movement that shifted party control of the chamber back to the Republicans in the midterm elections of 2010.

Although this new GOP majority was remarkably united about policy, deep fissures within the party over strategy emerged early in 2011, remained on full display for the remaining six years of the Obama administration, and if anything stepped up during the Trump years. The freshman class of 2011 demanded that the Republican Conference adopt a more aggressive posture toward bargaining with Obama, especially on spending and the deficit, even if such tactics endangered passage of traditionally "must-pass" debt limit hikes and appropriations bills. As a result of the ongoing conservative insurrection, Republican Majority Leader and former Whip Eric Cantor lost a primary challenge in June 2014 and left the House. The following year, Speaker John Boehner was forced from office. The House Republican Conference, many observers claimed, had become ungovernable.

Upon closer examination, though, the key ingredients of the whip systems of Congress remained in place within both parties and chambers. Consistent with the behavioral approach of this book, the conservative revolt was firmly rooted in the representational relationships that the insurgents had forged with important constituent audiences at home. Contrary to the claims of some, the factionalization that characterized the House Republican Conference following the 2010 midterm elections was more than an "ideological freak show" cast with prominent politicians.[6] Many of the insurgents were first elected to Congress in 2010 and 2012, as the national Tea Party movement exploded onto the American political scene. The House Republicans most likely to break with leaders like John Boehner, Eric Cantor, or even Paul Ryan, R-Wis., who replaced the deposed Boehner late in 2015, also tended to come from districts where Tea Party activists were prevalent.[7]

Mick Mulvaney, R-S.C., was an illustration. First elected in 2010 from the 5th District of South Carolina, Mulvaney defeated veteran Democrat John Spratt. Spratt was a respected moderate who chaired the Budget Committee, was second ranking Democrat on the Armed Services panel, and over the years had funneled millions of dollars of federal funding back to his constituents. In his first campaign, Mulvaney positioned himself as a deficit hawk who would operate independently of either party establishment. Like the many Tea Party supporters within the 5th district, he was adamantly in favor of repealing Obamacare. And periodically bucking pressure from accommodationist party leaders in Washington resonated with the expectations of his constituents, and was thus easily explainable at home.

Mulvaney commented on the linkages between his strategic posture in Washington and the attitudes of important audiences within his district.

> Folks didn't vote for me because I was a Republican. They voted for me because my ideas were different than my Democrat predecessor.... I hate the Republican Party talking points. They make me sick and tired.... "President Obama's failed policies are damaging job creators." What the hell does that mean? ... [If] I come down here and start spewing Republican talking points that come straight from the Speaker's office in a memo that we get every single week and the talking points haven't changed for the last eighteen months, I'd be a laughing stock.[8]

Importantly, the revolt on the right among contemporary House Republicans is best viewed as a continuation of the alienation on the conservative extreme that was apparent in the whip processes of the minority Republicans during period 3, and which took full form within the majority GOP Conferences of period 4. In that sense, Mulvaney and his colleagues were simply following in the footsteps of Tom Coburn, Newt Gingrich, and other conservative insurgents of the 1990s and 1980s.

Considered from the perspective of the behavioral model, there also are important indications of leadership effectiveness and efficacious whipping—even within the fractious House Republican Conferences of recent years. Most important, Republican leaders recognized that they needed to work with Mulvaney and other conservatives within the aforementioned context of constituent expectations and representational style. Regularly, the leadership was able to trade opportunities for the insurgents to air their legislative alternatives within the conference and on the floor in exchange for support on critical procedural votes. During summer 2011, for example, Mulvaney and other party conservatives refused to back efforts by Boehner to strike an agreement with the Obama administration to raise the debt limit and avert a potentially catastrophic default. As the deadline grew near and political pressure for an agreement intensified, party leaders convinced Mulvaney and his colleagues to vote for a procedural rule that enabled the leadership to bring a bipartisan accord to the floor. But on the substantive votes that followed, Mulvaney and other conservatives voted no and the measure passed instead with support from mainstream Republicans and most Democrats. Was the outcome a GOP loss and an indicator of coalition-building ineffectiveness by the whips, as many observers claimed? Not really. The party was able to avoid a federal default that would have damaged its name brand, while still enabling the most conservative elements of the Republican Conference to cast votes that were explainable at home.

The handiwork of the whips was even apparent during the most conspicuous case of majority party failure in many years—the inability of the Republican majority to comprehensively repeal the Obamacare law during 2017. With GOP majorities in both chambers and Republican Donald Trump ensconced in the White House (and Mulvaney serving as his Director of the Office of Management and Budget), most expected that the party would follow through on its long-held pledge to overturn the Affordable Care Act. That May, the House did pass a major revision of the statute by a narrow margin of 217–213. Throughout the coalition-building process, the House Republican whip operation was "in full blitz mode."[9] Two months previously, Speaker Paul Ryan, R-Wis., had pulled from the agenda an earlier version of the bill because whip counts came up short. As the floor vote neared on the revised measure, the party's counts again indicated that the leadership lacked the votes to win. So Ryan and his colleagues crafted substantive modifications aimed at picking up the support of both party moderates and the most ideologically conservative elements of the Republican Conference. Once again, the leadership confronted serious alienation at both extremes. Right up until the roll call, Trump, Vice President Mike Pence, and House Republican leaders called and texted with the members that whip intelligence indicated might bolt. By all accounts, these efforts were pivotal to the outcome.[10]

During summer 2017, the Obamacare repeal effort imploded in the Senate, as Majority Leader Mitch McConnell, R-Ky., and GOP Whip John Cornyn, R-Tex., failed to devise legislation with sufficient Republican support to overcome unanimous opposition from chamber Democrats.

Still, the whip apparatus was apparent—canvassing members during the weekly party lunches, providing the leadership with information about possible modifications to build support, and urging colleagues to vote with the party and otherwise promote the GOP name brand.[11]

In short, amid the legislative disorder of the early Trump era, the essential whip machinery chronicled in this book remained in place. In structure and size, the party whip systems resemble the networks that existed at the end of 2002. On both sides of the Capitol, even when partisan majorities are relatively large, member positions continue to be fluid and leaders often lack the votes necessary to prevail in the weeks and days prior to major votes. On matters important to the party program, where significant internal unity appears possible, and the outcome remains in doubt, there are incentives for leaders to engage the whips. Since presidents are also partisan leaders, the policy program of the White House strongly conditions whipped agendas on both sides of the aisle. When an issue bifurcates a party caucus, as civil rights did for congressional Democrats prior to the Voting Rights Act, and internal unity is not feasible, the whips likely will be inactive, and coalition leadership if it exists will have to come from other power centers within the chamber, the White House, or outside advocacy groups. For issues and periods where the majority party is fragmented along multiple dimensions, as often was the case for the large Democratic majorities of the 1970s, the whips provide leaders with critical political intelligence and otherwise help them build coalitions in the legislative equivalent of sand. And for the burgeoning portions of the legislative agenda where the parties are divided from the very beginning, the whips identify the subset of potentially pivotal lawmakers and are central to the lobbying, grassroots mobilization, rewards, and threats needed to grow the party vote.

In the Senate, the whip process continues to be a smaller, less formal version of the complex networks that have evolved within the House. The parties still caucus over lunch on Tuesdays, with the whips working the room. And for now, party coalition building within the Senate remains structured by the chamber's unique procedural context. The decision of Senate Democrats in 2011 to end filibusters on administrative and lower court nominations restricted use of the tactic somewhat. And in April 2017, the Senate Republican majority ended filibusters on Supreme Court nominees. Midway through the 115th Congress, however, dilatory tactics were still a regular feature of the Senate legislative process. Especially in the Senate, majority party whipping is often a defensive exercise, aimed at countering the minority's attempts to undermine the majority coalition, aided and abetted by the obstructionist potential of chamber rules. And compared to their House counterparts, Senate minorities are more likely to prevail on whipped questions because the threshold for victory (just 41 votes to defeat cloture motions or waive budget rules) can be low. Most important, on both sides of the Capitol whipping in the legislative process remains inseparable from the representational relationships of rank-and-file members at home. For more than half a century, now, the whip systems of Congress have not been solely, nor even primarily, a Washington story.[12]

As the Trump era continues, the divisions that have erupted among congressional Republicans will likely remain—indeed, their sources are longstanding and apparent in the whip process dating back to the 1990s. The potential for factionalization within the Democratic Caucuses of the House and Senate also should not be discounted, especially if the party regains majority control of one or both chambers. From discordant social media to energized party activists and a public fed up with political elites of all stripes, the remarkable permeability of the contemporary legislative process to forces outside the hallways of Congress is probably here to stay, which of course complicates the work of the whips. As we have seen, however, whipping becomes consequential precisely when leaders are challenged. Recall the careful balancing act required of Hale Boggs and the majority whips of the 1950s and 1960s because of their party's sectional cleavage; the complex machinations necessary to build floor majorities within the fractious parties of the O'Neill speakership; the dramatic victories and losses that occurred on the budget in 1990 and 1993 as the Congress turned toward polarization; and the almost surgical precision required of the DeLay and Nickles operations due to narrow majorities and intense partisanship during the late 1990s and early 2000s.

Simply put, most of the challenges confronting contemporary congressional leaders are not all that new. Deep divisions within and across parties condition what congressional leaders can accomplish, to be sure, but they also make possible a consequential role for the whips in the first place.

Conclusion

As we look to the future, the exploration of the whips at work provided in this book has a number of implications for scholars and citizens. First, the significant fluidity of member positions on the House and Senate floor is more than noise, and instead reflects attempts to balance often complex pressures and concerns, many of which derive from important constituent audiences at home. Moreover, the substantive content of the main alternatives often remains in flux, further contributing to the prevalence of position change in the weeks and days before major floor votes. The decision-making process on the House and Senate floor is more complicated, volatile, and important than is implied by most contemporary congressional scholarship. This stage of the process, the evidence shows, merits sustained inquiry and close public attention.

It is difficult to quantify, of course, but in recent years the scholarly community may have lost some interest in the internal operations of Congress as a field of study.[13] When cross-partisan coalitions were commonplace and more legislative decisions were made out in the open in committee, the legislative process seemed a lot less predictable and perhaps more intriguing. One result was a wealth of new scholarship about committee behavior, the impact of chamber rules, the foundations of legislative organization, and other aspects of the deep structure of Congress. What really is to be learned, scholars may now ask, if time and again members simply divide along party lines throughout the legislative process? The work of the whips, however, reveals just how volatile and fascinating the coalition-building process can be even within a Congress that at first blush appears to move in partisan lockstep. You just need to look in the right places.

Second, the end-game bargaining that occurs within both chambers of Congress must be viewed through a partisan lens, and the activities of the whips are integral to that process. On both sides of the aisle, and within both chambers, the lion's share of the position movement is toward the relevant party position. Through a combination of coordination, persuasion, the integration of outside interests and pressures, and threats and promises that target individual lawmakers, leaders are responsible for much of this tendency toward party support on votes. The importance of the whips within congressional politics has grown over time, as floor activity increased in quantity, the House and Senate became more open to outside interests, and the portion of the floor agenda capable of internally uniting each party expanded. But from the 1950s onward, there are important continuities to the whip machinery rooted in the strategic behavior of party leaders.

One last time—leaders are most inclined to whip on matters important to the party program, where significant internal agreement appears possible, and the outcome remains in doubt. In the 1950s and 1960s, that meant the majority Democrats would avoid taking action on items that tapped the deep sectional divide between southern members and the rest of the party. In the 1970s, as floor amendments and roll call votes exploded in number, that meant a substantial expansion of whip networks and whip activism. And in the 1980s and 1990s, as the partisan structure of congressional politics solidified and party margins narrowed, that meant greater focus on the subset of potentially wavering centrists and party extremists needed to win on the floor. The scope of the whipped agenda, the size and complexity of the whip networks, and the number and identity of potential defectors from the party line have changed over time, to be sure, but the basic mechanisms of the contemporary whip process have been in place for many decades now and continue to shape party politics in Congress.

Third, heightened partisanship is not tantamount to party government or majority party dominance. As 50 years of whip evidence reveals, even within chambers that are deeply polarized along partisan lines, majority party wins often depend on some level of crossover support from the minority. Moreover, member support generally trends toward the leadership position within both the majority *and* the minority party. Although the majority leadership has certain formal prerogatives and other internal resources that are not available to leaders of the minority, the minority leadership still has important institutional leverage (e.g., committee assignments and other internal patronage to dole out) that can be used to influence members. And critically, minority party strategy often is the politics of opposition, and members can oppose a majority party initiative for many different reasons. As a result, the minority party in Congress actually has certain tactical advantages relative to their majority counterparts. Not surprisingly, when both parties face-off and whip the same question in opposite directions, the two whip operations to some extent balance one another out.

Fourth, on both sides of the aisle, and particularly in the Senate, floor whipping does not primarily take the form of arm-twisting or otherwise inducing members to take actions that are contrary to their pre-formed legislative preferences. The evidence marshalled in this book shows that member positions develop and change as part of the lawmaking process. The positions members take and the votes they cast do not derive from spatial comparisons of ideal points and policy locations within some predetermined ideological space, but are instead strategies aimed at balancing competing pressures, the most important of which emanate from sources outside the halls of Congress. Within both chambers and over time, the whip process is inseparable from the representational relationships of lawmakers at home. Indeed, for a whip, the most important leverage is systematic knowledge of the districts or states represented by a potentially defecting member. Party leaders grow the vote by priming such considerations within member districts or states, altering legislation to make pro-party votes explainable back home and to outside constituencies of national party activists and donors, and by structuring the floor agenda to facilitate the aforementioned explanation process. Time and again, the evidence for whip effectiveness described in this book highlighted the broader partisan-electoral context within which the vote-gathering efforts of party leaders take place. Party theories based on premises about monopoly agenda control by the majority, or some conceptually framed caricature of Tom DeLay's hammer, cannot shed much light on the whip process in Congress.

Fifth, scholarly theories or journalistic accounts that conceptualize party influence as some spatial deviation of legislative outcomes from the exogenously determined preferences of the floor median (or any other legislator made pivotal by chamber rules) in the direction of the party program tend to obscure far more than they reveal. Too often, the spatial renditions of the cartel model, conditional party government, and other party theories that are so ubiquitous in contemporary congressional scholarship embrace precisely this benchmark. Indeed, every time a scholar includes within a statistical model both partisan factors and vote-based ideological indicators as competing explanatory variables, he or she implicitly buys into the notion that informative distinctions can be drawn between party effects and preference effects. But as the nuts and bolts of floor whipping reveal, such distinctions are not grounded in reality. What we have called the behavioral perspective provides a better foundation for constructing scholarly theories or popular understanding of party leadership influence in the legislative process.

Sixth, the history of the whips at work shows just how vulnerable majority coalitions are, even within the highly polarized congressional environment of the 2000s. Leaders routinely lack the votes necessary to prevail immediately prior to major votes in both chambers and that pattern extends across decades. Especially in the Senate, but also in the House, the aim of majority party whipping typically is to counter opposing forces, which often emanate from across the partisan aisle. Under the best of circumstances, then, passing legislation in Congress is really, really difficult. Or as John Dingell, D-Mich., once observed, lawmaking is "hard, pick-and-shovel work . . . and it takes a long time to do."[14]

As a result, the default outcome of the congressional legislative process should not be viewed as the chamber median preference or some other conceptualization of exogenously determined centrist viewpoints. When the whips fail, the reversion outcome is inaction, the status quo, or some other form of legislative gridlock. Rather than promoting spatial deviations from centrist preferences toward the majority party program, effective whipping helps overcome the gravitational attraction of legislative stasis. Instead of diverting outcomes away from median preferences, the whips help determine what comes to constitute the legislative middle ground as floor decision making unfolds.

For this reason, the focus of legislative scholarship should not be predominantly on ideal point estimates, or inferences about the ideological location of competing policy proposals based on who does or does not vote for them. Instead, in identifying how parties and leaders matter, the emphasis should be on the dynamics of lawmaking—on the substantive content of the competing legislative alternatives, the initial positions members take on such proposals, the substantive modifications that ensue as leaders attempt to grow their coalitions, the movements in member positions that result, and the contents of the legislation that emerges at the end of the process. By training a microscope on the fluidity of member positions during the bargaining endgame, our exploration of the whips suggests that scholarly attention should shift from statistical manipulations of the roll call record toward sustained inquiry about the contents of legislation and how these contents relate to the demands of important constituent audiences. Such a focus on legislative substance was a central feature of the behavioral tradition upon which this book rests.[15]

Finally, and again for scholars and citizens alike, the whip systems of Congress clarify what we can properly expect from parties and their leaders, and thus how we should evaluate the representation we receive from the national legislature. There has been a lot of loose talk of late about the evils of partisanship, self-interested politicians, and a broken Congress. Indeed, the standard toolkit of partisan coalition building in the House and Senate—pressure, inside deal making, grassroots mobilization and message politics, favors, threats, and other parochial side-payments—will strike many as unsavory, even corrupt. But in a large, diverse country with an institutionally fragmented federal government, and amid an electoral environment characterized by modern communication technologies and ample points of access for special interest money, this is what it takes to build coalitions in Congress. Tom DeLay, for example, was often vilified as unprincipled or worse by Democrats, much of the mainstream media, and many public interest organizations during his decade in the House GOP leadership. No doubt, DeLay periodically walked right up to the boundary of what constitutes appropriate behavior for an elected official, and on occasion appears to have crossed it.[16] But he was also the most effective whip in modern congressional history. Although occasionally heavy-handed, his blend of member-to-member pressure, intensive appeals to party loyalty, hardball management of the legislative agenda, and backroom alliances with interest groups harkened back to the styles embraced by other influential congressional leaders of the past, from Lyndon Johnson in the Senate to Sam Rayburn in the House. Although the internal operations of the whip systems of Congress seldom reflect the better angels of our nature, they do make feasible the passage of legislation, and the kinds of bargains and compromises necessary to hold together a free society.

Appendix

Archival and Other Sources

Much of the evidence in this book derives from materials included in the papers of former House and Senate party leaders, especially former whips. The sources are best delineated by party and time period. Since I made use of thousands of separate file folders and over 30,000 pages of photocopied documents, the location of the relevant materials is provided here at the box level. Where appropriate, citations at the folder level are provided for these and other archival sources in notes throughout the text.

House Democrats, 1955–61, 84th Congress through the 1st Session of the 87th Congress

The Carl Albert Collection, The Carl Albert Center, University of Oklahoma, Norman, Oklahoma, Legislative Files, Boxes 26–58. My visit to the Albert Center was funded in part from a Visiting Scholars Grant generously awarded to me by the Center. Many thanks to the Carl Albert Center for this support, as well as for the guidance of Carolyn Hanneman and Todd Kosmerick during my visit.

House Democrats, 1962–1970, 2nd Session of the 87th Congress through the 91st Congress

The Hale Boggs Congressional Collection, Howard-Tilton Memorial Library, Tulane University, New Orleans, Louisiana, Majority Whip Collection, Boxes 1–3. Leon Miller of the special collections division at Howard-Tilton Library greatly enhanced my work during three separate visits.

House Democrats, 1971–72, 92nd Congress

The Thomas P. O'Neill Papers, John J. Burns Library, Boston College, Boston, Massachusetts, Series V, Subseries A, Box 347. Access to the O'Neill papers was greatly assisted by John Atteberry.

The Carl Albert Collection, The Carl Albert Center, University of Oklahoma, Legislative Files, Box 151.

House Democrats, 1973–74, 93rd Congress

Democratic whip count records for this Congress were not available in the papers of the relevant whip, John J. McFall, D-Calif. I thank AnnElise Golden, Holt-Atherton Special Collections Library, University of the Pacific, Stockton, California, for devoting several days to searching through the papers of Rep. McFall (albeit unsuccessfully) for whip items on my behalf.

Instead, most of the whip data for the 93rd Congress in this database were coded from records provided to me by Professor Lawrence C. Dodd of the University of Florida. Professor Dodd was an American Political Science Association Congressional Fellow during the 1974–75 academic year, serving in the office of the House Democratic whip, and he originally secured these items during his time in the office. I am significantly indebted to Larry Dodd for his generosity in providing the documents. The master list of polled questions for this Congress is drawn from these records, but also from Dodd, Lawrence C., "The Expanded Roles of the House Democratic Whip System: The 93rd and 94th Congresses," *Capitol Studies* 7 (1979): 27–56.

The Dodd materials were supplemented by records from *The Carl Albert Collection*, The Carl Albert Center, University of Oklahoma, Legislative Files, Box 192.

House Democrats, January 1975–February 1976, 94th Congress

John J. McFall was also House Democratic whip during this Congress, and as mentioned, his papers do not include whip records. A partial set of records was obtained from *The Carl Albert Collection*, The Carl Albert Center, University of Oklahoma, Legislative Files, Box 237.

House Democrats, 1977–86, 95th through the 99th Congress

Congressional Papers of Thomas S. Foley, Manuscripts, Archives and Special Collections Department, Holland Library, Washington State University, Pullman, Washington, Boxes 197–203. During my visit to the Foley archives, I benefited from the financial support of the Thomas S. Foley Institute, as well as further assistance from Ed Weber and Holly Tate of the Foley Institute and Laila Miletic-Vejzovic, then Head of Manuscripts, Archives, and Special Collections at Holland Library.

House Democrats, 1989–90, 101st Congress

David Bonior Papers, Walter P. Reuther Library, Wayne State University, Detroit, Michigan, Boxes 24–25, 30, 51, 57, 78, 97–98, 125, 140, 154, 157, 175, 177. In navigating this collection, I was assisted by William LeFevere, Mike Smith, and especially Max Stepinak. I also appreciate the help of the unnamed IT staff at the Reuther Library who spent a morning attempting to restore data from several ancient hard drives that had been archived decades before by the Bonior whip office. Those efforts were unsuccessful, alas, but still above and beyond the call of archivist duty.

House Democrats, 1991–94, 102nd through the 103rd Congress

Butler Derrick Papers, South Carolina Political Collections, University Libraries, University of South Carolina, Columbia, South Carolina, Leadership Files, Boxes 46–49. My thanks to Chuck Finocchiaro and his student, Ben Kassow, for their assistance during my work with the Derrick collection.

House Republicans, 1975–80, 94th through the 96th Congress

The Robert H. Michel Collection, The Dirksen Congressional Center, Pekin, Illinois, Leadership Files, 1963–96, Boxes 1–3. Frank Mackaman, longtime Director of The Dirksen Congressional Center, provided critical assistance in securing copies of GOP whip records from Rep. Michel's papers, as well as during a follow-up visit to the Dirksen Center. I also benefited from conversations with Cindy Koeppel during my visit. A Congressional Research Award granted to me by the Center in 2011 made the visit possible.

House Republicans, 1989–94, 101st through the 103rd Congress

The Newt Gingrich Papers, Ingram Library, Special Collections, University of West Georgia, Carrollton, Georgia, Boxes 2426, 2662, 2673–74, 2677–79, 2683, 2690, and 2692–94. My thanks to former Speaker Gingrich for granting me access to his then-closed congressional papers, and also to Professor Melvin Steely, an emeritus member of the History Department at West Georgia, a longtime friend and colleague of Gingrich and the author of an informative biography of the former Speaker, for his guidance in making sense of the collection. Myron House, head archivist at the time, also provided valuable assistance.

House Republicans, 1995–2002, 104th through the 107th Congress

The Tom DeLay Papers, University of Houston Libraries, Special Collections Department, Houston, Texas, especially Boxes 85, 91–102, 132. My thanks to former Rep. DeLay for granting me access to his then-closed papers, and to Lee Rawls and Brett Loper for approaching Mr. DeLay on my behalf. During my visit, Pat Bozeman, the head of the special collections department, was of great assistance.

Senate Republicans, 1997–2002, 105th through the 107th Congress

The Don Nickles Senate Papers, Special Collections Department, Oklahoma State University, Stillwater, Oklahoma, Box 15. The Nickles papers were almost entirely unprocessed at the time of my visit in August 2008 and the box identifiers may change as archival work on the collection proceeds. My thanks to Senator Nickles for granting me access to his papers for the purpose of scholarly research and publication, and to Lee Rawls for approaching him and his staff for me. Kay Bost, head of the Special Collections Department at OSU during my week in Stillwater, was also very helpful.

Other Support

The archival research and extensive data coding necessarily to produce this book was assisted in part by financial support from the National Science Foundation (Award SES-04107759) and the Roy R. Charles Center of the College of William & Mary.

While constructing the data sets included in this study, I relied heavily on roll call and other data sets created by Keith Poole and his colleagues for the Voteview.com website, as well as ICPSR Study No. 7803, Roster of United States Congressional Officeholders and Biographical Characteristics of Members of the United States Congress, 1789–1996: Merged Data, Carroll McKibbin. Also important were the congressional voting databases constructed by David Rohde and his colleagues in the Political Institutions and Public Choice (PIPC) programs at Michigan State University and Duke University. The committee assignment evidence used in this book is from data sets compiled by David Canon, Garrison Nelson, and Charles Stewart III, and provided via Professor Stewart's website. In assigning whipped questions to committees, I leaned heavily on the bill specific jurisdictional data compiled by E. Scott Adler and John Wilkerson for the Policy Agendas Project. Gary Jacobson shared with me his uniquely valuable database on congressional election outcomes. Among other indicators, the measure of presidential voting at the district level used in Chapters 5–8 is from that source. My thanks to all of these scholars and organizations, but especially Professors Poole and Rohde. Without the remarkable resources provided by Voteview and the PIPC project, compiling the evidence for this volume would have been much more difficult.

Last and certainly not least, in coding whipped positions from the archival record I received superb research assistance from several dozen students at the College of William & Mary. In alphabetical order, my thanks go to Billy Abbott, Courtney Behringer, Nicky Bell, Pierce Blue, Erin Bradbury, Sarah Brown, J. Tyler Butts, Ryan Davidson, Tim Deering, Keith Devereaux, Amanda Downing, Rami Fakhouri, Logan Ferree, Nicole

Gaffen, Claire Grandy, Kristen Haase, David Husband, Anne Hyslop, Keith Klovers, Jessica Lane, Josh Litten, Will Marlow, Miguel Mataromos, Beth Materese, Walter McClean, Josh McHenry, Lauren Merrill, Laura Minnichelli, Mary Moll, Michael O'Neill, Angie Petry, Chris Renjilian, Patricia Ruane, Brent Schultheis, Jennifer Sykes, Paul Trifiletti, Ricky Trotman, Josh Turner, and Laura Whipple. For three decades now, working with them and other students at William & Mary has been an honor and a pleasure.

Notes

PREFACE

1. *Congressional Record*, October 13, 2009, 24550.

INTRODUCTION

1. "Whip Survey B," Box 97, Tom DeLay Papers. The appendix includes full information about the location of these and other archival sources not fully referenced in chapter notes.

2. Ibid. For the remainder of the book, regular references will be made to the response totals on particular whipped questions. Rather than cite each time the individual documents from which these totals were calculated via endnotes, source information for all such references is provided together in the appendix.

3. "Fast Track Group Meeting, 5/16/01" and "Gephardt Meeting, 5/17/01," Box 177, David Bonior Papers.

4. Chris Cillizza, "Labor Ads Target Trade," *Roll Call*, July 26, 2001.

5. Peter H. Stone, "Fury Over 'Fast-Track,' " *The National Journal*, July 28, 2001.

6. "American Trade Leadership: What is at stake," remarks as delivered by US Trade Representative Robert B. Zoellick at the International Economics Institute, Washington, D.C., September 24, 2001, Federal News Service.

7. "Rep. Rangel responds to USTR Zoellick's claim that Congress must pass 'Fast Track' to help in fight against terrorism," Press Release, September 26, 2001.

8. *Congressional Record*, December 6, 2001, 24176.

9. Although the legislation would be considered under a closed rule with no amendments, the Democrats were able to secure a vote on a Levin-Rangel substitute as the party's motion to recommit with instructions, where it was defeated, 162–267. Recommital instructions, because of their procedural cast, are generally viewed by the minority as a less valuable opportunity for modifying legislation than are floor amendments. The closed rule significantly advantaged the Thomas bill.

10. "The Fast Track Five," *The Hill*, December 12, 2001, 33; "Bush Reassures Skittish Legislators on Textile Promises," *National Journal's Congress Daily*, December 14, 2001.

11. "Gephardt Meeting," Box 177, David Bonior Papers.

12. Susan Ferrechio, "3-Minute Interview: Jerry Hartz," *The Washington Examiner*, March 9, 2009.

13. "The Fast Track Five," *The Hill*, December 12, 2001, 33.

14. "Final vote—Key contact information," Box 177, David Bonior Papers.

15. Susan Crabtree, "Dealing Divides GOP," *Roll Call*, December 10, 2001; "The Fast Track Five," *The Hill*, December 12, 2001, 33.

16. Ripley (1964) provides a superb history of the early House whip systems. For more recent changes, see Dodd (1978), Dodd and Sullivan (1981), Sinclair (1983, 1995), Rohde (1991), Burden and Frisby (2004), Meinke (2008, 2016), and Evans and Grandy (2009). Oleszek (1971) and Smith and Gamm (2002) describe the institutional development of Senate whip operations, while Bradbury et al. (2008) explores Democratic whip activities in the Senate during the late 1980s.

17. For an explanation, see Fenno (1978), Appendix.

CHAPTER 1

1. See Thomas (1971) and Gladstone (1927). Although Burke appears to be the first individual to refer to the hunting analogy within Parliament, it apparently had been in informal usage since at least the 1740s.

2. Consider, for example, these passages from floor remarks in the *Congressional Globe* from the period: January 22, 1866, p. 335; February 20, 1872, p. 1131; February 21, 1872, p. 74.

3. Alexander (1916), 104.

4. Ibid, 105.

5. Robinson (1930), 351–76.

6. Clinton and Lapinski (2006).

7. Sources for Table 1.1 include the Congressional Biographical Directory, history.house.gov, and Voteview.com.

8. See Jessee and Malhotra (2010).

9. Following the lead of Jessee and Malhotra (2010), the ideological ratings in Table 1.1 are based on W-NOMINATE scores, because the goal is to capture ideological positions in the Congress immediately prior to a member's selection as whip. The only exceptions are the entries for McCarthy, Scalise, and Hoyer (2011), which derive from DW-NOMINATE scores because W-NOMINATE data are not readily accessible for the previous Congress. All of the NOMINATE evidence used in this book was downloaded from Voteview.com.

10. Jessee and Malhotra (2010), Peabody (1976).

11. Interview by the author with a House leadership aide, July 2010.

12. See Harris (2006) and Connelly and Pitney (1994), Chapter 3.

13. "Tom DeLay Is Counting on Cracking the Whip," *Dallas Morning News*, November 27, 1994, 14A.

14. "Steve Scalise Elected Majority Whip," *Breitbart*, June 19, 2014.

15. Hardeman and Bacon (1987), 212.

16. Farrell (2001), 273–75.

17. Ibid, 279–91; Interview by the author with Gary Hymel, June 2010.

18. Barry (1990), 78.

19. The Caucus election to replace Bonior as whip took place in October 2001, but he did not formally step down until January 2002.

20. Karen Foerstel, "Hoyer's and Pelosi's 3-Year Race for Whip: It's All Over but the Voting," *CQ Weekly Report*, October 6, 2001, 2321.

21. Karen Forestel, "Pelosi's Vote-Counting Prowess Earns Her the House Democrats' No. 2 Spot," *CQ Weekly Report*, October 13, 2001, 2397.

22. My treatment of House whip organizations before the 1950s leans heavily on Alexander (1916) and especially Ripley's (1964, 1967) superb scholarship about early whip operations in the chamber.

23. This paragraph derives from Ripley (1964), which in turn is based on 1963 correspondence between Bachmann and the author.

24. "Letter from Rep. Charles A. Plumley to Joseph L. Martin, Jr., April 28, 1942." Folder 23.1, Box 22.6, Joseph W. Martin, Jr. Papers, Archives and Historical Collections, Martin Institute, Stonehill College, Easton, Massachusetts.

25. Ibid.

26. For details, consult Arends' February 5, 1951 floor statement about the Republican whip organization, which is cited and summarized in *Deschler's Precedents of the United States House of Representatives*, Ch. 3, Section 23.4.

27. Information about changes in the size and composition of the House Democratic and Republican whip organizations is from relevant issues of *Congressional Quarterly Almanac* and *Politics in America* (Washington, D.C.: CQ Press), supplemented by the archival records that have been gathered for this book. There are certain differences between these sources, and also with figures cited in published work about party leaders and the whips. For the most part, the differences are minor, and I generally use the higher number, albeit with one exception. For some reason, during Newt Gingrich's tenure as GOP whip, there are many Republicans listed as whips in the archival record that are not mentioned in the standard sources. It appears that the assistant whips responsible for counting positions were excluded. Here, I use the data from the archival record. In 2001, the Republican leadership stopped making public the participants in its whip system, and as a result the standard sources dropped the lists for both parties. In Figure 1.1, the 2001–02 data are from various materials in the personal papers of Tom DeLay and David Bonior, as well as Judy Schneider, "House Leadership: Whip Organization," *CRS Report for Congress*, updated February 12, 2002.

28. Consult Sinclair (1995), Chapter 7, for an overview of the changes that occurred in the House Democratic whip organization from the 1960s to the late 1980s. Also see Rohde (1991) and Meinke (2016).

29. See Meinke (2008) and Rohde (1991).

30. Clark (1920), v. 2, 337

31. Ibid, 338–39.

32. Alfred Steinberg, "Shepherds of Capitol Hill," *Nation's Business*, January 1952, 33.

33. "Verdict for a Tariff," *Washington Post*, March 1, 1900, 1.

34. Ibid.

35. Alexander (1916), 106.

36. Robert C. Albright, "74th Congress Smashed all Records with New Deal Legislation," *Washington Post*, August 25, 1935, B3.

37. Robert C. Albright, "Boland Seeks Frazier-Lemke Farm Mortgage Vote in House; Democratic Whip Recommends That Leaders 'Call Bluff' of Inflationists After Poll of Members; Sees Defeat of Measure," *Washington Post*, March 9, 1936, 1.

38. Robert C. Albright, "House Votes on Embargo Repeal Today," *Washington Post*, November 2, 1939, 1.

39. Robert C. Albright, "Predicting How the House Will Vote No Longer an Easy Job," *Washington Post*, November 16, 1941, B4.

40. On Rayburn's leadership style, consult Hardeman and Bacon (1987) and Cooper and Brady (1981).

41. Interview by the author with David Bonior, Summer 2004.

42. NOMINATE scores for individual members and Congresses change somewhat over time as new data from subsequent years are added. For the most part, the House NOMINATE data used in this book was accessed in Fall 2011 and covered the 1–111th Congresses. None of the relationships that are reported here, it should be emphasized, change significantly if different iterations of the NOMINATE measure are used.

43. Party sizes can vary over a Congress with membership changes and party switches. Here, party divisions are from the first day of the relevant Congress. The source is Vital Statistics on Congress, www.brookings.edu/VitalStats, Table 1-19. When appropriate, in the text we will occasionally reference party sizes at particular points in time that may diverge slightly from the entries in Table 1.3.

44. Smith (1989), 15–49.

45. Bach and Smith (1988), 38–87.

CHAPTER 2

1. Ben Pershing, "Time to Put a Nail in DeLay Moniker?" *Roll Call*, March 3, 2004, 20. Although Republican insiders during DeLay's time as whip were familiar with his nickname, none could remember a member or staffer actually using it in personal conversation. The moniker appears to be entirely a creation of the media.

2. Peter Pel, "The Gospel According to Tom DeLay," *Washington Post Magazine*, May 13, 2001, 14–34. DeLay responded that he only looked mean because "I have squinty eyes." Ibid, 16.

3. Richard E. Cohen, "The Silent Hammer," *National Journal*, February 2, 2002, 316.

4. For a superb and comprehensive analysis of scholarship about the congressional parties, see Smith (2007).

5. For a review, see Krehbiel (1988).

6. The map in Figure 2.1 was prepared by Daniel Maliniak, with much appreciated assistance also provided by Stuart Hamilton and Colleen Trusky of the Center for Geospatial Analysis at the College of William & Mary.

7. Interview with the author, January 12, 2012.

8. Michael Barone, Richard E. Cohen, and Grant Ujifusa, *The Almanac of American Politics 2002*, Washington D.C.: National Journal Group, 1155.

9. Ibid.

10. On roll calls and explainability, see also Kingdon (1973).

11. Hayes interview, January 12, 2012.

12. Ibid.

13. Steven R. Weisman, "In Old Textile District, the Free-Trade Issue Dominates," *New York Times*, October 26, 2006.

14. Hayes interview.

15. My account of national party and interest group efforts on Hayes's behalf in the 2002 campaign is drawn from Heberlig (2003).

16. For a systematic treatment of member preferences that includes undefined orderings, see Fishburn (1973).

17. This behavioral calculus follows closely the decision rules posited for members in Kingdon (1973), and especially Arnold (1990).

18. Compelling research by Lee (2009) likewise maintains that much of what appears as ideological reasoning in Congress actually derives from the partisan competition for power. See also Koger and Lebo (2017).

19. See Mayhew (2011). More generally, the influence of Mayhew's collective work on congressional lawmaking should be apparent throughout this book.

CHAPTER 3

1. Since records of majority whip counts were unavailable for much of the second session of the 94th Congress (after February 5, 1976), the entirety of the 100th Congress (1987–88), the second session of the 101st Congress (1990), and the first nine months of the 102nd Congress (until September 23, 1991), the roll calls that occurred during these gaps in the archival record were dropped to avoid biasing downward the percentages of votes linked to whip activity. For instance, the percentages for the 94th Congress only include roll calls that occurred on or before February 5, 1976. Restricting the vote data in this manner meant that a few whipped roll calls were dropped—considerable time may have passed between the count and the associated roll call and the vote occurred after the period for which whip evidence is available. These omissions are few in number, however, and do not affect the relationships illustrated in Figure 3.1.

2. In selecting key votes, *CQ* weighs the extent to which the underlying issue was "a matter of major controversy, a test of presidential or political power, or a decision of potentially great impact on the nation and lives of Americans." If there are multiple votes on such an issue or bill, *CQ* usually picks as a key vote the one it views as "most important in determining the outcome." http://library.cqpress.com/congress/html/help/Help_keyVote.htm

3. Scholars utilize a number of approaches for identifying the presidential legislative agenda. For example, Lee (2009) relied on the contents of presidential "State of the Union" speeches to identify Senate roll calls important to the White House. Beckmann (2010) focuses on coverage about major bills in the annual almanacs produced by *CQ* to create an indicator of presidential lobbying. Our goal here is to juxtapose the whipped agenda with presidential interest over nearly five decades of House roll calls, and fully implementing the Lee or Beckmann approaches is not feasible. The use of *CQ* presidential votes is more straightforward and is the

approach adopted by a number of major studies of legislative-executive relations (e.g., Bond and Fleischer, 1990). Data are from Rohde (2010).

4. The categorization of roll calls by question type is a collapsed version of the "vote" variable found in Rohde (2010). For purposes of comparison, the same question categories are used across the two tables, with the exception of "procedure." Certain of the whipped questions in the procedural category of Table 3.2 do not readily translate into roll call votes, so only votes on rules and previous question motions on rules are included. Most of the whipped procedural questions concerned such matters, in any event.

5. Differences in the table between the majority and the minority, it should be emphasized, do not derive from temporal differences in the evidentiary base. If we only consider evidence from periods where whip archives are available for both parties, the gist of the table remains.

6. Consult Kowalcky and LeLoup (1993) and especially Lee (2016).

7. In Congress, bills that create or continue an agency or policy are referred to as "authorizations" legislation, while measures that fund authorizations are called "appropriations." Certain important programs, like Social Security, are directly funded by their authorizing statutes and are referred to as "mandatory" or "entitlements."

8. Based on the issue codes in Rohde (2010), votes are collapsed into 13 policy areas—Congress/government operations, defense, foreign policy, the economy, trade, energy and environment, civil rights, social welfare, health, education, labor and consumer, appropriations, and other. Appropriations are treated as a separate policy area because they are omnibus measures that can encompass different issue areas, and because of the distinctiveness of appropriations politics during much of the time span covered by this book. Separate policy-specific cohesion scores are calculated for each of the four time periods that structure Chapters 5–8 (1955–72, 1973–82, 1983–94, and 1995–2002).

9. More precisely, because the categories for passage, procedure, and veto are logically related (a one for one implies a zero for the other two), for them marginal changes are calculated by first setting the relevant variable to zero and the others to their means, and then setting the variable of interest to one and the other two to zero.

10. Based on archived whip records, there are a small number of cases where the party position as determined by the leadership is not supported by a majority of the relevant rank and file on the floor. These instances are rare, however, and it is not feasible to identify analogous cases for the roughly 16,000 roll calls included in this part of the analysis. As a result, the balance of votes within the majority caucus/conference is always treated as the party position.

CHAPTER 4

1. With the majority Democrats, for instance, archival records about the positions of individual members are not available for most of the second session of the 94th Congress (1976), the entire second session of the 101st Congress (1990), and most of the first session of the 102nd Congress (1991). For the Republican majorities of 1995–2002, we have comprehensive information about what was

whipped for all eight years, but systematic evidence about the positions of individual members is lacking for most of the 104th Congress (1995–96). And for the minority Republicans, although we again have reliable lists of what was whipped during 1975–80 and 1989–93, response data at the member level are available for only a small portion of counts conducted during the 102nd and 103rd Congresses (1991–92 and 1993–94, respectively).

2. In classifying member responses during the whip process, one question concerns how to treat the many instances where there are multiple drafts of a count on an individual question. Much of the analysis in this book would be unwieldy without a summary measure producing a single member position per whipped question. The vast majority of observations are not complicated in this fashion, it should be emphasized, but position changes over multiple drafts do occur for a nontrivial minority. When there are position changes across drafts, the decision rule adopted here is to select the response that *maximizes the degree of ambiguity or indecision*. Basically, if we conceptualize the standard "yes" to "no" response spectrum as a scale, the summary decision rule is to choose the response closest to the midpoint of "undecided." For example, if a member is "undecided" on one draft and "leaning yes" on the second, the response for "undecided" is used as the summary position. If a member is "leaning yes" on one and "yes" on the other, then the summary response is "leaning yes," and so on. Substantive responses always dominate nonresponse, so if a member is missing from the first count, but recorded with a position in a later draft, the substantive position is used. If there is a tie in terms of distance from undecided (e.g. shifts from "no" to "yes" or "leaning no" to "leaning yes"), then I use the response that is furthest from the leadership. Unless there are reasons to do otherwise, members listed as with the leadership "if needed" are treated as initial opponents. Of course, there are other possible rules for selecting a summary response in the presence of multiple drafts with different positions, including using the earliest or the latest temporal position. There are advantages and disadvantages to all of the alternative rules, but based on my understanding of the raw evidence the maximization of response ambiguity seems to work best. The substantive findings reported in this book are not altered in any significant way if other reasonable summary rules are employed.

3. When we break the evidence down by congress or year, there is considerable fluctuation within periods and no general trend. The step up in leadership support only becomes apparent when the data are collapsed by period.

4. More concretely, to calculate the party sizes reported in Table 4.1, I determined the number of members in the relevant caucus or conference at the time a whip count was conducted and then took the average across the whipped items for that period. As a result, the party size entries reported in the table do not perfectly correspond with the sizes reported in Table 1.3.

5. The focus is on initial House passage, as opposed to conference reports, to avoid situations where non-centrist policy outcomes may result from the practical exigencies of bicameral bargaining. In other words, negotiations between the House and Senate may produce compromises that necessarily deviate from median preferences in one or both chambers. For initial passage questions in the House, though, median voter driven models imply an outcome located near the center of the chamber distribution.

6. The individual-level roll call data used in this book were downloaded from Voteview.com. In calculating loyalty rates, paired votes are treated as yes or no, depending on the direction of the pair. Other categories (announced yes or no, present, or not voting) are treated as missing data.

7. The estimator was an ordered probit with the four-level ordinal dependent variable ranging from 1 (a loss in Table 4.4) to a 4 (a win in the table). The independent variables were majority party size and indicators for periods 2, 3, and 4, with period 1 omitted.

8. The Fast Track fight of 2001, of course, meets the definition of a face-off. Comprehensive whip evidence is only available for both parties on Fast Track passage because the matter was a personal priority of then Democratic Whip David Bonior and whip records on the question happened to be included in his personal papers. Unfortunately, the Bonior collection does not include systematic whip materials after 1989, again with the exception of a few personal priorities like Fast Track. As a result, that question is treated elsewhere as a special case (the introduction and Chapter 2) and is not included in the face-off analysis here.

9. Especially prior to the 1990s, it was not unusual for members who reported positions during the whip process not to cast roll call votes. Perhaps they were out of town, ill, or otherwise chose not to vote yes or no or cast paired votes. Similarly, if a member was new to the chamber around the time of the roll call, she may not have reported a position to the whips. Since the "flow" concept attempts to capture individual-level movements between the count and the vote, only members who registered positions at both stages are included. For this reason, certain of the entries in Table 4.5 differ somewhat from the position and vote totals for these items mentioned in other chapters.

10. Unfortunately, we lose half of the face-off observations for 1989–93 because individual-level response data is unavailable for the GOP. The archival record includes a comprehensive listing of whipped questions, so we can identify all of the face-off events, but records about member responses on these items often were unavailable as the research for this book was completed.

CHAPTER 5

1. Bars are not included for the 88th and 90th Congresses due to missing presidential voting data at the district level, which in turn resulted from court-ordered reapportionment during the 1960s.

2. Interview with Gary Hymel, July 8, 2010.

3. Robert Michel Papers, Leadership Series, Box 1, Folders: 88th, 1963–64, Whip; 88th, 1963–64, Whip Count Rules Committee; 89th, 1965–66, Whip.

4. Although results are not reported here, the bivariate relationships apparent in Tables 5.3 and 5.4 are also statistically significant and of roughly the same comparative magnitude in a multivariate analysis, with the whip count response as the dependent variable and all of the factors in the table except region included as explanatory variables. For the whip count response, the multivariate analysis was conducted in two steps. First, results are obtained via ordered probit and a three-point leadership support scale ranging from Y/LY to U to N/LN, and then through a probit regression for members in the nonresponse category. For the roll

call choices summarized in Table 5.4, within each category member votes were regressed on the aforementioned explanatory variables, with probit as the estimator. Similar tests were conducted for the analogous relationships reported in Chapters 6–8 for other House periods, and for the Senate GOP evidence summarized in Chapter 9. In each case, the bivariate relationships reported in tables generally hold up to multivariate analysis.

5. Observations from the 88th and 90th congresses must be dropped because comprehensive and reliable presidential vote tallies at the district level are not available.

6. For Chapters 5–9, information about participation in the leadership and various party committees is from editions of the *Congressional Directory*, *CQ's Politics in America*, and the *Almanac of American Politics*.

7. For these cases, zone aggregates were reported for at least one draft of the whip count.

8. "Head-Count Leaks on Close Votes Provoke Revolt by 26 in House," *Washington Post*, April 5, 1966, A2.

9. One exception was the zone comprised of Georgia and South Carolina, which continued to report only aggregate tallies until the mid-1970s. One reason was that John Flynt, D-Ga., the longtime whip for the zone, continued in that position until 1975.

10. If whip outcomes are considered by question type, the differences are relatively minor, perhaps because such a large percentage of whipped questions during period 1 dealt with final passage.

11. Schickler's (2016) prize-winning volume is by far the best general treatment of civil rights politics in Congress.

12. "Powell is punched by House colleague," *New York Times*, July 21, 1955, 1.

13. The case also surfaced in Riker's collaborative research with Denzau and Shepsle (Denzau, Riker, and Shepsle, 1985), as well as in works as disparate as Brady and Sinclair (1984), Enelow (1981), Ordeshook (1986), Krehbiel and Rivers (1990), Poole and Rosenthal (1997), and Stewart (2001), as well as the additional works cited in the text. Munger and Fenno (1962) and Fenno (1962) provide a highly useful descriptive account.

14. Carl Albert Collection, Legislative Files, Box 26, Folder 39.

15. For an insightful analysis of the challenges that civil rights issues created for Boggs throughout his House career, see Balius (1992).

16. Balius (1992), 80.

17. Ibid, 118.

18. Ibid, 118.

19. Hale Boggs Papers, Majority Whip Collection, Box 3.

20. "Effective Lobbying Put Open Housing Bill Across." In *CQ Almanac 1968*, 24th ed., 14-166–14-168. Washington, D.C.: Congressional Quarterly, 1969.

21. *Congressional Record*, April 10, 1968, 9620.

22. For a study of the consequences of the changing farm economy for agricultural politics in Congress, consult Winders (2009).

23. "Farm Price Supports." CQ Electronic Library, CQ Almanac Online Edition, 1955.

24. "Price Support Legislation," Carl Albert Collection, Legislative Files, Box 26, Folder 21.

25. Notes on April 29 Whip Meeting on Price Support Program. Carl Albert Collection, Legislative Files, Box 26, Folder 21.

26. Memo for the Majority Leader, April 29, 1955, Ibid.

27. Memo for the Speaker, April 29, 1955, Ibid.

28. "First Farm Bill Beaten, Compromise Passed." CQ Electronic Library, CQ Almanac Online Edition, 1962.

CHAPTER 6

1. The reference to "building coalitions in sand" is from Sinclair (1981), and originally from King (1978). For a perceptive account of the majority whip process of the 1970s and early 1980s authored by a former whip aide, see Brown (1985). Consult also Dodd (1978).

2. See, for example, the essays included in Mann and Ornstein (1981).

3. Ibid, 215.

4. On the 1970s reforms, see especially Rohde (1991) and Zelizer (2004).

5. The 1974 Budget Act as enacted provided for two concurrent resolutions on the budget, but the requirement for the second resolution was eliminated in 1986.

6. The water pollution control bill of 1972 was whipped because the leadership was concerned about possible floor amendments from pro-environment Democrats that might undermine the fragile coalition supporting the committee-approved language. On the Clean Water Act of 1977, the Democrats whipped the vote on House passage and the rule, primarily because the procedure for the bill was unusual and complicated. To avoid a conference negotiation with the Senate that might preclude enactment, Democratic leaders used the rule to combine the measure with the Senate-passed version of a public works bill. The goal of the whips was not to grow their vote, but to inform rank-and-file members about the procedural strategy.

7. The analogy to independent contractors is from Loomis (1988).

8. The best treatment of the declining role played by "Yankee Republicans" in the House is Rae (1989).

9. Since the purpose of the pickup analysis is to capture changes in the size of the party's support between the whip count and the vote, the aggregate tallies include all lawmakers who were included in the whip count or cast a vote on the associated roll call, assuming one occurred. In other words, unlike the treatment of "flow" in Table 4.5, here we do not exclude members who either were not included during the whip stage or failed to cast votes on the floor. As a result, there are certain differences between the pickup numbers reported in Tables 6.9 and 6.10, on the one hand, and the entries in the "face-off" table of Chapter 4, on the other.

10. Clyde H. Farnsworth, "U.S. Debt Ceiling Raised; Threats of Default Ended," *New York Times*, April 3, 1979, 12.

11. "Debt Limit Extensions." In *CQ Almanac 1979*, 35th ed., 305–7. Washington, D.C.: Congressional Quarterly, 1980.

12. "House Approves Increase in Debt Limit after Concessions on Balanced Budget," Mary Russell, *Washington Post*, March 16, 1979, A4.

13. White and Wildavsky (1989) provide an excellent summary of congressional action on the Reagan budget and tax fights.

14. Thomas S. Foley Congressional Papers, Box 200, Folder 6174.

15. In summarizing administration and leadership lobbying activities, I draw on the excellent treatment in Farrell (2001), as well as relevant portions of the Reagan Diaries (2007) and contemporaneous coverage in *CQ Weekly Report* and the relevant annual *CQ Almanacs*.

16. "Congress Enacts President Reagan's Tax Plan." In *CQ Almanac 1981*, 37th ed., 91–104. Washington, D.C.: Congressional Quarterly, 1982.

17. Elizabeth Wehr, "White House's Lobbying Apparatus Produces Impressive Tax Vote Victory," *CQ Weekly Report*, August 1, 1981, 1372.

18. Wehr, "White House's Lobbying Apparatus Produces Impressive Tax Vote Victory," 1372.

19. "Congress Enacts President Reagan's Tax Plan." In *CQ Almanac 1981*, 37th ed., 91–104.

20. As quoted by Farrell (2001), 560.

21. The majority list also includes two items that are formally classified as tax votes in the Rohde (2010) database, but were critical to House deliberations over energy reform during 1977–78. Similarly, one item categorized as an antitrust/economic matter by Rohde (2010) is included in the minority list because the question was an important part of the 1977–78 energy reform debate.

22. The narrative that follows leans on excellent treatments of the House energy fight by Oppenheimer (1980), Jones and Strahan (1985), and Farrell (2001).

23. Jimmy Carter, Address to the Nation on Energy, April 18, 1977. *The American Presidency Project*, edited by John Wooley and Gerhard Peters, University of California, Santa Barbara: http://www.presidency.ucsb.edu.

24. *Gallup News: Energy*. http://news.gallup.com/poll/2167/energy.aspx.

25. An initial Democratic whip count on passage (July 27) is not included in Table 6.10 because that version was obviated by events and not assigned an outcome category.

26. "Carter Energy Bill Fails to Clear." In *CQ Almanac 1977*, 33rd ed., 708–45. Washington, D.C.: Congressional Quarterly, 1978.

27. "Energy Bill: The End of an Odyssey." In *CQ Almanac 1978*, 34th ed., 639–67. Washington, D.C.: Congressional Quarterly, 1979.

28. *Congressional Record*, April 13, 1978, 1030–35.

29. Robert M. Michel Collection, Leadership Series, Box 2.

30. As quoted in Farrell (2001), 506–7.

31. Ibid, 507–508.

CHAPTER 7

1. For an apt description, see Sinclair (1995), Chapter 7.

2. Archival records for the period include a form prepared by the staff of House Democratic Whip David Bonior, D-Mich., that portrayed the physical layout of the House floor, including stations where members of the whip team were expected to stand during the relevant roll call vote. Butler Derrick Papers, Box 48.

3. For a description, see Evans and Grandy (2009).

4. "House Party Committees, 101st Congress." In *CQ Almanac 1989*, 45th ed., 33-E–36-E. Washington, D.C.: Congressional Quarterly, 1990.

5. Table 7.9 also includes a question placed in the category for "appropriations" based on the issue codes in Rohde (2010). The matter is included here because it was a critical part of House debates over aid to the Nicaraguan "Contras," a central focus of this section.

6. As is the case with the "pickup" tables in other chapters, the aggregate tallies in Tables 7.9 and 7.10 include all lawmakers who participated in the whip count or cast a vote on the associated roll call. Unlike the treatment of flow in Table 4.5, we do not exclude members who either were not included during the whip stage or failed to cast votes on the floor. Consequently, there are differences between the pickup numbers reported in Tables 7.9 and 7.10 and certain of the entries in the "face-off" table of Chapter 4.

7. "Nicaragua Covert Aid Issue Compromised." In *CQ Almanac 1983*, 39th ed., 123–32. Washington, D.C.: Congressional Quarterly, 1984.

8. Boland was also the primary author of the 1982 amendment bearing his name.

9. The measure of military presence within districts is from E. Scott Adler, Congressional District Data, University of Colorado, Boulder.

10. Jon Felton, "Reagan Asks Hill to Approve Arms, Other Aid for 'Contras,'" *CQ Weekly Report*, March 1, 1986, 489.

11. John Felton, "Reagan Loses Ground on 'Contra' Aid Program," *CQ Weekly Report*, March 8, 1986, 536.

12. David Rapp, "Lack of Support from House Moderates Was Key to Reagan Nicaragua Setback," *CQ Weekly Report*, March 22, 1986, 650.

13. Milton Coleman and Lou Cannon, "Reagan Acts to Salvage Contra Aid," *Washington Post*, March 20, 1986, online version.

14. John Felton, "House Republicans Go for Broke on 'Contra' Aid," *CQ Weekly Report*, April 19, 1986, 835.

15. The item is not included in Table 7.9 because it was obviated by events and there is no clear outcome, at least on that question as whipped. The 1986 Contra aid item with 174 Y/LY that is referenced in the table is for a different, albeit related matter (the previous question and the rule for the underlying supplemental appropriations measure).

16. John Felton, "House Republicans Go for Broke on 'Contra' Aid," 835.

17. "Congress Agrees to Renew Contra Arms Aid." In *CQ Almanac 1986*, 42nd ed., 394–414. Washington, D.C.: Congressional Quarterly, 1987.

18. Ibid. Instead, the Speaker suggested that Reagan appear before a joint session of Congress, an offer that the president declined because his own coalition-building challenges concerned floor action in the House, not the Senate.

19. John Felton, "For Reagan, a Key House Win on 'Contra' Aid," *CQ Weekly Report*, June 28, 1986, 1447.

20. Ibid.

21. Robert D. Reischauer, "Taxes and Spending Under Gramm-Rudman-Hollings," *National Tax Journal*, September 1990, 223–32.

22. Background on House action on the budget resolution and reconciliation package in 1990 is from Janet Hook, "Anatomy of a Budget Showdown: The Limits

of Leaders' Clout," *CQ Weekly Report*, October 6, 1990, 3189–91. For a treatment of factional politics within the House Republican Conference of period 3, consult Connelly and Pitney (1994).

23. Pamela Fessler, "Summit Talks Go in Circles as Partisan Tensions Rise," *CQ Weekly Report*, July 21, 1990, 2276.

24. Janet Hook, "Anatomy of a Budget Showdown," 3189.

25. "Budget Adopted After Long Battle." In *CQ Almanac 1990*, 46th ed., 111–66. Washington, D.C.: Congressional Quarterly, 1991.

26. Ibid.

27. Details about leadership and White House lobbying on the measure are from materials included in files about reconciliation and the budget, Butler Derrick Papers, Box 49.

28. "Deficit-Reduction Bill Narrowly Passes." In *CQ Almanac 1993*, 49th ed., 107–24. Washington, D.C.: Congressional Quarterly, 1994.

29. Ibid.

30. The vote changes are described in Clifford Krauss, "Whips Use Soft Touch to Succeed," *New York Times*, August 7, 1993, A7.

31. Scholarly references to the Margolies-Mezvinsky vote as a paradigmatic example of legislative vote buying include Wiseman (2004) and Saiegh (2011).

32. Clifford Krauss, August 7, 1993, A7.

33. Michael Wines, "At the Congressional Brink: A Freshman Saves the Day," *New York Times*, August 5, 1993, A1.

34. Background on Thornton, his district, and his two House careers, is from *Congressional Quarterly's Politics in America 1994: The 103rd Congress*, edited by CQ's Political Staff and Phil Duncan. Washington, D.C.: Congressional Quarterly Inc., 1993.

35. Butler Derrick Papers, Box 49.

CHAPTER 8

1. For summaries of the House Republican reforms, see Evans and Oleszek (1997) and Aldrich and Rohde (1998b).

2. DeLay (2007), 46.

3. Tom Delay Papers, Box 102.

4. Tom DeLay Papers, "Whips-Master" (Binder), Box 102. The whip's office periodically tabulated the response rate of the counters on whip polls, the attendance of the whips at meetings, and their loyalty to the party on targeted roll calls.

5. Bivariate regressions of the DW-NOMINATE scores, first dimension, of members of the Republican Conference on the various forms of whip status did not generate statistically significant parameter estimates.

6. The day-to-day logistics of whipping were described in detail in a manual kept by the office: Tom DeLay Papers, untitled white notebook, Box 93. My description of the DeLay whip operations is also based on conversations with knowledgeable staff.

7. Tom DeLay Papers, "Whip Meetings 107th Congress (Binder), Box 93.

8. Tom DeLay Papers, untitled white notebook, Box 93.

9. For many congressional observers, DeLay's approach called to mind Tony Coelho's stretch as Democratic whip during the late 1980s. For colorful descriptions of Coelho as whip, see Barry (1989) and Jackson (1990).

10. DeLay was indicted in 2005 and convicted in 2010 of attempting to use corporate donations to influence electoral outcomes in Texas. The conviction was overturned on appeal in 2013 for insufficient evidence, and the appellate decision was affirmed in 2014.

11. Information on the organization of the House Democratic whip system for the 107th Congress is from various materials in the David Bonior Papers. See also Judy Schneider, "House Leadership: Whip Organization," *Congressional Research Service*, February 12, 2002.

12. Background about Morella and her district is from Michael Barone, with Richard E. Cohen, *The Almanac of American Politics 2002*, Washington, D.C.: National Journal, 2001, 728–30.

13. Mark Francis Cohen, "Angel from Montgomery," *Washington City Paper*, July 5, 2002.

14. Catherine Matacic, "Morella Sifts through 16 years of Memories, Looks Ahead after Loss," *Capital News Service*, November 27, 2002.

15. A fourth logically possible category—no GOP position, but a discernable Democratic position—did not surface in the data.

16. The main sources included *CQ Weekly Report* and other media accounts, whip records where available, and relevant passages in the *Congressional Record*.

17. Only questions where the majority leadership had a position and the outcome was classifiable are included in the configuration totals, but just a small number of observations were dropped for these reasons.

18. "After Initial Veto, GOP and Clinton Split the Differences on Commerce-Justice-State." In *CQ Almanac 1999*, 55th ed., 2-17-2-28. Washington, D.C.: Congressional Quarterly, 2000.

19. "Putting Differences Aside, Lawmakers Clear $69 Billion Agriculture Spending Bill." In *CQ Almanac 1999*, 55th ed. Washington, D.C.: Congressional Quarterly, 2000, Section 2, 5–16.

20. "Earmarks in Appropriations Acts: FY1994, FY1996, FY1998, FY2000, FY2002 FY2004, FY2005," *Congressional Research Service*, July 26, 2006.

21. Tom DeLay, "The Power of the Purse: Banning Earmarks Is Not the Right Reform," *Politico*, February 26, 2007.

22. Evans (2004), and also Frisch and Kelly (2011).

23. Strategic timing was also a feature of the appropriations process. The more popular bills were generally considered first (e.g., agriculture, defense). As expenditure caps were breached on the early bills, the larger and less popular measures waiting in queue would flounder or be vetoed. Then, as the October 1 deadline neared, the unpassed measures would be combined into an omnibus measure that evoked clear-cut partisan divisions and put enormous pressure on majority party members to vote yes and thereby avoid a governmental closure or other outcome embarrassing to the party. The contours of this temporal strategy are also apparent in the specific spending questions that were targeted for whipping.

24. Staff to the whip also referred to the partial counts as spot checks on occasion.

25. Two of the completed whip counts could not be assigned an outcome category and are excluded from Table 8.6.

26. The item is not included in Table 8.6 because it was a spot check, and not a full count.

27. Tom DeLay Papers, Box 97.

28. Ibid.

29. Joseph Schatz, "Bush Wins Key Victory before Recess," *CQ Weekly Report*, August 3, 2002, 2127–30.

30. Joanna Ramey, "DeMint in Middle of Textile Tussle," *WWD*, June 11, 2002, 18.

CHAPTER 9

1. Gamm and Smith (2002), 235.

2. This section draws on Bradbury, Davidson, and Evans (2008), as well as Evans and Grandy (2009).

3. Personal communication, December 29, 2009.

4. During these years, a top aide, Republican Party Secretary Howard Greene, conducted counts of member positions from his seat in the GOP cloakroom.

5. "Some Thoughts on the Whip Election," memo to Alan Simpson, November 25, 1994, Box 624, Folder 8, Alan Simpson Congressional Collection, American Heritage Center, University of Wyoming, Laramie, Wyoming.

6. Don Nickles Papers, Box 15. The archival record also includes traces of a few additional whip counts, but based on the lack of completed responses, or because the relevant questions are missing in the annual summaries of whip activities compiled by staff, these items are not treated as formal counts here.

7. My understanding of the internal operations of the Senate Republican leadership at the time and of the important party "lunches" derives from many conversations with W. Lee Rawls, who served as chief of staff to Senate Majority Leader Bill Frist, R-Tenn.

8. Personal interview, April 2009.

9. See Miller (1962).

10. On Nickles's priorities as leader and his relationship with Lott, see Peter H. Stone, "Playing Second Fiddle," *The National Journal*, July 11, 1998, 1612–16; and Chris Casteel, "Nickles Considered Own Power Play," *The Daily Oklahoman*, November 17, 1998, 7.

11. As with the House evidence, the policy categorizations for Senate votes are based on data compiled and provided by David Rohde and his colleagues at the Political Institutions and Public Choice program at Duke University. For an update, see PIPC Roll Call Datasets, The Carl Albert Center, University of Oklahoma: http://pipcvotes.cacexplore.org. For whipped questions that resulted in votes, I simply used the PIPC issue codes. For whipped questions that could not be directly or indirectly associated with a Senate roll call, I categorized issues based on the PIPC codebook and the policy types assigned for similar items.

12. As with the analogous presentation for the House in Chapters 5–8, the results reported in Tables 9.3 and 9.4 are bivariate and cross-tabular to make the

presentation accessible and transparent, but the implications drawn from the table generally hold up to more systematic multivariate analysis.

13. Lott (2005).

14. The four questions related to strategic matters (e.g., whether or not to cosponsor legislation produced by the Senate Republican healthcare task force or to forgo offering amendments to a measure) or broader policy matters where a clear threshold could not be identified.

15. For background on partisan struggles over managed care reform during 1997–2000, consult "Despite Lengthy Conference, Lawmakers Cannot Agree on Managed Care." In *CQ Almanac 2000*, 56th ed., 12-3–12-15. Washington, D.C.: Congressional Quarterly, 2001.

16. Lizette Alvarez, "Eye on Polling, G.O.P. Unveils a Patients' Bill," *New York Times*, July 15, 1998, A1.

17. "Lawmakers Agree on Need for Patients' Rights but Remain Divided on Methods." In *CQ Almanac 1999*, 55th ed., 16-3–16-30. Washington, D.C.: Congressional Quarterly, 2000.

18. Michael Grunwald and Eric Pianin, "Senate Democrats Make Threat for HMO Vote," *Washington Post*, June 22, 1999, A6.

19. Pickup requirements differ across the two questions because both were settled by motions to table. While the Republicans only needed 50 votes (for a tie) to defeat the motion to table their own proposal, 51 were required for them to successfully table the Kennedy alternative.

20. Alan Greenblatt, "Managed Care Initiative Slows Senate Consideration of Agriculture Spending Bill," *CQ Weekly Report*, June 26, 1999, 1535.

21. For a summary of party strategy on the matter, see Alison Mitchell, "Senate Approves Republicans' Plan for Health Care," *New York Times*, July 16, 1999, A1.

22. Karen Foerstel, "Managed Care Struggle Shifts to Unpredictable House," *CQ Weekly Report*, July 17, 1999, 1715.

23. Interview with the author, July 23, 1999.

24. Jackie Koszczuk, "GOP's Fragile Unity Factures in Managed Care Decision," *CQ Weekly Report*, October 9, 1999, 2354.

25. David Nather, "GOP Concession on Patients' Right to Sue is Unlikely to End Managed-Care Impasse," *CQ Weekly Report*, July 1, 2000, 1598.

CHAPTER 10

1. For example, consult Russell W. Mills, Nicole Kalaf-Hughes, and Jason A. MacDonald, "This Is What Will Make It Harder for Congress to Pass a Budget This Fall," *Monkey Cage, Washington Post*, August 18, 2015.

2. Ezra Klein, "Lessons from the Medicare Prescription Drug Benefit Vote," *Wonkbook, Washington Post*, March 8, 2010.

3. Darren Goode, "Three Anti-CAFTA Republicans Have Road Projects Slashed," *National Journal's Congress Daily PM*, August 5, 2005.

4. Jonathan Weisman, "Liberals Relent on Iraq War Funding," *Washington Post*, March 23, 2007.

5. Jonathan Cohn, "How They Did It," *The New Republic*, May 21, 2010.

6. Dana Milbank, "In the House's Dark Hour, Speaker Paul Ryan Offers a Glimpse of Hope," *Washington Post*, October 29, 2015.

7. For an analysis of the impact of the House Republican freshman class of 2011–12, see Evans (2014).

8. "Congressman Mick Mulvaney—Husband, Father, and Not Your Average Republican," Interview with *Crescent Magazine*, posted August 27, 2012.

9. MJ Lee, Deidre Walsh, Phil Mattingly, and Lauren Fox, "After Dramatic Day, GOP Fails to Reach Health Care Deal," *CNN Politics*, March 23, 2017.

10. Thomas Kaplan and Robert Pear, "Health Care Bill, Passed by House, Faces Senate Test," *New York Times*, May 5, 2017, A1.

11. John Breshnaham, Burgess Everett, Jennifer Haberkorn, and Seung Min Kim, "Senate Rejects Obamacare Repeal," *Politico*, July 27, 2017.

12. For that matter, very little that occurs during the congressional legislative process is solely, or even primarily, a "Washington story." See Fenno (2013).

13. One informal indicator—From the 1980s to the 2010s, there appears to have been a substantial decline in the number of panels focusing on the internal operations of Congress at annual meetings of the American Political Science Association.

14. Margaret Kris, "Still Charging," *National Journal*, December 6, 1997, 2462.

15. The penultimate chapter of Fenno (1973), for example, was about the legislative outcomes of the congressional committee process.

16. "Investigation of Certain Allegations Related to Voting on the Medicare Prescription Drug, Improvement, and Modernization Act of 2003," Report of the Committee on Standards of Official Conduct, House of Representatives, Report 108–722, October 4, 2004.

Bibliography

Aldrich, John H. 1995. *Why Parties?:The Origin and Transformation of Political Parties in America*. Chicago, IL: University of Chicago Press.

Aldrich, John H., and David W. Rohde. 1998a. "Measuring Conditional Party Government." Presented at the Annual Meeting of the Midwest Political Science Association, Chicago, IL, April 1998.

Aldrich, John H., and David W. Rohde. 1998b. "The Transition to Republican Rule in the House: Implications for Theories of Congressional Parties." *Political Science Quarterly* 112: 541–67.

Aldrich, John H., and David W. Rohde. 2000. "The Consequences of Party Organization in the House: The Role of the Majority and Minority Parties in Conditional Party Government." In *Polarized Politics: Congress and the President in a Partisan Era*, edited by Jon R. Bond and Richard Fleisher. Washington, DC: CQ Press.

Alexander, De Alva S. 1916. *History and Procedure of the House of Representatives*. Boston, MA: Houghton Mifflin.

Amer, Mildred. 2006. "Major Leadership Election Contests in the House of Representatives, 94th–109th Congress." Congressional Research Service, Library of Congress, Washington DC.

Arnold, R. Douglas. 1990. *The Logic of Congressional Action*. New Haven, CT: Yale University Press.

Bach, Stanley, and Steven S. Smith. 1988. *Managing Uncertainty in the House: Adaptation and Innovation in Special Rules*. Washington, DC: Brookings Institution Press.

Balius, Scott E. 1992. *The Courage of His Convictions: Hale Boggs and Civil Rights*. Unpublished dissertation. Department of History, Tulane University, New Orleans, LA.

Barry, John. 1989. *The Ambition and the Power*. New York, NY: Penguin.

Bawn, Kathleen. 1998. "Congressional Party Leadership: Utilitarian versus Majoritarian Incentives." *Legislative Studies Quarterly* 23(2): 221–45.

Beckmann, Matthew N. 2010. *Pushing the Agenda: Presidential Leadership in U.S. Lawmaking, 1953–2004*. New York, NY: Cambridge University Press.

Behringer, Courtney, C. Lawrence Evans, and Elizabeth R. Materese. 2006. "Parties, Preferences, and the House Whip Process." Presented at the Annual Meeting of the Southern Political Science Association, Atlanta, GA, January 2006.

Binder, Sarah A. 1995. "Partisanship and Procedural Choice: Institutional Change in the Early Congress, 1789–1823." *Journal of Politics* 57: 1093–117.

Binder, Sarah A. 1997. *Minority Rights, Majority Rule*. New York, NY: Cambridge University Press.

Black, Duncan. 1958. *The Theory of Committees and Elections*. Cambridge UK: Cambridge University Press.

Boatright, Robert G. 2014. *Getting Primaried: The Changing Politics of Congressional Primary Challenges*. Ann Arbor, MI: University of Michigan Press.

Bond, Jon R., and Richard Fleisher. 1990. *The President in the Legislative Arena*. Chicago, IL: University of Chicago Press.

Bradbury, Erin, Ryan Davidson, and C. Lawrence Evans. 2008. "The Senate Whip System: An Exploration." In *Why Not Parties?*, edited by Nathan Monroe, Jason Roberts, and David Rohde. Chicago, IL: University of Chicago Press.

Brady, David W., and Barbara Sinclair. 1984. "Building Majorities for Policy Changes in the House of Representatives." *Journal of Politics* 46: 1033–60.

Brady, David W., and Craig Volden. 2006. *Revolving Gridlock: Politics and Policy from Jimmy Carter to George W Bush (2nd edition)*. Boulder, CO: Westview Press.

Brown, Lynne P. 1985. *Dilemmas of Party Leadership: Majority Whips in the House of Representatives, 1962–1984*. Unpublished dissertation. Department of Political Science, The Johns Hopkins University, Baltimore, MD.

Brown, Sarah, Keith Devereaux, C. Lawrence Evans, Kristen Haase, William Marlow, and Joshua McHenry. 2005. "Tax Cuts, Contras, and Partisan Influence in the U.S. House." Presented at the Annual Meeting of the Midwest Political Science Association, Chicago, IL, April 2005.

Burden, Barry D., and Tammy M. Frisby. 2004. "Preferences, Partisanship, and Whip Activity in the House of Representatives."*Legislative Studies Quarterly* 29: 569–90.

Butts, Josiah, Amanda Downing, C. Lawrence Evans, Keith Klovers, and Mary Moll. 2007. "The Minority Whip System in the U.S. House." Presented at the Annual Meeting of the Midwest Political Science Association, Chicago, IL, April 2007.

Calvert, Randall L., and Richard F. Fenno, Jr. 1994. "Strategy and Sophisticated Voting in the Senate." *Journal of Politics* 56: 349–76.

Campbell, Andrea, Gary Cox, and Mathew McCubbins. 2002. "Agenda Power in the U.S. Senate, 1977–1986." In *Party, Process and Political Change in Congress*, edited by David Brady and Mathew McCubbins. Stanford, CA: Stanford University Press, 146–65.

Cherepanov, Vadim, Timothy Feddersen, and Alvaro Sandroni. 2013. "Rationalization." *Theoretical Economics* 8: 775–800.

Clark, Champ. 1920. *My Quarter Century in American Politics*. New York, NY: Harper & Brothers.

Clausen, Aage. 1973. *How Congressmen Decide: A Policy Focus.* New York, NY: St. Martin's Press.

Clausen, Aage, and Clyde Wilcox. 1987. "Policy Partisanship in Legislative Recruitment and Behavior." *Legislative Studies Quarterly* 12: 243–63.

Clinton, Joshua D., and John S. Lapinski. 2006. "Measuring Legislative Accomplishment, 1877–1994." *American Journal of Political Science* 50: 232–49.

Connelly, William F., Jr., and John J. Pitney, Jr. 1994. *Congress' Permanent Minority?* Lanham, MD: Rowman & Littlefield.

Cooper, Joseph, and David W. Brady. 1981. "Institutional Context and Leadership Style: The House from Cannon to Rayburn." *American Political Science Review* 75: 411–25.

Cooper, Joseph and Ulrich Sieberer. 2005. "The Importance of Majority Party Size in Congress," Manuscript, John Hopkins University, Baltimore, MD.

Covington, Cary R. 1987. "Staying Private: Gaining Congressional Support for Unpublicized Presidential Preferences on Roll Call Votes." *Journal of Politics* 49: 737–55.

Cox, Gary W. 2001. "Estimating Legislators' Preferences with Roll Call Data: Introduction to the Special Issue." *Political Analysis* 9: 189–91.

Cox, Gary W., and Eric Magar. 1999. "How Much Is Majority Status in the U.S. Congress Worth?" *American Political Science Review* 93: 293–309.

Cox, Gary W., and Mathew D. McCubbins. 1993. *Legislative Leviathan: Party Government in the House.* Berkeley, CA: University of California Press.

Cox, Gary W., and Mathew D. McCubbins. 2005. *Setting the Agenda: Responsible Party Government in the U.S. House of Representatives.* New York, NY: Cambridge University Press.

Crespin, Michael, and David R. Rohde. 2010. "Dimensions, Issues, and Bills: Appropriations Voting on the House Floor." *Journal of Politics* 72: 976–89.

Curry, James. 2016. *Legislating in the Dark: Information and Power in the House of Representatives.* Chicago, IL: University of Chicago Press.

Deering, Christopher J., and Steven S. Smith. 1997. *Committees in Congress.* Washington, DC: CQ Press.

DeLay, Tom. 2007. *No Retreat, No Surrender: One American's Fight.* New York, NY: Penguin Group.

Den Hartog, Chris, and Nathan W. Monroe. 2011. *Agenda Setting in the U.S. Senate: Costly Consideration and Majority Party Advantage.* New York, NY: Cambridge University Press.

Denzau, Arthur, William Riker, and Kenneth A. Shepsle. 1985. "Farquharson and Fenno: Sophisticated Voting and Home Style." *American Political Science Review* 79: 1117–34.

Dodd, Lawrence C. 1978. "The Expanded Roles of the House Democratic Whip System: The 93rd and 94th Congresses." *Congressional Studies* 7: 27–56.

Dodd, Lawrence C. 1985. "Congress and the Quest for Power." In *Studies of Congress,* edited by Glenn R. Parker, 489–520. Washington, DC: CQ Press.

Dodd, Lawrence C., and Terry Sullivan. 1981. "Majority Party Leadership and Partisan Vote Gathering: The House Democratic Whip System." In *Understanding Congressional Leadership,* edited by Frank H. Mackaman. Washington, DC: CQ Press.

Enelow, James M. 1981. "Saving Amendments, Killer Amendments, and an Expected Utility Theory of Sophisticated Voting." *Journal of Politics* 43: 1062–89.

Evans, C. Lawrence. 1991. *Leadership in Committee*. Ann Arbor, MI: University of Michigan Press.

Evans, C. Lawrence. 2001. "Committees, Leaders, and Message Politics." In *Congress Reconsidered*, 7th ed., edited by Lawrence C. Dodd and Bruce I. Oppenheimer. Washington, DC: CQ Press.

Evans, C. Lawrence. 2014. "Congressional Cohorts: The House Republican Class of 2010." *The Forum*, Fall.

Evans, C. Lawrence and Claire E. Grandy. 2009. "The Whip Systems of Congress." In *Congress Reconsidered*, 9th ed., edited by Lawrence C. Dodd and Bruce I. Oppenheimer, 189–216. Washington, DC: CQ Press.

Evans, C. Lawrence and Walter J. Oleszek. 1997. *Congress Under Fire: Reform Politics and the Republican Majority*. Boston, MA: Houghton Mifflin.

Evans, C. Lawrence and Walter J. Oleszek. 2000. "The Procedural Context of Senate Deliberation." In *Esteemed Colleagues: Civility and Deliberation in the U.S. Senate*, edited by Burdett A. Loomis, 79–104. Washington, DC: Brookings Institution.

Evans, Diana. 2004. *Greasing the Wheels: Using Pork Barrel Projects to Build Majority Coalitions in Congress*. New York, NY: Cambridge University Press.

Farrell, John A. 2001. *Tip O'Neill and the Democratic Century*. Boston, MA: Little, Brown.

Fenno, Richard F., Jr. 1962. "The House of Representatives and Federal Aid to Education." In *New Perspectives on the House of Representatives*, edited by Robert L. Peabody and Nelson W. Polsby. Chicago, IL: Rand McNally.

Fenno, Richard F., Jr. 1966. *The Power of the Purse*. Boston, MA: Little, Brown.

Fenno, Richard F., Jr. 1973. *Congressmen in Committees*. Boston, MA: Little, Brown.

Fenno, Richard F., Jr. 1978. *Home Style: House Members in Their Districts*. Boston, MA: Little, Brown.

Fenno, Richard F., Jr. 1985. "Observation, Context, and Sequence in the Study of Politics." *American Political Science Review* 80: 3–15.

Fenno, Richard F., Jr. 2013. *The Challenge of Congressional Representation*. Cambridge, MA: Harvard University Press.

Finocchiaro, Charles J., and David W. Rohde. 2008. "War for the Floor: Partisan Theory and Agenda Setting in the U.S. House of Representatives." *Legislative Studies Quarterly* 33: 35–62.

Fishburn, Peter. 1973. *The Theory of Social Choice*. Princeton, NJ: Princeton University Press.

Frisch, Scott A., and Sean Q. Kelly. 2011. *Cheese Factories on the Moon: Why Earmarks Are Good for American Democracy*. Boulder, CO: Paradigm Publishers.

Froman, Lewis A. 1967. *The Congressional Process: Strategies, Rules, and Procedures*. Boston, MA: Little, Brown.

Froman, Lewis A., and Randall B. Ripley. 1965. "Conditions for Party Leadership: The Case of the House Democrats." *American Political Science Review* 59: 52–63.

Gilmour, John B. 2001. "The Powell Amendment Voting Cycle: An Obituary." *Legislative Studies Quarterly* 26: 249–62.

Gladstone, Viscount. 1927. "The Chief Whip in the British Parliament." *American Political Science Review* 21: 519–28.

Goodwin, Richard. 1970. *The Little Legislatures: Committees of Congress*. Amherst, MA: University of Massachusetts Press.

Green, Matthew N. 2010. *The Speaker of the House: A Study of Leadership*. New Haven, CT: Yale University Press.

Grofman, Bernard, William Koetzle, and Anthony J. McGann. 2002. "Congressional Leadership 1965–96: A New Look at the Extremism versus Centrality Debate." *Legislative Studies Quarterly* 27: 87–105.

Grossmann, Matt, and David A. Hopkins. 2016. *Asymmetric Politics*. New York, NY: Oxford University Press.

Hall, Richard L. 1996. *Participation in Congress*. New Haven, CT: Yale University Press.

Hardeman, D. B., and Donald C. Bacon. 1987. *Rayburn: A Biography*. Austin, TX: Texas Monthly Press.

Harris, Douglas B. 2006. "Legislative Parties and Leadership Choice: Confrontation or Accommodation in the 1989 Gingrich-Madigan Whip Race." *American Politics Research* 34: 189–222.

Harris, Douglas B., and Garrison Nelson. 2008. "Middlemen No More? Emergent Patterns in Congressional Leadership Selection." *PS: Political Science and Politics* 41: 49–55.

Heberlig, Eric S. 2003. "The Survival of a Targeted Incumbent: Soft Money and Issue Advocacy in North Carolina's Eight and Ninth Districts." *PS Online*, July 2003.

Herrnson, Paul S. 2012. *Congressional Elections: Campaigning at Home and in Washington*. Washington, DC: CQ Press.

Hetherington, Marc. 2001. "Resurgent Mass Partisanship: The Role of Elite Polarization." *American Political Science Review* 95: 619–32.

Hinckley, Barbara. 1971. *The Seniority System in Congress*. Bloomington, IN: Indiana University Press.

Hurwitz, Mark S., Roger J. Moiles, and David W. Rohde. 2001. "Distributive and Partisan Issues in Agriculture Policy in the 104th House." *American Political Science Review* 95: 911–22.

Jackson, Brooks. 1990. *Honest Graft: Big Money and the American Political Process*. Washington, DC: Farragut Publishing Company.

Jackson, John E., and John W. Kingdon. 1992. "Ideology, Interest Group Ratings, and Roll Call Votes." *American Journal of Political Science* 36: 805–23.

Jenkins, J. A., and Nathan W. Monroe. 2012. "Buying Negative Agenda Control in the U.S. House." *American Journal of Political Science* 56: 897–912.

Jessee, Stephen and Neil Malhotra. 2010. "Are Congressional Leaders Middle Persons or Extremists? Yes." *Legislative Studies Quarterly* 35: 361–92.

Jones, Charles O. 1961. "Representation in Congress: The Case of the House Agriculture Committee." *American Political Science Review* 55: 358–67.

Jones, Charles O. 1964. *Party and Policy-Making: The House Republican Policy Committee*. New Brunswick, NJ: Rutgers University Press.

Jones, Charles O. 1970. *The Minority Party in Congress*. Boston, MA: Little, Brown.

Jones, Charles O. 1988. *The Trusteeship Presidency: Jimmy Carter and the United States Congress*. Baton Rouge: Louisiana State University Press.

Jones, Charles O., and Randall Strahan. 1985. "The Effect of Energy Politics on Congressional and Executive Organization in the 1970s." *Legislative Studies Quarterly* 10: 151–79.

Kelly, Andrew, and Robert Van Houweling. 2010. "Roll Calls and Representation." Presented at the Annual Meeting of the Western Political Science Association, San Franciso, CA, April 2010.

King, Anthony. 1978. "The American Polity in the Late 1970s: Building Coalitions in the Sand." In *The New American Political System*, edited by Anthony King. Washington, DC: American Enterprise Institute.

King, David C., and Richard J. Zeckhauser. 2002. "Punching and Counter-punching in the U.S. Congress: Why Party Leaders Tend to be Extremists." Presented at the Conference on Leadership 2002: Bridging the Gap between Theory and Practice. The Center for Public Leadership, Cambridge, MA.

Kingdon, John W. 1973. *Congressmen's Voting Decisions*. New York, NY: Harper and Row.

Koger, Gregory. 2010. *Filibustering: A Political History of Obstruction in the House and Senate*. Chicago, IL: University of Chicago Press.

Koger, Gregory, and Matthew J. Lebo. 2017. *Strategic Party Government: Why Winning Trumps Ideology*. Chicago, IL: University of Chicago Press.

Kowalcky, Linda, and Lance LeLoup. 1993. "Congress and the Politics of Statutory Debt Limitation." *Public Administration Review* 53: 14–27.

Krehbiel, Keith. 1988. "Spatial Models of Legislative Choice." *Legislative Studies Quarterly* 13: 259–319.

Krehbiel, Keith. 1991. *Information and Legislative Organization*. Ann Arbor, MI: University of Michigan Press.

Krehbiel, Keith. 1998. *Pivotal Politics: A Theory of U.S. Lawmaking*. Chicago, IL: University of Chicago Press.

Krehbiel, Keith and Douglas Rivers. 1990. "Sophisticated Voting in Congress: A Reconsideration." *Journal of Politics* 52: 548–78.

Lawrence, Eric D., Forrest Maltzman, and Steven S. Smith. 2006. "Who Wins? Party Effects in Legislative Voting." *Legislative Studies Quarterly* 31: 33–69.

Layman, Geoffrey C., and Thomas M. Carsey. 2002. "Party Polarization and 'Conflict Extension' in the American Electorate." *American Journal of Political Science* 46: 786–802.

Lee, Frances. 2009. *Beyond Ideology*. Chicago, IL: University of Chicago Press.

Lee, Frances. 2016. *Insecure Majorities*. Chicago, IL: University of Chicago Press.

Loomis, Burdett. 1988. *The New American Politician: Ambition, Entrepreneurship, and the Changing Face of Political Life*. New York, NY: Basic Books.

Mackie, Gerry. 2004. *Democracy Defended*. New York, NY: Cambridge University Press.

Mann, Thomas E., and Norman J. Ornstein. 1981. *The New Congress*. Washington, DC: American Enterprise Institute.

Manley, John F. 1970. *The Politics of Finance: The House Committee on Ways and Means*. Boston, MA: Little, Brown.

Mayhew, David R. 1966. *Party Loyalty among Congressmen*. Cambridge, MA: Harvard University Press.

Mayhew, David R. 1974. *Congress: The Electoral Connection*. New Haven, CT: Yale University Press.

Mayhew, David R. 2011. *Partisan Balance*. Princeton, NJ: Princeton University Press.

Mayhew, David R. 2014. "The Long 1950s as a Policy Era." In *The Politics of Major Policy Reform in Postwar America*, edited by Jeffery A. Jenkins and Sidney M. Milkis. New York, NY: Cambridge University Press.

McCarty, Nolan, Keith T. Poole, and Howard Rosenthal. 2001. "The Hunt for Party Discipline in Congress." *American Political Science Review* 95: 673–88.

McCarty, Nolan, Keith T. Poole, and Howard Rosenthal. 2006. *Polarized America*. Boston, MA: MIT Press.

Meinke, Scott R. 2008. "Who Whips: Party Government and the House Extended Whip Network." *American Politics Research* 36 (5): 639–68.

Meinke, Scott R. 2016. *Leadership Organizations in the House of Representatives*. Ann Arbor, MI: University of Michigan Press.

Miller, Clem. 1962. *Member of the House: Letters of a Congressman*, edited by John W. Baker. New York, NY: Scribner.

Munger, Frank J., and Richard F. Fenno, Jr. 1962. *National Politics and Federal Aid to Education*. Syracuse, NY: Syracuse University Press.

Oleszek, Walter J. 1971. "Party Whips in the United States Senate." *The Journal of Politics* 33 (4): 955–79.

Oppenheimer, Bruce I. 1977. "The Rules Committee: New Arm of Leadership in a Decentralized House." In *Congress Reconsidered*, edited by Lawrence C. Dodd and Bruce I. Oppenheimer. New York, NY: Praeger.

Oppenheimer, Bruce I. 1980. "Policy Effects of U.S. House Reform: Decentralization and the Capacity to Resolve Energy Issues." *Legislative Studies Quarterly* 5: 5–30.

Ordeshook, Peter. 1986. *Game Theory and Political Theory: An Introduction*. New York, NY: Cambridge University Press.

Ornstein, Norman J., and David W. Rohde. 1974. "The Strategy of Reform: Recorded Teller Voting in the U.S. House of Representatives." Presented at the Annual Meeting of the Midwest Political Science Association, Chicago IL, April 1974.

Peabody, Robert L. 1976. *Leadership in Congress: Stability, Succession, and Change*. Boston, MA: Little, Brown.

Pitkin, Hanna F. 1972. *The Concept of Representation*. Berkeley, CA: University of California Press.

Polsby, Nelson W. 1983. *Consequences of Party Reform*. New York, NY: Oxford University Press.

Polsby, Nelson W., and Eric Schickler. 2002. "Landmarks in the Study of Congress since 1945." *Annual Review of Political Science* 5: 333–67.

Poole, Keith T. 2005. *Spatial Models of Parliamentary Voting*. New York, NY: Cambridge University Press.

Poole, Keith T., and Howard Rosenthal. 1997. *Congress: A Political-Economic History of Roll Call Voting*. New York, NY: Oxford University Press.

Rae, Nicol D. 1989. *The Decline and Fall of the Liberal Republicans from 1952 to the Present*. New York, NY: Oxford University Press.

Rawls, W. Lee. 2009. *In Praise of Deadlock: How Partisan Struggle Makes Better Laws*. Baltimore, MD: John Hopkins University Press.

Reagan, Ronald W. 2007. *The Reagan Diaries*. Edited by Douglas Brinkley. New York, NY: HarperCollins.

Riker, William H. 1965. "Arrow's Theorem and Some Examples of the Paradox of Voting." In *Mathematical Applications in Political Science*, edited by John M. Claunch. Dallas, TX: Southern Methodist University Press.

Riker, William H. 1982. *Liberalism against Populism: A Confrontation between the Theory of Democracy and the Theory of Social Choice*. San Francisco, CA: W.H. Freeman.

Ripley, Randall B. 1964. "The Party Whip Organization in the United States House of Representatives." *American Political Science Review* 58: 561–76.

Ripley, Randall B. 1967. *Party Leaders in the House of Representatives*. Washington, DC: The Brookings Institution.

Roberts, Jason M., and Steven S. Smith. 2003. "Procedural Contexts, Party Strategy, and Conditional Party Voting in the U.S. House of Representatives, 1971–2000." *American Journal of Political Science* 47: 305–17.

Robinson, William A. 1930. *Thomas B. Reed: Parliamentarian*. New York, NY: Dodd, Mead & Co.

Rohde, David W. 1991. *Parties and Leaders in the Postreform House*. Chicago, IL: University of Chicago Press.

Rohde, David W. 2010. *PIPC Roll Call Database*. Durham, NC: Duke University.

Rohde, David W. 2013. "Reflections on the Practice of Theorizing: Conditional Party Government in the Twenty-First Century." *The Journal of Politics* 75: 849–64.

Saiegh, Sebastian. 2011. *Ruling by Statute: How Uncertainty and Vote Buying Shape Lawmaking*. New York, NY: Cambridge University Press.

Schick, Alan. 1980. *Congress and Money: Budgeting, Spending and Taxing*. Washington, DC: Urban Institute.

Schickler, Eric. 2016. *Racial Realignment: The Transformation of American Liberalism, 1932–1965*. Princeton, NJ: Princeton University Press.

Schneider, Judy. 2002. *House Leadership: Whip Organization*. CRS Report for Congress, updated February 12, 2002.

Shepsle, Kenneth A. 1987. "The Changing Textbook Congress." In *Can the Government Govern*, edited by John E. Chubb and Paul E. Peterson, 238–66. Washington, DC: Brookings Institution Press.

Shepsle, Kenneth A., and Barry R. Weingast. 1995. *Positive Theories of Congressional Institutions*. Ann Arbor, MI: University of Michigan Press.

Sinclair, Barbara. 1981. "Coping with Uncertainty: Building Coalitions in the House and the Senate." In *The New Congress*, edited by Thomas E. Mann and Norman J. Ornstein, 178–222. Washington, DC: The American Enterprise Institute.

Sinclair, Barbara. 1983. *Majority Leadership in the U.S. House*. Baltimore, MD: Johns Hopkins University Press.

Sinclair, Barbara. 1989. *The Transformation of the U.S. Senate*. Baltimore, MD: Johns Hopkins University Press.

Sinclair, Barbara. 1995. *Legislators, Leaders, and Lawmaking: The U.S. House of Representatives in the Postreform Era*. Baltimore, MD: Johns Hopkins University Press.

Sinclair, Barbara. 2006. *Party Wars: Polarization and the Politics of National Policy Making*. Norman, OK: University of Oklahoma Press.

Smith, Steven S. 1989. *Call to Order: Floor Politics in the House and Senate.* Washington, DC: Brookings Institution Press.

Smith, Steven S. 2007. *Party Influence in Congress.* New York, NY: Cambridge University Press.

Smith, Steven S. 2014. *The Senate Syndrome: The Evolution of Procedural Warfare in the Modern U.S. Senate.* Norman, OK: University of Oklahoma Press.

Smith, Steven S., and Gerald Gamm. 2002. "Emergence of the Modern Senate: Party Organizations, 1937–2002." Paper presented at the Annual Meeting of the American Political Science Association, Boston, MA, August 2002.

Stevens, Arthur G., Arthur H. Miller, and Thomas E. Mann. 1974. "Mobilization of Liberal Strength in the House, 1955–1970: The Democratic Study Group." *American Political Science Review* 68: 667–81.

Stewart, Charles, III. 2001. *Analyzing Congress.* New York, NY: W. W. Norton.

Strahan, Randall. 2007. *Leading Representatives: The Agency of Leaders in the Politics of the U.S. House.* Baltimore, MD: Johns Hopkins University Press.

Sullivan, Terry. 1990a. "Bargaining with the President: A Simple Game and New Evidence." *American Political Science Review* 84: 1167–95.

Sullivan, Terry. 1990b. "Explaining Why Presidents Count: Signaling and Information." *Journal of Politics* 52: 939–62.

Sundquist, James L. 1968. *Politics and Policy: The Eisenhower, Kennedy, and Johnson Years.* Washington, DC: Brookings Institution Press.

Theriault, Sean. 2008. *Party Polarization in Congress.* New York, NY: Cambridge University Press.

Thomas, P. D. G. 1971. *The House of Commons in the Eighteenth Century.* New York, NY: Oxford University Press.

Uslaner, Eric M. 1989. *Shale Barrel Politics: Energy and Legislative Leadership.* Stanford, CA: Stanford University Press.

Walker, Jack L. 1991. *Mobilizing Interest Groups in America: Patrons, Professions, and Social Movements.* Ann Arbor, MI: University of Michigan Press.

White, Joseph, and Aaron Wildavsky. 1989. *The Deficit and the Public Interest: The Search for Responsible Budgeting in the 1980s.* Berkeley, CA: University of California Press.

Winders, Bill. 2009. *The Politics of Food Supply: U.S. Agricultural Policy in the World Economy.* New Haven, CT: Yale University Press.

Wiseman, Alan. 2004. "Tests of Vote-Buyer Theories of Coalition Formation in Legislatures." *Political Research Quarterly* 57: 441–50.

Zaller, John R. 1992. *The Nature and Origins of Mass Opinion.* New York, NY: Cambridge University Press.

Zelizer, Julian E. 2004. *On Capitol Hill: The Struggle to Reform Congress and Its Consequences, 1948–2000.* New York, NY: Cambridge University Press.

Index

Made in the USA
Middletown, DE
27 January 2020